ROOTS OF
WESTERN CIVILIZATION
FROM THE ENLIGHTENMENT
TO THE 1980's

ROOTS OF
WESTERN
CIVILIZATION

VOLUME II
FROM THE ENLIGHTENMENT
TO THE 1980's

Edited by

WESLEY D. CAMP
Adelphi University

Translations, unless otherwise indicated,
are by the editor.

JOHN WILEY & SONS
New York   Chichester   Brisbane   Toronto   Singapore

Library of Congress Cataloging in Publication Data:
Main entry under title:

Roots of Western civilization.

  Bibliography: p.
  Includes index.
  Contents: v. 1. From ancient times to 1715 — v. 2.
From the Enlightenment to the 1980's
  1. Civilization, Occidental—History—Sources.
I. Camp, Wesley Douglass, 1915–
CB245.R63   1983   909'.09821   82-13576
ISBN 0-471-87642-9 (v. 1)
ISBN 0-471-87641-0 (v. 2)

Printed in the United States of America

10 9 8 7 6 5 4 3 2 1

for Matthew Douglass

PREFACE

Man has no nature; what he has is history.

—*Ortega y Gasset*

Historical sources provide entree into the past that only a visit to places like Athens or Rome might rival. Students learn to discover and explore history as a foreign country. The raw materials of the past—rather than being simple, neat, and orderly, like a textbook—are rarely above dispute and always subject to interpretation. Whereas the smooth flow of a narrative may give the impression that history is somehow predetermined, the documents themselves offer students the kind of situation confronting an archaeologist at a dig, filled with bits and pieces of the past that seldom fit together. Once students begin to see how history is "made"—out of whole cloth, so to speak—they may come to question not only the textbook but even the polished lectures of the instructor. *Caveat magister!* Gertrude Stein, asked for her solution to the "German problem" after World War II, recommended that children speak back to their parents and contradict their teachers at least once a day.

To do so with authority, however, the child would need reliable sources, and, as the Renaissance humanist Lorenzo Valla demonstrated, even the best of them are not above suspicion. But they do provide a basis for rational argument and criticism, which are central activities in the intellectual process. Also, the student who learns to see history as a series of problems to be explored may find that many of today's controversial questions can be illuminated by similar issues from the past. Such a student will be well on the way to becoming a mature and useful citizen.

"History, to be above dispute or evasion," said Lord Acton, "must stand on documents, not on opinion." Novice historians should learn this lesson early on. If they read Hammurabi's code, the Epic of Gilgamesh, and the book of Genesis all in the first week of class, they may change their minds about the meaning of "history."

Some students may be impressed with the literary quality of many of the sources: for example, Erasmus's "Julius II Excluded from Heaven" or Mary Wollstonecraft's "Rights of Woman." Or the conflict between Antigone and Creon in Sophocles' play, giving an immediacy to Greek civilization that few modern sources can convey. Once students find that history involves issues and ideas as well as names and dates, when they discover that even its heroes make mistakes, then their enthusiasm is sufficient reward for the teacher.

We in the History Department of Adelphi University have long followed the above philosophy in teaching the "Introduction to Western Civilization" course. But when we found various source books inadequate for one reason or another, I offered to compile a new anthology following certain principles now incorporated in the present work:

¶ Organize documents and sources by themes into chapters corresponding to standard textbook divisions.

¶ Keep excerpts as short as feasible, in order to focus on central issues and hold the student's interest.

¶ Where possible, choose the more familiar source over the less familiar, capitalizing on the student's shock of recognition: for example, the Bible, Aristotle, Galileo, Marx, Freud, Hitler.

¶ Make each chapter short enough to be covered in one assignment.

¶ Offer as wide a range of viewpoints as possible; the 250-odd documents in these volumes also provide some latitude of choice on the part of instructors and students.

¶ Write brief, provocative headnotes and introductions in order to arouse the student's curiosity while at the same time providing the necessary background information.

¶ Choose documents covering a broad spectrum of cultural phenomena: religion, art, literature, science, philosophy, mythology, as well as records of social, political, and economic life.

¶ Select a diversity of sources: monuments, chronicles, and biographies; satires, poems, and plays; letters, diaries, and speeches; essays and tracts, laws and decrees, architecture and sculpture, painting and photography.

¶ Carefully edit all sources, using ellipses and brackets [. . .] to eliminate extraneous material, for example, unkeyed names, parenthetical remarks.

¶ Revise or retranslate inadequate versions; the editor doubles as professional translator. For translations from the Russian, I thank my colleague Professor Devlin, who also compiled and edited the chapter "Lenin and tthe Russian Revolution."

Similarly, I thank my other colleagues in the Adelphi History Department who graciously adopted these readings in preliminary form for use in their classes and gave me the benefit of their own and their students' criticisms. I am also deeply indebted to Professor Frank L. Kidner of San Francisco State University and to Professor Howard R. Holtzer of California State University, Dominguez Hills, both of whom read an earlier version of this anthology and made many excellent criticisms and suggestions, from which I have greatly profited. The errors and shortcomings that remain are, of course, entirely my own.

Wesley D. Camp
Garden City, New York

NOTE TO THE TEACHER

Our experience in the use of sources has convinced us that, rather than their being merely "supplemental," they can be an integral or central feature of the course. First, however, it is necessary to insure that students *read* the sources, so we require them to submit brief "reaction papers"—one or two pages—before any topic is discussed. Volunteers are then asked to tell the class frankly what they thought of the various documents—what they liked, disliked, understood, or did not understand; also what they discovered that was not in the textbook or was at variance with it. Since not all students have the same reactions, arguments and discussions often ensue, leaving the instructor little to do except to act as moderator and make the final summation.

Later, the papers are read by the instructor or the graduate assistant or, preferably, both. Except for a check mark ($\sqrt{}$) to indicate "assignment completed," papers are not usually graded, although some instructors may wish to reward brevity-cum-insight with *two* checks. Overly ambitious students should be informed that lengthy papers gain nothing, since only the first two pages will be read, in any case.

For the instructor, reaction papers often provide valuable feedback, indicating where students may have missed the point or become confused. For the students, there are several advantages: In addition to their improved "stage presence" from giving reactions in class, the mere act of writing a paper a week helps to improve their English composition, even when grades are not assigned. Some teachers provide guidance in the form of marginal notations, for example,   ? , "Verbiage?" "Logic?" or even, "What is your source here?"

Students also report that their reading speed and comprehension increase as they learn to look for ideas to record in their reaction papers, rather than getting bogged down in details. Some students, of course, may need to be warned that mere summaries are not acceptable.

Finally, when students once discover that historical documents are not sacred but may be evaluated and criticized like any other, they are well along toward proving Carl Becker's dictum: Every person his, or her, own historian.

W.D.C.

NOTE TO THE STUDENT

You are about to discover History! Like Columbus, who thought he was bound for India, you too may discover a whole new world. By the time you have finished reading the documents in this book, you should have acquired a new discipline as well. Does the word "discipline" scare you? It shouldn't. Almost everything we do, except sleep, involves some kind of control, coordination, and concentration: for example, sports. And thinking may also be a sport; it requires training, practice, coaching, and testing under pressure. One way to begin real thinking is to ask some hard questions: How do I know what I know? What evidence do I have for my opinions? Are my sources reliable? How may I test them? Many questions are similar to those a good lawyer would use in the courtroom: Is this witness reliable? Does the witness have a bias? Does other evidence rebut this witness's testimony?

Why should you read *original* sources? Why isn't the textbook enough? Some of the advantages of a textbook, in fact, supply arguments for the reading of source documents. Textbooks are usually well written, noncontroversial, factual, and biased—biased, that is, in favor of our own contemporary, Western culture whose values we always have to question, as John Stuart Mill says, in order to keep from holding them as mere prejudices. When we read history directly from the sources, without a textbook or a historian to smooth out the rough spots, we discover some new insights into human behavior, such as the Crusaders' killing 10,000 men, women, and children in Solomon's Temple after the fall of Jerusalem in 1099; or Susan B. Anthony's crusade for women's rights supported by such men as J. S. Mill and J. B. Shaw.

But probably the chief advantage of reading original sources is for the better understanding and interpretation of the past—how its story is written and how it relates to life in the present. Historians themselves have to work from documents like these and also, of course, from such physical remains as monuments, buildings, art, and artifacts.

Not all documents are easy to read, but some can be very exciting. For instance, when you read Socrates's own defense at his trial, you will get a heightened sense not only of an original folk hero but also of the life of Athens four centuries before the birth of Christ. Or when you read Cellini's story of his difficulties in creating a masterpiece, you will understand more about the meaning of art and the function of the artist. Finally, when you study the documents in English history from the king's charters to the Bill of Rights, you will see how far "we" had come before Washington and Jefferson were born.

W.D.C.

CONTENTS

CHAPTER 16

THE ENLIGHTENMENT: AGE OF IDEAS

Enlightenment is Man's quitting the nonage occasioned by himself. Nonage or minority is the inability to make use of one's own understanding without the guidance of another. This nonage is occasioned by one's self when the cause of it is not from lack of understanding but of resolution and courage to use one's own understanding without the guidance of another. *Sapere aude!* Dare to use thy own understanding! is therefore the dictum of Enlightenment.

—*Immanuel Kant, 1784.*

As Kant implies in the above quotation, the Enlightenment was a European, if not a worldwide, phenomenon; as pervasive in its effects as the Renaissance or the Reformation. Dare to think! Dare to use your mind! That is the message of the *philosophes*—the intellectuals of the eighteenth century.

We today are living the Enlightenment dream, at least we in the United States in the 1980s: we are not persecuted for daring to think original religious, political, or even social ideas. We may read anything we choose and, although it may be banned in one or more school districts, we can also write what we please and usually find a publisher for it.

The battles of the philosophes seem rather remote in the United States today, though not in many other parts of the world. Montesquieu's fight for the separation of powers to prevent tyranny; Rousseau's struggle for the humane treatment of children; Voltaire's lifelong campaign against religious bigotry and intolerance— all those battles we take for won. What may surprise us, however, is the sense of humanity of the eighteenth century, as in Voltaire's *Candide*, for example, which has been translated into almost all modern languages, has been produced in several movies, and was recently seen on Broadway as a musical comedy! It was Albert Schweitzer, in our own time, who said that Western Civilization has been derailed ever since the Enlightenment and that it is our task to put it back on the right track again. What do you think he meant by his comment? Do you agree?

Voltaire, bust by Houdon, one of France's greatest portrait sculptors, who seems to have caught the philosopher's wit and joie de vivre. *(Victoria and Albert Museum.)*

VOLTAIRE: ON NEWTONIAN SCIENCE (1733)

Letters Concerning the English Nation (London, 1733), pp. 83f., 122f., 132f., 136f., 140f.

Thrown in the Bastille for a witticism about a nobleman, François Marie Arouet de Voltaire was freed on his promise to go to England. After spending more than two years in that country, he came back impressed by its freedom of expression and by the ideas of men such as Bacon, Newton, and Locke—ideas he popularized in his *Lettres philosophiques,* which was first published in English.

[Recently] the trite and frivolous question following was debated in a very polite and learned company: Who was the greatest man, Caesar, Alexander, Tamerlane, Cromwell, &c. Somebody answered that Sir Isaac Newton excelled them all. The gentleman's assertion was very just; for if true greatness consists in having received from heaven a mighty genius, and having used it to enlighten our own minds and that of others, a man like Sir Isaac Newton, whose equal is hardly found in a thousand years, is the truly great man. And those politicians and conquerors were . . . generally so many illustrious wicked men. That man commands our respect who commands over the minds of the rest of the world by the force of truth, not those who enslave their fellow creatures; he who is acquainted with the universe, not they who deface it. . . .

The discoveries which gained . . . Newton so universal a reputaton relate to the system of the world, light, geometrical infinities [the calculus], and chronology. . . . Disputes were long . . . maintained on the cause that turns the planets and keeps them in their orbits, and on those causes which make all bodies here below descend toward the surface of the earth . . .

Sir Isaac Newton has demonstrated by experiments [that] the power of gravitation acts proportionally to the quantity of matter in bodies. This new discovery has been of use to show that the sun . . . attracts them all in a direct ratio [to] their quantity of matter combined with their nearness. From hence, Sir Isaac, rising by degrees to discoveries which seemed not to be formed for the human mind, is bold enough to compute the quantity of matter contained in the sun and in every planet; and in this manner shows, from the simple law of mechanics, that every celestial globe ought necessarily to be where it is. . . .

This is attraction, the great spring by which all nature is moved. . . . Newton, after having demonstrated the existence of this principle, plainly foresaw that its very name would offend, and therefore . . . gives his readers some caution about it, [to] beware of confusing it with what the ancients called occult qualities, . . . but that there is in all bodies a central force which acts to the utmost limits of the universe, according to invariable laws of mechanics. Give me leave . . . to introduce Sir Isaac speaking: ". . . I have discovered a new property of matter, one of the secrets of the Creator, and have calculated and discovered the effects of it. . . . Shall people quarrel with me about the name I gave it?"

MONTESQUIEU: THE SPIRIT OF LAWS (1748)

Trans. T. Nugent (London, 1878), 1:1–6, 162–164.

As a judge from 1716 to 1728 in the Sovereign Court (Parlement) of Bordeaux, Charles Louis de Secondat, Baron de Montesquieu, became an expert in the nature and function of laws. Finally, he sold his judgeship and made a grand tour of Europe including, especially, England. There he came to admire what he mistakenly assumed to be a system of checks and balances and separation of powers. Nevertheless, our founding fathers, who were students of Montesquieu, wrote these concepts into the American Constitution of 1787, a living monument to the baron from Bordeaux.

Of Laws in General

In the broadest sense, laws are the relationships that necessarily result from the nature of things. All beings therefore have their laws: the Deity His laws, the material world its laws, intellects higher than man their laws, the beasts theirs, and man his. . . .

As a physical being, man is like other bodies governed by laws, [but] as an intelligent being he incessantly transgresses the laws established by God, and also changes those of his own making. Though a limited being subject . . . to ignorance and error, he is left to his own devices; even imperfect knowledge he loses, and as a sensitive being he is carried away by violent passions. Such a creature would constantly forget his Creator, who must therefore remind him of his duty by the laws of religion. Such a creature is liable to forget himself at every minute. Formed by nature to live in society, he would forget his fellow creatures; legislators therefore have held him to his duty by laws civil and political. . . .

As soon as man enters a state of society, he loses his feeling of weakness, all equality ceases, and there begins a state of war. Each particular society begins to feel its strength, whence arises a state of war among different nations. The individuals in each of these societies also become aware of their power and try to convert the principal advantages of that society to their own use, thereby constituting a state of war between individuals.

These two different types of states give rise to human laws. As inhabitants of this great planet, which necessarily contains a variety of nations, they have laws relating to their mutual intercourse, called [collectively] the law of nations. Then, as members of a society that must maintain itself properly, they have laws relating to the governors and the governed, and this we call *politic* law; they also have another sort of laws governing their relations with one another, and that is called *civil* law. . . .

In What Liberty Consists

In every government there are three sorts of powers. . . . By virtue of the first, the prince or magistrate enacts temporary or permanent laws, and amends or abrogates those already enacted. By the second, he makes peace or war, sends or receives ambassadors, establishes the public security, and provides against invasions. By the third, he punishes criminals, or determines the disputes that arise between individuals. . . .

The political liberty of the subject is a tranquillity of mind due to the assurance he has of his own safety. For this liberty to exist, the government must be so constituted that no man need fear any other.

If the legislative and executive powers are combined in the same person or in the same body of magistrates, there can be no liberty, because of apprehensions that the same monarch or senate might enact tyrannical laws and execute them in a despotic manner.

Again, there is no liberty if the judicial power is not separate from the legislative and executive. Were it joined with the legislative, the life and liberty of the subject would be exposed to arbitrary control, for the judge would then be the legislator. Were it joined to the executive power, the judge might act with violence and oppression.

There would be an end of everything if the same man or body of men, whether noble or common, were to exercise all three powers—enacting the laws, executing the public resolutions, and trying the suits of individuals.

Most kingdoms in Europe enjoy a moderate government because the prince, who is invested with the first two powers, leaves the third to his subjects. In Turkey, however, where the three powers are united in the sultan, the subjects groan under the most dreadful oppression.

In the republics of Italy, where these three powers are united, there is less liberty than in our monarchies. Hence their government is obliged to resort to methods for its support as violent as those of the Turks; witness the state inquisitors and the system whereby informers can toss their written accusations at any time into the lion's mouth. What a terrible situation for the poor subjects in those republics! The same body of magistrates possess, as executors of the law, the whole power they have given themselves as legislators. They may not only plunder the state by their general decisions, but since they also have the judicial power, they can ruin any private citizen by their particular decisions.

The whole power is there united in one body, and although there is no external pomp to indicate a despotic rule, yet the people feel its effects every moment. Hence it is that many princes of Europe, aiming at despotic power, have constantly set out to unite in their own person all the branches of the magistracy and all the great offices of the state.

VOLTAIRE: ON RELIGION

Dictionnaire philosophique, article "Religion."

Since Voltaire, like Montesquieu, had a rationalist's view of religion, he was horrified at the outrages committed in its name throughout history. As a deist, he believed in a Supreme Intelligence pervading the universe, in sharp contrast to the vengeful deity of the Old Testament. Voltaire's *Philosophical Dictionary,* first published in 1764 but to which he kept adding more articles of all kinds, contains several selections such as the following that treat religion seriously with a light touch.

Last night I meditated, dreaming while awake. I was lost in the contemplation of nature, admiring the immensity, the orbits, and the harmony of those spheres which the vulgar cannot appreciate.

Still more did I admire the Intelligence which directs those vast forces. One would have to be blind not to be dazzled by this spectacle, I said to myself, one would have to be stupid not to recognize the Author of it; one would have to be mad not to worship Him. What tribute should I offer Him? Should not such tribute be the same throughout space, since the same power reigns equally everywhere? Should not a thinking being on a star in the Milky Way offer Him the same homage as a thinking being on this little globe of ours? Light is the same for the star Sirius as for us, so moral philosophy must be the same. If a sentient thinking creature is born of a tender father and mother who are concerned about his happiness, he owes them as much love and care as we owe our parents. If someone in the Milky Way sees a needy cripple, if he can help him and does not, he is guilty toward all globes. Everywhere the heart has the same duties: on the steps of God's throne, if He has a throne, and in the depths of the abyss, if there is an abyss.

I was absorbed in these ideas when one of those genii who occupy the interstellar spaces came down to me. I recognized him as the same aerial creature who had appeared to me on another occasion to teach me how God's judgments differed from our own and how a good deed is preferable to a controversy.

He transported me to a wasteland piled high with bones, and between those heaps of the dead were walks of evergreens; at the end of each walk a tall man of august mien contemplated these sad remains with sorrow.

"Alas! my archangel," said I, "where have you brought me?"

"To desolation," he replied.

"And who are those fine patriarchs, sad and mute, that I see at the ends of these green walks? They seem to be weeping over these legions of dead."

"You shall know, poor human creature," said the genius, "but first you must weep."

Starting with the first pile, he said, "These are the 23,000 Jews who danced before a calf, with the 24,000 who were killed while lying with Midianitish women. The number of those massacred for such errors and crimes comes to almost 300,000.

"In other walks are the bones of Christians slaughtered by each other for metaphysical disputes. They are divided into several piles of four centuries each; one pile would have reached up to the sky, so they had to be divided."

"What!" I cried, "brothers have treated brothers this way and I have the misfortune to belong to this brotherhood!"

"Here," said the spirit, "are 12 million American Indians killed in their homeland because they were not baptized."

"Heavens! Why not leave these frightful bones to whiten in the hemisphere where they were born and where they were consigned to so many different deaths? Why gather here all these terrible monuments to barbarism and fanaticism?"

"To instruct you. [Come,] . . ." I saw a man of gentle countenance, who appeared to be about 35 years old. From afar he looked compassionately at these piles of whitened bones, beside which I had had to walk to reach the sage's abode. I was amazed to discover that his feet were swollen and bleeding, his hands likewise, his side pierced, and his ribs flayed with whip cuts.

"Good heavens!" I said to him, "is it possible for a just person, a sage, to be in such a condition? I have just seen [Socrates,] who was treated very hatefully, but there is no comparison between his torture and yours. Wicked priests and wicked judges poisoned him; did priests and judges so cruelly assassinate you?"

"Yes," he replied very courteously.

"And who were those monsters?"

"They were hypocrites."

"Ah! that says it all; by that single word I understand that they must have condemned you to death. Had you then proved to them, as Socrates did, that the moon was not a goddess and Mercury not a god?"

"No, those planets were not involved. My compatriots had no idea what a planet was; they were all errant ignoramuses. Their superstitions were quite different from those of the Greeks."

"You wanted to teach them a new religion, then?"

"No, not at all. I simply said, 'Love God with all your heart and your fellow-creatures as yourself, for that is man's whole duty.' Tell me if that precept is not as old as the universe; judge whether I brought them a new religion. . . ."

"Then why did they put you in the state I now see you?"

"What can I say? They were arrogant and selfish. They saw that I knew them and they knew that I was acquainting the people with them. They were the stronger, they took my life, as such people always do, if they can, to whomever does them too much justice."

"Did you do or say anything that could have served them as a pretext?"

"To the wicked everything serves as a pretext."

"Did you not once say that you were come not to send peace but a sword?"

"That was a copyist's error; I told them I sent peace and *not* a sword. I have never written anything; what I said might have been changed without evil intent."

"So you contributed in no way by your speeches, however badly reported and interpreted, to these frightful piles of bones I saw on my way to you?"

"Only with horror have I looked upon those guilty of such murders."

"What about those monuments of wealth and power, of pride and greed; all those ornaments and symbols of grandeur that I saw piled along the way as I was seeking wisdom? Do they come from you?"

"Impossible! I and my people lived in poverty and simplicity; my only grandeur was in virtue."

I was about to ask him who he was, but my guide warned me not to, for I was not made to understand such sublime mysteries. So I asked him only in what true religion consisted.

"Have I not told you already? Love God and your fellow man as yourself."

'What! If I love God, I can eat meat on Friday?"

"I always ate what was given to me; I was too poor to give food to anyone."

"In loving God and being just, should I not be cautious about confiding all my life's adventures to an unknown man?"

"That was always my policy."

"By doing good, may I forgo making a pilgrimage to Santiago de Compostello?"

"I have never been there."

"Should I shut myself up in a retreat with fools?"

"As for me, I always made little excursions from place to place."

"Should I take sides for either the Greek church or the Roman?"

"When I was on earth I never made any distinction between Jews and Samaritans."

"Well, if that is the case, then I take you for my sole master." He made a sign with his head that filled me with consolation. The vision disappeared but a clear conscience remained.

VOLTAIRE: CANDIDE, OR OPTIMISM (1759)

Although Voltaire would undoubtedly wince, *Candide* is the only work of his that is widely known outside of France today. But that work has become one of the masterpieces of world literature. The number of its editions, translations, and representations on stage and screen attest to its universal appeal. Incredibly, Voltaire dashed it off in eight weeks, inspired by two phenomena: the Lisbon earthquake of 1755 that killed thirty thousand people, and the philosophy of Leibniz and others that this is "the best of all possible worlds." Like a musician, Voltaire played on the two themes of violence and optimism in as many variations as J. S. Bach might have developed on his famous clavichord.

Chapter 1. How Candide Was Brought up in a Magnificent Castle and How He Was Driven from It

In the castle of the baron of Thunder-ten-Tronckh in Westphalia lived a youth whom nature had endowed with the gentlest disposition. His face was a veritable reflection of his soul. He combined good judgment with the greatest simplicity. And that, I imagine, is why he was named Candide. The old servants of the household suspected that he was the son of milord's sister by a most respectable gentleman of the region, whom that lady had refused to marry because he could produce only 71 quarterings of nobility, the rest of the family's genealogical tree having been lost through the ravages of time.

Monsieur le Baron was one of the greatest lords in Westphalia, for his castle had not only a door but windows as well, and his great hall was hung with a tapestry. When he went hunting, instead of hounds he made do with all the dogs in his stableyard and his grooms served as huntsmen. The parish priest officiated as his grand almoner. He was called Your Lordship by all of his people, who invariably laughed at all his little stories.

Madame la Baronne weighed 350 pounds and commanded, therefore, no little consideration; she did the honors of the house with a dignity that won universal respect. Her daughter Cunegonde was 17 years old, fresh-colored, comely, plump, and delicious. . . . Pangloss, the tutor, was the family oracle, whose precepts Candide listened to with the simple faith befitting his age and disposition.

Doctor Pangloss taught metaphysico-theologo-cosmolo-nigology. He proved to perfection that there is no effect without a cause, and that in this best of all possible worlds the baron's castle was the most magnificent of all castles, and milady the best of all possible baronesses.

It is demonstrable, said he, that things cannot be other than what they are, for since all things have been created for some end, they must necessarily be created for the *best* end. Note, for example, that noses were made for wearing glasses and therefore we have spectacles; legs were obviously made for stockings, hence we have hosiery; stones were made to be quarried and used for castle-building, wherefore milord has a magnificent castle, for the greatest baron in the province should be the best housed. Pigs were intended to be eaten, so we eat pork the year round. Those who say that all is *well* do not know what they are talking about; they should say, All is for the *best*.

Candide paid close attention and believed in all innocence; for he thought Mlle. Cunegonde exceedingly beautiful, although he had never had the nerve to tell her so. He concluded that next to the joy of being born Baron of Thunder-ten-Tronckh was that of being Mlle. Cunegonde; next, that of seeing her every day; and finally, that of listening to Doctor Pangloss, the greatest philosopher in the province and hence in the entire world.

One day when Mlle. Cunegonde was strolling in a nearby wood called The Park, she saw through the bushes the sage Doctor Pangloss giving a lesson in experimental philosophy to her mother's chambermaid, a dark-haired lass, very pretty and very tractable. Endowed with a special aptitude for science, Mlle. Cunegonde watched breathlessly the experiments repeated under her very eyes. She saw clearly the doctor's sufficient reason, its causes and its effects. She went away greatly flustered, very pensive, and imbued with the desire to learn more, thinking she might be the sufficient reason for young Candide and he for her.

On her way back, whom should she meet but Candide! She blushed, so did he. She wished him good morning with a catch in her throat and he replied without knowing what he was saying. Next day, on leaving the dinner table, Cunegonde and Candide slipped behind a screen. She dropped her handkerchief; he picked it up. She innocently took his hand; he innocently kissed hers with a warm, feeling, and grace that were all very special. Their lips met, their eyes sparkled, their knees trembled, their hands strayed. The baron happened by. He beheld this cause and that effect and drove Candide out of the castle with some notable kicks on the backside. Cunegonde fainted. When she came to, the baroness slapped her cheeks very smartly. Thus general consternation reigned in the most magnificent and delightful of all possible castles.

ROUSSEAU: EMILE, A TREATISE ON EDUCATION (1762)

From *Emile* (1762), in *Oeuvres complètes*, 38 vols. (Paris, 1788−1793), 10:50−51, 53−60.

Jean Jacques Rousseau (1712−1778) has been called the father of modern Progressive Education, popularized by John Dewey in the 1920s and 30s and still alive and well today. The following excerpt from the *Emile* illustrates some of the advantages as well as, by implication, some of the disadvantages of "learning by doing."

What is the use of that? . . . This is the sacred formula by which Emile and I test every action. This is how I invariably answer all his questions; it serves to check the stream of a child's foolish and tiresome questions, . . . which produce no result, but are designed to get a hold over you. . . . The pupil who has been taught to want to know only what is useful will ask questions like those of Socrates—never a question without a reason, because he knows he will have to give a reason before getting an answer.

See what a powerful instrument I have given you for use with your pupil. Since he does not know the reason for anything, you can reduce him to silence almost at will. And what advantage do your knowledge and experience offer him to prove the usefulness of your suggestions. For, make no mistake about it, when you put the question to him, you are teaching him to put it to you, and you must expect that whatever you suggest to him in the future, he will ask, following your example, "What is the use of that?" . . .

I do not like verbal explanations. Young people pay them little heed and remember them even less. Things! things! I cannot repeat it too often: We teachers rely too much on words; we babble, and our students follow our example.

Suppose we are studying the path of the sun and how to find our bearings, when all at once Emile interrupts: "What is the use of that?" What a fine lecture I might make; how many things might I not take that opportunity to teach him in answer to his question, especially if other people were present. I could speak of the advantages of travel, the importance of foreign trade, the special products of different countries as well as their strange customs, the use of the calendar, how to reckon the seasons in farming, the art of navigation and steering a course at sea, how to find your way without knowing exactly where you are. Politics, natural history, astronomy, even morals and international law might come into it, so as to give my pupil an idea of all these sciences and the motivation to learn them. When I had finished, I should have shown myself a great pedant. I should have made a fine display of learning without his having understood one single idea. He would love to ask me again, "What is the use of taking one's bearings?" if he were not afraid of annoying me. So he finds it best to pretend to listen to what he is forced to endure. This is the net result of your fine system of education.

But Emile is educated in a simpler fashion. When we take such pains to teach him a difficult idea, ... at the first word he does not understand he prances around the room, runs away, and leaves us to speechify by ourselves. Let us pursue a more ordinary procedure; our scientific knowledge is of no use to him.

We were observing the position of the forest north of Montmorency when he interrupted me with the usual, "What is the use of that?" "You are right," I said "Let us take time to think about it and if we still find it is of no use, we will drop it, for we want only useful games." We found something else to do and put geography aside for the day.

Next morning I suggested a walk before breakfast; there is nothing he would like better, for children are always ready to gad about and he is a good walker. We climbed up to the forest, wandered through its clearings, and lost ourselves; we had no idea where we were, and when we wanted to retrace our steps we could not find the way. Time passed, we were hot and hungry; rushing vainly this way and that, we found nothing but woods, quarries, and plains, with no landmark in sight. Very hot, very tired, very hungry, we only went further astray. At last we sat down to rest and consider our situation. I assume Emile to have been brought up like any ordinary child: he does not think, but starts to cry. He had no idea how close we were to Montmorency, which was hidden from us by a mere thicket; but this thicket was a forest to a person his size, who was lost among the bushes. After a few minutes' silence, I began, in an anxious tone of voice:

"My dear Emile, how shall we get out of here?"

"I'm sure I don't know. I'm tired, I'm hungry, I'm thirsty. I can't go any further," he said, bathed in tears.

"Do you suppose I am any better off? I would cry too, if I could eat tears for breakfast. But crying is no use, we must look around us. Let me see your watch; what time is it?"

"It's noontime and I am so hungry!"

"Just so; it is noon and I am so hungry too."

"You must be very hungry indeed," he replied.

"Yes, but unfortunately, my dinner won't come to find me. It is 12 o'clock. This time yesterday we were observing the position of the forest from Montmorency. If only we could find the position of Montmorency from the forest. . . ."

"Yesterday we could see the forest, but from here we can't see the town."

"That is just it; if only we could find it without seeing it."

"Oh! my dear friend!" he cried.

"Did we not say that the forest was . . ."

"North of Montmorency."

"Then Montmorency must be . . ."

"South of the forest."

"Do we know how to locate the north at midday?"

"Yes, by the direction of the shadows."

"But south?"

"What shall we do?"

"South is opposite of north."

"That is true," he cried, "we have only to find the opposite of the shadows. *That's* the south! Montmorency must be over there! Let's look for it that way."

"Maybe you are right; let us follow this path through the woods."

Emile, clapping his hands, said, "I can see Montmorency! There it is, quite plain, just ahead. Come to lunch, come to dinner, hurry! Astronomy is of some use after all."

You may be sure he thinks this even if he does not say it; no matter, provided I do not say so myself. He will never forget this day's lesson as long as he lives. But if I had simply had him think about this at home, my lecture would have been forgotten the next day. Teach by doing whenever you can, and resort to words only when doing is out of the question.

ADAM SMITH: THE WEALTH OF NATIONS (1776)

An Inquiry into the Nature and Causes of the Wealth of Nations (London, 1776), Book 4, chapter 1 passim.

The Wealth of Nations is a classic that everybody knows but few ever read. Its influence has been extensive, right down to the present day, when to question its tenets in certain schools and groups is to be labeled a "radical." When Newton had done for celestial mechanics Adam Smith was trying to do for worldly economics—find a formula that would explain it all as simply as Newton's

$$f = \frac{M_1 M_2}{d^2}$$

Smith's law: Each person pursuing his enlightened self-interest in the marketplace benefits everyone, provided there are no extraneous forces such as monopolies or government interference.

That wealth consists in money, or in gold and silver, is a popular notion which naturally arises from the double function of money as the instrument of commerce and as the measure of value. In consequence of its being the instrument of commerce, when we have money we can more readily obtain whatever else we have occasion for, than by means of any other commodity. The great affair, we always find, is to get money. When that is obtained, there is no difficulty in making any subsequent purchase. In consequence of its being the measure of value, we estimate that of all other commodities by the quantities of money which they will exchange for. We say of a rich man that he is worth a great deal, and of a poor man that he is worth very little. . . .

A rich country, in the same manner as a rich man, is supposed to be a country abounding in money; and to heap up gold and silver in any country is supposed to be the readiest way to enrich it. For some time after the discovery of America, the first inquiry of the Spaniards, when they arrived upon any unknown coast, used to be if there was any gold or silver to be found in the neighborhood? By the information they received they judged whether it was worth while to make a settlement there, or if the country was worth conquering. . . .

Nations have been taught that their interest consisted in beggaring all their neighbors. Each nation has been made to look with an invidious eye upon the prosperity of all the nations with which it trades, and to consider their gain as its own loss. Commerce, which ought naturally to be, among nations as among individuals, a bond of union and friendship, has become the most fertile source of discord and animosity. The capricious ambition of kings and ministers has not . . . been more fatal to the repose of Europe than the impertinent jealousy of merchants and manufacturers. The violence and injustice of the rulers of mankind is an ancient evil, . . . [without] remedy. But the mean rapacity, the monopolizing spirit of merchants and manufacturers, who neither are, nor ought to be, the rulers of mankind, though it cannot perhaps be corrected, may very easily be prevented from disturbing the tranquillity of anybody but themselves.

That it was the spirit of monopoly which originally both invented and propagated this doctrine, cannot be doubted; and they who first taught it were by no means such fools as they who believed it. In every country it always is and must be the interest of the great body of the people to buy whatever they want of those who sell it cheapest. The proposition is so very manifest that it seems ridiculous to take any pains to prove it; nor could it ever have been called in question had not the interested sophistry of merchants and manufacturers confounded the common sense of mankind. Their interest is, in this respect, directly opposite to that of the great body of the people. As it is the interest of the freemen of a corporation to hinder the rest of the inhabitants from employing any workmen but themselves, so it is the interest of the merchants and manufacturers of every country to secure to themselves the monopoly of the home market. Hence in Great Britain, and in most other European countries, the extraordinary duties upon almost all goods imported by alien merchants. Hence the high duties and prohibitions upon all those foreign manufactures which can come into competition with our own. Hence too the restraints upon the importation of almost all sorts of goods from those countries with which the balance of trade is supposed to be disadvantageous: that is, from those against whom national animosity happens to be most violently inflamed.

  The wealth of a neighboring nation, however, though dangerous in war and politics, is certainly advantageous in trade. In a state of hostility it may enable our enemies to maintain fleets and armies superior to ours; but in a state of peace and commerce it must likewise enable them to exchange with us to a greater value, and to afford a better market, either for the immediate produce of our own industry, or for whatever is purchased with that produce. As a rich man is likely to be a better customer to the industrious people in his neighborhood than a poor, so is likewise a rich nation. A rich nation, indeed, who is himself a manufacturer, is a very dangerous neighbor to all those who deal in the same way. All the rest of the neighborhood, however, by far the greatest number, profit by the good market which his expense affords them. They can even profit by his underselling the poorer workmen who deal in the same way with him. The manufacturers of a rich nation, in the same manner, may no doubt be very dangerous rivals to those of their neighbors. This very competition, however, is advantageous to the great body of the people, who profit greatly besides by the good market which the great expense of such a nation affords them in every way. . . .

Consumption is the sole end and purpose of all production; and the interest of the producer ought to be attended to only so far as it may be necessary for promoting that of the consumer. . . . But in the mercantile system, the interest of the consumer is almost constantly sacrificed to that of the producer; and it seems to consider production and not consumption as the ultimate end and object of all industry and commerce.

In the restraints upon the importation of all foreign commodities which can come into competition with those of our own growth, or manufacture, the interest of the home-consumer is evidently sacrificed to that of the producer. It is altogether for the benefit of the latter, that the former is obliged to pay that enhancement of price which this monopoly almost always occasions.

CHAPTER 17

THE FRENCH REVOLUTION, 1787–1799: RIGHTS AND WRONGS

For two years prior to the calling of the Estates General in 1789 Louis XVI and his ministers tried desperately to solve the Government's financial crisis—an annual deficit of 100 million francs on a budget of 475 million. On the face of it that should not have been impossible, since France was then one of the richest nations on earth. But the Government was handicapped by the fact that the nobles and clergy—the two privileged classes—had obtained almost total immunity from taxation.

The problem was, therefore, to get them to agree to tax themselves in order to save the Government from bankruptcy. For this purpose the king's chief minister, Calonne, called a meeting, in 1787, of selected aristocrats, an "Assembly of Notables," including, among others, seven princes of the blood, 14 prelates, 36 great nobles (including our hero, Lafayette), 37 judges of the *parlements* or sovereign courts, and 25 city mayors; in all, 144 members. Although they met faithfully from February to May 1787, in the end they refused to approve any new taxes on the grounds that only the parlements or the Estates had the necessary authority.

The Government then took its case to the highest court in the realm, the Parlement of Paris. But they also refused to help, pleading similar lack of authority and recommending that the king call the Estates General, which had not met for 175 years!

Louis XVI had no choice. He sent out the order for elections to be held early in 1789 for representatives of the three "orders," or classes: clergy, nobles, and Third Estate ("commons"). Electors were also instructed to bring the traditional lists of grievances *(cahiers)* that representatives since the Middle Ages had always presented to the king at meetings of the Estates.

The following documents illustrate how the Revolution went from love and respect for the king to eventual distrust, hatred, and deposition; how a foreign war led to the establishment of a republic that soon turned into a dictatorship under

Robespierre and the Committee of Public Safety (pleasantly so named). Finally, after he had executed thirty to forty thousand Frenchmen of all classes (but mostly Third Estate), Robespierre was overthrown by his own party. A new constitution was drafted, designed to prevent future dictatorships: the executive power was divided among five independently elected "Directors." But five years later this government overthrew itself, with the help of the abbé Sieyès and a twenty-nine-year-old general named Napoleon Bonaparte.

Finally, the ongoing "debate" on the French Revolution was begun by Edmund Burke's "Reflections," answered by Thomas Paine's "Rights of Man," which in turn provoked a great feminist, Mary Wollstonecraft, to counter with "The Rights of Woman."

To what extent did the Revolution accomplish the goals it set for itself? If France was governed by kings and emperors for two-thirds of the nineteenth century, who won the Revolution?

THE COMING CRISIS

ASSEMBLY OF NOTABLES (1787)

When Calonne tried to convince the Notables of the Government's deficit, they refused to believe him. After all, Necker, their hero, had indicated only two years earlier that there was a treasury surplus. So when Calonne asked the nobles and clergy to help bail out the monarchy by taxing themselves, they refused. If there *was* a deficit, they said, the minister must have created it himself.

Archbishop Boisgelin Attacks the Chief Minister

Archives Nationales M788 (57), in J. Egret, *La Pré-Révolution française* (Paris, 1962), p. 40.

It is true that . . . the clergy dictate opinions everywhere [and] our opinions will save the nation. But this infamous bankrupt [Calonne] . . . dares to tell us that we should be responsible for *his* bankruptcy. Take a good look at him, remember all the features of his face. It has not yet been decided that this man will not be hanged by decree.

Lafayette Issues a Call for the Estates General, May 1787

Mémoires, correspondances et manuscrits, 6 vols. (Paris, 1837), 2:177; Arsenal, MS3976, in Egret, p. 59.

"Our own" Lafayette, who fought beside Washington in the American Revolution was one of the great nobles of France, with an annual income of about $500,000 (US 1980).

And he was the first to call for a meeting of the Estates General in the following exchange between himself and the king's brother, the Comte d'Artois.

"It seems to me," [said Lafayette,] "that . . . we should ask His Majesty to gather reports of all [government] operations and consolidate . . . the result by convening a truly national assembly." The Comte d'Artois asked if Monsieur le Marquis de Lafayette was asking for the convocation of the Estates General. He replied that that was precisely the intent of his request.

CAHIER OF GRIEVANCES OF THE THIRD ESTATE OF CARCASSONNE (1789)

Archives parlementaires (Paris, 1879ff.), 2:532ff.

In calling for meetings of the Estates, the king traditionally requested lists of grievances, or *cahiers de doléances,* to be drawn up at the same time. Several hundred such lists were presented at Versailles in 1789: they fill six volumes of the official record. Following is a small portion of one of these.

The Third Estate . . . of Carcassonne, wishing to give a beloved monarch . . . the most unmistakable proof of its love and respect, [and] desiring to cooperate with the whole nation in repairing the successive misfortunes which have overwhelmed it, . . . declares that the happiness of the nation must, in their opinion, depend upon that of its king, on the stability of the monarchy, and the preservation of the orders that compose it and the fundamental laws that govern it. . . . The Third Estate of Carcassonne very humbly petitions His Majesty to consider . . . the following:

1. Public worship should be limited to the Roman Catholic apostolic religion, to the exclusion of all other forms of worship. . . .

2. But the civil rights of those . . . subjects who are not Catholic should be confirmed and they should be admitted to public offices and positions. . . .

3. The nation should find some way to abolish the . . . dues paid to the holy see [papacy] to the detriment, and despite the protests, of the whole French nation. . . .

8. The nation should be subject only to such laws and taxes as it shall itself freely enact.

9. Meetings of the Estates General should be regular . . . and the monies needed for the State and public administration should be voted for a period no longer than the close of the year in which the next meeting of the Estates General is to occur.

10. To give the Third Estate the authority to which it is entitled in view of its numbers, its contribution to the public treasury, and its manifold functions in the national assemblies, its votes should be taken and counted by head.

11. No order, corporation, or individual citizen may claim any tax exemption whatever. . . .

SIEYÈS: WHAT IS THE THIRD ESTATE?

Qu'est-ce que le Tiers Etat? (Paris, 1888) passim.

More philosopher than priest, the abbé Sieyès won immediate recognition with this pamphlet, published in January 1789, just before the voting for delegates to the Estates General. It sold thirty thousand copies in the first three weeks. Sieyès, occupying the middle ground between Jacobins and Girondins, eventually conspired with Napoleon to overthrow the Directory and establish the Consulate in 1799.

We have three questions before us:

What is the Third Estate?—*Everything.*

What has it been in the political arena up to now?—*Nothing.*

What does it want to be?—*Something.*

The Third Estate Is a Complete Nation

What does a nation need in order to survive and prosper?—Private businesses and public services.

Private businesses may be divided into four classes:

1) Since land and water furnish the raw materials for man's needs, the first class includes all families who work on the land.

2) Between the first sale of raw materials and their final consumption, labor gives them added value, as industry perfects the gifts of nature. . . .

3) Between production and consumption, a variety of intermediate agents—dealers and merchants—intervene to help both producers and consumers. . . .

4) In addition, . . . society needs many specialized functions and services, either useful or pleasurable to the individual. This class includes occupations from the most distinguished . . . professions to the lowest menial tasks.

Such are the activities that maintain society. And who performs them?—the Third Estate.

Public services may also . . . be divided into four well-known categories: The Armed Forces, the Law, the Church, and the Bureaucracy. . . . Everywhere the Third Estate constitutes nineteen-twentieths of these, but it is burdened with all the arduous tasks that the privileged class refuses to perform. They occupy only the honorific and lucrative positions. . . .

We have [therefore] shown that the alleged usefulness of the privileged classes in service to the public is a myth; that without them the higher positions could be infinitely better filled; that those posts should normally be the reward for talent and recognized service; and that if the privileged have succeeded in usurping all the lucrative positions, that is both a heinous crime against the citizens in general and an act of treason against the State.

Who then dares to say that the Third Estate does not contain within itself all that is necessary to constitute a complete nation? . . . If the privileged order were removed, the nation would not be less but more. So what is the Third Estate?—Everything. But an "everything" shackled and oppressed. What would it be without the privileged?—Everything, but free and flourishing. Nothing can get along without it; everything would get along much better without the other two orders. . . .

What Does the Third Estate Want To Be?—Something

The people want to be *something,* and in truth the least thing possible. It wants to have genuine representatives in the Estates General: that is, *deputies from its own ranks,* who can interpret its will and protect its interests. . . . It cannot participate in the Estates General *unless its influence is at least equal to that of the privileged.* So it asks for a number of representatives equal to that of the other two [houses] combined. But this equality of representation would be nullified if each chamber were to vote separately. Therefore the Third Estate asks that the votes be taken and counted *by head and not by order.*

Caricature of disgruntled aristocrat cursing the Revolution while a happy democrat, holding a copy of the Declaration of Rights in her hand, exclaims, "What a fine act!" (Historical Pictures Service.)

NATICAL ASSEMBLY

DECLARATION OF THE RIGHTS OF MAN AND THE CITIZEN
(1789)

Trans. Thomas Paine, *The Rights of Man* (London, 1792), 1:49–50.

This document was drawn up and adopted as one of the first major acts of the National Assembly (formerly Estates General). Are there any rights listed here which should have been included in the American list?

The National Assembly doth recognize and declare, in the presence of the Supreme Being, and with the hope of his blessing and favor, the following sacred rights of men and citizens:

1. Men are born, and always continue, free and equal in respect of their rights. . . .

2. The end of all political associations in the preservation of the natural imprescriptible rights of man, and these are liberty, property, security, and resistance of oppression.

3. The nation is essentially the source of all sovereignty; nor can any individual, or any body of men, be entitled to any authority which is not expressly derived from it.

4. Political liberty consists in the power of doing whatever does not injure another. . . .

5. The law ought to prohibit only actions hurtful to society. What is not prohibited by the law, should not be hindered; nor should anyone be compelled to that which the law does not require.

6. The law is an expression of the will of the community. All citizens have a right to concur, either personally or by their representatives, in its formation. It should be the same to all, whether it protects or punishes; and all being equal in its sight, are equally eligible to all honors, places, and employments, according to their different abilities, without any other distinction than that created by their virtues and talents. . . .

10. No man ought to be molested on account of his opinions, not even on account of his religious opinions, provided his avowal of them does not disturb the public order. . . .

13. A common contribution being necessary for the support of the public force, and for defraying the other expenses of government, it ought to be divided equally among the members of the community according to their abilities. . . .

17. The right to property being inviolable and sacred, no one ought to be deprived of it, except in cases of evident public necessity, legally ascertained, and on condition of a previous indemnity.

CIVIL CONSTITUTION OF THE CLERGY (NOVEMBER 1789)

Archives parlementaires (Paris, 1879ff.), 21:80–81.

To have nationalized the lands of the Catholic Church—estimated at 10 percent of all the land in France—to have offered those lands for sale to solve the Government debt, and to have put all clergy on the national payroll as civil servants—that would have been bad enough. But the National Assembly went one step further and committed the supreme blunder of the Revolution: It required a loyalty oath of all clergy, swearing allegiance to the new constitution above any other commitment.

Article 1

The bishops, former archbishops, and priests shall be required to take an oath . . . by which they swear to watch over the faithful of the diocese or parish entrusted to them, to be faithful to the Nation, the Law, and the King, and to maintain the Constitution with all their ability. . . .

Article 6

If the said bishops, former archbishops, priests, and other ecclesiastical functionaries . . . fail in their respective oaths, either by refusing to obey the decrees of the National Assembly . . . or in stirring up opposition to the National Assembly, they shall be prosecuted . . . as rebels against the law, punished by deprivation of salary, and forfeit the rights of active citizenship.

WAR AND TERROR

MANIFESTO OF THE DUKE OF BRUNSWICK (JULY 1792)

Archives parlementaires, 16:378.

After the first assault on the Tuileries Palace by the Parisian populace on June 20, 1792, the Duke of Brunswick, who was marching on France at the head of the combined Imperial and Prussian armies, made his contribution to the list of revolutionary blunders: he issued the following proclamation warning the Parisians to restore Louis XVI to full power or face annihilation. When the Duke's manifesto reached Paris, it led to the second storming of the Tuileries on August 10 and the total collapse of the monarchy in France. (P.S. The Duke never got to Paris to carry out his threat; he was defeated at the battle of Valmy, on September 20.)

Their Majesties, the Emperor [HRE] and the King of Prussia, having assigned me the command of their united armies, . . . I hereby announce to the French people that: . . . the City of Paris and all its inhabitants without distinction shall submit immediately . . . to their king, restore [him] to full and perfect freedom, and assure him . . . the respect and inviolability which the law of nations and of Man requires; . . . their Imperial and Royal Majesties will hold responsible . . . all members of the National Assembly, of the department, district, and municipality . . . of Paris, all the judges and all others that shall be involved . . . if the Tuileries be entered by force or attacked, if the least violence or outrage be perpetrated against the King, the Queen, and the royal family; . . . [we] will . . . deliver the city of Paris over to a military execution and complete destruction.

A JACOBIN CIRCULAR (12 SEPTEMBER 1792)

From *The Constitutions of . . . France, 1789–1901*, ed. F.M. Anderson (Minneapolis, 1904), pp. 127–128.

Note the date: one month after Louis's attempted flight on August 10, a week after the September Massacres, and ten days before the opening of the National Convention. How would you have responded if you had belonged to a Patriotic Society receiving such a letter from your "Mother Society" in Paris?

The Mother Society has had to suspend its correspondence since the 10th of August. . . . [Now] the conspirators have expiated their crimes; the public morale has risen once more; and the sovereign [people], having recovered its rights, is finally triumphant over the scoundrels combining against its freedom and welfare. However, the people of Paris felt it necessary to maintain . . . vigilance over the minions of that traitor, Louis the Last. . . . The head, cause, and pretext of the machinations still lives! . . .

The great interests of the people are about to be discussed in the National Convention; let us prepare and make known the national opinion, which alone should direct their actions. Let us especially prevent . . . these new legislators from asserting . . . their personal interests or opinions in place of the sovereign will of the nation. . . .

SPREADING THE GOSPEL: DECREE OF 15 DECEMBER 1792

From *Le Moniteur Universel* (Paris, 1858), 14:755.

It was one of the myths of the French Revolution that their hard-won freedoms were to be shared with the rest of mankind, or at least with their European neighbors. Had they not proclaimed the Rights of *Man* and not just Frenchmen? Only slowly did they discover that other nations had different ideas about human rights. As Edmund Burke pointed out, there are no such things as rights in the abstract, only privileges handed down through time by each people, as an "entailed" inheritance.

In regions occupied by the armies of the French Republic, the generals shall immediately proclaim the abolition of all existing taxes, tithes, feudal dues, . . . real or personal serfdom, exclusive hunting rights, the nobility and all its privileges. They shall tell the people that they bring them peace, assistance, brotherhood, freedom, and equality.

Sans culotte Parisien.

Parisian sans-culotte with his pike in hand, sword at his side, and Revolutionary cockade in his hat. (Lauros-Giraudon/Art Reference Bureau.)

WHAT IS A SANS-CULOTTE?

Archives Nationales, Document $F^7 4775^{48}$, May 1793.

Literally, one who did not wear knee-breeches, the dress of aristocrats. The Sans-culotte wore workers' trousers because that is what they were: artisans, tradesmen, small shopkeepers, day laborers—the "little people" who took control of the Revolution in August 1792 and supported Robespierre during the Reign of Terror. The following Sans-culotte speech shows how the term, originally applied in derision, became a badge of honor.

Reply to the Impertinent Question: What Is a Sans-culotte?

. . He is a person who goes everywhere on foot and has none of the money the rest of you are after. He has no fine houses and no servants to wait on him. He lives quite simply with his wife and children, if he has any, on the fourth or fifth floor. He is useful because he knows how to plow a field or work a forge, a saw, a file; he knows how to cover a roof, make shoes, and shed the last drop of his blood to save the

Republic. Since he is a working man, you won't find him in the Café de Chartres, nor in the back rooms where people gamble and plot, nor at the National Theatre. . . . Evenings he spends at his Section, not all dolled up with powder and perfume to impress the *citoyennes* in the gallery, but to give his vigorous support to sound resolutions and beat down the faction of vile politicians. Furthermore, the Sans-culotte keeps an edge on his sword to give salutary lessons to troublemakers. Sometimes he carries his pike and, at the first roll of the drum, he will take off for the Vendée, the Army of the Alps, or the Army of the North.

LEVÉE EN MASSE (23 AUGUST 1793)

Archives parlementaires, 72:674–675.

This is the first general conscription in history. Only with the rise of modern nationalism in the Revolutionary era did governments find that they could put the whole nation under arms, instead of having to hire their soldiers or shanghai them. Note that this conscription is *really* general, including women and children as well as men, both old and young.

Henceforth, until the enemy shall have been driven from the . . . Republic, all French people are on permanent call for army service. Young men will go to battle, married men will forge arms and transport supplies, women will make tents and clothing and work in hospitals, children will make lint from old linen, and old men will go to public places to encourage the soldiers and foster the hatred of kings and the unity of the Republic.

ROBESPIERRE DEFENDS THE TERROR (5 FEBRUARY 1794)

Oeuvres, ed. M. Bouloiseau, 10 vols. (Paris, 1967), 10:352.

Try to imagine an American president delivering such a speech as this, perhaps during a wartime emergency. Could it happen here? Or is there some historical-sociological difference between the American and French cultures?

We are seeking an order of things in which all mean and base impulses will be suppressed by law and all charitable and generous feelings stimulated; where ambition will be the desire to serve one's country; where distinction will arise out of equality; where citizens will be subject to the magistrates, magistrates to the people, and the people to Justice; where the nation will protect the welfare of the individual, and the individual will be proud to share in his country's wealth and glory; where every mind will be stimulated by the continual exchange of republican ideas and the will to earn the respect of a great nation; where the arts will be the ornament of liberty [and] business the source of public welfare, rather than the luxurious monopoly of the few.

We will substitute morality for egotism, honesty for renown, principles for customs, duties for amenities, the rule of reason for the tyranny of tradition, aversion to vice for aversion to misfortune, self-respect for arrogance, love of honor for love of money, . . . in other words, all the virtues and marvels of the Republic for all the vices and absurdities of the monarchy. We want to satisfy nature's requirements, accomplish man's destiny, and fulfill philosophy's promises. . . .

Now what is the basic principle of democratic or popular government, the mainspring . . . that makes it work? It is virtue . . . public virtue, which is simply the love of one's country and its laws. . . .

[But,] if the basis of popular government in peace-time is virtue, its basis during a revolution is virtue *and terror*—virtue, without which terror is barbaric; and terror, without which virtue is impotent. Terror is simply stern, swift, inexorable justice; it springs, therefore, from virtue itself.

REVOLUTIONARY JUSTICE: LAW OF 22 PRAIRIAL (10 June 1794)

From *The Constitutions of France*, ed. Anderson, pp. 154–156.

From what you know of the American legal system, can you see any problems in the judicial procedures outlined here? This is the Reign of Terror at its height.

1. The revolutionary tribunal shall have one president, four vice-presidents, one prosecutor with four assistants, and twelve associate justices.

2. There shall be fifty jurors. . . .

3. The revolutionary tribunal is established in order to punish the enemies of the people. . . .

4. The reputed enemies of the people are those who have:

Promoted the reestablishment of royalty or sought to denigrate or dissolve the National Convention and the revolutionary government; . . .

Deceived the people, [leading] them into activities contrary to the interests of liberty;

Tried to spread pessimism, thereby aiding and abetting the tyrants who are in league against the Republic;

Spread false rumors to divide and demoralize the people;

Sought to mislead public opinion and prevent the instruction of the people, to corrupt their morals and destroy the public conscience, to impair the vitality and purity of revolutionary and republican principles—by hindering their progress or by insidious, counterrevolutionary writings, or by any other kind of intrigue. . . .

A Woman of the Revolution (1795), by Jacques-Louis David, illustrates his remarkable sensitivity to people of the lower classes. In this case he seems to have captured his subject's fears and apprehension mixed with her courage and defiance. (Musée des Beaux-Arts, Lyon.)

7. The penalty for all offenses is death.

9. Proofs needed to convict the enemies of the people shall be any kind of evidence—material, moral, verbal, or written—which will naturally persuade a just and reasonable mind; the criterion for all judgments shall be the conscience of the jurors, enlightened by the love of country. . . .

16. The law [provides] counsel for calumniated patriots [but] not for conspirators.

GRACCHUS BABEUF: CONSPIRACY OF THE EQUALS

Conspiration pour l'Egalité, dite de Babeuf, ed. P. Buonarroti (Brussels, 1828), 2:130–136 passim.

There were numerous groups and parties to the left of Robespierre. The most extreme was the "Conspiracy of the Equals," led by "Gracchus" Babeuf. The following manifesto, written by one of his disciples after his arrest in 1796, makes the aims of the party explicit. The police of the Directory maintained informers within the organization: when it moved to overthrow the government, the leaders were seized and either executed or deported. In spite of their failure, however, they later became the heroes of Marxian Socialism.

People of France! For fifteen centuries you lived as slaves, [but] in the last six years you have been able to breathe a little easier in the hope of independence, happiness, and equality. . . . From time immemorial, hypocrites have said, *Men are equal,* but the most monstrous inequality still weighs upon the human race. . . . Now that we are demanding equality with a louder voice, they say, "Be quiet, wretches! Real equality is an illusion; be satisfied . . . that you are equal before the law. What more do you want?"

Well! We want to live and die equal, just as we were born equal. Real equality or death—that is what we want. . . . The French Revolution is but the precursor of another, larger, and more important revolution, which will be the last. . . .

What do we want more than equal rights? We want an equality that is not just written into the Declaration of the Rights of Man and the Citizen: We want it here, among us, where we live. . . .

The land reform was the goal of soldiers without principle and of people governed by their emotions rather than their minds. We aim at something more sublime and more fair—the Common Good, the Community of Property. No more private ownership of land: *the land belongs to no one.* We demand—we shall have—communal sharing of the products of the earth, *products that belong to all.*

. . . We can no longer allow the vast majority of mankind to sweat and toil for the service and pleasure of a small minority. For too long now, less than a million people have disposed of what belongs to 20 million. . . . Away with the odious distinctions of rich and poor, great and small, masters and servants. . . . Let there be no difference among human beings except age and sex. . . .

The time has come to found the REPUBLIC OF EQUALS, that great haven for all people. . . . The establishment of true equality—the only kind that meets every need without making any victims . . .—may not satisfy everyone in the beginning. The egoist, the pretentious person, will fly into a rage. Those who hold land unjustly will scream, "Injustice!"

People of France, by what sign shall you know an excellent constitution?—If it is based entirely on equality. . . . Those aristocratic constitutions of 1791 and '95 riveted your chains instead of breaking them. The constitution of 1793 did make a giant step towards true equality; never before had it been approached so closely, but it did not reach the goal. . . .

People of France, open your eyes and hearts to the achievement of happiness: Proclaim with us the REPUBLIC OF EQUALS.

CONTEMPORARY COMMENTS

BURKE: REFLECTIONS ON THE REVOLUTION IN FRANCE (1790)

(London, 1790), pp. 47–50, 55–56, 88–90, 143–144.

Edmund Burke, MP, who had strongly supported the rights of the American colonists before the Revolution, was expected to give equal encouragement to the French. Instead, in response to a request from one of the revolutionaries, he penned one of the strongest attacks on the idea of revolution of any modern thinker.

You will observe that from Magna Charta to the Declaration of Right it has been the uniform policy of our constitution to claim and assert our liberties as an *entailed inheritance* derived to us from our forefathers, and to be transmitted to our posterity, as . . . specially belonging to the people of this kingdom without any reference to any other more general or prior right. By this means our constitution preserves a unity in so great a diversity of its parts. We have an inheritable crown; an inheritable peerage; and a house of commons and a people inheriting privileges, franchises, and liberties, from a long line of ancestors.

This policy appears to me to be the result of profound reflection; or rather the happy effect of following nature, which is wisdom without reflection, and above it. A spirit of innovation is generally the result of a selfish temper and confined views. People will not look forward to posterity, who never look backward to their ancestors. Besides, the people of England well know that the idea of inheritance furnishes a sure principle of conservation, and a sure principle of transmission, without at all excluding a principle of improvement. It leaves acquisition free, but it secures what it acquires. . . .

You [Frenchmen] might, if you pleased, have profited by our example and given to your recovered freedom a correspondent dignity. Your privileges, though discontinued, were not lost to memory. Your constitution, . . . whilst you were out of possession, suffered waste and dilapidation; but you possessed in some parts the walls, and in all, the foundations of a noble and venerable castle. You might have repaired those walls; you might have built on those old foundations. . . .

Remember that your parlement of Paris told your king that, in calling the [Estates] General he had nothing to fear but . . . the excess of their zeal in support of the throne. It is right that these men should hide their heads. It is right that they should bear their part in the ruin which their counsel has brought on their sovereign and their country. . . . They have seen the French rebel against a mild and lawful monarch, with more fury, outrage, and insult, than ever any people has been known to rise against the most illegal usurper, or the most sanguinary tyrant. Their resistance was made to concession; . . . their blow was aimed at a hand holding out graces, favors, and immunities.

This was unnatural. The rest is in order: They have found their punishment in their success. Laws overturned; tribunals subverted; industry without vigor; commerce expiring; [taxes] unpaid, yet the people impoverished; a church pillaged, and a state not relieved; civil and military anarchy made the constitution of the kingdom; everything human and divine sacrificed to the idol of public credit, and national bankruptcy the consequence. . . .

Government is not made in virtue of natural rights, which may and do exist in total independence of it; and exist in much greater clearness, and in a much greater degree of abstract perfection: but their abstract perfection is their practical defect. By having a right to everything they want everything. Government is a contrivance of human wisdom to provide for human *wants*. Men have a right that these wants should be provided for by this wisdom. Among these wants is . . . the want, out of civil society, of a sufficient restraint upon their passions. Society requires not only that the passions of individuals should be subjected, but that . . . the inclinations of men should frequently be thwarted, their will controlled, and their passions brought into subjection. . . . In this sense the restraints on men, as well as their liberties, are to be reckoned among their rights. But as the liberties and restrictions vary with times and circumstances, . . . they cannot be settled upon any abstract rule; and nothing is so foolish as to discuss them upon that principle.

The moment you abate anything from the full rights of men, each to govern himself, and suffer any artificial positive limitation upon those rights, from that moment the whole organization of government becomes a consideration of convenience. This . . . makes the constitution of a state, and the due distribution of its powers, a matter of the most delicate and complicated skill. . . . The science of government being so practical . . . and intended for such practical purposes, a matter which requires experience, . . . more than any man can gain in his whole life, . . . it is with infinite caution that any man ought to . . . pull down an edifice which has answered in any tolerable degree for ages the common purposes of society, . . . or [build] it up again without having models of approved utility before his eyes. . . .

Society is indeed a contract . . . but the state ought not to be considered as nothing better than a partnership agreement in a trade of pepper and coffee, calico or tobacco, . . . to be taken up for a little temporary interest, and to be dissolved by the fancy of the parties. . . . It is a partnership in all science; a partnership in all art; a partnership in every virtue, and in all perfection. As the ends of such a partnership cannot be obtained in many generations, it becomes a partnership not only between those who are living, but between those who are living, those who are dead, and those who are to be born.

THOMAS PAINE: THE RIGHTS OF MAN

(London, 1792), pp. 1:7–10, 70–71.

After the American Revolution, our old friend Thomas Paine went to France, where he became an honorary citizen and member of the National Convention. His *Rights of Man* was intended to refute Burke.

There never did, there never will, and there never can exist a parliament or any description of men, or any generation of men in any country, possessed of the right or the power of binding and controlling posterity to the *end of time*, or of commanding forever how the world shall be governed, or who shall govern it; and therefore, all such claims, acts or declarations, by which the makers of them attempt to do what they have neither the right nor the power to do, nor the power to execute, are in themselves null and void. Every age and generation must be as free to act for itself, *in all cases*, as the ages and generations which preceded it. The vanity and presumption of governing beyond the grave, is the most ridiculous and insolent of tyrannies. Man has no property in man; neither has any generation a property in the generations which are to follow. The parliament or the people of 1688, or of any other period, had no more right to dispose of the people of the present day, or to bind or to control them *in any shape whatever,* than the parliament or the people of the present day have to dispose of, bind or control those who are to live a hundred or a thousand years hence. Every generation is, and must be, competent to all the purposes which its occasions require. It is the living, and not the dead, that are to be accommodated. When man ceases to be, his power and his wants cease with him; and having no longer any participation in the concerns of the world, he has no longer any authority in directing who shall be its governors, or how its government shall be organized, or how administered. . . .

It requires but a very small glance of thought to perceive, that although laws made in one generation often continue in force through successive generations, yet they continue to derive their force from the consent of the living. A law not repealed continues in force, not because it *cannot* be repealed, but because it *is not* repealed; and the non-repealing passes for consent. . . .

It was not against Louis XVI, but against the despotic principles of the government, that the nation revolted. These principles had not their origin in himself, but in the original establishment, many centuries back; and they were become too deeply rooted to be removed, and the Augean stable of parasites and plunderers too abominably fithly to be cleansed, by anything short of a complete and universal revolution. When it becomes necessary to do anything, the whole heart and soul should go into the measure, or not attempt it. That crisis was then arrived, and there remained no choice but to act with determined vigor, or not to act at all. The king was known to be the friend of the nation, and this circumstance was favorable to the enterprise. Perhaps no man bred up in the style of an absolute king, ever possessed a heart so little disposed to the exercise of that species of power as the present King of France. But the principles of the government itself still remained the same. The Monarch and the Monarchy were distinct and separate things; it was against the established despotism of the latter, and not against the person or principles of the former, that the revolt commenced, and the revolution has been carried. . . .

As it is not difficult to perceive, from the enlightened state of mankind, that hereditary Governments are verging to their decline, and that Revolutions on the broad basis of national sovereignty, and Government by representation, are making their way in Europe, it would be an act of wisdom to anticipate their approach, and produce Revolutions by reason and accommodation, rather than commit them to the issue of convulsions.

From what we now see, nothing of reform in the political world ought to be held improbable. It is an age of Revolutions, in which everything may be looked for. The intrigue of Courts, by which the system of war is kept up, may provide a confederation of Nations to abolish it; and an European Congress, to patronize the progress of free Government, and promote the civilization of Nations with each other, is an event nearer in probability, than once were the Revolutions and alliance of France and America.

MARY WOLLSTONECRAFT: A VINDICATION OF THE RIGHTS OF WOMAN (1792).

The first great document of the feminist movement was written by an English woman who went to Paris to observe the French Revolution first-hand. There she had a daughter, Fanny, by an American who deserted her a year later. In 1797 she married the

Mary Wollstonecraft, an early champion of women's rights, both at home and in France. This portrait shows a very determined woman. ("Mary Wollstonecraft" by the British School, Walker Art Gallery, Liverpool.)

English radical, William Godwin, and died giving birth to a second daughter, Mary. It was this daughter who later married the poet Percy Bysshe Shelley.

. . . When men contend for their freedom and to be allowed to judge for themselves respecting their own happiness, [is] it not unjust to subjugate women—even though you [the Legislator] believe that you are acting in the manner best calculated to promote their happiness? Who made man the exclusive judge, if woman partake with him the gift of reason.

In this style argue tyrants of every denomination, from the weak king to the weak father of a family; they are all eager to crush reason; yet always assert that they usurp its throne only to be useful. Do you not act a similar part when you *force* all women, by denying them civil and political rights, to remain immured in their families groping in the dark? for surely, sir, you will not assert that a duty can be binding which is not founded on reason? If, indeed, this be their destination, arguments may be drawn from reason; and thus augustly supported, the more understanding women acquire the more they will be attached to their duty—comprehending it—for unless they comprehend it, unless their morals be fixed on the same immutable principles as those of men, no authority can make them discharge it in a virtuous manner. They may be convenient slaves, but slavery will have its constant effect, degrading the master and the abject dependent.

But if women are to be excluded, without having a voice, from participation of the natural rights of mankind, prove first, to ward off the charge of injustice and inconsistency, that they want reason—else this flaw in your NEW CONSTITUTION will ever show that man must, in some shape, act like a tyrant; and tyranny . . . will ever undermine morality.

I have repeatedly asserted and produced . . . arguments [and] facts to prove my assertion that women cannot, by force, be confined to domestic concerns; for they will, however ignorant, intermeddle with more weighty affairs, neglecting private duties only to destroy, by cunning tricks, the orderly plans of reason which rise above their comprehension.

Besides, whilst they are only made to acquire personal accomplishments, men will seek for pleasure in variety, and faithless husbands will make faithless wives; such ignorant beings, indeed, will be very excusable when, not taught to respect public good, nor allowed any civil rights, they attempt to do themselves justice by retaliation. . . .

Let there be, then, no coercion *established* in society, and the common law of gravity prevailing, the sexes will fall into their proper places. And, now that more equitable laws are forming your citizens, marriage may become more sacred; your young men may choose wives from motives of affection, and your maidens allow love to root out vanity. . . .

CHAPTER 18

NAPOLEON: FOR AND AGAINST

Born in Corsica in 1769, of petty-noble parents, Napoleon spoke Italian until he was ten years old, when he was sent to the Brienne military academy. Seven years later he graduated, as an artillery officer, from the Ecole Militaire in Paris. After winning his first laurels at the battle of Toulon, Napoleon became a hero of the National Convention by defending it against a counterrevolutionary insurrection in 1795, firing cannons loaded with grapeshot into the mob on the Rue St. Honoré.

This action won him command of the Army of Italy. It also won him a wife, Josephine, a merry widow with two children and nine years his senior. In Italy Bonaparte displayed his military genius by defeating the Austrian armies and threatening to storm Vienna if the Emperor did not accept his peace terms. Thus Napoleon added a "diplomatic" triumph to his military successes.

Later, when he was given command of an army to invade England, he found that too difficult but invaded Egypt instead—"to cut the British lifeline." That campaign turned into a disaster, however, when Admiral Nelson sank the French fleet in Abukir Bay. Nothing daunted, Napoleon abandoned his army and returned to France just in time to be made First Consul of a new government replacing the Directory, in 1799. Still under thirty years of age, Bonaparte found himself in control of all France and half of Europe.

In 1804, he established the First French Empire. An emperor needs an heir, so Napoleon divorced Josephine and married the Austrian Princess Marie Louise, who bore him a son in 1810. By then, though, he had other problems: the Spanish were in revolt, Germany was resisting French control, and the Russian Tsar was openly defiant.

Therefore Napoleon crossed Germany with one of the largest armies ever seen and invaded Russia in 1812. He captured Moscow but could not defeat the Tsar, whose armies scorched the earth and retreated. The next year Napoleon lost the Battle of Nations at Leipzig, the Allies entered Paris and exiled the French Emperor to the island of Elba. Finally, in 1815, Napoleon escaped, returned to Paris, and reigned France again until the battle of Waterloo, a Hundred Days later. His last exile was to the little island of St. Helena, where he died in 1821, but not before having written his memoirs and established the legend that others would profit from.

Some questions for thought: How do you think Machiavelli would have judged Napoleon?

What advantages and disadvantages do Napoleon's own words offer in evaluating his historic role?

Compare his contemporaries' opinions of him with his own evaluations. Was he a "son of the Revolution" or its antithesis? Hero or villain?

NAPOLEON SPEAKS

From his diaries, letters, proclamations, etc.

June 17, 1800. I have just reached Milan. . . . Some Hungarians and Germans, who were prisoners in my campaigns of 1796−97, recognized the First Consul and shouted enthusiastically, ''Vive Bonaparte!'' Imagination! what a thing it is! Here are men who do not know me, have never seen me before, and are still moved by my presence. They would do anything for me. The same thing happens all over, in all centuries! Such is fanaticism. Yes, imagination rules the world. But our modern institutions do not appeal to the imagination. By it alone can man be ruled; without it he is an animal.

December 30, 1802. My power comes from my reputation and my reputation from my victories. It would collapse if I did not bolster it with ever more victories and more glories. Conquest has made me what I am and it alone sustains me.

Friendship is only a word. I love nobody; no, not even my brothers. Joseph a little, perhaps, but even that is a matter of habit, because he is my older brother. Duroc [Napoleon's aide-de-camp]—Oh, yes, I do love him. But why? Because his character appeals to me: he is cool, dry, gruff, and never sheds a tear.

. . . I know perfectly well that I have no real friends. . . . But for appearance's sake, I will have as many as I need. Let the women whimper, that's the way they are, but as for me, give me no sentiment. A man must be firm, with a stout heart, or else leave war and government alone.

November 4, 1804. It is from a sense of justice that I will not divorce [Josephine]. Perhaps my personal interest or that of my system will argue that I should remarry. But . . . how can I put away this excellent woman just because I am becoming great? No, that is beyond me. I have the heart of a man; I was not born of a tigress. When [Josephine] dies, I shall remarry and have children perhaps. But I will not make her unhappy. . . .

Power is my mistress. I have done too much to capture her to let her be snatched away. Although some will say that power came to me naturally, I know what work it took, what sleepless nights, what scheming.

November 30, 1809. To Josephine, on the divorce: Will you do it of your own accord or won't you? My mind is made up!

December 1. Josephine sent word that she has consented. As we sat down to dinner, she suddenly cried aloud and fainted.

December 3. To Josephine: I am going to Paris, dear friend; I want to hear that you are happy. I will see you some time this week. I have received your letters which I shall read in the carriage.

December 15. The day of the divorce: The ceremony took place in the state apartments of the Tuileries Palace. It was very touching; everybody wept.

My Empire and its program, my people's needs and interests, which have guided all my actions, require that I should leave the throne to my children. . . . But for some years I despaired of having any children by my beloved wife the Empress Josephine. That is what led me to sacrifice my dearest affections, to consider only the good of the State, and to seek the dissolution of our marriage. At age 40 I may yet hope to live long enough to bring up in my own way the children Providence may be pleased to give me. God knows how much my present decision has cost me, but no sacrifice is beyond my courage if it can be shown to be in the interest of France.

March 3, 1817. Saint Helena. Despite the libels, I have no fear for my fame; posterity will do me justice. The truth will out and the good I have done will be weighed against my faults. I am not worried about the results. Had I succeeded, . . . my reputation would have been that of the greatest man who ever lived. As it is, although I failed, I shall still be considered extraordinary. My rise was unique, being unaccompanied by crime. I fought 50 pitched battles and won. I framed and carried out a code of laws that will bear my name through all posterity. I rose from nothing to become the most powerful monarch in the world. Europe was at my feet. I have always considered sovereignty to reside in the people: the Imperial government was, in fact, a kind of republic. Called to head it by the voice of the nation, I had the maxim, *Careers open to talent,* with no distinctions of birth or wealth. That system of equality is why your oligarchy hates me so.

August 28. Jesus was hanged like so many fanatics who posed as prophets; there were several each year. What is certain is that opinion was then moving toward one God. . . . It is the same in my case: sprung from the lower ranks of society, I became emperor because circumstances and opinion were with me.

January 29, 1818. To be a good general one must know mathematics; it is a daily help in organizing the mind. Maybe I owe my success to my mathematical conceptions. A general must never imagine things. . . . My great talent is to see things clearly. The same with eloquence, I can see the crux of a question from all sides. The great art in warfare is to change the mode of operations in the middle of a battle; that is my own idea and entirely new.

The art of war does not require complicated maneuvers; the simplest are the best and common sense is essential. From which you might wonder why generals make mistakes; it is because they try to be too clever. The hardest thing is to guess the enemy's plan, to sift the truth from all the reports coming in. The rest is just common sense; like a boxing match, the more you punch the better. You must also know how to read a map.

ON THE MANAGEMENT OF AFFAIRS AT HOME AND ABROAD

December 26, 1799. To Lucien Bonaparte, Minister of the Interior: If it were not for the war, my first consideration would be to base the prosperity of France on its communes. In rebuilding a nation, it is much easier to deal with a thousand inhabitants at a time than to strive romantically for the happiness of every individual. Since each commune represents 1,000 people, working for the prosperity of 36,000 communes is working for the prosperity of the 36 million inhabitants of France. . . .

The Minister of the Interior will consider carefully the following: Before the Revolution the commune belonged to the nobleman and the priest. Serfs and parishioners had no right to the roads nor to the fields for pasturing their cows or sheep. Since 1790, when those rights . . . were suddenly and rightfully taken away from the feudal lords, each municipality became a separate entity with the right, under protection of the law, to own, buy, and sell property and perform acts under the law for the benefit of the community. So France was immediately divided into 36,000 individualities, each motivated by the instincts of a proprietor to increase its holdings, improve its products, boost its income. That was the root of France's prosperity.

The reason why nothing grew from that root is because, while an individual proprietor is always alert to his own interests, a community, by contrast, is dormant and sterile; the interests of the individual are a simple matter of instinct, while those of a commune require virtue, and virtue is rare. Since 1790 the 36,000 communes are so many orphans, heirs to the old feudal privileges, alternately plundered or neglected these ten years by the municipal guardians sent out by the National Convention and the Directory. They have plundered the roads, trees, churches. What will happen if this continues another ten years? The first duty of the Minister of the Interior is to arrest a disease that will otherwise infect all 36,000 members of the body politic.

In dealing with an epidemic, one must begin by diagnosing its incidence and seriousness. The Minister of the Interior will therefore start by preparing a general survey of all 36,000 communes. We have never had such a survey. These are the main guidelines: There are three types of communes: those in debt, those whose accounts balance, and those with a surplus. The last two are not very many. . . . The major problem is how to relieve those that are in debt.

After the survey, the prefects will be notified that the thrust is on the communes in debt; mayors that do not go along with this idea will be removed. Each prefect is to visit those communes at least twice a year, and the subprefect four times, under penalty of removal from office. A monthly report of what is being done and what remains to be done shall be forwarded to the Minister.

Nominations may be sent to me for a prize to be awarded those mayors who free their communes from debt within two years, and the Government will appoint a special commission to administer any commune that is not free from debt in five years. Every year the 50 mayors who have done the most to rid their communes of debt or to increase their resources will be brought to Paris at government expense and ceremonially presented to the three Consuls. A column bearing the mayor's name will be erected by the Government at the entrance to his city or village with the inscription:

A GRATEFUL COUNTRY TO THE GUARDIAN OF HIS COMMUNE

May 14, 1802. Decree. "Pursuant to Clause 87 of the Constitution, concerning military awards, and in recognition of civilian distinction and service, a Legion of Honor shall be established."

Napoleon's comment. Where is the republic, ancient or modern, that has not conferred honors? Call them trifles if you will, it is by trifles that men are moved. I would not say such a thing in public, but here, among statesmen and thinkers, things should be seen in their true light. In my opinion, the French do not care a fig for liberty or equality; they have only one sentiment: Honor. That sentiment must therefore be gratified; they must be given distinctions. Do you think you can persuade men to fight by logical reasoning? A soldier wants glory, distinctions, awards.

August 17, 1806. To his brother Joseph, King of Naples. It would be a good thing if the Neapolitan rabble attempted to revolt. So long as you have not made an example, you will not be their master. Every conquered nation should revolt at least once, and I would look upon an insurrection at Naples as a father looks upon measles in his children. Provided the patient is not too seriously weakened, it makes a healthy crisis.

April 4, 1807. To his brother Louis, King of Holland. A prince who gains such a great reputation for benevolence in his first year is a prince who will be despised in his second. The affection inspired by kings must be virile, a blend of respectful fear and high esteem. When it is said of a king that he is a good man, his reign is a failure.

November 15. To his brother Jerome, King of Westphalia. The enclosed constitution for your kingdom contains the conditions under which I forgo my rights, won by conquest, over your country. You must observe it strictly. Do not listen to anyone who says that your people, accustomed to servitude, will be thankful for your benefits. What the people of Germany expect is that those who are not born noble but have ability should have an equal right to your consideration and to employment, and that all forms of serfdom should be abolished. The benefits of the Napoleonic Code, publicity for trials, establishment of juries will distinguish your monarchy.

ON THE CHURCH AND THE FAITH

June 5, 1800. Speech to the priests of Milan. Convinced as I am that the Roman Catholic faith is the only one that can assure real happiness in a well-ordered society and strengthen the foundations of government, I assure you that I shall endeavor to protect and defend it at all times and in every way. I regard you, ministers of a religion that is also mine, as my dearest friends. It is my firm intention that the Christian religion, Catholic and Roman, shall be maintained intact. Now that I have the power, I am determined to do whatever is necessary to secure and guarantee the faith. Do not be alarmed by the way the late pope was treated: Pius VI's misfortunes were due partly to the intrigues of his advisers and partly to the cruel policy of the Directory. When I am able to discuss matters with the new pope, I hope to remove any obstacles remaining in the way of a reconciliation between France and the head of the Church.

August 13. Paris. How can a state be well governed without the aid of religion? Society cannot exist unless there is inequality of wealth, and inequality of wealth is intolerable without religion. When a man is starving to death beside another who is gorged, he cannot accept that disparity without some authority who says: God has decreed that there must be rich and poor in this world, but in the next and throughout eternity, it will be the other way round.

It was by becoming a Catholic that I pacified the Vendée, and a Moslem that I established myself in Egypt; by becoming ultramontane I won over public opinion in Italy. If I ruled a people of Jews, I would rebuild Solomon's temple.

March 11, 1806. I respect what religion respects, but as a statesman I dislike the fanaticism of celibacy; it was one means by which the court of Rome tried to rivet the chains of Europe by preventing the clergy from being citizens. Military fanaticism is the only kind that is of any use to me; a man needs it to get himself killed.

July 22, 1807. To Prince Eugene, Napoleon's stepson, Viceroy of Italy. I have received the pope's letter, which you forwarded. Answer His Holiness in some such terms as the following:

Holy Father, I have placed your Holiness's letter before the Emperor, my reverend father and my Sovereign, who has replied to me in a long letter from Dresden, from which I quote an extract to show Your Holiness His Majesty's views, so as not to conceal the real issue in these matters:

"My son, I perceive from His Holiness's letter, which he certainly never wrote himself, that I am threatened. I would not tolerate this from any other pope. What is Pius VII trying to do by denouncing me to Christendom? Put my throne under an interdict? Excommunicate me? Does he imagine that my soldiers' muskets will fall from their hands? Or does he intend to put an assassin's dagger into the hands of my people?

"Frantic popes, born for men's misfortunes, have already preached that infamous doctrine. Next I shall probably hear that the Holy Father intends to tonsure me and shut me up in a monastery! Does he think the present century has reverted to the ignorance and brutality of the ninth? . . .

"The present pope has too much power; priests are not made to rule; let them follow the example of St. Peter, St. Paul, and the holy Apostles, who were certainly worth any Julius, Boniface, Gregory, or Leo. Jesus Christ declared that his kingdom was not of this world. Why will not the pope render unto Caesar that which is Caesar's? Is he something greater on earth than was Jesus Christ?

"Is there anything in common between the interests of religion and the prerogatives of the Court of Rome? Is religion to be based on anarchy, civil war, revolt? Is *that* preaching the doctrine of Jesus Christ? The pope threatens me with an appeal to the people. In truth, I begin to blush and feel alarmed at all the foolery that the Court of Rome makes me endure; and perhaps it will not be long, if they insist on creating disturbances in my States, before I refuse to recognize the pope as anything more than bishop of Rome, the equal of any of the bishops in my States. I would not hesitate to convene the Gallican, Italian, German, and Polish churches in a Council to settle affairs without the Court of Rome. My crown proceeds from God and the will of my people; I am answerable only to God and the will of my people for it. . . ."

Holy Father, this was not intended to be seen by Your Holiness. I beg you to end this quarrel. The Emperor's complaint is justified.

Send this letter to the pope and inform me when it is presented.

June 8, 1816. St. Helena. Everything proclaims the existence of a God; that is beyond doubt; but all of our religions are clearly Man's creations. While no one can swear to what he will do during his last moments, my own belief is that I shall die without a confessor. I am certainly far from being an atheist, but I cannot believe all that is taught, contrary to reason, without being dishonest and hypocritical. During the Empire and especially after my marriage to Marie Louise, the greatest efforts were made to persuade me to go to Notre Dame in full state for communion, after the manner of our kings; my faith was not strong enough for that to do me any good, but it was too strong for me to commit a sacrilege in cold blood. To know whence I come, what I am, and whither I go is beyond me, but there it is! I am a clock that exists without knowing itself. I can appear before God's tribunal and await his judgment without fear. I worked only for the glory, power, and splendor of France; that is where all my abilities, efforts, and time were spent. This cannot have been a crime; to me it seemed a virtue!

ON PUBLIC OPINION AND ITS CONTROL

September 10, 1800. To Lucien Bonaparte, Minister of the Interior. Please send me a list of our ten best painters, ten best sculptors, ten best composers, ten best musicians, ten best architects, and the names of any other artists who deserve public recognition.

April 24, 1805. To Fouché, during the war of the Third Coalition. Have some well-written articles published describing the military movements of the Russians, the interview between the Emperors of Russia and Austria, and the absurd reports . . . born of the fogs and spleen of England. Get busy keeping up public opinion. Tell the newspaper editors that I still read the newspapers even though I am far away [Napoleon was in Lyons]. Tell them that if they keep on their present tack I shall close their accounts.

August 6. It is my intention to turn art towards subjects tending to memorialize the events of the last fifteen years. I am amazed that I have not been able to persuade the Gobelin [tapestry makers] to abandon sacred history and let their artists work on all the actions that have won glory for the army and the Nation, events that have created our throne.

September 3, 1808. At the beginning of the Spanish Campaign. Give orders for the city of Metz to entertain the troops when they pass through. If the city cannot afford it, I will grant three francs per man, but it must all be done in the name of the city itself.

Have the prefects on the line of march look after the troops well and bolster their loyalty and love of glory in every way possible. Speeches, songs, free theatre performances, dinners—that is what I expect from our citizens for our soldiers. . . .

Have songs composed in Paris and sent to the major cities, proclaiming the glory the army has already won, the glories it still has to win, and the freedom of the seas that will result from its victory [in Spain].

September 18. Proclamation. Soldiers, after your triumphs on the banks of the Danube and the Vistula, you have crossed Germany by forced marches. Now I order you through France without a moment's respite. Soldiers, I need you! The Leopard's hideous apparition has sullied the mainland of Spain and Portugal. He should flee in terror at your approach. We shall carry our triumphant Eagles to the columns of Hercules: there too we have scores to settle. Soldiers, you have surpassed the fame of all modern armies! But have you equalled the glory of the armies of Ancient Rome—armies that won victories on the Rhine, the Euphrates, the Tagus, and in Illyria, all in the same campaign!

May 1, 1816. St. Helena. Change, chop, and suppress as they will, they will find it pretty hard to make me disappear altogether. No French historian can easily avoid dealing with the Empire, and if he has a heart, he will have to give me back something of my own. I capped the well of anarchy, brought order out of chaos, purified the Revolution, raised up nations, strengthened the throne. I stimulated every ambition, rewarded merit, and expanded the limits of glory!

THE NAPOLEONIC CATECHISM (1806)

From *Grand dictionnaire universel du XIXe siècle*, 3:567.

When Napoleon renewed relations with the papacy by the Concordat of 1801, he included a clause giving his government the authority to issue "police regulations" affecting the church. On this basis he promulgated a set of Organic Articles for the Catholic Religion that went far beyond what Pius VII had understood by the Concordat. Included in those Articles was the provision that there be only one catechism for all of France. Characteristically, Napoleon took an active part in drawing it up.

Q. What are the duties of Christians toward the princes who govern them, and what in particular are our duties toward Napoleon I, our Emperor?
A. . . . Love, respect, obedience, fidelity, military service, and taxes levied for the preservation and defense of the Empire and of his throne; we also owe him fervent prayers for his well-being and for the spiritual and temporal prosperity of the State.

Q. Why do we owe these duties to our Emperor?
A. First, because God, who created empires, distributed them according to his will and blessed our Emperor with gifts of both peace and war. He established him as our sovereign and made him the agent of His power and image on earth. To honor and serve our Emperor, then, is to honor and serve God himself. Secondly, because our Lord Jesus Christ . . . has taught us what we owe to our sovereign . . . by ordering us to render unto Caesar that which is Caesar's.

Q. Are there not special reasons that bind us even more strongly to our Emperor Napoleon I?
A. Yes, for he is the one whom God raised up in difficult times to reestablish public worship of the holy religion of our fathers and to be its protector. By his profound and

active wisdom he has restored and defended public order; he defends the State with his powerful arm; and he has become the anointed of the Lord by the consecration he received from the sovereign pontiff, head of the universal Church.

Q. What should we think of those who are remiss in their duties toward our Emperor?
A. According to the apostle Paul, they are resisting the established order of God himself and are therefore worthy of eternal damnation.

Q. Do our duties toward our Emperor bind us equally toward his successors?
A. Yes, certainly, for we read in Holy Scripture that God, Lord of heaven and earth, . . . gives empires not only to one person in particular but also to his family.

VIEWED BY CONTEMPORARIES

MADAME DE STAËL'S OPINION

Oeuvres complètes (Paris, 1820–1821), 13:250–259, 319–320.

Daughter of Jacques Necker, the former Minister of Finance, Germaine Necker Baronne de Staël (d. 1817) was a gifted writer and a strong believer in the ideals of 1789. She had originally supported Napoleon when she thought he too was "a child of the Revolution" but, quickly disillusioned, she soon became his foremost critic—in exile. The following excerpts are from her posthumous *Considerations on the Events of the French Revolution.*

Bonaparte's most potent magic in establishing his power . . . was the terror inspired by the mere mention of *Jacobinism.* . . . Anybody attempting to establish despotism will call up all the crimes committed by demagogues. It is an easy way. Bonaparte paralyzed all resistance by saying simply, "Do you want me to hand you over to the Jacobins?" At which France surrendered, with no one bold enough to say, "But we can fight both the Jacobins *and* you!" . . . He almost always offered himself as an alternative to some other danger in order to gain power as the lesser of two evils.

A commission of 50 members of the [former Directory] was charged to discuss the new constitution [of the Consulate] with General Bonaparte. Some of those members had recently jumped out the windows to escape the bayonets [of Napoleon's soldiers in the Brumaire coup] . . . .

Bonaparte let these men, accustomed to talking from the rostrum, dissipate in words whatever was left of their characters. But if they went beyond the theoretical and got too close to the practical, he threatened to have nothing more to do with them; in other words, to end it by resorting to force. He could be agreeable enough in those lengthy discussions because he likes to talk. His method of dissimulation in politics is not silence; rather, he befuddles the mind by a whirlwind of words, making people believe alternately the most contradictory things. In fact, sometimes a person deceives better by talking than by keeping quiet. The slightest sign may betray those who keep still, whereas those who have the effrontery to lie aggressively may challenge convictions more effectively. . . .

Tyranny establishes itself almost always after long civil disturbances, because it offers the hope of protection for all the exhausted and frightened parties. Bonaparte said of himself, with good reason, that he knew very well how to play upon the instrument of power. Since he is in fact attached to no principle and unrestrained by any obstacle, he enters the arena of fortune like a tough, vigorous athlete. He senses immediately what in each man or group of men will serve his purpose.

His plan to gain control of France had three elements: To appeal to people's egoism at the expense of their virtue; to deprave public opinion by means of sophistry; and to substitute war for freedom as the nation's objective. . . .

Bonaparte stirred up [the nation's] passions without having to struggle against its principles. He had it in his power both to honor France and to establish himself by respectable means, but his distrust of the human race had dried up his soul and he believed there was nothing profound outside the realm of evil.

We have seen that General Bonaparte decreed a constitution with no guarantees [of rights]. Furthermore, he was careful to preserve the laws passed during the Revolution, so that he might use whatever weapons he needed from that arsenal. The special committees, the deportations, the exiles, the enslavement of the press—measures taken in the name of liberty—also served the purposes of tyranny only too well. . . . When he became so spiritually bankrupt as to see no greatness without despotism, it was probably impossible for him to escape from continual warfare; in a country like France, what would a despot be without military glory?

LOUIS BOURRIENNE: MEMOIRS OF NAPOLEON BONAPARTE

(Paris, 1829), trans. R. Phipps, 4 vols. (New York, 1895), 1:313–328 passim, 2:112, 233, revised.

Louis Bourrienne, schoolmate of Napoleon, later became his personal secretary (1797–1802) and diplomatic representative in Germany. He eventually fell out of favor and supported the restoration of Louis XVIII.

My long and intimate association with Bonaparte from boyhood, my close relations with him when he was General, Consul, and Emperor, enabled me to see and appreciate all that was . . . done during that momentous period. I not only had the opportunity of being present at the conception and execution of the extraordinary deeds of one of the ablest men nature ever formed, but . . . I was able to use the moments of leisure at my disposal to make notes, collect documents, and record for posterity facts that would otherwise be difficult to verify. . . .

Bonaparte had two ruling passions: glory and war. He was never more happy than in the camp, and never more morose than in the idleness of peace. Plans for building public monuments also satisfied his imagination and helped fill the void. . . . He knew that monuments form part of the history of nations. . . . In all the activities he lost sight of the present moment, thinking only of the future. . . .

Bonaparte did not esteem mankind, whom he despised more and more in proportion as he became more acquainted with them. . . . One of his greatest misfortunes was that he neither believed in friendship not felt the necessity of loving. . . .

In his social relations Bonaparte's temper was bad, but his fits of ill-humor passed away like a cloud and spent themselves in words. His violent language and bitter imprecations were often premeditated. . . . He had every quality for being what is called in society an agreeable man, except the will to be so. His manner was imposing rather than pleasant and those who did not know him experienced an involuntary feeling of awe in his presence. . . .

He often talked a great deal and sometimes a little too much, but nobody ever told a story in a more interesting way. His conversation, which was seldom gay or humorous, never dealt in trivial matters. So fond of arguing was he that in the heat of discussion it was easy to draw out secrets he wanted to conceal. . . .

Having no faith in medicine, Bonaparte spoke of it as an art that was entirely conjectural and his opinion on the subject was fixed and incontrovertible. His vigorous mind rejected all but demonstrative proofs.

He had little memory for proper names, words, or dates, but he had almost total recall of facts and places. . . . He was insensible to the charms of poetry, lacking any ear for harmony; he could never recite a verse without violating the meter. But the grand ideas and concepts of poetry fascinated him. . . .

Gallantry toward women was no part of Bonaparte's character. He seldom said anything agreeable to them and often said rude and extraordinary things, instead . . . [such as] "Do you never change your gown? I have seen you in that one twenty times." . . . But he was neither malignant nor vindictive. . . . Only those blinded by fury would call him a Nero or a Caligula. . . .

To judge impartially, we must take into account the influence of time and circumstance, and distinguish between the different characters of the collegian, the general, the First Consul, and the Emperor. . . . He had no idea of power except as direct force. All benevolent men who speculate on the amelioration of human society Bonaparte regarded as dangerous, because their maxims and principles were diametrically opposed to the harsh and arbitrary system he had adopted. . . . Men, he always said, were to be governed only by fear and interest. . . . He held freedom of the press in the greatest horror; great man that he was, he was sorely afraid of little paragraphs. . . . He held all literary men in low esteem, calling them mere "phrasemongers." He was never able to forgive them for excelling in a pursuit in which he himself had no claim to distinction.

MEMOIRS OF MADAME DE RÉMUSAT (1802–1808)

Trans. C. Hoey and J. Little (New York, 1880), pp. 1–15, 334–337.

The Comtesse de Rémusat was another of the many gifted women of this period. The wife of a high Napoleonic official, she was also a close friend of the Empress Josephine.

In addition to her intimate memoirs of the Imperial Court, from which the following excerpts are taken, she also published an essay on the education of women.

I am far from saying that [Bonaparte] always appeared to me in the light in which I now see him; my opinions have progressed, even as he did, but I am so far from being influenced by personal feelings that I do not think it possible for me to deviate from the exact truth. . . .

There was a certain charm in the smile of Bonaparte, but during all the time when I was accustomed to see him, he seldom evinced that particular charm. Gravity was the foundation of his character; not the gravity of a dignified and noble manner, but that which arises from profound thought. In his youth he was a dreamer; later in life he became moody, and still later habitually ill tempered. . . .

The rational turn of his mind disposed him to analyze even his own emotions. No man has ever meditated more deeply than Bonaparte on the ''wherefore'' that rules human actions. He could never understand that natural nonchalance which leads some people to act without a plan and without aim. He always judged others by himself and was often mistaken.

Bonaparte was deficient in education and in manners; it seemed as if he must have been destined to live either in a tent where all men are equal, or on a throne where everything is permitted. . . .

In trying to depict Bonaparte, it seems necessary . . . to separate him into three parts: his soul, his heart, and his mind, for no one of these ever blended completely with the others. Although very remarkable for certain intellectual qualities, no man . . . was ever less lofty of soul. There was no generosity, no true greatness in him. . . .

I ought now to speak of Bonaparte's heart, but if it were possible to believe that a being . . . could exist without that portion of our system that makes us desire to love and be loved, I should say that in his creation the heart was left out. Perhaps the truth is that he succeeded in suppressing it: he was always too engrossed by himself to be influenced by any sentiment of affection. . . . The Emperor despised women, and contempt cannot coexist with love. He regarded their weakness as irrefutable evidence of their inferiority, and the power they have in society as an intolerable usurpation. . . . I am inclined to believe that Bonaparte was never awakened to love except by vanity. . . .

The intellect of Bonaparte was most remarkable. It would be difficult . . . to find among men a more powerful or comprehensive mind. It owed nothing to education, for in reality, he was ignorant, reading but little and that hurriedly. But he quickly seized upon the little he had learned and his imagination developed it so extensively that he might easily have passed for well educated. . . . With him one idea gave birth to a thousand others and a word would lift his conversation into elevated regions of fancy in which logic no longer kept him company but in which his intellectual power never failed to shine. . . .

I have said that Bonaparte was incapable of generosity; yet his gifts were immense and the rewards he bestowed gigantic. But when he paid for a service, he made it plain that he expected to buy another, and there always remained a vague uneasiness about the conditions of the bargain. He believed that we French would not grumble if our slavery were glamorous and that we would gladly exchange all the freedom the

Revolution had won for us, for his dazzling military successes. . . He found in war a means of stifling the thoughts his style of government was sure to evoke sooner or later and he maintained it [war] in order to dazzle us or reduce us to silence, at least. Feeling himself to be the perfect master of the science of war, he did not fear its consequences. . . . His chief, his real ambition was for power; he would have preferred peace if that would have increased his authority. . . .

Only with disdain did he look upon the progress recently achieved through the French Revolution, which was such a grave warning to sovereigns. He saw it merely as an event which might be turned to his advantage and he came to despise the cry for liberty, uttered by the people at intervals for 20 years. He thought he could trick them by destroying what had existed and replacing it with new, original creations that would satisfy the longing for equality, which he believed, correctly, to be the ruling passion of the day. He tried to turn the Revolution into a mere quirk of fate, a useless disturbance that had simply upset everyone. . . .

It seems as if Napoleon were two different men at once: the first, gigantic rather than great, but still prompt to conceive and to execute. . . . Actuated by a single idea, unaffected by any other impressions, this man, if he had taken the good of humanity for his goal, would have become, with his abilities, one of the greatest men on earth; even now, he remains through his shrewdness and will power, one of the most extraordinary.

The other Bonaparte, a kind of guilty conscience to the first, was consumed by anxiety and suspicion, a slave to insatiable passions, distrustful, fearing every rival success or glory. . . .

JEAN CHAPTAL: RECOLLECTIONS OF NAPOLEON

Mes souvenirs sur Napoléon, ed. A. Chaptal (Paris, 1893), pp. 224–231, 270f., 291, 341.

Jean Chaptal was Napoleon's Minister of the Interior from 1801 to 1809. He was also a recognized scholar and scientist who pioneered in the application of chemistry to industry. He had occasion to observe Napoleon in action as head of the largest empire since Charlemagne.

When Bonaparte took over the government, he was not only profoundly ignorant of the principles of administration, jurisprudence, geography, etc., but he knew nothing whatever about the government that existed before the Revolution. Bonaparte had ruminated a lot but never studied. Military glory had carried him to the supreme eminence; that alone had surrounded him with all the glamour of enthusiasm and illusion, and it sustained him to the end.

Bonaparte had one virtue which is more unusual the higher a man has risen. He was not ashamed of knowing so little of the details of administration. He put many questions, asking the definitions and sense of the most ordinary words. He stimulated discussion and kept it going till his opinion was formed. . . .

In the four years of his Consulate he held several Councils of State every day. There all questions of administration, finance, and jurisprudence were debated. Because he had great acumen, he would often throw out profound comments, judicious reflections, which astonished those most experienced in these matters. . . .

But as soon as Bonaparte had formed an opinion, right or wrong, on these questions of government, he no longer consulted anyone, or if he did so, it was no longer to embrace the other viewpoint. He always followed his own ideas; his opinion was his one rule of conduct, and he made bitter sport of all who expressed a different view. Tapping himself on the head, he would hold them up to ridicule by saying, "This sound instrument is more useful than the advice of men who are supposed to be more educated and experienced."

Once he had succeeded in concentrating the whole government in his own hands and taking counsel only with himself, Bonaparte hit on the idea of molding a generation of henchmen. He often said that men of 40 were imbued with the principles of the Old Regime, and could not therefore be devoted to his person or policies. He took a dislike to them and immediately started a "nursery" of five or six hundred young men, whom he appointed in turn to every office. A young man of 23 was put in charge of a department; others were sent out to administer conquered territory; another, barely 30, with no previous study, discharged the important functions of chief judge and minister of justice. Not all of these young men had the capacity, the prestige, or the decorum required for these positions. But he judged them sufficiently devoted to his person and his government, and that was enough. He applied the same principles to the organization of the army. The glory of the older generals irked him, their advice offended him, and in his later years he was less concerned to make use of ability than to reward devotion to himself. . . .

This conduct of Bonaparte's had no small share in alienating the minds of the French. A department placed under the control of a schoolboy feels humiliated; its confidence in the head of the government is weakened and its trust in the magistrature is at an end. . . .

He encouraged the arts, but only from policy or ostentation, never from the feeling that a country is judged by its monuments and its works of genius. . . . It was curious to observe him walking through the [Louvre] and confronting each masterpiece with the same impassivity. He never stopped before any of them. If his attention was directed to one, he would ask coldly, "Whose is it?" without offering any comment. Told that David was the finest painter of the age, he believed it and repeated it, but never entered into any detail on his talent or ventured a comparison with other artists of the day. . . .

Napoleon was afraid of the masses. He dreaded insurrection and this fear always drove him to wrong measures. He made it a policy that grain should be very cheap, since riots are nearly always caused by the high price and scarcity of bread. Consequently, he did not allow the export of grain until the farmers threatened to stop growing it. No one could get it into his head that since the price of all commodities had risen by [half] since the Revolution, it was natural for grain to follow suit. He did not see that well-to-do farmers meant a wealthy nation. . . .

Napoleon never knew a generous feeling. That is what made him such boring company. That was the reason he had no friends. He regarded men as base coin with which to gratify his whims and ambitions. . . .

CHAPTER 19
ROMANTIC REACTION (ca. 1800–1835)

Romanticism, in one sense, is a timeless philosophy that prefers emotion and sentiment to logic; the individual and the particular to the type and the general; religion and mystical experiences to agnosticism. The Romanticist therefore strenuously opposes the Classicist. Mankind then tends to fluctuate between these polar extremes, which have been called "the systole and diastole of the human conscience."

But *Romantic* also has a historical meaning; it signifies the *Zeitgeist,* or spirit, animating the generation that came after the French Revolution—the generation that could no longer accept the old values of the Age of Reason, but found they had nothing to put in their place. So they frequently spent their lives seeking new values, most of which were, naturally, opposed to those of the eighteenth century. Called "Romantic," these values were often the result of the wildest kind of experimentation in styles of living, thinking, and writing. One is reminded of Walt Whitman or Henry David Thoreau in the United States, or their predecessors: Goethe, Heine, Hegel in Germany: Jean-Jacques Rousseau in France; and Wordsworth, Coleridge, Byron in England. It is not surprising, given the French leadership in the Age of Reason, that most of the leaders of Romanticism were German and English.

The Age of Romanticism was also an Age of Reaction and Reconstruction. The victorious powers—Austria, Russia, Prussia, and England—would have liked to turn the clock back to 1789, before the Revolution and the twenty-five years of warfare and dictatorship that had cost them all so dear, not only in lives and money, but also in those same values the Romantics were struggling with, except that where Romantics tended to favor liberal principles, the governing classes favored conservative, if not reactionary, principles. Their leader from behind the scenes was the Austrian Premier Prince Metternich, who managed to hold the line against the threat of nationalism, liberalism, and democracy until almost mid-century, although he lost the battle in Greece, Belgium, and Latin America; which last defeat of the Holy Alliance, as the victorious powers were known, was by an American President named Monroe and a doctrine proposed by John Quincy Adams.

DOCUMENTS

First we turn to an old friend, Jean-Jacques Rousseau, whose life was an example of the unrequited Romantic, although we hasten to add that most of his writings are superb illustrations of the application of Reason to life's biggest problems. Then we look to Goethe and Heine for the best in German poetic vision and expression, followed by some examples of English Romantic poetry in Blake, Wordsworth, and Coleridge. Finally we turn to politics in Metternich's thought, the Holy Alliance, and some ideas on the reconstruction of society.

REVOLT AGAINST THE EIGHTEENTH CENTURY

ROUSSEAU: CONFESSIONS (1770ff.)

Livre premier, passim.

The Father of Modern Romanticism, Jean-Jacques Rousseau sought for, longed for, a harmony with nature. He discovered the beauty of mountains, trees, birds, and flowers. He cultivated his heart the way others cultivate their minds. Not that he was anti-intellectual, far from it! Self-taught, he became the great teacher of others, including such varied personages as Immanuel Kant, Wolfgang von Goethe, Maximilien Robespierre, Karl Marx, Leo Tolstoy, and John Dewey. His *Confessions*, the most widely read of all his works, is unique, as Rousseau himself indicates: "God made me and then broke the mold!"

I am undertaking a project without precedent, one which will not have any imitators. I intend to set before my fellow creatures the likeness of a man in the full light of his true nature. And that man is myself.

Myself alone! I know the feelings of my heart and I know Mankind. I am not made like the men I have seen; I dare say I am not like any man in existence. If I am not better, at least I am different. Whether Nature did well to break the mold in which I was cast is for others to decide after reading me.

Whenever the trumpet sounds the Last Judgment, I shall go before the Sovereign Judge with this book in my hand. Boldly I will say, "Here is what I have done, what I have thought, and what I have been. I have set down the good and the bad with equal candor. I have omitted nothing bad; neither have I exaggerated the good. . . . I have shown myself as I was: mean and contemptible, on the one hand; good, high-minded, and sublime, on the other. I have revealed my innermost self, as Thou hast known me. O Eternal Spirit, gather round me the countless host of my fellow men. Let them hear my confessions, and blush with shame at my villanies or groan in agony at my misfortunes. Then let each of them in turn reveal his heart at the foot of Thy throne with the same sincerity, and say, who dares: 'I was a better man than he!' "

I felt before I thought: that is the common lot of humanity. But I experienced it more than others. I do not know what I did before the age of five or six. I do not know how I learned to read; I only remember my earliest reading and the effect it had on me. I date from then the development of my uninterrupted self-awareness. My mother had left behind some romances, which my father and I began reading after supper. At first it was simply a matter of practicing my reading on some interesting books, but soon we became so absorbed that we read by turns without stopping and spent whole nights that way. We could not close a book until we had finished it. Sometimes my father, hearing the birds chirp in the morning, would say, shamefacedly, "We must go to bed, I am a bigger child than you are."

With this dangerous method, I soon acquired not only great facility in reading and understanding, but a knowledge of emotions that was unique in one of my years. I had no idea of things in themselves, but all feelings and passions were known to me. I conceived of nothing, but felt everything. Those chaotic emotions which I experienced one after another did not affect my reason, which had not yet developed, but they helped to give me a mind of a different stamp and notions of human life that were both odd and romantic—notions that neither experience nor reflection have been able to cure me of. . . .

How could I become wicked when I saw nothing but gentleness and was surrounded by the finest people in the world? My father, my aunt, my nurse, my relatives, our friends and neighbors, all those around me did not obey me, it is true, but they loved me and I loved them in return. My will was so little stimulated and so seldom contradicted that it did not occur to me to have any. Up until the day that I served under a master, I never knew what a whim might be. Except for the time I spent in reading or writing, or when my father took me for a walk, I was always with my aunt, standing or sitting by her side, watching her embroider or listening to her sing, and I was happy. Her good cheer, her gentleness, her sweet face made such a strong impression on me that I can still see her appearance, her attitude, her expression; I remember her endearing little words and phrases; I could describe the clothes she wore and how her hair was done, not forgetting the two little curls on her temples, after the fashion of the time.

I am convinced that I owe to her the taste—passion, rather—for music, which only developed to the full long afterward. She knew a prodigious number of melodies and songs, which she would sing in a thin but gentle voice. This excellent woman's cheerful disposition banished all moodiness and melancholy, not only from herself but also from those around her. . . . Even now, when I have lost her and as I grow older, many of [her songs] totally forgotten since childhood, return to my mind with inexpressible charm. Would anyone believe that an old dotard like myself, plagued with cares and troubles, sometimes find myself weeping like a child while mumbling through one of those little songs in a voice already broken and trembling?

. . . I have spent my life in idle longing, without saying a word, in the presence of those I loved the most. Not daring to declare my taste, I at least satisfied it in relationships that gave me the sense of it. To lie at the feet of an imperious mistress, to obey her commands, to ask her forgiveness—that was pure pleasure, and the more my vivid imagination heated up my blood, the more I had the aspect of a bashful lover.

One can well imagine that this manner of making love does not lead to very speedy results, and is not very dangerous to the virtue of those who are its object. Hence, I have seldom possessed, but have nonetheless enjoyed myself after my fashion, which is to say, in imagination. That is how it happens that my senses, in keeping with my timid disposition and romantic spirit, have kept my sentiments pure and my morals blameless, owing to the very tastes which, with a bit more daring, might have plunged me into the most brutal sensuality. . . .

I am a man of very strong passions, and when I am stirred by them nothing can equal my impetuosity; I forget all discretion, all feelings of respect, fear, and decency; I am cynical, impudent, violent, and intrepid; no feeling of shame restrains me, no danger frightens me; except for the single object that occupies my mind, the universe no longer exists. But all this lasts only a moment, and the next moment plunges me into complete annihilation. In my calmer moments I am indolence and timidity personified; everything frightens and repels me; a fly buzzing past alarms me; something I want to say or do terrifies my apathy; fear and shame overwhelm me to such an extent that I want to hide myself completely from my fellows. If I have to speak, I do not know what to say; if I have to act, I do not know what to do; if anyone looks at me, I am mortified. . . .

Add to this, that none of my prevailing interests have to do at all with things that can be bought. I want nothing but pure pleasures and money poisons everything. For instance, I am fond of the pleasures of the table, but since I cannot endure the constraint of good society nor the drunkenness of the tavern, I can enjoy them only with a friend; alone, I cannot do so, for my imagination then flies to other things and eating affords me no pleasure. If my overheated blood longs for women, my warm heart cares more for affection. Women bought for money lose their charm for me. . . . It is the same with all pleasures within my reach: unless they are free, I find them insipid. I like only those pleasures that belong to the first one who knows how to enjoy them.

. . . I worship freedom; I abhor restraint, confinement, subjugation. As long as I have money in my wallet, I am assured my independence. . . . The money we possess is an instrument of freedom; that which we pursue is an instrument of slavery. . . .

My disinterestedness is therefore nothing but laziness; the pleasure of possession is not worth the trouble of acquisition. . . . Money tempts me less than things: between money and a desired object there is always an intermediary, but between the thing itself and the enjoyment of it there is none.

GOETHE: POETRY AND TRUTH (1811–1833)

Dichtung und Wahrheit, trans. J. Oxenford (London, 1848), pp. 419–425.

The nearest to an all-round man since the Renaissance, Wolfgang von Goethe (1749–1832) rivals Shakespeare in his literary output and exceeds him in such areas as science, philosophy, music, and politics. His collected works number 140 volumes, but his greatest work is said to have been his life! The following excerpts from his autobiography show the gulf between him and the Age of Reason and indicate something of the new spirit he helped bring about, although he never accepted Romanticism uncritically.

We young men, with our German love of truth and nature, considered honesty toward ourselves and others as the best rule in life and art. Hence Voltaire's partisan dishonesty and his constant debasement of noble subjects became more and more distasteful and our aversion to him grew daily. He seemed never to have done with degrading religion and the Holy Scriptures on which it is grounded, for the sake of injuring priestcraft, so-called. That aroused my irritation, but when I learned that, to weaken the tradition of the Flood, he had denied the existence of fossilized shells, . . . he entirely lost my confidence, for my own eyes had seen, plainly enough on the Bastberg, that I stood on what had been the floor of an ancient sea. . . . These mountains had certainly once been covered with waves, whether before or during the Flood did not concern me. . . .

Diderot was sufficiently akin to us, since on all the points for which the French criticize him, he is a true German. But even his point of view was too lofty, his range of vision too wide for us to place . . . ourselves at his side. . . . But he, like Rousseau, by emanating a disgust of social life, quietly paved the way for those enormous world-wide changes affecting all hitherto existing forms.

But . . . what influence did these two men have on art? Here again they pointed to Nature and urged us to turn from art to follow her. Now, the greatest problem in all art is to produce, by illusion, the semblance of a higher reality. But it is a false endeavor to push the realization of the illusion so far that only a commonplace reality remains in the end. . . .

We had neither the desire nor the inclination to be enlightened or improved with the aid of philosophy. On religious questions we felt we had sufficiently enlightened ourselves, looking askance at the violent quarrel between the *philosophes* and the French priesthood. Prohibited books condemned to the flames, of which so much was heard, had no effect on us: As a typical instance, [Holbach's] *Système de la nature,* we did not see how such a book could be dangerous. It seemed so gloomy, so Cimmerian, so deathlike, . . . that we shuddered at it as at a spectre. The author thinks he is giving his book a great recommendation when he announces in the preface that, as a decrepit old man just sinking into the grave, he wants to proclaim the truth to his contemporaries and to posterity.

We laughed at him, for we thought old people incapable of appreciating whatever is good and desirable in the world. "Old churches have dark windows: to know how cherries and berries taste, ask children and sparrows"—those were our gibes and maxims. So that book, as the quintessence of senility, seemed to us insipid, offensive even. "Everything had to be, of necessity," said the book, "therefore there was no God." But could not God also exist of necessity? we asked. At the same time we admitted that we could not escape from the necessity of day and night, the seasons, the influence of climate, physical and animal conditions. Still, we felt within us something like perfect freedom of will, as well as something that sought to counteract that freedom.

We could not abandon the hope of making ourselves more and more rational, more and more independent of external things, nay, even of ourselves. The word freedom has so fair a sound that we cannot do without it, even if it designates an error.

None of us read the book through, for it disappointed the expectations with which we had opened it. It announced a "system of nature," so we had hoped to learn something of Nature, our idol. Physics and chemistry, descriptions of heaven and world with its wealth of beauty, and we would fain have heard more, both in general and in particular: of suns and stars, of planets and moons, of mountains, valleys, rivers, and seas, with all that live and move in them. That in the course of this, much must occur which would appear to the common man as pernicious, to the clergy as dangerous, and to the State as inadmissible, we had no doubt. . . . But how hollow and empty did we feel this melancholy, atheistic half-night to be, in which earth vanished with all its creatures, heaven with all its stars. Matter was supposed to have existed and to have been in motion from all eternity, and this motion, to right and left and in every direction, was supposed to have produced the infinite phenomena of existence. We might have allowed all this to pass if the author, out of his matter in motion, had really built up the world before our eyes. But he seemed to know as little about nature as we did. . . .

If this book did us any harm at all, it was in giving us a hearty dislike of all philosophy, especially metaphysics, while on the other hand we threw ourselves into living knowledge, experience, action, and poetry, with all the more zeal and passion.

Thus on the very borders of France, we at one blow got rid of everything French about us. The French way of life we found too defined and genteel, their poetry cold, their criticism annihilating, and their philosophy abstruse. . . .

HEINE: THE ROMANTIC SCHOOL (1833)

From *Die romantische Schule* (Halle a. S., 1836), pp. 2–3, 17. Trans. S. Fleischmann (New York 1882).

German poet, critic, and satirist, Heinrich Heine emigrated to Paris in 1831 to escape German anti-Semitism, among other things. He was not only a leading lyrical poet but he was also able to criticize the excesses of the Romantic movement. An international personage, Heine combined the best of French, German, and English thought.

What was the Romantic School in Germany? It was nothing else than the reawakening of the poetry of the Middle Ages as it manifested itself in the . . . art and life of those times. This poetry, however, had developed out of Christianity, it was a passion-flower that blossomed from the blood of Christ . . .—that flower in whose calyx one may behold a counterfeit presentment of the tools used at the Crucifixion, . . . hammer, pincers, nails. This flower is by no means unsightly, only spectral; its aspect fills our hearts with a dread pleasure, like those convulsive, sweet emotions that arise from grief. In this respect the passion-flower would be the fitting symbol of Christianity itself, whose awe-inspiring charm consists in the voluptuousness of pain . . .

I refer to that religion whose earliest dogmas contained a condemnation of all flesh, not only admitting the supremacy of the spirit over the flesh but seeking also to mortify the latter in order to glorify the former. I refer to that religion through whose unnatural mission vice and hypocrisy came into the world, for through the odium which it cast on the flesh, the most innocent gratification of the senses was accounted sinful; and, since it was impossible to be entirely spiritual, the growth of hypocrisy was inevitable. I refer to that religion which, by teaching the renunciation of all earthly pleasures, and by inculcating abject humility and angelic patience, became the most efficacious support of despotism. Mankind now recognizes the nature of that religion and will no longer allow itself to be put off with promises of a heaven hereafter; it knows that the material world has also its good and is not wholly given over to Satan; now man vindicates the pleasures of the world, this beautiful garden of the gods, our inalienable heritage. . . .

The political condition of Germany was particularly favorable to the tendencies of the Romantic School, which sought to introduce a national-religious literature similar to that . . . of the Middle Ages. "Need teaches prayer," they say, and the need was never greater. More than ever were the masses inclined toward prayer, toward religion, toward Christianity. No people is more devoted to its rulers than the German people, and the awful condition to which the country was reduced through war and foreign rule, combined with the sorrowful spectacle of their vanquished princes creeping at the feet of Napoleon, afflicted and grieved the Germans. . . .

We would have submitted to Napoleon quietly enough, except that our princes . . . thought the united strength of their subjects might be useful, [so] they sought to awaken a sense of homogeneity in the German people; even the most exalted magnates now spoke of a German nationality, a common German fatherland, a union of the Christian-Germanic races, and the unity of Germany. We were ordered to be patriotic, and straightway we became patriots—for we always obey when our princes command.

ROMANTIC POETRY

Many students find it difficult to read poetry, especially the lyric poetry of the last century. Maybe it would help if you simply read the poem through to see if there is a line or two that appeals to you for whatever reason. Then concentrate on that portion, reading and rereading it until you get it into your head as you would a popular song. That is what lyric poetry is, after all: a song, usually celebrating something the poet has strong feelings about and wants to share. That is what makes these poems Romantic— the sense of the personal, the unique, the once-in-a-lifetime experience.

BLAKE: MOCK ON, MOCK ON, VOLTAIRE, ROUSSEAU

An engraver who became a poet and illustrated his own books, William Blake (1757–1827) was also a revolutionary thinker and a mystic who exerted great influence on the Romantic movement. He taught his wife to read and write, after which she

The Dream of Reason Produces Monsters
(1797), by the Spanish painter Goya, illus-
trates the Romantic attack on the Age of
Enlightenment, which had played down or
neglected the emotions. (Brooklyn Museum
Collection.)

became his active partner in all his work. Blake's powerful drawings and paintings recall those of Michelangelo in the Sistine Chapel. The following poem illustrates his revolt against the eighteenth century.

Mock on, mock on, Voltaire, Rousseau;
Mock on, mock on; 'tis all in vain!
You throw the sand against the wind,
And the wind blows it back again.

And every sand becomes a gem
Reflected in the beams divine;
Blown back they blind the mocking eye
But still in Israel's path they shine.

The Atoms of Democritus
And Newton's Particles of Light
Are sands upon the Red Sea shore
Where Israel's tents do shine so bright.

WORDSWORTH: THE TABLES TURNED

After a rather wild boyhood, William Wordsworth (1770—1850) went to France in 1791 and was enthralled by the Revolution. He returned to England filled with the spirit of

Rousseau and Romanticism. In 1798 he and Coleridge published *Lyrical Ballads,* which became a manifesto for the new poetry, characterized by the language of people rather than the stiff and formal structures of the earlier age. But it is the content of their poetry, especially, that illustrates the Romantic Protest against the Age of Reason.

Up! up! my Friend, and quit your books;
Or surely you'll grow double:
Up! up! my Friend, and clear your looks;
Why all this toil and trouble?
. . . . . .

Books! 'tis a dull and endless strife:
Come, hear the woodland linnet,
How sweet his music! on my life,
There's more of wisdom in it.

And hark! how blithe the throstle sings!
He too, is no mean preacher:
Come forth into the light of things,
Let Nature be your teacher.
. . . . . .

One impulse from a vernal wood
May teach you more of man,
Of moral evil and of good,
Than all the sages can.

Sweet is the lore which Nature brings;
Our meddling intellect
Mis-shapes the beauteous forms of things:—
We murder to dissect.

Enough of Science and of Art;
Close up those barren leaves;
Come forth, and bring with you a heart
That watches and receives.

COLERIDGE: KUBLA KHAN

Poet, critic, philosopher—Samuel Taylor Coleridge (1772–1834) was one of the most original minds of the nineteenth century. The power of his imagination is displayed in all his work, perhaps nowhere more graphically than in "The Rime of the Ancient Mariner," part of the *Lyrical Ballads* mentioned above and his most widely read work. The following poem, written in 1816, is favored by students of elocution; it should be read aloud.

In Xanadu did Kubla Khan
A stately pleasure-dome decree:
Where Alph, the sacred river ran
Through caverns measureless to man
   Down to a sunless sea.
. . . . . .

   The shadow of the dome of pleasure
   Floated midway on the waves;
   Where was heard the mingled measure
   From the fountain of the caves.
It was a miracle of rare device,
A sunny pleasure-dome with caves of ice!
   A damsel with a dulcimer
   In a vision once I saw:
   It was an Abyssinian maid,
   And on her dulcimer she played,
   Singing of Mount Abora.
   Could I revive within me
   Her symphony and song,
   To such a deep delight 'twould win me,
That with music loud and long,
I would build that dome in air,
That sunny dome! those caves of ice!
And all who heard should see them there,
And all should cry, Beware! Beware!
His flashing eyes, his floating hair!
Weave a circle round him thrice,
And close your eyes with holy dread,
For he on honey-dew hath fed,
And drunk the milk of paradise.

ROMANTICISM IN POLITICS

"Our constitution . . . is the result of . . . following nature, which is wisdom without reflection, and above it."—Edmund Burke.

THE HOLY ALLIANCE (1815)

From Robinson and Beard, *Readings in Modern European History*, 1:384.

One of the more bizarre documents in international relations, the Holy Alliance was the brainchild of Czar Alexander I and his spiritualist, Madame Krudener. Eventually all the

Liberty Leading the People, by Eugene Delacroix (1831). Liberty, a buxom goddess, and the French freedom fighters—swarthy workers, bourgeois in top hats, and children wielding pistols—all stride nonchalantly over their fallen comrades, toward the Romantic goal of a popular revolution to overthrow the Bourbon monarchy of Charles X in July 1830. (Alinari/Editorial Photocolor Archives.)

European heads of state signed it, except the Pope, the Sultan, and the King of England. The Pope did not sign, he said, because he saw nothing holy about an alliance among a schismatic Russian Orthodox Emperor, an heretical Protestant King of Prussia, and a Roman Catholic Emperor of Austria. The Sultan of Turkey did not sign it: being an "infidel," he was not asked. And the King of England would not sign it because, he said, he did not know what it meant and, besides, he thought the Quadruple Alliance was adequate by itself.

It is true, of course, that the alliance of the four powers—England, Austria, Prussia, and Russia—that had won the war also controlled the peace, prevented revolutions from succeeding, and generally maintained the *status quo ante bellum*. But in the public's mind it was the Holy Alliance that was the real instrument of repression. Like George III as a target of the American Declaration of Independence, the Holy Alliance was a propagandist's delight in the years after Waterloo.

Their Majesties the Emperor of Austria, the King of Prussia, and the Emperor of Russia, having, in consequence of the great events which have marked the course of

The Executions of May 3rd, one of a series of paintings by Goya based on the Peninsular War of 1808–1812. Here another Romantic feeling—nationalism—comes into play. Goya's indignation, however, seems to be directed more at mankind in general for failing to prevent this kind of insanity, than at the French, who are doing the actual killing. (Museo del Prado.)

the last three years in Europe, and especially of the blessings which it has pleased Divine Providence to shower down upon those States which place their confidence and their hope on it alone, acquired the intimate conviction of the necessity of settling the rules to be observed by the Powers, in their reciprocal relations, upon the sublime truths which the Holy Religion of our Saviour teaches:

They solemnly declare . . . their fixed resolution, both in the administration of their respective States and in their political relations with every other Government, to take for their sole guide the precepts of that Holy Religion, namely, the precepts of Justice, Christian Charity, and Peace, which . . . must have an immediate influence on the councils of princes, and guide all their steps, as being the only means of consolidating human institutions and remedying their imperfections. . . .

Art. 1. Conformably to the words of the Holy Scriptures, which command all men to consider each other as brethren, the three contracting Monarchs will always remain united by the bonds of a true and indissoluble fraternity, and . . . they will, on all occasions and in all places, lend each other aid and assistance; and, regarding themselves towards their subjects and armies as fathers of families, they will lead them, in the same spirit of fraternity with which they are animated to protect Religion, Peace, and Justice.

Art. 2. . . . The three allied Princes, looking on themselves as merely delegated by· Providence to govern three branches of the one family, namely, Austria, Prussia, and Russia, thus confessing that the Christian world, of which they and their people form a part, has in reality no other Sovereign than Him to whom alone power really belongs, because in Him alone are found all the treasures of love, science, and infinite wisdom, that is to say, God, our Divine Saviour, the Word of the Most High, the Word of Life. Their Majesties consequently recommend to their people, with the most tender solicitude, as the sole means of enjoying that Peace which arises from a good conscience, and which alone is durable, to strengthen themselves every day more and more in the principles and exercise of the duties which the Divine Saviour has taught to mankind.

Art. 3. All the Powers who shall choose solemnly to avow the sacred principles which have dictated the present Act, and shall acknowledge how important it is for the happiness of nations, too long agitated, that these truths should henceforth exercise over the destinies of mankind all the influence which belongs to them, will be received with equal ardor and affection into this Holy Alliance.

Done in triplicate and signed at Paris, the year of Grace 1815, 14/26th September.

Signed: Francis [Emperor of Austria]
Frederick William [King of
Prussia]
Alexander [Emperor and Czar
of Russia]

METTERNICH: CONSERVATIVE PHILOSOPHY (1815−1848)

From *Memoirs of Prince Metternich* (New York, 1880−1889), 3:474f.

The Chancellor of Austria, Prince Metternich, was the leading light in the union of the powers to maintain peace after the Congress of Vienna in 1815. His philosophy and political acumen dominated Europe until the Revolutions of 1848. The following excerpts from his *Memoirs* tell how he did it.

The world wants to be governed by facts and according to justice, not by phrases and theories; the first need of society is to be maintained by strong authority . . . and not to govern itself. . . . The first and chief concern of the great majority of every nation is the stability of the laws and their uninterrupted action—never their change. Therefore let governments govern, let them maintain the foundations of their institutions, both ancient and modern. . . .

Let governments announce this determination to their people and demonstrate it by facts. Let them reduce the doctrinaires to silence at home and show their contempt for them abroad. Let them not foster the suspicion of being tolerant of error or indifferent to it. Let them not encourage the belief that experience will be supplanted by experiments, which are, to say the least, dangerous. Let them . . . not seek by concessions to placate parties whose aim is the destruction of all power but their own, whom concessions will never win over, but only further embolden in their pretensions to power.

In these troublous times, let them be more than usually cautious in attempting any real ameliorations not absolutely required by the needs of the moment, to the end that good itself may not turn against them, which is the case whenever a government measure seems to be inspired by fear.

Let them not confuse concessions made to parties with the good they ought to do for their people in modifying, according to their recognized needs, such branches of the administration as require it.

Let them give minute attention to the financial state of their kingdoms, so that their people may enjoy, by the reduction of public burdens, the real, not imaginary, benefits of a state of peace.

Let them be just, but strong; beneficent, but strict.

Let them maintain religious principles in all their purity, and not allow the faith to be attacked and morality interpreted according to the social contract or the visions of foolish sectarians.

Let them suppress secret societies, the gangrene of society.

In short, let the great monarchs strengthen their union and prove to the world that while it exists, it is beneficent and insures the political peace of Europe; that it is powerful only for the maintenance of tranquillity at a time when so many attacks are directed against it; that the principles which they profess are paternal and protective, menacing only the disturbers of public tranquillity. . . . The people will take courage and the most profound and salutary peace . . . will have been effected.

THE CARLSBAD DECREES (1819)

From Meyer, *Corpus juris confoederationis Germanicae*, 2:138ff.

The practical side of Metternich's conservatism is illustrated by the following measures designed to deal with "the restless disposition of men's minds." On Hallowe'en 1817 the *Burschenschaften*, or German students' association, held a monster celebration of the 400th anniversary of Luther's Ninety-five Theses, replete with the burning of various symbols of repression. Not long afterward a reactionary poet-historian was murdered by a demented student of theology. Metternich seized upon these incidents to call a conference of the leading German princes at Carlsbad, in Bohemia, where they drew up the following resolutions. Adopted by the Diet of the Confederation, they successfully repressed liberalism and nationalism in Germany until the Revolutions of 1848.

I. Measures to be Adopted Regarding the Universities

Art. 1. A special governmental representative shall be appointed for each university and he shall reside in the place where the university is located; he is to be given appropriate instructions and extensive powers. [His] function shall be to see to the strict enforcement of the existing laws and rules of discipline; to observe carefully the spirit in which the instructors conduct their public lectures and classroom courses; to give a salutary direction to the instruction, without, however, interfering with matters of scholarship or methods of education, always having in view the future attitudes of the students; finally, to give constant attention to all that might promote morality, good order, and propriety. . . .

Art. 2. The confederated governments . . . pledge to remove from the universities or other public educational institutions all teachers who, by obvious deviation from their duty, or by exceeding the limits of their functions, or by the abuse of their legitimate influence over the minds of youth, or by propagating harmful doctrines hostile to public order or subversive of existing governmental institutions, shall have unmistakably proven their unfitness for the important offices entrusted to them. . . . No teacher so dismissed shall be appointed to any other institution of learning in any of the states in the Confederation.

Art. 3. The laws which have existed for some time against secret and unauthorized societies in the universities shall be strictly enforced, and especially they shall apply to the association established some years under the name of *Allgemeine Burschenschaften* (Universal Students' Union), since this society is based on the utterly unacceptable conception of permanent fellowship and communication among the universities. . . . The governments agree that no individual who shall be shown to have remained in such unauthorized associations . . . shall be admitted to any public office.

Art. 4. No student expelled from a university by a decision of the university senate, ratified or prompted by the governmental agent, or who shall have left in order to escape expulsion, may be admitted to any other university. . . .

II. Measures Concerning the Press

Art. 1. . . . No publication which appears in the form of a daily newspaper or periodical, or as a serial of less than 20 pages, may be sent to press in any state . . . without the previous knowledge and approval of the government officials. . . .

Art. 4. Each state is responsible not only to the state against which an offense is directed but also to the whole Confederation for every publication appearing within its jurisdiction in which the honor or security of another state is infringed or their constitution or administration is attacked. . . .

Art. 6. The Diet shall have the right to suppress on its own authoriy, without being petitioned, such writings included in Art. 1, in whatever German state they may appear, . . . as are inimical to the honor of the union, the safety of individual states, or the maintenance of peace and quiet in Germany. There shall be no appeal from such decisions and the governments involved shall see that they are put into exectuion. . . .

Art. 7. When a newspaper or periodical is suppressed by a decision of the Diet, the editor thereof may not, within a period of five years, edit a similar publication in any state of the German Confederation.

ALFRED DE MUSSET: THE CONFESSION OF A CHILD OF THE CENTURY (1835)

La confession d'un enfant du siècle (Paris, 1887), pp. 6–10, 14–15, 18–21.

Musset (1810–1857) represents what might be called the Romanticism of politics. In his *Confession,* written at age twenty-five after an ill-starred love affair with George Sand, that *femme fatale* of so many young men, Musset describes the "sickness" *(mal du siècle)* of the generation growing up too late—too late to know Napoleon, too late to have any heroes. But his generation did two things well: they made love and they made literature—out of their love affairs. Musset wrote his best play, *On ne badine pas avec l'amour* ("Don't Trifle with Love"), based on his affair with George Sand. And she developed the same theme in *Elle et lui* ("She and He"). Moral: If you are a Romanticist, your suffering may pay royalties.

The King of France [Louis XVIII] was on his throne, looking to see if he could find a bee [symbol of Napoleon] in the royal tapestry. Some people held out their hats and he gave them money; others showed him a crucifix and he kissed it; others merely shouted great resounding names at him and he told those people to go into the Great Hall where the echoes were better; . . . still others showed him their old cloaks, after they had carefully removed the bees, and to them he gave new ones.

The youths saw all this, thinking that the spirit of Caesar would soon land at Cannes and blow away this chaff. But the silence was unbroken and they saw only the paleness of the lily [symbol of the Monarchy] floating in the sky. When these youths asked about glory, they were told, "Become priests"; when they asked about hope, love, power, Life: "Become priests.". . .

Some people said, "The Emperor fell because they wanted no more of him." Others added, "The people wanted the King; no, Freedom; no, Reason; no, Religion; no, the English Constitution; no, Absolutism." And the last one said, "No, none of those things, just peace and quiet."

Three factors affected the lives of these young people: Behind them, a past forever discredited, thrashing about on its throne, with the fossils of centuries-old absolutism; before them, the dawning of a new horizon, the first glimmer of the future; and in between, something like the Ocean separating the Old World from Young America, something vague and floating, a troubled sea filled with wreckage and traversed now and then by some distant sail or a ship belching heavy smoke; the present, in a word, which separates the past from the future, neither the one nor the other but resembling both—where one never knows at each step whether he is treading on a seed or a dungheap.

It was amidst this chaos that a choice had to be made; this was the choice facing young men who were full of energy and courage, sons of the Empire, grandsons of the Revolution. As for the past, they wanted none of it, they had no faith in it; the future they loved, but how?—as Pygmalion loved Galatea: the future was their loved one in marble and they waited for the breath of life to animate her breast, for the blood to color her cheeks. . . .

Just as on the approach of a mighty storm there passes through the forest a terrible noise, making all the trees shudder, followed by profound silence; so Napoleon, in passing, had shaken the world. Kings felt their crowns trembling in the storm and, raising their hands to steady them, found only their own hair, bristling with terror. The pope traveled 300 leagues to bless Napoleon in the name of God and crown him with the diadem; but Napoleon took it from the pope's hands. And so everything trembled in that dismal forest of old Europe, followed by silence. . . .

A feeling of extreme discomfort began growing in all these young men's breasts. Condemned to idleness by the powers governing the world, delivered up to vulgar pedants of all kinds, . . . these gladiators suffered an intolerable anguish in the depths of their being. . . .

About this time two poets, whose genius was second only to Napoleon's, devoted their lives to collecting all the elements of agony and grief scattered through the universe. Goethe, the patriarch of the new literature, after having depicted in *Werther* the passion that leads to suicide, presented in *Faust* the most somber character ever to represent evil and unhappiness. . . . From his studio, surrounded by paintings and statues, rich, happy, and comfortable, he watched with a paternal smile as his gloomy creatures marched in dismal procession across the frontiers into France. Lord Byron replied with a cry of grief that made Greece tremble; he suspended *Manfred* over the abyss as if nothingness were the answer to the hideous enigma in which he clothed himself.

It was a degeneration of all things in heaven and earth, . . . as if humanity in a trance had been pronounced dead by those who took her place. Like a soldier who was asked, In what do you believe? replied: Myself; so the youth of France hearing that question replied: Nothing.

They split into two camps: On the one hand, the exalted spirits, the sufferers, all the expansive souls who had need of the infinite, bowed their heads and wept; they wrapped themselves in unwholesome dreams; and on an ocean of bitterness one saw nothing but broken reeds.

On the other hand, the men of flesh remained upright, inflexible amid material pleasures, caring for nothing but counting the money they had accumulated. One heard only a sob and a laugh, the one from the soul, the other from the body.

CHAPTER 20

THE INDUSTRIALIZATION OF SOCIETY, 1770–1830

The classic definition of the "Industrial Revolution" was provided almost a century ago by Arnold Toynbee (1852–1883). The following paragraphs are excerpted from his *Lectures on the Industrial Revolution of the 18th Century in England* (London, 1884), pp. 87ff.

An agrarian revolution plays as large part in the great industrial change of the end of the eighteenth century as does the revolution in manufacturing. . . . The agricultural changes which led to the decrease in the rural population . . . were: the destruction of the common-field system of cultivation; the enclosure, on a large scale, of common and waste lands; and the consolidation of small farms into large. . . . Between 1760 and 1843 nearly seven million acres . . . were enclosed. Connected with the enclosure system was the substitution of large for small farms. . . . The consolidation of farms reduced the number of farmers, while the enclosures drove the laborers off the land, as it became impossible for them to exist without their rights of pasturage for sheep and geese on common lands.

Severely, however, as these changes bore upon the rural population, they wrought . . . distinct improvement from an agricultural point of view. They meant the substitution of scientific for unscientific culture. . . . Enclosures brought an extension of arable cultivation and the tillage of inferior soils; and in small farms, where the land was exhausted by repeated corn [grain] crops, consolidation into farms of 100 to 500 acres meant rotation of crops, leases of 19 years, and good farm buildings. The period was one of great agricultural advance: the breed of cattle was improved, rotation of crops was generally introduced, the steam plow was invented, [and] agricultural societies were instituted. . . .

Passing to manufacturers, the all-prominent fact here [is] the substitution of the factory for the domestic system. . . . Four great inventions altered the character of the cotton manufacture: the spinning jenny, patented by Hargreaves in 1770; the waterframe, invented by Arkwright the year before; Crompton's mule introduced in 1779, and the self-acting mule. . . . None of these inventions by themselves would have revolutionized the industry. But in 1769—the year in which Napoleon and Wellington were born—James Watt took out his patent for the steam engine. In 1785 [he] and Boulton made a steam engine for a cotton mill, . . . and in the same year Arkwright's patent expired. These two facts taken together mark the introduction of the factory system. But the most famous invention of all, and the most fatal to domestic industry, the power-loom, . . . did not come into use for several years, and till the power-loom was introduced the workman was hardly injured. At first, in fact, machinery raised the wages of the spinners and weavers owing to the great prosperity it brought to the trade. In 15 years the cotton trade trebled itself; from 1788 to 1803 has been called "its golden age.". . . Meanwhile, the iron industry had been equally revolutionized by the invention of smelting by pit-coal brought into use between 1740 and 1750, and by the application in 1788 of the steam engine to blast furnaces. . . .

A further growth of the factory system owed its origin . . . to the expansion of trade, an expansion which was itself due to the great advance made . . . in the means of communication. The canal system was being rapidly developed throughout the country. In 1777 the Grand Trunk canal, 96 miles in length, connecting the Trent and Mersey, was finished; Hull and Liverpool were connected by one canal while another connected them both with Bristol; and in 1792, the Grand Junction canal, 90 miles in length, made a waterway from London through Oxford to the chief midland towns. Some years afterwards, the roads were greatly improved under Telford and Macadam; between 1818 and 1829 more than a thousand miles of turnpike road were constructed; and the next year, 1830, saw the opening of the first railroad. These improved means of communication caused an extraordinary increase in commerce, and to secure a sufficient supply of goods it became the interest of merchants to collect weavers around them in great numbers, to get looms together in a workshop, and to give out the warp themselves to the workpeople. To these latter this system meant a change from independence to dependence; at the beginning of the century the report of a committee asserts that the essential difference between the domestic and the factory system is that in the latter the work is done "by persons who have no property in the goods they manufacture." Another direct consequence of this expansion of trade was the regular recurrence of periods of overproduction and of depression, a phenomenon quite unknown under the old system, and due to this new form of production on a large scale for a distant market.

These altered conditions in the production of wealth necessarily involved an equal revolution in its distribution. In agriculture the prominent fact is an enormous rise in rents. . . . largely the effect of the enclosure system, of the consolidation of farms, and of the high price of corn during the French war. Whatever its causes, however, it represented a great social revolution, a change in the balance of political power and in the relative position of classes. The farmers shared in the prosperity of the landlords; for many of them held their farms under beneficial leases, and made large profits by them. In consequence, their character completely changed; they ceased to work and live with their laborers, and became a distinct class. The high prices of the war-time thoroughly demoralized them, for their wealth then increased so fast that they were at a loss what to do with it. Cobbett has described the change in their habits, the new food and furniture, the luxury and drinking, [resulting from] more money coming into their hands than they knew how to spend. Meanwhile, the effect . . . [on] the laborer was an exact opposite and most dangerous one. He felt all the burden of high prices, while his wages were steadily falling, and he had lost his common-rights. It is from this period, viz., the beginning of the nineteenth century, that the alienation between farmer and laborer may be dated.

Exactly analogous phenomena appeared in the manufacturing world. The new class of great capitalist employers made enormous fortunes, they took little or no part personally in the work of their factories, their . . . workmen were individually unknown to them, . . . the old relations between masters and men disappeared, and a "cash nexus" was substituted for the human tie.

CHANGES IN AGRICULTURE

ARTHUR YOUNG ON THE IMPROVEMENTS IN AGRICULTURE (1771)

The Farmer's Tour through the East of England (London, 1771), 2:150ff.

A member of the lesser English gentry, Arthur Young (d. 1820) never had to work with his hands; instead he spent most of his life as a publicist for the new agriculture, meaning large-scale, scientific, and experimental, as he indicates in the following excerpt. His writing on this subject was extensive and popular, winning him an appointment as Secretary to the new Board of Agriculture in 1793.

Pointing out the practices which have succeeded so nobly here [in Norfolk County] may perhaps be of some use to other counties possessed of the same advantages, but unknowing in the art to use them.

From 40 to 60 years ago, the northern and western, and a part of the eastern tracts of the county, were sheep-walks, let so low as from 6d. to 2s.6d. and 2s. an acre. Much of it was in this condition only 30 years ago. The great improvements have been made by means of the following circumstances.

First.   By inclosing without assistance of parliament.

Second.   By a spirited use of marle and clay.

Third.   By the introduction of an excellent course of crops.

Fourth.   By the culture of turnips well hoed.

Fifth.   By the culture of clover and ray-grass.

Sixth.   By landlords granting long leases.

Seventh.   By the country being divided chiefly into large farms.

In this recapitulation, I have inserted no article that is included in another. Take any one from the seven, and the improvement of Norfolk would never have existed. . . .

After the best managed inclosure, and the most spirited conduct in marling, still the whole success of the undertaking depends on this point: No fortune will be made in Norfolk by farming unless a judicious course of crops be pursued. That which has been chiefly adopted by the Norfolk farmers is,

a. Turnips.
b. Barley.
c. Clover; or clover and ray-grass.
d. Wheat.

. . . If the preceding articles are properly reviewed, it will at once be apparent that no small farmers could effect such great things as have been done in Norfolk. Inclosing, marling, and keeping a stock of sheep large enough for folding, belong absolutely and exclusively to great farmers. None of them could be effected by small ones—or such as are called middling ones in other counties. Nor should it be forgotten that the best husbandry in Norfolk is that of the largest farmers. . . . Great farms have been the soul of the Norfolk culture: split them into tenures of an hundred pounds a year, you will find nothing but beggars and weeds in the whole county. The rich man keeps his land rich and clean.

These are the principles of Norfolk husbandry, which have advanced the agriculture of the greatest part of that county to a much greater height than is anywhere to be met with over an equal extent of country.

THE ENCLOSURE MOVEMENT: GENERAL REPORT OF THE AGRICULTURAL STATE, AND POLITICAL CIRCUMSTANCES, OF SCOTLAND (1814)

A major agricultural development for both Young and Toynbee is *enclosure*. To understand this, one has to recall the medieval manor with its open-field system of strip farming and its common lands. As the Middle Ages declined, with the rise of towns and more efficient farming, there began a movement to fence in those lands, but each enclosure took an act of Parliament, of which 2,183 were passed in 1714–1801.

The following report by the British Board of Agriculture and Internal Improvement indicates some of the results of this procedure. Since it represents the British landed gentry, the report does not tell the whole story, especially the effect on the small farmers and cottagers, most of whom could no longer live on the land that had supported them for generations. What happened to them? We must defer that question until later.

The advantages of inclosures ought to be considered as connected with climate, soil, and occupancy.

1. A climate that is naturally warm or mild, will hardly require artificial shelter; but if cold, and backward for the production of crops, and hazardous . . . to livestock, shelter ought to be one of the . . . most important objects held in view.

2. A dry and kindly soil gives encouragement for plans of improvement by cultivation, and the fences and inclosures ought to be adapted for that purpose. . . . If the soil be wet, a large proportion of the fences ought to be . . . constructed for the additional purpose of drainage.

3. If the lands to be inclosed are to be occupied in pasture, the plan must [take] into consideration the particular kind of stock, [since] the same kind of fence that may sufficiently confine cattle, does not answer for sheep. . . . The general objects . . . are, to save expense in herding and attendance, to arrange the stock, to enable them to pasture quietly, undisturbed by dogs or other violence, and to shelter them . . . from cold and storms.

4. If the lands are to be chiefly occupied under grain, or other cultivated crops, the great objects of inclosure must be, a good arrangement of the fields for easy and correct access and cultivation, and for the effectual protection of the crops from trespass and depradation.

5. When a mixed mode of occupancy is in view, embracing both cultivation and pasture, a combination of the foregoing must form the basis for a proper plan of inclosure.

Advantages to Proprietors [Landlords]

. . . Inclosures are considered so necessary and useful by all practical farmers that, in consideration of having their land properly inclosed and fenced, they readily agree to pay a liberal percentage to the landlord for the expense, and to uphold the fences at their own charges during the occupancy. . . .

Advantages to Farmers

In the pasturage of livestock, the farmer is relieved, by means of inclosures, from the very considerable expense of herding and attendance, which is materially diminished in the management of sheep, and almost entirely saved in that of cattle, when the fences are all good. . . . By means of inclosures the pasturing stock is . . . allowed in peace to eat up the food upon the pastures to its utmost limits; and thus it improves much faster and better on the same extent of land, and of course returns more ample profit to the farmer. . . .

In the management of his arable lands, the farmer derives other solid advantages from inclosures. The important idea of security against trespass, from his own livestock or those of his neighbors, gives a stimulus towards improvement, enabling him to adopt a correct rotation of crops, to proceed with vigor in their cultivation, and to reap their fruits in safety. . . .

Advantages to the Laborers

Laborers find a great source of employment . . . in the execution of plans of inclosure, . . . besides which, there is a great extension of work provided for them, in consequence of the various improvements required upon inclosed land, far beyond what is called for in open lands; for the same waste[land] that afforded only the miserable wages and bare subsistence of a herd-boy . . . becomes capable, when inclosed, cultivated, and improved, to give employment and bread to many. . . .

Advantages to the Public

From what has already been stated, respecting wages and subsistence, . . . and the subsequent great increase of food for mankind, which the inclosed land afterwards produces, it necessarily follows that the population of the kingdom must be proportionally encouraged, increased, and supported, and that a numerous and hardy peasantry will thereby be trained up in the most productive and most valuable species of labor. As the physical strength of the nation evidently depends on the numbers of its hardy peasantry, everything that tends to increase their numbers, and to contribute towards their comfortable subsistence is deserving of the utmost encouragement.

POPULATION GROWTH

The following table shows the rate of population change in England during the eighteenth century. After a loss in 1700–1710, there is a rather obvious acceleration by the end of the century. Afterwards the rate went even higher, reaching 14 percent in 1801-1811 and 18 percent in 1811–1821. This increase helped to supply cheap labor for the new factories, while depressing the living standards for those affected by the enclosures and the periodic depressions mentioned by Toynbee.

Table 1
Population Growth of England and Wales in the Eighteenth Century

Year	Population (in millions)	Percentage Change
1700	5.5	**
1710	5.2	−5.4%
1720	5.6	+7 7
1730	5.8	+3.6
1740	6.0	+3.4
1750	6.5	+8.3
1760	6.7	+3.0
1770	7.4	+10.5
1780	7.9	+6.8
1790	8.7	+10.1
1801	9.2	+5.7

1700-1801—Net change in population = +3.7 million
          —Percentage change   = +67.3%

Source: *Observation on the Results of the Population Act,* 41 Geo. III, 9 (London, 1802).

THE FACTORY SYSTEM

RICHARD ARKWRIGHT AND THE FACTORY SYSTEM (1771ff)

From E. Baines, *History of Cotton Manufacture in Great Britain* (London, 1835), pp. 193ff.

Although he shamelessly stole other men's inventions, Richard Arkwright is credited with being the "Father of the Modern Factory System." Edward Baines, who was a prominent journalist and a member of Parliament, describes the nature of Arkwright's involvement in the rise of the modern factory.

Hitherto the cotton manufacture had been carried on almost entirely in the houses of the workmen; the hand or stock cards, the spinning wheel, and the loom required no larger apartment than that of a cottage. A spinning jenny of small size might also be used in a cottage, and in many instances was so used; when the number of spindles was considerably increased, adjacent workshops were used. But the water frame, the carding engine, and the other machines which Arkwright brought out in a finished state required both more space than could be found in a cottage and more power than could be applied by the human arm. The weight also rendered it necessary to place them in strongly built mills, and they could not be advantageously turned by any power then known but that of water.

The use of machinery was accompanied by a greater division of labor than existed in the primitive state of the manufacture; the material went through many more processes, and, of course, the loss of time and the risk of waste would have been much increased if its removal from house to house at every stage of the manufacture had been necessary. It became obvious that there were several important advantages in carrying on the numerous operations of an extensive manufacture in the same building. Where water power was required it was economy to build one mill, and put up one water wheel rather than several. This arrangement also allowed the master spinner himself to superintend every stage of the manufacture; it gave him a greater security against the wasteful or fraudulent consumption of the material; it saved time in the transference of the work from hand to hand; and it prevented the extreme inconvenience which would have resulted from the failure of one class of workmen to perform their part, when several other classes of workmen were dependent upon them. Another circumstance which made it advantageous to have a large number of machines in one manufactory was, that mechanics must be employed on the spot to construct and repair the machinery, and that their time could not be fully occupied with only a few machines.

All these considerations drove the cotton spinners to that important change in the economy of English manufactures, the introduction of the *factory system;* and when that system had once been adopted, such were its pecuniary advantages that mercantile competition would have rendered it impossible, even had it been desirable, to abandon it. . . .

Although Arkwright, by his series of machines, was the means of giving the most wonderful extension to the system, yet he did not absolutely invent it. Mills for the throwing of silk had existed in England, though not in any great number, from . . . 1719, at Derby, on the model of those . . . in Italy.

. . . Arkwright's first mill, at Nottingham, was moved by horses; his second, at Cromford, by water. During a period of ten or fifteen years after Mr. Arkwright's first mill was built (in 1771) at Cromford, all the principal works were erected on the falls of considerable rivers; no other power than water having been found practically useful. There were a few exceptions, where Newcomen's and Savery's steam engines were tried. But the principles of these machines were defective and their construction bad, the expense in fuel was great and the loss by frequent stoppages was ruinous. . . .

Arkwright was now rapidly making a large fortune, not merely by the sale of his patent machines and of licenses to use them, but much more by the profits of his several manufactories, for, having no less enterprise than judgment and skill, and being supported by large capital and very able partners, he greatly extended his concerns, and managed them all with such ability as to make them eminently prosperous. He offered the use of his patents by public advertisements, and gave many permission to use them on receiving a certain sum for each spindle. In several cases he took shares in the mills erected; and from these various sources he received a large annual tribute. . . .

I have found myself compelled to form a lower estimate of the inventive talents of Arkwright than most previous writers. [My] investigations . . . have shown that the splendid inventions, which even to the present . . . are ascribed to Arkwright, . . . belong in great part to other and much less fortunate men. In appropriating those inventions as his own, and claiming them as the fruits of his unaided genius, he acted dishonorably, and left a stain upon his character, which the acknowledged brilliance of his talents cannot efface. . . .

Table 2
Rate of Increase in the Importation of Raw Cotton into
Great Britain by Decades from 1741 to 1831 (% rounded)

Decade	Increase (%)	Decade	Increase (%)
1741–1751	81	1791–1801	68
1751–1761	22	1801–1811	40
1761–1771	26	1811–1821	93
1771–1781	76	1821–1831	85
1781–1791	320		

Source: Baines, History of the Cotton Manufacture, p. 348.

Baine's comment on the above table is also revealing:

From 1697 to 1741 the increase was trifling; between 1741 and 1751 the manufacture, though still insignificant in extent, made a considerable spring; during the next twenty years the increase was moderate; from 1771 to 1781, owing to the invention of the jenny and the water-frame, a rapid increase took place; in the ten years from 1781 to 1791, being those which immediately followed the invention of the mule and the expiration of Arkwright's patent, the rate of advancement was prodigiously accelerated, being nearly 320%; and from that time to the present [1835], and especially since the close of the war [with Napoleon], the increase, though considerably moderated, has been rapid and steady far beyond all precedent in any other manufacture.

THE ENGLISH FACTORY ACT OF 1802

From Statutes at Large, 43:632f., George III, c. 73.

There remains a nagging question behind all these discussions of agricultural and industrial "improvements": What happened to the common people, the farmers and cottagers, who were driven off the land by the inclosures, and also what about the new bodies of workers produced by the rapid population growth?

Although we do not know what happened to them in the aggregate, we suspect that many of them—or their children—ended up in the expanding mills and factories, where they were forced to work under conditions indistinguishable from slavery. The following act of 1802 was supposed to regulate their working conditions, but the Parliamentary reports three decades later show how much, or how little, was accomplished.

An Act for the preservation of the health and morals of apprentices and others employed in cotton and other mills. . . .

Be it enacted that . . . all such mills and factories within Great Britain and Ireland, wherein three or more apprentices or 20 or more other persons shall at any time be employed, shall be subject to the . . . rules and regulations contained in this act:

. . . The rooms and apartments in or belonging to any such mill or factory shall, twice at least in every year, be well and sufficiently washed with quick lime and water . . . [and] due care and attention shall be paid by the master and mistress of such mills or factories to provide a sufficient number of windows and openings . . . to insure a proper supply of fresh air. . . .

No apprentice . . . bound to any such master or mistress shall be employed or compelled to work for more than 12 hours in any one day . . . and after the first day of June, 1803, no apprentice shall be . . . compelled to work upon any occasion whatever between the hours of 9 o'clock at night and 6 o'clock in the morning. . . .

Every apprentice shall be instructed . . . in reading, writing, and arithmetic. . . .

The room or apartment in which any male apprentice shall sleep shall be entirely separate . . . from the room or apartment in which any female apprentice shall sleep, and . . . not more than than two apprentices shall in any case sleep in the same bed. . . .

Every apprentice . . . shall, for the space of one hour at least every Sunday, be instructed and examined in the principles of the Christian religion. . . .

And be it further enacted that the justices of the peace for every county [shall] appoint two persons, not interested in or . . . connected with any such mills or factories, to be visitors [with] full power and authority to enter into and inspect any such mill or factory at any time of the day [and] report from time to time in writing to the quarter sessions of the peace the state and condition of such mills and factories.

LIFE OF THE INDUSTRIAL WORKER

IN THE FACTORY

From *Parliamentary Papers*, 1831–1832, 15:95–97, 195–197, 339–341.

In 1832 Michael Sadler was chairman of a committee to investigate factory working conditions. His report not only produced some major reforms in a new factory act (1833), but it also provided Karl Marx with valuable evidence for his tracts on the capitalist system.

Mr. Matthew Crabtree, Called in and Examined

What age are you?—22.

What is your occupation?—A blanket manufacturer.

Have you ever been employed in a factory?—Yes.

At what age did you first go to work in one?—Eight.

How long did you continue in that occupation?—Four years.

Will you state the hours of labor . . . when you first went to the factory, in ordinary times.—From 6 [AM] to 8 [PM].

Fourteen hours?—Yes.

With what intervals for refreshment and rest?—An hour at noon.

When trade was brisk, what were your hours?—From 5 in the morning to 9 at night.

Sixteen hours?—Yes.

How far did you live from the mill?—About two miles.

Was there any time allowed for you to get your breakfast in the mill?—No.

Did you take it before you left your home? — Generally.

[How] could you be punctual; how did you awake?—I seldom did awake spontaneously; I was most generally awoke or lifted out of bed, sometimes asleep, by my parents.

Were you always in time?—No.

What were the consequences if you had been too late?—I was most commonly beaten.

Severely?—Very severely, I thought.

In those mills is chastisement towards the latter part of the day going on perpetually?—Perpetually. . . .

Do you think that if the overlooker were naturally a humane person it would still be found necessary for him to beat the children, in order to keep up their attention and vigilance at the termination of those extraordinary days of labor?—Yes, . . . they must keep up with the machine, and therefore however humane the slubber may be, as he must keep up with the machine or be found fault with, he spurs the children to keep up also by various means, but that which he commonly resorts to is to strap them when they become drowsy. . . .

When you got home at night after this labor, did you feel much fatigued?—Very much so.

Had you any time to be with your parents and to receive instruction from them?—No.

What did you do?—All that we did . . . was to get the little bit of supper that was provided for us and go to bed immediately. If the supper had not been ready directly, we should have gone to sleep while it was preparing. . . .

Elizabeth Bentley, Called in and Examined

What age are you?—23. . . .

What time did you begin to work in a factory?—When I was 6 years old. . . .

What were your hours of labor? . . .—From 5 in the morning till 9 at night, when they were thronged.

For how long have you worked that excessive length of time?—For about half a year.

What were your usual hours of labor when they were not so thronged?—From 6 in the morning till 7 at night.

What time was allowed for your meals?—40 minutes at noon.

Had you any time to get your breakfast or drinking?—No, we got it as we could.

And when your work was bad, you had hardly any time to eat at all?—No, we were obliged to leave it or take it home, and when we did not take it, the overlooker took it and gave it to his pigs. . . .

Explain what you had to do.—When the frames are full, they have to stop the frames, and take the flyers off, and take the full bobbins off, and carry them to the roller; and then put empty ones on, and set the frames going again.

Does that keep you constantly on your feet?—Yes, there are so many frames, and they run so quick.

Your labor is very excessive?—Yes, you have no time for anything.

Suppose you flagged a little, or were too late, what would they do?—Strap us. . . .

Girls as well as boys?—Yes.

Have you ever been strapped?—Yes.

Severely?—Yes. . . .

Did you live far from the mill?—Yes, two miles.

Had you a clock?—No, we had not. . . .

Were you also beaten for being too late?—No, I was never beaten myself, I have seen the boys beaten for being too late.

Were you generally there in time?—Yes; my mother has been up at four o'clock in the morning and at two o'clock; the colliers used to go to their work at about three or four o'clock, and when she heard them stirring she has got up out of her warm bed, and gone out and asked them the time; and I have sometimes been at Hunslet Car at 2 o'clock when it was steaming down with rain, and we have had to stay till the mill was opened [at 5 A.M.].

Peter Smart, Called in and Examined

. . You say you were locked up night and day?—Yes.

Do the children ever attempt to run away?—Very often.

Were they pursued and brought back again?—Yes, the overseer pursued them and brought them back.

Did you ever attempt to run away?—Yes, I ran away twice.

And were you brought back?—Yes; and I was sent up to the master's loft and thrashed with a whip for running away.

Were you bound to this man?—Yes, for six years.

By whom were you bound?—My mother got 15 shillings for the six years.

Do you know whether the children were . . . compelled to stop during the whole time for which they were engaged?—Yes, they were.

By law?—I cannot say by law; but they were compelled by the master; I never saw any law used there but the law of their own hands.

To what mill did you go next?—To Mr. Webster's. . . .

In what situation did you act there?—I acted as an overseer.

At 17 years of age?—Yes.

Did you inflict the same punishment that you yourself had experienced?—I went as an overseer; not a slave, but a slave-driver.

What were your hours of labor in that mill?—My master told me that I had to produce a certain quantity of yarn; the hours were at that time fourteen; I said I was not able to produce the quantity of yarn that was required; I told him if he took the timepiece out of the mill I would produce the quantity.

How long have you worked per day in order to produce the quantity your master required?—I have wrought nineteen hours. . . .

To what time have you worked?—I have seen the mill going till it was past 12 o'clock on the Saturday night.

So that the mill was still working on the Sabbath morning?—Yes.

Were the workmen paid by the piece or by the day?—No, all had stated wages.

Did not that almost compel you to use great severity to the hands then under you?—Yes, I was compelled often to beat them in order to get them to attend to their work. . . .

Were not the children exceedingly fatigued at that time?—Yes, exceedingly fatigued. . . .

Did you find that the children were unable to pursue their labor properly? . . .—Yes; they have been brought to that condition that I have gone and fetched up the doctor to them, to see what was the matter with them, and to know whether they were able to rise or not; [and] they were not able to rise; we have had great difficulty in getting them up.

TESTIMONY BEFORE THE ASHLEY MINES COMMISSION (1842)

Parliamentary Papers, 1842, 16:252, 258, 386, 461 (App. 1 and 2).

Just as the Sadler's Commission report resulted in regulatory factory legislation, so Lord Ashley's Commission report resulted in the Mines Act of 1842, prohibiting the employment of all women in the mines, and of boys under thirteen years of age.

No. 116.—Sarah Gooder, aged 8 years. I'm a trapper in the Gawber pit. It does not tire me, but I have to trap without a light and I'm scared. I go at four and sometimes half-past three in morning, and come out at half-past five [P.M.] I never go to sleep. Sometimes I sing when I've light, but not in the dark; I dare not sing then. I don't like being in the pit. I am very sleepy when I go sometimes in the morning. I go to Sunday-schools and read Reading made Easy. (She knows her letters and can read little words.) They teach me to pray. . . . I have heard tell of Jesus many a time. I don't know why he came on earth, I'm sure, and I don't know why he died, but he had stones for his head to rest on. I would like to be at school far better than in the pit.

No. 137—Thomas Wilson, Esq., of the Banks, Silkstone, owner of three collieries.
. . . I object on general principles to government interference in the conduct of any trade, and I am satisfied that in mines it would be productive of the greatest injury and

injustice. The art of mining is not so perfectly understood as to admit of the way in which a colliery shall be conducted being dictated by any person, however experienced, with such certainty as would warrant an interference with the management of private business. . . .

No. 14.—Isabella Read, 12 years old, coal-bearer. I carry about 125 pounds on my back; have to stoop much and am frequently in water up to the calves of my legs. When first [went] down, fell frequently asleep while waiting for coal and from heat and fatigue. I do not like the work nor do the lassies, but they are made to like it. When the weather is warm, there is difficulty in breathing and frequently the lights go out.

No. 134.—Isabel Wilson, 38 years old, coal putter. When women have children thick (fast), they are compelled to take them down early, I have been married 19 years and have had ten [births]; seven are in life. When [I] was a carrier of coals, which caused me to miscarry five times from the strains, I was gai ill after each. [But] putting is not so oppressive; last child was born on Saturday morning and I was at work on the Friday night. . . . None of the children read, as the work is no regular. I did read once, but no able to attend to it now; when I go below, lassie ten years of age keeps house and makes the broth or stir-about.

No. 26.—Patrice Kershaw, aged 17. My father has been dead about a year; my mother is living and has ten children. . . . All my sisters have been hurriers, but three went to the mill. . . . I hurry the corves [carts] a mile and more underground and back; they weigh 300cwt. [sic]; I hurry eleven a day; I wear a belt and chain at the workings to get the corves out; the getters [miners] that I work for are naked except [for] their caps; they pull off all their clothes; I see them at work when I go up; sometimes they beat me, if I am not quick enough, with their hands; they strike me upon my back; the boys take liberties with me sometimes they pull me about; I am the only girl in the pit; there are about 20 boys and 15 men; all the men are naked; I would rather work in mill than in coalpit.

This girl is an ignorant, filthy, ragged, and deplorable-looking object, and such an one as the uncivilized natives of the prairies would be shocked to look upon.

ANDREW URE: PHILOSOPHY OF MANUFACTURES (1835)

(p. 301)

Apologists for the new industrial system, of course, were numerous and none waxed more enthusiastic in his praise of child labor and factory working conditions than Andrew Ure, a Scottish chemist who turned his talents to the study of industry.

[The children] seemed to be always cheerful and alert, taking pleasure in the light play of their muscles—enjoying the mobility natural to their age. The scene of industry, so far from exciting sad emotions in my mind, was always exhilirating. It was delightful to observe the nimbleness with which they pieced the broken ends . . . and to see them at leisure, after a few seconds' exercise of their tiny fingers, to amuse themselves in any attitude they chose. . . . The work of these lively elves seemed to resemble a sport, in which habit gave them a pleasing dexterity. Conscious of their skill, they were delighted to show it off to any stranger. As to exhaustion by the day's work, they evinced no trace of it on emerging from the mill in the evening; for they immediately began to skip about any neighboring playground, and to commence their little amusements with the same alacrity as boys issuing from a school. . . .

Of all the common prejudices that exist with regard to factory labor, there is none more unfounded than that which ascribes to it excessive tedium and irksomeness above other occupations, owing to its being carried on in conjunction with the "unceasing motion of the steam engine." . . . The most irksome . . . are those [mills] in which steam engines are not employed, as in lace-running and stocking-weaving.

MR. COBBETT'S DISCOVERY (1833)

Hansard's *Parliamentary Debates*, July 18, 1833, 3d Ser. 19:912.

A publicist and reformer who lived some time on Long Island, William Cobbett entered Parliament in 1833, just in time to take part in the spirited debate on the factory legislation of that year.

Mr. Cobbett said a new discovery had been made in the House that night, which would doubtless excite great astonishment in many parts; at all events it would in Lancashire. It had formerly been said that the Navy was the great support of England; at another time that our maritime commerce was the great bulwark of our country; at another time that our colonies; it had even been whispered that the Bank was; but now it was admitted that our great stay and bulwark was to be found in three hundred thousand little girls, or rather in one-eighth of that number. Yes; for it was asserted, that if these little girls worked two hours less per day, our manufacturing superiority would depart from us.

THE ENGLISH FACTORY ACT OF 1833

From *Statutes of the United Kingdom*, 73:985f.:3−4. William IV, c. 103.

The Sadler's Committee investigations resulted in the following legislation, which should be compared with the Factory Act of 1802 (pp. 70−71, above).

An act to regulate the labor of children and young persons in the mills and factories of the united kingdom. . . .

No person under 18 years of age shall be allowed to work in the night—that is to say, between the hours half-past eight o'clock in the evening and half-past five o'clock in the morning—. . . in or about any cotton, woolen, worsted, hemp, flax, tow, linen, or silk mill or factory. . . .

No person under the age of 18 shall be employed in any such mill or factory . . . more than 12 hours in any one day, nor more than 69 hours in any one week. . . . There shall be allowed in the course of every day not less than one and a half hours for meals. . . .

It shall not be lawful for any person whatsoever to employ in any factory or mill as aforesaid, except in mills for the manufacture of silk, any child who shall not have completed his or her ninth year of age.

It shall not be lawful for any person . . . to employ . . . in any factory or mill . . . for a longer time than 48 hours in any one week, nor for [more] than nine hours in any one day . . . any child who shall not have completed his or her eleventh year of age. . . .

And whereas, by an act . . . passed in the forty-second year of George III [1802], it was . . . provided that the justices of the peace . . . should appoint yearly two persons . . . to be visitors of . . . mills and factories; . . . and whereas it appears that the provisions . . . were not duly carried into execution: . . . it shall be lawful for His Majesty . . . to appoint . . . four persons to be inspectors of factories and places where the labor of children and young persons under 18 is employed. . . . And such inspectors . . . are hereby empowered to enter any factory or mill, and any school attached or belonging thereto at all times and seasons, by day or by night . . . and to examine therein the children and any other person or persons employed therein, and to make inquiry respecting their condition, employment, and education. And such inspectors . . . are hereby empowered to . . . call to their aid in such examination and inquiry such persons as they may choose, and . . . to require any person . . . to give evidence upon such examination and inquiry. . . .

CHAPTER 21

LAISSEZ-FAIRE

> As every individual . . . endeavors as much as he can
> both to employ his capital in the support of domestic
> industry, and so to direct that industry that its produce
> may be of the greatest value; every individual necessar-
> ily labors to render the annual revenue of the society as
> great as he can. He generally, indeed, neither intends to
> promote the public interest, nor knows how much he is
> promoting it. By preferring the support of domestic to
> that of foreign industry, he intends only his own security;
> and by directing that industry in such a manner as its
> produce may be of the greatest value, he intends only his
> own gain, and he is in this, as in many other cases, led
> by an invisible hand to promote an end which was no
> part of his intention.
>
> —Adam Smith, *The Wealth of Nations.*

Laissez-faire, or "Hands off!" was a concept of the separation of State and Business that developed in the eighteenth century in opposition to mercantilism, the theory that all economic power should be concentrated in the State. Adam Smith in England, and the Physiocrats in France, developed the theory that economic forces were "natural," like the laws of physics and mathematics. Just as Newton had discovered the law of universal gravitation, the laissez-faire school "discovered" the law of supply and demand, the iron law of wages, the laws of population growth—all controlled by the "Unseen Hand" of God who, at the beginning of time, had ordained these and the other laws governing the universe.

In the nineteenth century these doctrines of "economic liberalism" came to predominate to such an extent that they took on the quality of holy writ. To question them, even to the extent of trying to regulate the labor of women and children, was to question the very foundations of society.

BENTHAM: A MANUAL OF POLITICAL ECONOMY (1789)

From *The Works of Jeremy Bentham,* 11 vols., ed. J. Bowring (Edinburgh, 1843), 3:33–34.

The following summary statement of the laissez-faire philosophy was provided by Jeremy Bentham (1748-1832), whose name is usually associated with the idea of

Utilitarianism, "the greatest happiness for the greatest number," but he also made significant contributions to prison reform, judicial organization, and changes in the Parliamentary electorate.

Political Economy is at once a *science* and an *art*. . . .

According to the principle of utility in every branch of the art of legislation, the object or end in view should be the production of the maximum of happiness in a given time in the community in question.

In the instance of this branch of the art, the object or end in view should be the production of that maximum of happiness, in so far as this more general end is promoted by the production of the maximum of wealth and maximum of population.

The practical questions, therefore, are—How far the measures respectively suggested by these two branches of the common end agree?—How far they differ, and which requires the preference?—How far the end in view is best promoted by individuals acting for themselves? And in what cases these ends may be best promoted by the hands of government?

Those cases in which, and those measures or operations by which, the end is promoted by individuals acting for themselves, and without any special interference exercised with this special view on the part of government, beyond the distribution made and maintained, and the protection afforded by the civil and penal branches of the law, may be said to arise *sponte acta* [by the exercise of free choice]. . . .

With the view of causing an increase to take place in the mass of national wealth, or with a view to increase of the means of subsistence or enjoyment, without some special reason, the general rule is that nothing ought to be done or attempted by government. The motto or watchword of government on these occasions ought to be—*Be quiet.*

For this quietism there are two main reasons:—1. Generally speaking, any interference for this purpose on the part of government is *needless*. The wealth of the whole community is composed of the wealth of the several individuals belonging to it taken together. But to increase his particular portion is, generally speaking, among the constant objects of each individual's exertions and care. Generally speaking, there is no one who knows what is for your interest so well as yourself—no one who is disposed with so much ardor and constancy to pursue it.

2. Generally speaking, it is moreover likely to be pernicious, *viz.* by being unconducive, or even obstructive, with reference to the attainment of the end in view. Each individual bestowing more time and attention upon the means of preserving and increasing his portion of wealth, than is or can be bestowed by government, is likely to take a more effectual course than what, in his instance and on his behalf, would be taken by government.

It is, moreover, universally and constantly pernicious in another way, by the restraint or constraint imposed on the free agency of the individual. Pain is the general concomitant of the sense of such restraint, wherever it is experienced. . . .

In coercive measures, so called, it is only to the individual that the coercion is applied. In the case of measures of encouragement, the field of coercion is vastly more extensive. Encouragements are grants of money or money's worth, applied in some shape or other to this purpose. But for this, any more than any other purpose, money is not raised but by taxes, and taxes are the produce of coercive laws applied to the most coercive purpose. . . .

To estimate the good expected from the application of any particular mass of government money, compare it always with the mischief produced by the extracton of an equal sum of money by the most burdensome species of tax; since, by forbearing to make application of that sum of money, you might forbear levying the amount of that same sum of money by that tax, and thereby forbear imposing the mass of burden that results from it.

MALTHUS: AN ESSAY ON THE PRINCIPLE OF POPULATION AS IT AFFECTS THE FUTURE IMPROVEMENT OF SOCIETY
(London, 1798), pp. 1−3, 7, 11−14; (2d ed., 1803), pp. 9−11, 16, 505−506, 523−524.

Thomas Robert Malthus, an Anglican clergyman and a gentle soul, formulated a theory of population that made him at once very controversial and very influential. Even today his name is spoken with passion by his advocates and his enemies alike. In the nineteenth century such diverse figures as Karl Marx, Charles Darwin, and Herbert Spencer all proclaimed their debt to him.

Malthus's theory is stated in the form of a Newtonian-type law, complete with a mathematical formulation. But it is not only the theory that is controversial; it is also the conclusions that Malthus and others drew from it.

The great and unlooked-for discoveries that have taken place of late years in [science]; the increasing diffusion of general knowledge from the extension of the art of printing; . . . the new and extraordinary lights that have been thrown on political subjects, . . . and particularly that tremendous phenomenon in the political horizon, the French Revolution, . . . have all concurred to lead able men into the opinion that we are touching upon a period big with the most important changes. . . .

It has been said, that the great question is now at issue, whether man shall henceforth start forwards with accelerated velocity towards illimitable, and hitherto unconceived improvement; or be condemned to a perpetual oscillation between happiness and misery, and after every effort remain still at an immeasurable distance from the wished-for goal. . . .

I have read some of the speculations on the perfectibility of man and of society with great pleasure. . . . I ardently wish for such happy improvements. But I see great, and, to my understanding, unconquerable difficulties in the way of them. These difficulties it is my present purpose to state. . . .

I think I may fairly make two postulata.

First, That food is necessary to the existence of man.

Secondly, That the passion between the sexes is necessary, and will remain nearly in its present state.

These two laws, ever since we have had any knowledge of mankind, appear to have been fixed laws of our nature. . . .

Assuming, then, my postulata as granted, I say that the power of population is indefinitely greater than the power of the earth to produce subsistence for man.

Population, when unchecked, increases in a geometrical ratio. Subsistence only increases in an arithmetical ratio. A slight acquaintance with numbers will show the immensity of the first power in comparison with the second.

By that law of our nature which makes food necessary to the life of man, the effects of these two unequal powers must be kept equal.

This implies a strong and constantly operating check on population from the difficulty of subsistence. This difficulty must fall somewhere; and must necessarily be severely felt by a large portion of mankind. . . .

Of the General Checks to Population, and the Mode of their Operation

The ultimate check to population appears then to be a want of food, arising necessarily from the different ratios according to which population and food increase. But this ultimate check is never the immediate check, except in cases of actual famine.

The immediate check may be stated to consist in all those customs, and all those diseases, which seem to be generated by a scarcity of the means of subsistence; and all those causes, independent of this scarcity, whether of a moral or physical nature, which tend prematurely to weaken and destroy the human frame.

These checks to population . . . may be classed under two general heads—the preventive and the positive checks.

The preventive check . . . is peculiar to man, and arises from that distinctive superiority in his reasoning faculties which enables him to calculate distant consequences. The checks to the indefinite increase of plants and irrational animals are all either positive, or, if preventive, involuntary. But man cannot look around him and see the distress which frequently presses upon those who have large families; he cannot contemplate his present possessions or earnings, which he now nearly consumes himself, and calculate the amount of each share, when with very little addition they must be divided, perhaps, among seven or eight, without feeling a doubt whether, if he follow the bent of his inclinations, he may be able to support the offspring which he will probably bring into the world. . . . Will he not lower his rank in life, and be obliged to give up in great measure his former habits? Will he not be unable to transmit to his children the same advantages of education and improvement that he himself possessed? Does he even feel secure that, should he have a large family, his utmost exertions can save them from rags and squalid poverty? . . . And may he not be reduced to the grating necessity of forfeiting his independence, and of being obliged to the sparing hand of Charity for support?

These considerations are calculated to prevent, and certainly do prevent, a great number of persons in all civilized nations from pursuing the dictate of nature in an early attachment to one woman.

If this restraint do not produce vice, it is undoubtedly the least evil that can arise from the principle of population. Considered as a restraint on a strong natural inclination, it must be allowed to produce a certain degree of temporary unhappiness; but evidently slight, compared with the evils which result from any of the other checks to population; and merely of the same nature as many other sacrifices of temporary to permanent gratification. . . .

When this restraint produces vice, the evils which follow are but too conspicuous. A promiscuous intercourse to such a degree as to prevent the birth of children seems to lower, in the most marked manner, the dignity of human nature. It cannot be without its effect on men, and nothing can be more obvious than its tendency to degrade the female character, and to destroy all its most amiable and distinguishing characteristics. . . .

The positive checks to population are extremely various, and include every cause, whether arising from vice or misery, which in any degree contributes to shorten the natural duration of human life. Under this head, therefore, may be enumerated all unwholesome occupations, severe labor and exposure to the seasons, extreme poverty, bad nursing of children, great towns, excesses of all kinds, the whole train of common diseases and epidemics, wars, plague, and famine.

On examining these obstacles to the increase of population which I have classed under the heads of preventive and positive checks, it will appear that they are all resolvable into moral restraint, vice, and misery.

Of the preventive checks, the restraint from marriage which is not followed by irregular gratifications may properly be termed moral restraint.

Promiscuous intercourse, unnatural passions, violations of the marriage bed, and improper acts to conceal the consequences of irregular connections, are preventive checks that clearly come under the head of vice.

Of the positive checks, those which appear to arise unavoidably from the laws of nature, may be called exclusively misery; and those which we obviously bring upon ourselves, such as wars, excesses, and many others which it would be in our power to avoid, are of a mixed nature. They are brought upon us by vice, and their consequences are misery. . . .

The following propositions are intended to be proved:

1. Population is necessarily limited by the means of subsistence.

2. Population invariably increases where the means of subsistence increase, unless prevented by some very powerful and obvious checks.

3. These checks, and the checks which repress the superior power of population, and keep its effects on a level with the means of subsistence, are all resolvable into moral restraint, vice and misery.

Of the Only Effectual Mode of Improving the Condition of the Poor

He who performs his duty faithfully . . . [will] not bring beings into the world for whom he cannot find the means of support. . . . If he cannot support his children they must starve; and if he marry in the face of a fair probability that he shall not be able to support his children, he is guilty of all the evils which he thus brings upon himself, his wife, and his offspring. It is clearly in his interest, and will tend greatly to promote his happiness, to defer marrying till by industry and economy he is in a capacity to support the children that he may reasonably expect from his marriage; and as he cannot in the meantime gratify his passions without violating an express command of God, and running a great risk of injuring himself, or some of his fellow-creatures, considerations of his own interest and happiness will dictate to him the strong obligation to a moral conduct while he remains unmarried.

Of the Consequences of Pursuing the Opposite Mode

Among the lower classes of society . . . the poor-laws afford a direct . . . encouragement to marriage, by removing from each individual that heavy responsibility, which he would incur by the laws of nature, for bringing beings into the world which he could not support. Our private benevolence has the same direction as the poor-laws, and almost invariably tends to encourage marriage, and to equalize as much as possible the circumstances of married and single men. . . .

[Until] the poor are undeceived with respect to the principal cause of their poverty, and taught to know that their happiness or misery must depend chiefly upon themselves, it cannot be said that, with regard to the great question of marriage, we leave every man to his free and fair choice.

RICARDO: PRINCIPLES OF POLITICAL ECONOMY AND TAXATION (1817)

Ed. E. Gonner (London, 1891), pp. 5–6, 70–77.

A successful English businessman during the Napoleonic Wars, David Ricardo was intrigued by the questions of economics in Smith's *Wealth of Nations* and Malthus's *Essay on Population,* which led him in turn to carry the arguments further in his *Principles of Political Economy.* Ricardo is most noted for his "iron law" of wages and labor theory of value.

I. *The Value of a commodity, or the quantity of any other commodity for which it will exchange, depends on the relative quantity of labor which is necessary for its production, and not on the greater or less compensation which is paid for that labor.*

It has been observed by Adam Smith that "the word *value* has two different meanings, and sometimes expresses the utility of some particular object, and sometimes the power of purchasing other goods which the possession of that object conveys. The one may be called *value in use;* the other *value in exchange.*" "The things," he continues, "which have the greatest value in use, have frequently little or no value in exchange; and, on the contrary, those which have the greatest value in exchange, have little or no value in use.'' Water and air are abundantly useful; they are indeed indispensable to existence, yet, under ordinary circumstances, nothing can be obtained in exchange for them. Gold, on the contrary, though of little use compared with air and water, will exchange for a great quantity of other goods. . . .

Possessing utility, commodities derive their exchangeable value from two sources: from their scarcity, and from the quantity of labor required to obtain them.

There are some commodities the value of which is determined by their scarcity alone. No labor can increase the quantity of such goods, and therefore their value cannot be lowered by an increased supply. Some rare statues and pictures, scarce books and coins, wines of a peculiar quality . . . are all of this description. . . .

[But] by far the greatest part of those goods which are the objects of desire are produced by labor; and they may be multiplied . . . almost without any assignable limit. . . .

V. On Wages

Labor, like all other things which are purchased and sold, and which may be increased or diminished in quantity, has its natural and its market price. The natural price of labor is that price which is necessary to enable the laborers, one with another, to subsist and to perpetuate their race, without either increase or diminution.

The power of the laborer to support himself, and the family which may be necessary to keep up the number of laborers, does not depend on the quantity of money he receives for wages, but on the quantity of food, necessaries, and conveniences become essential to him from habit, which that money will purchase. The natural price of labor, therefore, depends on the price of food, necessaries, and conveniences required for the support of the laborer and his family. . . .

The market price of labor is the price which is really paid for it, from the natural operation of the proportion of the supply to the demand; labor is dear when it is scarce and cheap when it is plentiful. However much the market price of labor may deviate from its natural price, it has, like commodities, a tendency to conform to it.

It is when the market price of labor exceeds its natural price that the condition of the laborer is flourishing and happy, that he has it in his power to command a greater proportion of the necessaries and enjoyments of life, and therefore to rear a healthy and numerous family. When, however, by the encouragement which high wages give to the increase of population, the number of laborers is increased, wages again fall to their natural price, and indeed . . . sometimes far below it.

When the market price of labor is below its natural price, the condition of the laborers is most wretched; then poverty deprives them of those comforts which custom renders absolute necessaries. It is only after their privations have reduced their number, or the demand for labor has increased, that the market price of labor will rise to its natural price, and that the laborer will have the moderate comforts which the natural rate of wages will afford. . . .

It is not to be understood that the natural price of labor . . . is absolutely fixed and constant. It varies at different times in the same country, and very materially differs in different countries. It essentially depends on the habits and customs of the people. . . .

Many of the conveniences now enjoyed in an English cottage, would have been thought luxuries at an earlier period of our history. . . .

It appears then that wages are subject to a rise or fall from two causes:

First, the supply and demand of laborers.

Secondly, the price of the commodities on which the wages of labor are expended. . . .

Under favorable circumstances population may be doubled in 25 years; but under the same favorable circumstances the whole capital of a country might possibly be doubled in a shorter perod. In that case, wages, during the whole period would have a tendency to rise, because the demand for labor would increase still faster than the supply. . . .

[But] with a population pressing against the means of subsistence, the only remedies are either a reduction of people or a more rapid accumulation of capital. In rich countries, where all the fertile land is already cultivated, the latter remedy is neither very practicable nor very desirable, because its effect would be, if pushed very far, to render all classes equally poor. But in poor countries, where there are abundant means of production in store, from fertile land not yet brought into cultivation, it is the only safe and efficacious means of removing the evil, particularly as its effect would be to elevate all classes of the people.

CARLYLE: PAST AND PRESENT (1843)

(3d ed., New York, 1895), pp. 103–105, 108–110, 114, 124, 187–188.

After having written the first nonpartisan history of the French Revolution, Thomas Carlyle turned to the "condition of England" question, the growing split between the working and the propertied classes. He wanted to give them a historical lesson: that an irresponsible ruling class could be swept away by a revolution, but such a revolution in the end would accomplish nothing but destruction.

A former Calvinist minister, Carlyle found the answer in "the gospel of work." In *Past and Present* he criticized materialism ("Mammonism") and looked back romantically to the Good Old Days of the medieval guilds, manors, and monasteries, with a place for everybody and everybody in his or her place. In the New Age (nineteenth century), Carlyle would replace Bentham's "Greatest Happiness" principle with the ideals of justice and participation in society, for the workers; self-sacrifice and leadership for the "Captains of Industry," replacing the medieval aristocracy.

Gospel of Mammonism

We for the present, with our Mammon-Gospel, have come to strange conclusions. We call it a Society [but] our life is not a mutual helpfulness; . . . rather, cloaked under the . . . laws-of-war named "fair competition," it is a mutual hostility. . . . We have forgotten that Cash-payment is not the sole relation of human beings; we think . . . that *it* absolves and liquidates all engagements of man. "My starving workers?"—answers the rich Mill-owner: "Did not I hire them fairly in the market? Did I not pay them to

the last sixpence, the sum covenanted for? What have I to do with them more?''—
Verily Mammon-worship is a melancholy creed. When Cain . . . had killed Abel, and
was questioned, "Where is thy brother?" he too made answer, "Am I my brother's
keeper?" Did I not pay my brother *his* wages, the thing he had merited from me?

O sumptuous Merchant Prince, illustrious game-preserving Duke, is there no way
of "killing" thy brother but Cain's rude way!

. . . [Once] a poor Irish Widow, her husband having died in one of the lanes of
Edinburgh, went forth with her three children, bare of all resource, to solicit help from
the Charitable Establishments of that City. At this Charitable Establishment and then
at that she was refused; referred from one to the other, helped by none;—till she had
exhausted them all; till her strength and heart failed her: she sank down in typhus-fever;
died, and infected her Lane with fever, so that "seventeen other persons" died of fever
in consequence. The humane Physician asks thereupon, as with a heart too full for
speaking, Would it not have been *economy* to help this poor Widow? She took
typhus-fever, and killed seventeen of you!—Very curious. The forlorn Irish widow
applies to her fellow-creatures, as if saying, "Behold I am sinking, bare of help: ye
must help me! I am your sister, bone of your bone; one God made us: ye must help
me!" They answer, "No, impossible; thou art no sister of ours!" But she proves her
sisterhood; her typhus-fever kills *them:* they actually were her brothers, though
denying it! Had human creature ever to go lower for a proof? . . .

Happy

Does not the whole wretchedness, the whole *Atheism* as I call it, of man's ways, in
these generations, shadow itself for us in that unspeakable Life-philosophy of his: The
pretension to be what he calls "happy!" . . .

We construct our theory of Human Duties, not on any Greatest-Nobleness
Principle, never so mistaken; no, but on a Greatest-Happiness Principle. "The word
Soul with us . . . seems to be synonymous with *Stomach.*" We plead and speak, in our
Parliaments and elsewhere, not as from the Soul, but from the Stomach;—wherefore
indeed our pleadings are so slow to profit. We plead not for God's Justice; we are not
ashamed to stand clamoring and pleading for our own "interests," our own rents and
trade-profits; we say, They are the "interests" of so many; there is such an intense
desire in us for them! We demand Free-Trade with much just vociferation and
benevolence, That the poorer classes, who are terribly ill-off at present, may have
cheaper New-Orleans bacon. Men ask on Free-Trade platforms, How can the
indomitable spirit of Englishmen be kept up without plenty of bacon? We shall become
a ruined Nation!—Surely, my friends, plenty of bacon is good and indispensable: but, I
doubt, you will ever get even bacon by aiming only at that. You are men, not animals
of prey, well-used or ill-used! Your Greatest-Happiness Principle seems to me fast
becoming a rather unhappy one. . . .

The only happiness a brave man ever troubled himself with asking much about was,
happiness enough to get his work done. Not "I can't eat!" but "I can't work!" that
was the burden of all wise complaining among men. It is, after all, the one unhappiness
of a man, That he cannot work; that he cannot get his destiny as a man fulfilled. . . .

The English

Bull is a born conservative; for this . . . I inexpressibly honor him. All great Peoples are conservatives; slow to believe in novelties; . . . deeply and forever certain of the greatness that is in Law, in Custom once solemnly established, and now long recognized as just and final.—True. O Radical Reformer, there is no Custom that can, properly speaking, be final; none. And yet thou seest *Customs* which, in all civilized countries, are accounted final; nay, under the Old-Roman name of *Mores,* are accounted *Morality,* Virtue, Laws of God Himself. . . . And greatly do I respect the solid character . . . who esteems all "Customs once solemnly acknowledged" to be ultimate, divine, and the rule for a man to walk by. . . .

Unworking Aristocracy

. . . Our Governing Class, called by God and Nature . . . either to do something toward government, or to die and be abolished,—have not yet learned even to sit still and do no mischief! For no Anti-Corn-Law League yet asks more of them than this: . . . not Do something; but Cease your destructive misdoing, Do ye nothing! . . .

The Working Aristocracy; Mill-owners, Manufacturers, Commanders of Working Men: alas, against them also much shall be brought in accusation. . . . [They] must understand that money alone is *not* the representative either of man's success in the world, or of man's duties to man; and reform their own selves from top to bottom, if they wish England reformed. England will not be habitable long, unreformed. . . .

Captains of Industry

The leaders of industry, if Industry is ever to be led, are virtually the Captains of the World! If there be no nobleness in them, there will never be an Aristocracy more. But let [them] consider: . . . are they born of other clay than the old Captains of Slaughter; doomed forever to be no Chivalry, but a mere gold-plated *Doggery,*—what the French well name *Canaille,* "Doggery" with more or less gold carrion at its disposal? Captains of Industry are the true Fighters . . . against Chaos. . . . Let them retire into their own hearts and ask solemnly, if there is nothing but vulturous hunger for fine wines, valet reputation and gilt carriages, discoverable there? . . . Our England, our world cannot live as it is. It will connect itself with a God again, or go down with nameless throws and fire-consummation to the Devils. . . .

SMILES: SELF-HELP (1859)

(Boston, 1860), pp. 15–17, 191–192, 265–267.

Author of the most popular book of the nineteenth century, Samuel Smiles (1812–1904) exemplifies the optimism of the rising bourgeoisie. The fact that he was the eldest of eleven children and that, after his father's death, his mother raised them all on a shoestring, may have something to do with his philosophy as well as with his own success in overcoming adversity—giving up a failing medical practice and eventually finding his place in journalism and literature. He wrote major works in history and biography, all in the same direct style.

"Heaven helps those who help themselves," is a well-worn maxim, embodying in a small compass the results of vast human experience. The spirit of self-help is the root of all genuine growth in the individual; and, exhibited in the lives of many, it constitutes the true source of national vigor and strength. Help from without is often enfeebling in its effects, but help from within invariably invigorates. Whatever is done for men or classes, to a certain extent takes away the stimulus and necessity of doing for themselves; and where men are subjected to over-guidance and over-government, the inevitable tendency is to render them comparatively helpless.

Even the best institutions can give a man no active aid. Perhaps the utmost they can do is, to leave him *free* to develop himself and improve his individual condition. But in all times men have been prone to believe that their happiness and well-being were to be secured by means of institutions rather than by their own conduct. Hence the value of legislation as an agent in human advancement has always been greatly overestimated. To constitute the millionth part of a legislature, by voting for one or two men once in three or five years, however conscientiously this duty may be performed, can exercise but little active influence upon any man's life and character. Moreover, it is every day becoming more clearly understood, that the function of government is negative and restrictive, rather than positive and active; being resolvable principally into protection—protection of life, liberty, and property. Hence the chief "reforms" of the last fifty years have consisted mainly in abolitions and disenactments. But there is no power of law that can make the idle man industrious, the thriftless provident, or the drunken sober; though every individual can be each and all of these if he will, by the exercise of his own free powers of action and self-denial. Indeed, all experience serves to prove that the worth and strength of a state depend far less upon the form of its institutions than upon the character of its men. For the nation is only the aggregate of individual conditions, and civilization itself is but a question of personal improvement.

National progress is the sum of individual industry, energy, and uprightness, as national decay is of individual idleness, selfishness, and vice. What we are accustomed to decry as great social evils, will, for the most part, be found to be only the outgrowth of our own perverted life; and though we may endeavor to cut them down and extirpate them by means of law, they will only spring up again with fresh luxuriance in some other form, unless the individual conditions of human life and character are radically improved. If this view be correct, then it follows that the highest patriotism and philanthropy consist, not so much in altering laws and modifying institutions, as in helping and stimulating men to elevate and improve themselves by their own free and independent actions as individuals.

Practical industry, wisely and vigorously applied, never fails of success. It carries a man onward and upward, brings out his individual character, and powerfully stimulates the action of others. All may not rise equally, yet each, on the whole, very much according to his deserts. "Though all cannot live on the piazza," as the Tuscan proverb has it, "everyone can feel the sun."

We have already referred to some illustrious commoners raised from humble to elevated positions by the power of application and industry; and we might point to even the peerage itself as affording equally instructive examples. One reason why the peerage of England has succeeded so well in retaining its vigor and elasticity, arises from the fact that, unlike the peerages of other countries, it has been fed from time to time by the best industrial blood of the country—the very "liver, heart, and brain of Britain.". . .

It is will—force of purpose—that enables a man to do or be whatever he sets his mind on being or doing. A holy man was accustomed to say, "Whatever you wish, that you are: for such is the force of our will, joined to the Divine, that whatever we wish to be, seriously, and with a true intention, that we become. No one ardently wishes to be submissive, patient, modest, or liberal, who does not become what he wishes." The story is told of a working carpenter, who was observed one day planing a magistrate's bench, which he was repairing, with more than usual carefulness, and when asked the reason, he replied, "Because I wish to make it easy against the time when I come to sit upon it myself." And singularly enough, the man actually lived to sit upon that very bench as a magistrate. . . .

Any class of men that lives from hand to mouth will ever be an inferior class. They will necessarily remain impotent and helpless, hanging on to the skirts of society, the sport of times and seasons. Having no respect for themselves, they will fail in securing the respect of others. . . .

Sound was the advice given by Mr. Bright to an assembly of working men at Rochdale in 1847, when, after expressing his belief that "so far as honesty was concerned, it was to be found in pretty equal amount among all classes," he used the following words:

> There is only one way that is safe for any man, or any number of men, by which they can maintain their present position if it be a good one, or raise themselves above it if it be a bad one—that is, by the practice of the virtues of industry, frugality, temperance, and honesty. . . . What is it that has made, that has in fact created, the middle class in this country, but the virtues to which I have alluded? . . . When I speak of the middle class, I mean that class which is between the privileged class, the richest, and the very poorest in the community; and I would recommend every man to pay no attention whatever to public writers or speakers, whoever they may be, who tell them that this class or that class, that this law or that law, that this government or that government, can do all these things for them. I assure you, after long reflection and much observation, that there is no way for the working classes of this country to improve their condition but that which so many of them have already availed themselves of—that is, by the practice of those virtues, and by reliance upon themselves.

CHAPTER 22

POLITICAL LIBERALISM AND ITS ENEMIES, 1832–1867

Liberalism in the nineteenth century generally meant faith in the middle classes, in political compromise to avoid revolution, and in rational progress through economic growth. Its traditional enemies were absolutism on the one hand and radicalism on the other.

In England, the nineteenth century is divided into almost equal time periods by the first and second reform acts of 1832 and 1867. The interval between them is appropriately known as the Victorian Compromise. Although the new queen did not ascend the throne until 1837, her personality and philosophy coincide so well with the "Spirit of 1832" that her name precedes her rule. The Reform Act of 1832 was designed to take the pressure off a drive for the democratization of Parliament, a drive that had begun in the 1760s under George III.

So effective, indeed, was the first reform act that the great Chartist movement of the 1840s was not able to budge it, whereas other governments, like that of Louis Philippe in France, were being overthrown by similar democratic forces. However, the Second Republic of 1848 lasted only three years, when it was replaced by an authoritarian regime under Prince Louis Napoleon, himself having been elected President of the Republic by universal male suffrage.

In Germany, the year 1848 saw the Frankfurt Assembly attempt to establish a liberal regime, only to be frustrated by absolutist forces in Austria and Prussia. Later Bismarck would cynically use the device of universal suffrage to outmaneuver his enemies.

By 1867 in England, however, the pressure for change in the Reform Act of 1832 had built up to such an extent that it could no longer be resisted, and a new act was passed providing universal male suffrage, in spite of the fact that neither party had intended to go that far. And so the Victorian Compromise was exploded and a new era began: the era of the common man. The Second Reform Act was aptly termed "a leap in the dark," because nobody knew whether the common man would use his vote to support responsible leaders or demagogues. An answer was already being provided in France, where Louis Napoleon used plebiscites to win support for his programs. In the twentieth century similar answers would be provided by Mussolini and Hitler.

Is Liberalism still alive and well? As long as people will make compromises in order to protect individual rights and equality of opportunity, Liberalism survives. In the Third World, many countries find it useful in balancing opposing groups. Despite the Liberals' uncomfortable position on the fence, they continue to hold off the extremists on both sides.

THE ENGLISH REFORM ACT OF 1832

Parliamentary representation in England had not been significantly changed since the days of Elizabeth I. By 1831, out of a total population of 24,000,000 only about 400,000 were qualified to vote. The new industrial cities, such as Manchester and Birmingham, were wholly unrepresented, while "rotten boroughs" continued to send members to the Commons.

Agitation for reform had begun before the American Revolution, but the wars of the French Revolution and Napoleon had pushed it aside. Afterward it revived stronger than ever, and by 1830 it was the leading issue of the day. The middle classes were seeking their share of power, and the masses joined them in the hope that they too would benefit from an extension of the suffrage, although they were not included in the reform petitions. Economic depression fomented unrest and the continental revolutions of 1830 further stimulated British agitation. In his speech introducing the reform bill, Lord Russell indicates its aims.

LORD JOHN RUSSELL INTRODUCES THE FIRST REFORM BILL (MARCH 1, 1831)

From *Parliamentary Debates,* Third Series, 2:1061f.

. . . The measure I have now to bring forward is a measure, not of mine, but of the government in whose name I appear—the deliberate measure of a whole cabinet, unanimous upon this subject and resolved to place their measure before this house in redemption of their pledge to their sovereign, the parliament, and the country. . . .

It will not be necessary on this occasion that I should go over the arguments which have been so often urged in favor of parliamentary reform; but it is due to the question that I should state shortly the chief points of the general argument on which the reformers rest their claim. Looking at the question then as a question of right, the ancient statutes of Edward I contain the germ and vital principle of our political constitution. The 25th of Edward I. c. 6, declares in the name of the king that "for no business from henceforth we should take such manner of aids, tasks, nor prises, but by the common assent of the realm and for the common profit thereof, saving the ancient aids and prises due and accustomed." The 34th Edward I, commonly called the Statute de Tallagio Concedendo, provides "that no tallage or aid shall be taken or levied by us or our heirs in our realm without the good will and assent of archbishops, bishops, earls, barons, knights, burgesses, and other freemen of the land.''. . .

To revert again to ancient times, the assent of the commonalty of the land, thus declared necessary for the grant of any aid or tax, was collected from their representatives consisting of two knights from each county, from each city two citizens, and from every borough two burgesses. For 250 years the constant number of boroughs so sending their representatives was about 120. Some 30 or 40 others occasionally exercised or discontinued that practice or privilege, as they rose or fell in wealth or importance. How this construction of the house of commons underwent various changes, till the principle on which it was founded was lost sight of, I will not now detain the house by explaining. There can be no doubt, however, that at the beginning of the period I have alluded to the house of commons did represent the people of England. No man of common sense pretends that this assembly now represents the commonalty or people of England. If it be a question of right, therefore, right is in favor of reform.

Let us now look at the question as one of reason. Allow me to imagine, for a moment, a stranger from some distant country, who should arrive in England to examine our institutions. . . . He would have been told that the proudest boast of this celebrated country was its political freedom. If, in addition to this, he had heard that once in six years this country, so wise, so renowned, so free, chose its representatives to sit in the great council where all the ministerial affairs were discussed and determined, he would be not a little curious to see the process by which so important and solemn an operation was effected. What then would be his surprise if he were taken by his guide, whom he had asked to conduct him to one of the places of election, to a green mound and told that this green mound sent two members to parliament, or to be taken to a stone wall with three niches in it and told that these three niches sent two members to parliament; or, if he were shown a green park with many signs of flourishing vegetable life, but none of human habitation, and told that this green park sent two members to parliament! But his surprise would increase to astonishment if he were carried into the north of England, where he would see large flourishing towns, full of trade and activity, containing vast magazines of wealth and manufactures, and were told that these places had no representatives in the assembly which was said to represent the people. Suppose him, after all, for I will not disguise any part of the case—suppose him to ask for a specimen of popular election, and to be carried for that purpose to Liverpool; his surprise would be turned into disgust at the gross venality and corruption which he would find to pervade the electors. After seeing all this, would he not wonder that a nation which had made such progress in every kind of knowledge, and which valued itself for its freedom, should permit so absurd and defective a system of representation any longer to prevail? But whenever arguments of this kind have been urged, it has been replied—and Mr. Canning placed his opposition to reform on this ground—''We agree that the house of commons is not, in fact, sent here by the people; we agree that, in point of reason, the system by which it is sent is full of anomaly and absurdity; but government is a matter of experience, and so long as the people are satisfied with the actual working of the house of commons, it would be unwise to embark in theoretical change.'' Of this argument, I confess, I always felt the weight, and so long as the people did not answer the appeals of the friends of reform, it was indeed an argument not to be resisted. But what is the case at this moment? The whole people call loudly for reform. . . .

I arrive at the last objections which may be made to the plan we propose. I shall be told, in the first place, that we overturn the institutions of our ancestors. I maintain that, in departing from the letter, we preserve the spirit of those institutions. Our opponents say our ancestors gave Old Sarum representatives; therefore we should give Old Sarum representatives. We say our ancestors gave Old Sarum representatives because it was a large town. . . .It has been asserted also, if a reform were to be effected, that many men of great talents, who now get into this house for close boroughs, would not be able to procure seats. I have never entertained any apprehensions of the sort, for I believe that no reform that can be introduced will have the effect of preventing wealth, probity, learning, and wit from having their proper influence upon elections. . . .

It may be said, too, that one great and injurious effect of the measures I propose will be to destroy the power and privilege of the aristocracy. This I deny. . . . Wherever the aristocracy reside, receiving large incomes, performing important duties, relieving the poor by charity, and evincing private worth and public virtue, it is not in human nature that they should not possess a great influence upon public opinion and have an equal weight in electing persons to serve their country in parliament. Though such persons may not have the direct nomination of members under this bill, I contend that they will have as much influence as they ought to have. But if by aristocracy those persons are meant who do not live among the people, who know nothing of the people, and who care nothing for them—who seek honors without merit, places without duty, and pensions without service—for such an aristocracy I have no sympathy. . . .

To establish the constitution on a firm basis, you must show that you are determined not to be the representatives of a small class or of a particular interest, but to form a body who, representing the people, springing from the people, and sympathizing with the people, can fairly call on the people to support the future burdens of the country. . . . I conclude, sir, by moving for leave to bring in a bill for amending the state of the representation in England and Wales.

CHARTISM: PRO AND CON

Despite the violent Tory opposition to the first English Reform Bill (1832), it was immediately branded as totally inadequate by the English working classes. In the same year, then, agitation began for additional reforms. This took the form of a People's Charter or Constitution that would include provision for universal manhood suffrage, the secret ballot, annual meetings of parliament, equal electoral districts, pay for members and abolition of property qualifications. But the leaders of the movement were aiming at much more radical reforms, as the following excerpts from an 1832 pamphlet indicate.

THE PEOPLE'S CHARTER

(London, 1832), pp. 29–48 passim, quoted in Robinson and Beard, *Readings,* 2:245–249.

Aristocratic government. The abolition of aristocratic and exclusive, plundering and inefficient government, and the substitution of representative and liberal, cheap and efficient government. . . . The adoption especially of universal suffrage (for the man excluded from this is a slave); of the [secret] ballot (for the man who cannot thus vote may be oppressed by the superior to whom he refuses his vote); and of annual Parliaments. . . .

Taxes on knowledge. The abolition especially of all taxes on paper, printed and unprinted, and of all official embarrassment to the printing and publishing of newspapers, and to their cheap conveyance by post. . . .

The establishment of a system of national education, unfettered and untainted by religious tenets.

Peerage. The abolition of hereditary peerage and hereditary legislation.

(The application of such a principle to the government of nations is an insult to common sense; and a hereditary legislator is a far greater absurdity than a hereditary poet. . . .)

Privileges. The abolition of privileged classes. (A peer may send and receive all letters free, may frank those of his friends, and may send by post on Sunday as on other days. He may vote by proxy, though not present at a debate, and ignorant of its purport. He may give a verdict, not on oath, but honor, as if he alone were honorable, and other men were villains. He may not be arrested, made bankrupt, or have his estate sequestrated. He may, with perfect impunity, defraud his creditors, by borrowing, buying houses and lands, and leaving them to whom he pleases, as the lenders cannot touch his real estate. . . .)

Titles. The abolition of hereditary nobility, titles, honors, and distinctions.

Kingship. The abolition of the evils with which kingship is accompanied. (. . . Kings have every motive to remain ignorant; they generally are so in a degree that would surprise even a peasant; and the report of their having any sort of talent is always a mere flattery of courtiers.

The intellectual organs of kings are so small, and their faculties are so feeble, as always to border on fatuity. . . .)

Insolence. The interdiction of all insulting and slavish language, as "subjects," "humbly petitioning," "praying," etc.

The Church. The prevention of public plunder by the priesthood.

(The English are dupes to their priesthood in a degree that is quite incredible to strangers. There is actually no other nation, however debased by superstition, in which the clergy enjoy such prodigious wealth. There is no other nation in which such enormous Church property supports so unprincipled and immoral a priesthood. . . .

Abolition of State Church and State religion, leaving priests, parsons, preachers, ministers, etc., to be paid by those who choose to employ them.

The cessation of every species of persecution for religious opinions, and the punishment of such persecution when exercised by the followers of any creed.

REV. EVAN JENKINS: CHARTISM UNMASKED

(London, 1840), pp. 25ff; in Robinson and Beard, *Readings,* pp. 249–250.

The following popular tract is typical of those provoked by the Chartist literature in its attacks on the government, the monarchy, and the clergy.

That the Church of England and Chartism totally oppose each other, produce wholly different effects, and lead to widely and utterly different destinations, will appear if we just consider to what they each lead.

Chartism	*The Church of England*
Leads to *unholy* desires, wicked counsels, and unjust works.	Leads us to pray to that God from whom "all *holy* desires, all good counsels, and all just works proceed."
Leads to perils, dangers, evil, and mischief.	Leads us "to pray to be kept from all perils and dangers, from all evil and mischief."
Leads "to battle, murder, and sudden death."	Leads us to pray to be delivered "from battle, and murder, and from sudden death."
Leads us to curse and oppose the magistrates in the execution of their duties, in punishing wickedness and vice.	Leads us to beseech God "to bless and keep the magistrates, giving them grace to execute justice and to maintain truth."
Leads all nations to war, hatred, and discord.	Leads us to ask God "to give to all nations unity, peace, and concord."
Leads to the murder of fathers and husbands; and leaves the fatherless children and widows, desolate and oppressed.	Leads us to ask God "that it may please Him to defend and provide for the fatherless children and widows, and all that are desolate and oppressed."
Leads to the disturbance of public worship, to the immediate dispersion of the congregation when in the middle of their devotions, at the sight of the pike, pistol, scythe, gun, etc.	Leads us to pray thus: "Grant, O Lord, we beseech thee, that the course of this world may be so peaceably ordered by thy governance, that thy Church may joyfully serve thee in all godly quietness."

Chartism	*The Church of England*
Leads to skepticism, infidelity, and disbe-lief of the Scriptures.	Leads us to pray God "to grant us grace to hear, read, mark, learn, and inwardly digest them."
Leads to anarchy; to disobey and rebel against the powers that be; and to the subversion of all good government.	Leads us and all subjects duly to consider whose authority the Queen hath, that we may "faithfully serve, honor, and humbly obey her."
Leads to poverty, misery, and transportation; the gallows, death, and hell.	Leads to wealth, peace, freedom, pardon; and beseeches the Lord in his boundless mercy and love to "deliver us from wrath and from everlasting damnation."

JOHN STUART MILL

CONSIDERATIONS ON REPRESENTATIVE GOVERNMENT

John Stuart Mill (1806–1873) was one of the most important and versatile British thinkers of the nineteenth century. His father, James Mill, a noted Benthamite economist, had educated him not only in Utilitarianism but also in logical thinking and criticism, so that John Stuart became both one of the great champions of liberal reform and also one of its most incisive critics.

The younger Mill was fortunate in having, during most of his life, a secure position with the East India Company, which provided not only political experience but leisure for study and writing as well. Elected to Parliament in 1865, he supported the Reform Bill of 1867 and other liberal measures, such as the extension of the suffrage to the working classes and to women and the Irish home rule bill.

Chapter III. That the Really Best Form of Government is Representative Government

There is no difficulty in showing that the ideally best form of government is that in which the sovereignty, or supreme controlling power in the last resort, is vested in the entire aggregate of the community; every citizen not only having a voice in the exercise of that ultimate sovereignty, but being, at least occasionally, called on to take an actual part in the government, by the personal discharge of some public function, local or general. . . .

A completely popular government. . . . is both more favorable to present good government, and promotes a better and higher form of national character, than any other polity whatsoever. Its superiority in reference to present well-being rests upon two principles: . . . The first is that the rights and interests of every or any person are only secure from being disregarded, when the person interested is himself able, and habitually disposed, to stand up for them. The second is, that the general prosperity attains a greater height, and is more widely diffused, in proportion to the amount and variety of the personal energies enlisted in promoting it. . . .

Chapter V. Of the Proper Functions of Representative Bodies

Instead of the function of governing, for which it is radically unfit, the proper office of a representative assembly is to watch and control the government: to throw the light of publicity on its acts: to compel a full exposition and justification of all of them which anyone considers questionable; to censure them if found condemnable, and, if the men who compose the government abuse their trust, or fulfill it in a manner which conflicts with the deliberate sense of the nation, to expel them from office, and either expressly or virtually appoint their successors. . . . Representative assemblies are often taunted by their enemies with being places of mere talk and *bavardage*. There has seldom been more misplaced derision. I know not how a representative assembly can more usefully employ itself than in talk, when the subject of talk is the great public interest of the country, and every sentence of it represents the opinion either of some important body of persons in the nation, or of an individual in whom some such body have reposed their confidence. A place where every interest and shade of opinion in the country can have its cause even passionately pleaded, in the face of the government and of all other interests and opinions can compel them to listen, and either comply, or state clearly why they do not, is in itself, if it answered no other purpose, one of the most important political institutions that can exist anywhere, and one of the foremost benefits of free government. Such "talking" would never be looked upon with disparagement if it were not allowed to stop "doing"; which it never would, if assemblies knew and acknowledged that talking and discussion are their proper business, while *doing,* as the result of discussion, is the task not of a miscellaneous body, but of individuals specially trained to it. . . .

The very fact which most unfits such bodies for a Council of Legislation, qualifies them the more for their other office—namely, that they are not a selection of the greatest political minds in the country, from whose opinions little could with certainty be inferred concerning those of the nation, but are, when properly constituted, a fair sample of every grade of intellect among the people which is at all entitled to a voice in public affairs. Their part is to indicate wants, to be an organ for popular demands, and a place of adverse discussion for all opinions relating to public matters, both great and small; and, along with this, to check by criticism and eventually by withdrawing their support, those high public officers who really conduct the public business, or who appoint those by whom it is conducted. . . .

Chapter VI. Of the Infirmities and Dangers to which Representative Government Is Liable

The defects of any form of government may be either negative or positive. It is negatively defective if it does not concentrate in the hands of the authorities, power sufficient to fulfill the necessary offices of a government; or if it does not sufficiently develop by exercise the active capacities and social feelings of the individual citizens.

The *positive* evils and dangers of the representative, as of every other form of government, may be reduced to two heads: first, general ignorance and incapacity, or, to speak more moderately, insufficient mental qualifications, in the controlling body; secondly, the danger of its being under the influence of interests not identical with the general welfare of the community. . . .

One of the greatest dangers, therefore, of democracy, as of all other forms of government, lies in the sinister interest of the holders of power: it is the danger of class legislation; of government intended for (whether really effecting it or not) the immediate benefit of the dominant class, to the lasting detriment of the whole. And one of the most important questions demanding consideration, in determining the best constitution of a representative government, is how to provide efficacious securities against this evil.

If we consider as a class, politically speaking, any number of persons who have the same sinister interest,—that is, whose direct and apparent interest points towards the same description of bad measures; the desirable object would be that no class and no combination of classes likely to combine, should be able to exercise a preponderant influence in the government. A modern community, not divided within itself by strong antipathies of race, language, or nationality, may be considered as in the main divisible into two sections, which, in spite of partial variations, correspond on the whole with two divergent directions of apparent interest. Let us call them (in brief general terms) laborers on the one hand, employers of labor on the other: including however along with employers of labor, not only retired capitalists, and the possessors of inherited wealth, but all that highly paid description of laborers (such as the professions) whose education and way of life assimilate them with the rich, and whose prospect and ambition it is to raise themselves into that class. With the laborer, on the other hand, may be ranked those smaller employers of labor, who by interests, habits, and educational impressions, are assimilated in wishes, tastes, and objects to the laboring classes; comprehending a large proportion of petty tradesmen. In a state of society thus composed, if the representative system could be made ideally perfect, and if it were possible to maintain it in that state, its organization must be such, that these two classes, manual laborers and their affinities on one side, employers of labor and their affinities on the other, should be, in the arrangement of the representative system, equally balanced, each influencing about an equal number of votes in Parliament: since, assuming that the majority of each class, in any difference between them, would be mainly governed by their class interests, there would be a minority of each in whom that consideration would be subordinate to reason, justice, and the good of the whole; and this minority of either, joining with the whole of the other, would turn the scale against any demands of their own majority which were not such as ought to prevail. The reason why, in any tolerably constituted society, justice and the general interest mostly in the end carry their point, is that the separate and selfish interests of mankind are almost always divided: some are interested in what is wrong, but some, also, have their private interest on the side of what is right: and those who are governed by higher considerations, though too few and weak to prevail against the whole of the others, usually after sufficient discussion and agitation become strong enough to turn the balance in favor of the body of private interests which is on the same side with them. The representative system ought to be so constituted as to maintain this state of things: it ought not to allow any of the various sectional interests to be so powerful as to be capable of prevailing against truth and justice and the other sectional interests combined. There ought always to be such a balance preserved among personal interests, as may render any one of them dependent for its successes, on carrying with it at least a large proportion of those who act on higher motives, and more comprehensive and distant views.

ON LIBERTY (1859)

(Boston, 1864), pp. 22–23, 27–28, 101–102, 142–143.

The object of this Essay is to assert one very simple principle. . . . The principle is, that the sole end for which mankind are warranted, individually or collectively, in interfering with the liberty of action of any of their number is self-protection. That the only purpose for which power can be rightfully exercised over any member of a civilized community, against his will, is to prevent harm to others. . . .

The appropriate region of human liberty . . . comprises, *first,* the inward domain of consciousness: demanding liberty of conscience, in the most comprehensive sense; liberty of thought and feeling; absolute freedom of opinion and sentiment on all subjects practical or speculative, scientific, moral, or theological. The liberty of expressing and publishing opinions may seem to fall under a different principle, since it belongs to that part of the conduct of an individual which concerns other people; but, being almost of as much importance as the liberty of thought itself, and resting in great part on the same reasons, is practically inseparable from it. *Secondly,* the principle requires liberty of tastes and pursuits; of framing the plan of our life to suit our own character; of doing as we like, subject to such consequences as may follow—without impediment from our fellow-creatures so long as what we do does not harm them, even though they should think our conduct foolish, perverse, or wrong. *Thirdly,* from this liberty of each individual follows the liberty, within the same limits, of combination among individuals; freedom to unite, for any purpose not involving harm to others, the persons combining being supposed to be of full age, and not forced or deceived. . . .

We have now recognized the necessity to the mental well-being of mankind (on which all their other well-being depends) of freedom of opinion, and freedom of the expression of opinion, on four distinct grounds:

First, if any opinion is compelled to silence, that opinion may, for aught we can certainly know, be true. To deny this is to assume our own infallibility.

Secondly, though the silenced opinion be an error, it may, and very commonly does, contain a portion of truth; and since the general or prevailing opinion on any subject is rarely or never the whole truth, it is only by the collision of adverse opinions that the remainder of the truth has any chance of being supplied.

Thirdly, even if the received opinion be not only true, but the whole truth, unless it is suffered to be, and actually is, vigorously and earnestly contested, it will, by most of those who receive it, be held in the manner of a prejudice, with little comprehension or feeling of its rational grounds. And not only this, but, *fourthly,* the meaning of the doctrine itself, will be in danger of being lost, or enfeebled, and deprived of its vital effect on the character and conduct. . . .

A more powerful agency than even all these, in bringing about a general similarity among mankind, is the complete establishment, in this and other free countries, of the ascendancy of public opinion in the State. As the various social eminences which enabled persons entrenched on them to disregard the opinion of the multitude gradually become levelled; as the very idea of resisting the will of the public, when it is positively known that they have a will, disappears more and more from the minds of practical politicians; there ceases to be any social support for nonconformity—any substantive power in society, which, itself opposed to the ascendance of numbers, is interested in taking under its protective opinions and tendencies at variance with those of the public. . . . The demand that all other people shall resemble ourselves grows by what it feeds on. If resistance waits till life is reduced *nearly* to one uniform type, all deviations from that type will come to be considered impious, immoral, even monstrous and contrary to nature. Mankind speedily become unable to conceive diversity, when they have been for some time unaccustomed to see it.

A CRITIQUE OF LIBERALISM

ALEXIS DE TOCQUEVILLE: DEMOCRACY IN AMERICA (1840)

From *De la démocratie en Amérique* (2 vols., Paris, 1835–1840)

A "liberal conservative" nobleman, Tocqueville was a member of the French Parliament under Louis Philippe and elected to the French Academy in 1841. After a visit to the United States in the 1830s, he wrote an incisive commentary on his experiences. As the following excerpt shows, he did not see universal suffrage as the answer to the problems of democracy.

The power of the majority itself is not unlimited. Above it in the moral realm are humanity, justice, and reason; and in the political realm, vested rights. . . . Until our own time, it had been thought that despotism was odious, under whatever form it might appear. But our age has discovered that there are such things as legitimate tyranny and sanctified injustice, provided they are done in the name of the people. . . . I know of no country where there is so little independence of mind and so little freedom of discussion as in America. In any constitutional state in Europe, every kind of religious and political idea may be freely preached and spread abroad; for there is no country in Europe so cowed by any one authority as not to protect the man who raises his voice in the cause of truth, in order to shield him from the consequences of his boldness. If he has the misfortune to live under an absolute government, the people are often on his side; if he lives in a free country, he can, if necessary seek shelter behind the throne. . . . But in a nation where democratic institutions exist, . . . like those of the United States, there is but one authority, one element of strength and success, with nothing beyond it. . . .

Equality stimulates several propensities in people which are extremely dangerous to freedom. . . . People living in democratic ages do not readily understand the usefulness of forms, . . . which provoke their contempt and often hatred; since they usually aspire to none but easy and immediate gratifications, they rush towards the object of their desires, exasperated by the slightest delay. This same attitude, carried into political life, also makes them hostile to forms there—forms which are perpetually retarding or arresting them in their plans. But this objection that people in democracies make to forms is the very thing that makes forms so useful to freedom, for their chief advantage is to serve as a buffer between the strong and the weak, the ruler and the people, retarding the one and giving the other time to look about him. Forms become more necessary as the government becomes more active and powerful, while individual people are becoming more indolent and weaker. Thus democratic nations stand in greater need of forms than any other, and by their nature they respect them less.

UNIVERSAL SUFFRAGE IN AUTOCRATIC REGIMES

LOUIS NAPOLEON: PROCLAMATION TO THE PEOPLE (1851)

From Anderson, *Constitutions and Other Documents*, pp. 539–540.

After the French revolutions of 1848, the new president of the Second Republic, elected by manhood suffrage, turned out to be a man named Napoleon—*Louis* Napoleon, a nephew of Napoleon I. But the constitution of the new Republic, to insure against despotism, provided that the president could not succeed himself: after one four-year term he would have to go back to private citizenship. What a fortunate coincidence, therefore, that in his third year in office Louis Napoleon discovered a plot against the State, right in the Parliament itself, and dealt with it so adeptly, as his proclamation indicates!

Frenchmen!

The present situation cannot last much longer. Each passing day increases the danger to the country. The Assembly, which ought to be the firmest support of order, has become a center of conspiracies. The patriotism of 300 of its members was not able to arrest its fatal tendencies. Instead of making laws in the public interest, it forges weapons for civil war; it attacks the authority that I hold directly from the people; it encourages all evil passions; it jeopardizes the peace of France: I have dissolved it and I make the whole people judge between it and me.

The constitution, as you know, was intended to weaken in advance the power that you were about to confer upon me. Six million votes were an impressive protest against it, but I faithfully observed it nevertheless. Provocations, calumnies, outrages left me unmoved. But now that the fundamental compact is no longer respected even by those who incessantly invoke it, and the men who have already destroyed two monarchies wish to bind my hands, in order to overthrow the Republic; it is my duty to defeat their wicked designs, and to save the country by invoking the solemn judgment of the only sovereign I recognize in France, the people.

I therefore make a loyal appeal to the whole nation, and I say to you: If you wish to continue this state of uneasiness which degrades us and makes our future uncertain, choose another in my place, for I no longer wish an authority which is powerless to do good, makes me responsible for acts I cannot prevent, and chains me to the helm when I see the vessel speeding toward the abyss.

If, on the contrary, you still have confidence in me, give me the means to accomplish the great mission that I hold from you. This mission consists in bringing to a close the era of revolutions by satisfying the legitimate wants of the people and by protecting them against subversive passions. It consists, especially, in creating institutions that may survive men and that may be at length foundations on which something durable can be established.

Persuaded that the instability of authority and the preponderance of a single Assembly are permanent causes of trouble and discord, I submit to you the following fundamental bases of a constitution which the Assemblies will develop later.

1. A responsible chief selected for ten years.

2. Ministers dependent upon the executive power alone.

3. A Council of State composed of the most distinguished men to prepare the laws and discuss them before the legislative body.

4. A legislative body to discuss and vote the laws, elected by universal suffrage. . . .

5. A second assembly, composed of all the illustrious persons of the country, predominant authority, guardian of the fundamental compact and of the public liberties.

This system, created by the First Consul [Napoleon I] at the beginning of the century, has already given France calm and prosperity; it will guarantee them to her again.

Such is my profound conviction. If you share it, declare that fact by your votes. If, on the contrary, you prefer a government without force, monarchical or republican, borrowed from I know not what past or from what chimerical future, reply in the negative.

Thus, for the first time since 1804, you will vote with knowledge of the case, knowing well for whom and for what.

If I do not obtain a majority of your votes, I shall then convoke a new assembly, and I shall resign to it the mandate that I received from you. But if you believe that the cause of which my name is the symbol, that is, France regenerated by the revolution of 1789 and organized by the Emperor, is forever yours, proclaim it by sanctioning the powers that I ask from you. Then France and Europe will be saved from anarchy, obstacles will be removed, rivalries will disappear, for all will respect the decree of Providence in the decision of the people.

OTTO VON BISMARCK: ON UNIVERSAL SUFFRAGE

From Bismarck, *His Reflections and Reminiscences,* trans. A. Butler (2 vols., London, 1898).

After his forced retirement from office following the death of the Emperor Frederick III, Bismarck (d. 1898) spent the last years of his life criticizing the regime of the new emperor (William II) and defending his own policies. Such a defense is illustrated by his remarks on universal suffrage below.

Looking to the necessity, in a fight against an overwhelming foreign Power, of being able . . . to use even revolutionary means, I had no hesitation in throwing into the frying-pan, by means of the circular dispatch of June 10, 1866, the most powerful ingredient known at that time to liberty-mongers, namely, universal suffrage, so as to frighten off foreign monarchies from trying to stick a finger into our national omelette. I never doubted that the German people would be strong and clever enough to free themselves from the existing suffrage as soon as they realized that it was a harmful institution. If they cannot, then my saying that Germany can ride when once she has got into the saddle was erroneous. The acceptance of universal suffrage was a weapon in the war against Austria and other foreign countries, in the war for German unity, as well as a threat to use the last weapons in a struggle against coalitions. In a war of this sort, when it becomes a matter of life and death, one does not look at the weapons that one seizes; nor at the value of what one destroys in using them: one is guided at the moment by no other thought than the issue of the war, and the preservation of one's external independence; the settling of affairs and reparation of the damage has to take place after the peace. Moreover, I still hold that the principle of universal suffrage is a just one, not only in theory but also in practice, provided always that voting is not secret, for secrecy is a quality that is indeed incompatible with the best characteristics of German blood.

The influence and dependence on others that the practical life of man brings in its train are God-given realities which we cannot and must not ignore. If we refuse them to political life, and base that life on a faith in the secret insight of everybody, we fall into a contradiction between public law and the realities of human life which practically leads to constant frictions, and finally to an explosion, and to which there is no theoretical solution except by way of the insanities of [Socialism], whose support rests on the fact that the judgment of the masses is sufficiently stultified and undeveloped to allow them, with the assistance of their own greed, to be continually caught by the rhetoric of clever and ambitious leaders.

The counterpoise to this lies in the influence of the educated classes which would be greatly strengthened if voting were public, as for the Prussian Diet. It may be that the greater discretion of the more intelligent classes rests on the material basis of the preservation of their possessions. The other motive, the struggle for gain, is equally justifiable, but a preponderance of those who represent property is more serviceable for the security and development of the state. A state, the control of which lies in the hands of the greedy, of the new rich, and of orators who have in a higher degree than others the capacity for deceiving the unreasoning masses, will constantly be doomed to a restlessness of development, which so ponderous a mass as the commonwealth of the state cannot follow without injury to its organism. Ponderous masses, and among these the life and development of great nations must be reckoned, can only move with caution, since the road they travel to an unknown future has no smooth iron rails. Every great state-commonwealth that loses the prudent and restraining influence of the propertied class, whether that influence rests on material or moral grounds, will always end by being rushed along at a speed which must shatter the coach of state, as happened in the course of the French Revolution. . . .

I should regard it as a serious misfortune . . . if we in Germany were driven into the vortex of that French cycle. Absolutism would be the ideal form of government . . . were not the king and his officials ever as other men are, to whom it is not given to reign with superhuman wisdom, insight, and justice. The most experienced and well-meaning absolute rulers are subject to human imperfections, such as overestimation of their own wisdom, the influence and eloquence of favorites, not to mention petticoat influence, legitimate and illegitimate. . . . The most ideal monarch, if his idealism is not to be a common danger, stands in need of criticism, . . . [which] can only be exercised through the medium of a free press and parliaments in the modern sense of the term.

THE ENGLISH REFORM ACT OF 1867

From *Public General Statutes*, 2:1082f: 30–31 Victoria, c. 102.

This second reform bill was called a "leap in the dark" at the time it was passed, because it went further than either party intended. Each was trying to outmaneuver the other by making the bill so broad that it would have to be voted down, but instead it passed, giving England almost universal manhood suffrage; and the Reform Act of 1884 completed the democratization of the electorate by enfranchising males in rural areas.

An Act further to amend the laws relating to the representation of the people in England and Wales. . . . Be it enacted [that]: Every man shall, in and after the year 1868, be entitled to be registered as a voter and, when registered, to vote for a member or members to serve in parliament for a borough, who is qualified as follows: that is to say, (1) is of full age, and not subject to any legal incapacity; and (2) is on the last day of July in any year and has during . . . the preceding 12 calendar months been an inhabitant occupier, as owner or tenant of any dwelling-house within the borough; and (3) has during the time of such occupation been rated as an ordinary occupier in respect of the premises so occupied by him within the borough to all rates, if any, made for the relief of the poor in respect of such premises; and (4) has, on or before the 20th day of July in the same year, *bona fide* paid an equal amount in the pound to that payable by other ordinary occupiers in respect of all poor rates that have become payable by him in respect of the said premises up to the preceding 5th day of January. Provided, that no man shall under this section be entitled to be registered as a voter by reason of his being a joint occupier of any dwelling-house.

Every man shall, in and after the year 1868, be entitled to be registered as a voter and, when registered, to vote for a member or members to serve in parliament for a borough, who is qualified as follows: that is to say, (1) is of full age and not subject to any legal incapacity; and (2) as a lodger has occupied in the same borough separately and as sole tenant for the 12 months preceding the last day of July in any year the same lodgings, such lodgings being part of one and the same dwelling-house, and of a clear yearly value, if let unfurnished, of £10 or upwards; and (3) has resided in such lodgings during the 12 months immediately preceding the last day of July, and has claimed to be registered as a voter at the next ensuing registration of voters. . . .

From and after the end of this present parliament, no borough which had a less population than 10,000 at the census of 1861 shall return more than one member to serve in parliament. . . .

In all future parliaments the university of London shall return one member to serve in parliament. Every man whose name is for the time being on the register of graduates constituting the convocation of the university of London shall, if of full age and not subject to any legal incapacity, be entitled to vote in the election of a member to serve in any future parliament for the said university. . . .

CHAPTER 23

SOCIALISM IN THE NINETEENTH CENTURY: UTOPIANISM, MARXISM, REVISIONISM, ET AL.

Modern socialism stems from the Industrial and French Revolutions. As we have seen, Babeuf was an early egalitarian, and the social and economic transformations by the Industrial Revolution of the traditional agrarian society in England produced an environment that was ripe for radical reforms. While the new millowners were accumulating enormous wealth, the millworkers and their families were ground down into slums and poverty.

One of the first of the reformers—later dubbed "utopian" by Karl Marx—was Robert Owen, himself a millowner with a conscience. His plan was so successful in New Lanark, Scotland, that he attempted to set up a similar socialistic community in the United States, but it failed.

In France, following Babeuf and the French Revolution, the first major social reform movement was led by the Count de Saint-Simon (1760–1825). Combining socialism with Christianity, he and his followers not only influenced later French socialists, among them Louis Blanc, but they also laid the groundwork for the modern socialist movement in France.

Meanwhile, across the Channel Marx and Engels were collaborating on the development of a socialist program that was destined to outlast most of the others. In 1848 they published the *Communist Manifesto,* calling on the workmen of all countries to unite and overthrow the bourgeoisie. But at the time nobody was listening, and in the next generation several schools of "revisionist" thinking challenged many of the assumptions in the Manifesto.

On the other hand, a different kind of attack on the social problem was developed by a line of thinkers known as Anarchists. Their ideas were based on cooperation, mutual aid, and the concept of the General Strike, designed to produce the fall of the whole capitalist system by peaceful means. Two of the leading thinkers in this school were the Russians Peter Kropotkin and Michael Bakunin.

Finally, the Catholic Church became involved when Pope Leo XIII issued his famous encyclical *Rerum Novarum*. Rejecting socialism in all its forms, Leo also criticized industrialists for their lack of humanity and advocated unionization for the workers to achieve their goals—at a time when unions were anathema to almost everybody in the middle and upper classes.

UTOPIANISM

OWEN: PLAN FOR THE RELIEF OF THE MANUFACTURING AND LABORING POOR (1817)

From *The Life of Robert Owen, Written by Himself* (London, 1858), 1A:68–73.

Robert Owen worked his way up from child-millhand to successful cotton manufacturer, first in Manchester, England, and then in New Lanark, Scotland. Like many of his contemporaries, he was troubled by the workers' wretched state of working and living. But unlike most of the others, Owen did something about it. In the early years of the century he developed New Lanark into a model community, with good working conditions, housing, sanitation, schools, and nonprofit stores. And the mill-profits increased! When he tried to set up a similar community in New Harmony, Indiana, it failed. Why? That question is still being debated. All in all, Owen has several significant credits to his name: he was instrumental in the factory legislation of 1819, played a major role in the rise of British trade-unionism, influenced English educational reform, and is supposed to have been the first to use the word "socialism." The following "dialogue" provides some insight into his originality.

Q. To what causes do you attribute the distress existing among the poor and working classes?
A. To a misapplication of the existing powers of production in the country . . . when compared to the wants and demands for those productions. . . .

Q. Does your experience enable you to suggest a more advantageous application of these productive powers?
A. They may, with ease, be so directed as to remove speedily the present distress of the laboring poor and . . . carry the prosperity of the country to a point much higher than it has ever yet attained.

Q. How can this be done?

A. By forming well-digested arrangements to occupy the apparent surplus of the laboring poor, who are competent to work, in productive employment, in order that they may maintain themselves first, and afterwards contribute to bear their proportion of the expenses of the state.

Q. Do the means exist by which employment could be given to the unoccupied of the working class?

A. The country possesses the most ample means to attain this object. . . . land unemployed; land imperfectly cultivated; money employed unprofitably; manual powers of labor idle. . . .

Q. How can they be put into action?

A. By bringing them all into useful and profitable combinations, so as to create limited communities of individuals, on the principle of united labor and expenditure, having their basis in agriculture and in which all should have mutual and common interests.

Q. What are your reasons for recommending such a combination of human powers?

A. . . . The very superior advantages which each person could derive by this means beyond any application of his own exertions for his own exclusive purposes. . . . Communities of 500 to 1,500 persons, founded on the principles of united labor and expenditure, and having their basis in agriculture, might be arranged so as to give the following advantages to the laboring poor, and through them to all the other classes. . . . All the labor . . . would be . . . directed first to procure . . . abundance of all that was necessary for their comfortable existence; next, they would obtain the means to enable them to unlearn many . . . of the bad habits which the present defective arrangements of society have forced upon them; then, to give only the best habits and dispositions to the rising generation, and thus withdraw those circumstances from society which separate man from man, and introduce others, whose entire tendency shall be to unite them in one general interest. . . . It is found that when men work together for a common interest, each performs his part more advantageously for himself and for society, than when employed for others. . . .

Q. But will not the parties dispute perpetually about the division and possession of the property?

A. Certainly not. . . . Now the mass of mankind cannot procure sufficient to support themselves in ordinary comfort without great exertion and anxiety; they therefore acquire . . . a tenacious love of that property which costs them so much to procure; thus making the feeling itself appear . . . as one implanted by nature. . . . No conclusion can, however, be more erroneous. . . .

Q. [Will not] such arrangements produce a dull uniformity of character, repress genius?

A. . . . Quite the reverse. . . . From the hour they are born, treated with uniform kindness, directed by reason, . . . physical powers trained . . . mental faculties furnished with adequate data, . . . children so trained . . . would become . . . full of health, activity, and energy. [Genius] will . . . exert itself with unrestrained delight.

EARLY FRENCH SOCIALISM: THE SAINT-SIMONIANS

Louis Blanc, *Histoire de dix ans*, 5 vols. (Paris, 1841–1844).

Count Henri de Saint-Simon (d. 1825) fought in the American Revolution and returned to France to support the French Revolution and surrender his title. Having made a fortune in land speculation, he lost it all in social experiments and lived the rest of his life in poverty. After his death a socio-religious cult developed among his followers, laying the foundation for modern French socialism. One of his disciples was Louis Blanc, who originated the idea of "National Workshops," and wrote the following account of Saint-Simonism in Paris in the 1830s.

The July Revolution [1830] gave Saint-Simonism a burst of new energy. What had originally been only a school became a family. The early adepts combined the authority of lofty intellect and solid achievements with a passion for proselytism. Men of the world and ardent sectaries, they spread themselves about in all directions, holding out to orators the promise of a noble arena and a stirring theme; to poets and artists, the bait of a reputation easily acquired; to scientists, the message that the science of liberalism was false and hollow, without aim or scope, heart or feeling; to women, the promise of such things as the arts, love, and liberty. The success of these efforts was immediate; they made so many individual conquests that they began to think of collective triumphs. The hierarchy was founded: first the college, then the second degree, then the third. The *Globe* [newspaper] . . . became the daily journal of the school, which already had the *Organisateur*. It was no sooner hinted that money was wanting than money flowed in. . . . In a world permeated by the coarsest and most narrow-minded commercialism, there was something very marvellous and touching in this burst of generous enthusiasm. The great majority of journals in this period were mere trading ventures: the *Globe* was distributed gratuitously.

The zeal of the adepts spurred them on to the most vigorous exertions. The modest conferences which, before the July Revolution, had been held in the Rue Taranne, were now succeeded by the vehement and noisy harangues of the Rue Taitbout. Here men full of eloquence . . . repaired to exercise, in turns, the sovereignty of the mighty sermon. Nothing could be more curious than the spectacle offered by these assemblies. Around a vast hall under a glass roof, there arose three tiers of boxes. On the stage in front of these boxes and the large orchestra area, were three rows of red benches. Every Sunday at 12 o'clock these benches were occupied by a number of serious-looking young men dressed in blue suits and accompanied also by some ladies dressed in white with purple scarves. After the hall was filled with an eager audience, there appeared the two supreme fathers of the society, Messrs. Bazard and Enfantin, leading forward the preacher of the day. As they advanced to the front, the disciples rose with looks of tender veneration, while among the spectators there reigned a profound silence, either contemplative or ironical, according to the mood in which they came. After a short pause the preacher began. Many among the audience listened at first with a smile on their lips and mockery in their eyes, but after the orator had spoken a while, there would be a feeling among his hearers of astonishment mixed with admiration; and the most sceptical found themselves drawn irresistibly into serious thought about the discourse, if not into a secret feeling of sympathy with it.

Everything tended to make this propaganda effective and successful. The family established in the Rue Monsigny was like a glowing hearth, reflecting strong light on those whom its genial warmth attracted. Here the doctrine was developed amidst gallant soirées, under the powerful influence of fascinating women. Here engineers, artists, physicians, lawyers, and poets—abandoning their occupations, their dreams of fortune, their earlier romantic attachments—all rushed to put their most exalted hopes into one common association; some brought their books, others their furniture; their meals were taken in common and they assiduously studied this new religion of human brotherhood.

The name of *father* was given to the members of each superior degree by those of the inferior degree; and the women who had entered this intellectual colony were addressed by the gentle names of *mother, sister, daughter*. Here were centered the relations, constantly expanding, between the Parisian innovators and their provincial allies, an uninterrupted correspondence; and this was the point from which there set forth, bent on sowing the seed of Saint-Simonism throughout the length and breadth of France, the missionaries who left their traces everywhere; who made their way into shops and drawing rooms, into huts, hotels and castles; here received with enthusiasm, there with hoots, but everywhere unflagging in their zeal. . . .

According to the Saint-Simonians, humanity was headed for a situation in which individuals would be classified according to their capacity and salaried according to their work. Property as it now exists was to be abolished because it allowed a certain class of men to live by the labor of others; because it sanctioned the division of society into workers and idlers; because, violating all concepts of equity, it placed those who produce much and consume little in the hands of those who consume much and produce little, or even nothing. . . .

The existing system of inheritance was not only unjust in itself, said the Saint-Simonians, . . . but it also caused wages to be depressed and rents and interest rates to rise. . . . As the laborers gained power, they would demand the reduction of interest and rents. This being the case, what would become of the proprietors when those reductions became so great that they could no longer live on their interest and rents? They would go to work, replied the Saint-Simonians.

MARXISM

MARX AND ENGELS: MANIFESTO OF THE COMMUNIST PARTY
(1848)

Manifesto of the Communist Party: Authorized English Translation by S.F. Morse (London, 1888), pp. 7–29, 32–34, 48.

Issued by an organization called The Communist League, the Manifesto was the work of Karl Marx and Friedrich Engels. Marx, the son of a well-to-do German Jewish family, had been expelled from Germany in 1843 for his revolutionary activity; Engels, the son of a German industrialist, had been sent to England to manage a branch factory near Manchester, where he was shocked by the working conditions. Marx and he met in 1844 to begin a collaboration that lasted the rest of their lives. The Manifesto was largely ignored at the time it was written, but later became the torch for revolutionary fires around the world.

A specter is haunting Europe—the specter of Communism. All the powers of old Europe have entered into a holy alliance to exorcise this specter; Pope and Czar, Metternich and Guizot, French Radicals and German police-spies. . . .

The history of all hitherto existing society is the history of class struggles. . . .

The modern bourgeois Society that has sprouted from the ruins of feudal society, has not done away with class antagonisms. It has but established new classes, new conditions of oppression, new forms of struggle in place of the old ones.

Our epoch, the epoch of the bourgeoisie, however, possesses this distinctive feature: it has simplified the class antagonisms. Society as a whole is more and more splitting up into two great hostile camps, into two great classes directly facing each other: Bourgeoisie and Proletariat. . . .

The bourgeoisie, historically, has played a most revolutionary part. The bourgeoisie, wherever it has got the upper hand, has put an end to all feudal, patriarchal, idyllic relations. It has pitilessly torn asunder the motley feudal ties that bound man to his "natural superiors," and has left remaining no other nexus between man and man than naked self-interest, than callous "cash payment." It has drowned the most heavenly ecstacies of religious fervor, of chivalrous enthusiasm, of philistine sentimentalism, in the icy water of egotistical calculation. It has resolved personal worth into exchange value, and in place of the numberless indefeasible chartered freedoms, has set up that single, unconscionable freedom—Free Trade. In a word, for exploitation, veiled by religious and political illusions, it has substituted naked, shameless, direct, brutal exploitation. . . .

In proportion as the bourgeoisie, *i.e.,* capital, is developed, in the same proportion is the proletariat, the modern working-class, developed, a class of laborers, who live only so long as they find work, and who find work only so long as their labor increases capital. These laborers, who must sell themselves piece-meal, are a commodity, like every other article of commerce, and are consequently exposed to all the fluctuations of the market. . . .

Modern industry has converted the little workshop of the patriarchal master into the great factory of the industrial capitalist. Masses of laborers, crowded into the factories, are organized like soldiers. As privates of the industrial army they are placed under the command of a perfect hierarchy of officers and sergeants. Not only are they the slaves of the bourgeois class, and of the bourgeois State, they are daily and hourly enslaved by the machine, by the overlooker, and above all, by the individual bourgeois manufacturer himself. The more openly this despotism proclaims gain to be its end and aim, the more petty, the more hateful and the more embittering it is. . . .

But with the development of industry the proletariat not only increases in number, it becomes concentrated in greater masses, its strength grows, and it feels that strength more. The various interests and conditions of life within the ranks of the proletariat are more and more equalized, in proportion as machinery obliterates all distinctions of labor, and nearly everywhere reduces wages to the same level. The growing competition among the bourgeois, and the resulting commercial crises, make the wages of the workers ever more fluctuating. The unceasing improvement of machinery, ever more rapidly developing, makes their livelihood more and more precarious; the collisions between individual workmen and individual bourgeois take more and more the character of collisions between two classes. Thereupon the workers begin to form combinations (Trades' Unions) against the bourgeoisie. . . .

This organization of the proletarians into a class, and consequently into a political party, is continually being upset again by the competition between the workers themselves. But it ever rises up again, stronger, firmer, mightier. . . .

It [is] evident that the bourgeoisie is unfit any longer to be the ruling class in society, and to impose its conditions of existence upon society as an overriding law. It is unfit to rule, because it is incompetent to assure an existence to its slave within his slavery, because it cannot help letting him sink into such a state that it has to feed him, instead of being fed by him. Society can no longer live under this bourgeoisie, in other words, its existence is no longer compatible with society.

The essential condition for the existence, and for the sway of the bourgeois class, is the formation and augmentation of capital; the condition for capital is wage-labor. Wage-labor rests exclusively on competition between the laborers. The advance of industry, whose voluntary promoter is the bourgeoisie, replaces the isolation of the laborers, due to competition, by their involuntary combination, due to association. The development of Modern Industry, therefore, cuts from under its feet the very foundation on which the bourgeoisie produces and appropriates products. What the bourgeoisie therefore produces, above all, are its own gravediggers. Its fall and the victory of the proletariat are equally inevitable. . . .

The immediate aim of the Communists is the same as that of all the other proletarian parties; formation of the proletariat into a class, overthrow of the bourgeois supremacy, conquest of political power by the proletariat. . . .

The distinguishing feature of Communism is not the abolition of property generally, but the abolition of bourgeois property. But modern bourgeois private property is the final and most complete expression of the system of producing and appropriating products, that is based on class antagonism, on the exploitation of the many by the few.

In this sense, the theory of the Communists may be summed up in the single sentence: Abolition of private property. . . .

The Communists are . . . reproached with desiring to abolish countries and nationalities.

The workingmen have no country. We cannot take from them what they have not got. Since the proletariat must first of all acquire political supremacy, must rise to be the leading class of the nation, must constitute itself the nation, it is, so far, itself national, though not in the bourgeois sense of the word. . . .

The proletariat will use its political supremacy to wrest, by degrees, all capital from the bourgeoisie, to centralize all instruments of production in the hands of the State, i.e., of the proletariat organized as the ruling class; and to increase the total of productive forces as rapidly as possible.

Of course, in the beginning, this cannot be effected except by means of despotic inroads on the rights of property, and on the conditions of bourgeois production. . . . These measures will be different for different countries [but] in the most advanced countries the following will be pretty generally applicable:

1. Abolition of property in land and application of all rents of land to public purposes.

2. A heavy progressive or graduated income tax.

3. Abolition of all right of inheritance.

4. Confiscation of the property of all emigrants and rebels.

5. Centralization of credit in the hands of the State, by means of a national bank with State capital and an exclusive monopoly.

6. Centralization of the means of communication and transport in the hands of the State.

7. Extension of factories and instruments of production owned by the State. . . .

8. Equal liability of all to labor. Establishment of industrial armies, especially for agriculture.

9. Combination of agriculture with manufacturing industries; gradual abolition of the distinction between town and country, by a more equable distribution of population over the country.

10. Free education for all children in public schools. Abolition of children's factory labor in its present form. Combination of education with industrial production, etc., etc.

When in the course of development, class distinctions have disappeared, and all production has been concentrated in the hands of a vast association of the whole nation, the public power will lose its character. Political power, properly so called, is merely the organized power of one class for oppressing another. If the proletariat during its contest with the bourgeoisie is compelled, by force of circumstances, to organize itself as a class, if, by means of a revolution, it makes itself the ruling class, and, as such, sweeps away the old conditions of production, then it will, along with these conditions, have swept away the conditions for the existence of class antagonisms, and of classes generally, and will thereby have abolished its own supremacy as a class.

In place of the old bourgeois society, with its classes and class antagonisms, we shall have an association, in which the free development of each is the condition for the free development of all. . . .

The Communists disdain to conceal their views and aims. They openly declare that their ends can be attained only by the forcible overthrow of all existing social conditions. Let the ruling classes tremble at a Communist revolution. The proletarians have nothing to lose but their chains. They have a world to win.

Workingmen of all countries, unite!

REVISIONISM ET AL.

In the years after the publication of the Communist Manifesto, there arose a school of thought that argued against the necessity for violent revolution. Working independently in various countries, these "revisionists," as they were called, sought to bring about a democratic socialism by winning elections, educating the people, and gradually gaining a majority in the legislatures.

One such group was the Fabian Society in England. As a middle-class movement interested in social reform, the Fabians attracted luminaries such as Sidney and Beatrice Webb, George Bernard Shaw, and H.G. Wells. In 1900, they joined forces with the labor movement to create the British Labor Party of the present day.

FABIAN SOCIETY: STATEMENT OF PRINCIPLES

The Basis of the Fabian Society (London, 1886).

The Fabian Society consists of Socialists.

It therefore aims at the reorganization of Society by the emancipation of Land and Industrial Capital from individual and class ownership, and the vesting of them in the community for the general benefit. In this way only can the natural and acquired advantages of the country be equitably shared by the whole people.

The Society accordingly works for the extinction of private property in Land and of the consequent individual appropriation, in the form of Rent, of the price paid for permission to use the earth, as well as for the advantages of superior soils and sites.

The Society, further, works for the transfer to the community of the administration of such industrial Capital as can conveniently be managed socially. For, owing to the monopoly of the means of production in the past, industrial inventions and the transformations of surplus income into Capital have mainly enriched the proprietary class, the worker being now dependent on that class for leave to earn a living.

If these measures can be carried out, without compensation (though not without such relief to the expropriate individuals as may seem fit to the community), Rent and Interests will be added to the reward of labor, the idle class now living on the labor of others will necessarily disappear, and practical equality of opportunity will be maintained by the spontaneous action of economic forces with much less interference with personal liberty than the present system entails.

For the attainment of these ends the Fabian Society looks to the spread of Socialist opinions, and the social and political changes consequent thereon. It seeks to achieve these ends by the general dissemination of knowledge as to the relation between the individual and Society in its economic, ethical, and political aspects.

EDUARD BERNSTEIN: EVOLUTIONARY SOCIALISM (1898)

From *Die Voraussetzungen des Sozialismus und die Aufgaben des Sozialdemokratie* (Stuttgart, 1899, 1921), pp. 6−7, 9−10.

Eduard Bernstein came into contact with Fabian Socialist ideas in England during his exile from Bismarck's anti-Socialist crusade of the 1880s. Returning to Germany in

1896, Bernstein argued the reformist position in a series of articles titled "Problems of Socialism." The following statement is from a letter to the German Social Democratic Party in 1898.

. . . I disagree with the idea that we should look forward to a collapse of the bourgeois economy in the near future, and that the Social Democratic Party should base its strategy on the assumption of such an imminent social catastrophe. The proponents of this catastrophe theory base it primarily on the conclusions of the *Communist Manifesto*. That is a mistake from every point of view.

The theory of the evolution of modern society set forth in the *Communist Manifesto* was correct insofar as it characterized the general tendency of that evolution. But it was mistaken in several particulars, above all in the estimate of the *time* that that evolution would require. This has been candidly admitted by Friedrich Engels . . . in his preface to the *Class Struggles in France*. Now it is obvious that if social evolution takes much longer than was assumed, it must also take on forms and lead to developments that were not foreseen, and could not have been foreseen, then.

Social conditions have not developed into the violent opposition among classes that was predicted in the *Manifesto*. To try and hide this fact from ourselves is not only useless, it is also the greatest folly. The propertied classes today are not smaller but larger. The enormous increase of social wealth is accompanied not by a declining number of large capitalists but by an increasing number of capitalists of all sizes. The middle classes may change their character, but they do not disappear from the social scale.

Even today industrial concentration is not proceeding at the same rate and to the same extent in all areas. In many branches of production, of course, it certainly justifies the forecasts of the Socialist critics, but in other branches it still lags behind them. Concentration in agriculture is proceeding even more slowly. Trade statistics reveal an extraordinary gradation of enterprises in regard to size. No rung of the ladder is disappearing. Changes in the inner structures of these enterprises and in their interrelationships cannot avoid this reality.

In all advanced countries we find the privileges of the capitalist bourgeoisie yielding little by little to democratic organizations. Under this pressure, combined with that of the working classes, whose movement becomes stronger almost daily, there is a growing social reaction against capitalistic exploitation—a counteraction which, though still proceeding timidly and feebly, yet does exist and continues to exert its influence over more and more segments of economic life. Factory legislation, the democratization of local government, the extension of its jurisdiction, the freeing of trade unions and cooperatives from legal restraints, the standardization of working conditions for public employees—all these are indications of this evolution.

However, the more the political organizations of modern nations are democratized the fewer are the chances and the necessity for great political catastrophes. Anyone who is committed to the catastrophe theory of social evolution must resist with all his might the developments described above—which, indeed, the defenders of that theory used to do. But must the gaining of political power by the proletariat be by political catastrophe only? Must its appropriation and utilization of the power of the State be used exclusively against the whole nonproletarian world? . . .

No one questions the need for the working classes to gain control of the government. The point at issue is between the theory of a social cataclysm and the question of whether, given the social development in Germany and the advanced state of its working classes, in town and country alike, a sudden catastrophe would be to the interest of Social Democracy. I have denied it before and I deny it again, because in my judgment a greater chance for long-term success lies in a steady advance than in the opportunities offered by a social catastrophe.

Convinced as I am that important periods in a nation's development cannot be skipped over, I put great emphasis on the next tasks of Social Democracy, on the struggle for the political rights of the workingman, on his political activity in town and country for the interests of his class, as well as on the workers' industrial organization.

This is the sense in which I wrote that the movement means everything to me and that what is *usually* termed "the final aim of socialism" is nothing. And this is the sense in which I write it again today. . . . I have never had excessive interest in the future, beyond general principles; I have never been able to picture it with much precision. My thoughts and efforts are concerned with the present and the immediate future. Perspectives beyond that interest me only if they offer a line of conduct for suitable action now.

The conquest of political power by the working classes, the expropriation of the capitalists, are not ends in themselves but only means for the achievement of certain aims and endeavors. As such they are demands in the program of Social Democracy and are not attacked by me. Nothing can be said beforehand as to how they will be achieved; we can only fight for their realization. But the conquest of political power requires the possession of political *rights;* and the most important problem of tactics for German Social Democracy at present seems to me to be to devise the best means for extending the political and economic rights of the German working classes. . . .

KROPOTKIN: ANARCHISM, ITS PHILOSOPHY AND IDEAL

(London, 1897), pp. 19—21.

The most extreme of the nineteenth-century social reform movements, anarchism, proposed to substitute cooperation for governmental restraint and laissez-faire competition. Peter Kropotkin was one of the movement's leading spokesmen. Also acclaimed by many for his personal, scientific, and literary qualities, he wrote the book *Mutual Aid,* a major work of the period.

Educated men . . . tremble at the idea that society might some day be without judges, police, or jailers. But, frankly, do you need them as much as you have been told in musty books? Books written, be it noted, by scientists who generally know well what [was] written before them, but, for the most part, know nothing about the people and their everyday lives.

If we can wander, without fear, not only in the streets of Paris, which bristle with police, but especially in rustic walks where you rarely meet passers-by, is it to the police that we owe this security? Or rather to the absence of people who care to rob or murder us? I am evidently not speaking of someone who carries millions about with him. That one . . . is soon robbed, by preference in places where there are as many policemen as lamp-posts. . . .

In our everyday relations with our fellow-citizens, do you think that it is really judges, jailers, and the police that hinder anti-social acts from multiplying? The judge, ever ferocious, because he is a maniac of law, the accuser, the informer, the police spy, all those interlopers that live from hand to mouth around the Law Courts, do they not scatter demoralization far and wide into society? Read the trials, glance behind the scenes, push your analysis further than the exterior façade of law courts, and you will come out sickened.

Have not prisons—which kill all will and strength of character in man, which enclose . . . more vices than are met with on any other spot of the globe—always been universities of crime? . . .

When we ask for the abolition of the State and its organs, we are always told that we dream of a society composed of men better than they are in reality. But no; a thousand times, no. All we ask is that men not be made worse than they are, by such institutions! . . .

If by following the very old advice given by Bentham, you begin to think of the fatal consequences . . . of legal coercion, then like Tolstoy, like us, you will begin to hate the use of force, and you will begin to say that society possesses a thousand other means for preventing anti-social acts. If it neglects those means today, it is because, being educated by Church and State, our cowardice and apathy of spirit hinder our seeing clearly on this point. When a child has committed a fault, it is so easy to punish it; that puts an end to all discussion. It is so easy to hang a man, and it dispenses us from thinking of the causes of crime.

LEO XIII: DE RERUM NOVARUM (1891)

From the *American Catholic Review*, July 1891.

When Pope Leo XIII published his famous encyclical "On the Condition of the Workers," he was responding to the Socialist challenge on the one hand and to the unfeeling laissez-faire attitude of the employers on the other. This major pronouncement of the Catholic Church on the "social question" was a significant break with the past, and especially with the "medieval" attitude of Leo's predecessor, Pius IX (d. 1878).

After the old trade guilds had been destroyed in the last century, . . . it gradually came about that the present age handed over the workers, each alone and defenseless, to the inhumanity of employers and the unbridled greed of competitors. . . . The whole process of production as well as trade in every kind of goods has been brought almost entirely under the power of a few, so that a very few rich and exceedingly rich men have laid a yoke almost of slavery on the unnumbered masses of non-owning workers.

To cure this evil, the Socialists, exciting the envy of the poor toward the rich, contend that it is necessary to do away with private possession of goods, and in its place to make the goods of individuals common to all, and that the men who preside over a municipality or who direct the entire State should act as administrators of these goods. They hold that, by such a transfer of private goods from private individuals to the community, they can cure the present evil through dividing wealth and benefits equally among all citizens.

But their program is so unsuited for terminating the conflict that it actually injures the workers themselves. Moreover, it is highly unjust, because it violates the rights of lawful owners, perverts the functions of the State, and throws government into utter confusion.

. . . The fundamental principle of Socialism which would make all possessions public property is to be utterly rejected because it injures the very ones whom it seeks to help, contravenes the natural rights of individual persons, and throws the functions of the State and public peace into confusion. Let it be regarded, therefore, as established that in seeking help for the masses this principle before all is to be considered as basic, namely that private ownership must be preserved inviolate.

It is a capital evil with respect to the question we are discussing to take for granted that the one class of society is of itself hostile to the other, as if nature had set rich and poor against each other to fight fiercely in implacable war. This is so abhorrent to reason and truth that the exact opposite is true. . . . Neither capital can do without labor, nor labor without capital. . . .

The entire body of religious teaching and practice, of which the Church is the interpreter and guardian, can pre-eminently bring together and unite the rich and the poor . . . by recalling the two classes of society to their mutual duties. . . .

Private ownership is the natural right of man; and to exercise that right, especially as members of society, is not only lawful, but absolutely necessary. "It is lawful," says St. Thomas Aquinas, "for a man to hold private property; and it is also necessary for the carrying on of human life." But if the question be asked, How must one's possessions be used? . . . the holy Doctor [replies]: "Man should not consider his outward possessions as his own, but as common to all, so as to share them without hesitation when others are in need. . . ."

Whenever the general interest of any particular class suffers, or is threatened with evils which can in no other way be met, the public authority must step in to meet them. . . . The richer population have many ways of protecting themselves and stand less in need of help from the State; those who are badly off have no resources of their own to fall back upon, and must chiefly rely upon the assistance of the State. And it is for this reason that wage-earners, who are undoubtedly among the weak and necessitous, should be cared for and protected by the commonwealth. . . .

History attests what excellent results were effected by the . . . Guilds of a former day. . . . Such associations should be adapted to the requirements of the age in which we live. . . . There are actually in existence not a few associations of this nature, . . . but it were greatly to be desired that they should multiply and become more effective. . . . [But] many of these societies are in the hands of invisible leaders and are managed on principles far from compatible with Christianity and public well-being; and that they [try to control] the whole field of labor and force workmen either to join them or starve. Under these circumstances Christian workmen must . . . either join associations in which their religion will be in peril, or form associations among themselves to . . . shake off the yoke of an unjust . . . oppression. . . .

CHAPTER 24
DARWINISM: SCIENCE AND POLITICS

There are certain ideas that sometimes take hold of an age and give it a character and an impulse that are unique. Such an idea was that of the evolution of species through competition for a limited food supply, which competition leads to the survival of the fittest and the elimination of the less fit. The nineteenth century became so fascinated with the idea of "nature red in tooth and claw" that it was difficult for anyone to stand against the tide.

Some did, however. One was the Russian Prince Kropotkin, who offered a contrary theory of evolution, a theory of mutual aid rather than mutual competition. Another was Thomas Henry Huxley, "Darwin's bulldog," so-called because he was an early defender of Darwin, especially against the clerical establishment. Huxley argued that the history of mankind demonstrated not the survival of the fittest but the fitting of as many as possible to survive, as illustrated, for example, by the history of medicine.

But the dominant note of the age had been struck a decade before Darwin's *Origin of Species* by the founder of modern sociology, Herbert Spencer. Following the lead of Adam Smith, David Ricardo, and Thomas Malthus, Spencer advocated the elimination of the unfit not only by giving free rein to competition but also by stopping government aid to the poor in order to force them to work or starve. Only the "new imperialists" of the end of the century would carry Social Darwinism to a higher pitch of inhumanity by advocating the use of war to prove which nations were the fittest to survive.

At the end of the century there was another thinker, Nietzsche, who rejected the materialism and mindlessness of Darwinism, but found in it the hope for a self-created type of higher man who, in the future, would be self-selected by intelligence and will-power to rise above the herd and develop new values and new virtues. Nietzsche's major work is called, significantly, *Beyond Good and Evil: Prelude to a Philosophy of the Future* (1886).

Charles Darwin, Author of the Origin of Species (1859). His publisher thought he should change the title: "Nobody would ever buy a book with a name like that." He suggested making it "something about pigeons; there is a lot about pigeons in the book and everybody is interested in them nowadays." (That was when carrier pigeons were in vogue—before the invention of the Bell System.) (American Museum of Natural History).

CHARLES DARWIN: ON THE ORIGIN OF SPECIES BY MEANS OF NATURAL SELECTION, OR THE PRESERVATION OF FAVORED RACES IN THE STRUGGLE FOR LIFE (1859)

(London, 1859), pp. 63–67, 83f.

The influence of Malthus's doctrines on population and its limitation by the food supply is apparent in this excerpt from the *Origin of Species*. The struggle for survival leads to competition for food and the natural selection of certain "favorable" variations. These then reproduce themselves and eventually produce new species.

A struggle for existence inevitably follows from the high rate at which all organic beings tend to increase. Every being, which during its natural lifetime produces several eggs or seeds, must suffer destruction during some period of its life, and during some season or occasional year; otherwise on the principle of geometrical increase, its numbers would quickly become so inordinately great that no country could supply the product. Hence, as more individuals are produced than can possibly survive, there must in every case be a struggle for existence, either one individual with another of the same species, or with the individuals of distinct species, or with the physical conditions of life. It is the doctrine of Malthus applied with manifold force to the whole animal and vegetable kingdoms; for in this case there can be no artificial increase of food, and no prudential restraint from marriage. Although some species may be now increasing, more or less rapidly, in numbers, all cannot do so, for the world would not hold them.

There is no exception to the rule that every organic being naturally increases at so high a rate, that if not destroyed, the earth would soon be covered by the progeny of a single pair. Even slow-breeding man has doubled in 25 years, and at this rate, in a few thousand years, there would literally not be standing room for his progeny. . . . If an annual plant produced only two seeds—and there is no plant so unproductive as this—and their seedlings next year produced two, and so on, then in 20 years there would be a million plants. . . .

In looking at Nature, it is most necessary to keep the foregoing considerations always in mind—never to forget that every single organic being around us may be said to be striving to the utmost to increase in numbers; that each lives by a struggle at some period of its life; that heavy destruction inevitably falls either on the young or old, during each generation or at recurrent intervals. Lighten any check, mitigate the destruction ever so little, and the number of species will almost instantaneously increase to any amount. The face of Nature may be compared to a yielding surface, with ten thousand sharp wedges packed close together and driven inwards by incessant blows, sometimes one wedge being struck, and then another with greater force. . . .

As man can produce . . . a great result by his methodical and unconscious means of selection, what may not nature effect? Man can act only on external and visible characters: nature cares nothing for appearances, except in so far as they may be useful to any being. She can act on every internal organ, on every shade of constitutional difference, on the whole machinery of life. Man selects only for his own good; Nature only for that of the being which she tends. Every selected character is fully exercised by her; And the being is placed under well-suited conditions of life. Man keeps the natives of many climates in the same country; he seldom exercises each selected character in some peculiar and fitting manner; he feeds a long- and a short-beaked pigeon on the same food; he does not exercise a long-backed or long-legged quadruped in any peculiar manner; he exposes sheep with long and short wool to the same climate. He does not allow the most vigorous males to struggle for the females. He does not rigidly destroy all inferior animals, but protects during each varying season, as far as lies in his power, all his productions. . . . How fleeting are the wishes and efforts of man! how short his time! and consequently how poor will his products be, compared with those accumulated by nature during whole geological periods. . . .

It may be said that natural selection is daily and hourly scrutinizing, throughout the world, every variation, even the slightest; rejecting that which is bad, preserving and adding up all that is good; silently and insensibly working, whenever and wherever opportunity offers, at the improvement of each organic being. . . . We see nothing of these slow changes in progress, until the hand of time has marked the long lapse of ages, and then so imperfect is our view into long past geological ages, that we see only that the forms of life are now different from what they formerly were.

CHARLES DARWIN: THE DESCENT OF MAN (1871)

2 vols. (London, 1871), 2:385f, 404f.

In the *Origin of Species* Darwin had avoided any question of human evolution, but twelve years later he met the issue head-on, thereby joining the growing ranks of those, like Herbert Spencer, who had been preaching the doctrine of "survival of the fittest" in such realms as politics and economics.

The main conclusion here arrived at . . . is that man is descended from some less highly organized form. The grounds upon which this conclusion rests will never be shaken, for the close similarity between man and the lower animals in embryonic development, as well as in innumerable points of structure and constitution, both of high and of the most trifling importance—the rudiments which he retains, and the abnormal reversions to which he is occasionally liable—are facts which cannot be disputed. They have long been known, but until recently they told us nothing with respect to the origin of man. Now when viewed by the light of our knowledge of the whole organic world, their meaning is unmistakable. The great principle of evolution stands up clear and firm when these groups of facts are considered in connection with others, such as the mutual affinities of the same group, their geographical distribution in past and present times, and their geological succession. It is incredible that all these facts should speak falsely. He who is not content to look, like a savage, at the phenomena of nature as disconnected, cannot any longer believe that man is the work of a separate act of creation. . . .

[This] conclusion . . . will, I regret to think, be highly distasteful to many people. But there can hardly be a doubt that we are descended from barbarians. The astonishment which I felt on first seeing a party of Fuegians on a wild and broken shore will never be forgotten by me, for the reflection at once rushed into my mind—such were our ancestors. These men were absolutely naked and bedaubed with paint, their long hair was tangled, their mouths frothed with excitement, and their expression was wild, startled, and distrustful. They possessed hardly any arts, and like wild animals lived on what they could catch; they had no government, and were merciless to every one not of their own small tribe. He who has seen a savage in his native land will not feel much shame if forced to acknowledge that the blood of some more humble creature flows in his veins. . . .

Man may be excused for feeling some pride at having risen, though not through his own exertions, to the very summit of the organic scale; and the fact of his having thus risen, instead of having been aboriginally placed there, may give him hopes for a still higher destiny in the distant future. But we are not here concerned with hopes or fears, only with the truth as far as our reason permits us to discover it. I have given the evidence to the best of my ability; and we must acknowledge, as it seems to me, that man with all his noble qualities, with sympathy which feels for the most debased, with benevolence which extends not only to other men but to the humblest living creature, with his godlike intellect which has penetrated into the movements and constitution of the solar system—with all these exalted powers—Man still bears in his bodily frame the indelible stamp of his lowly origin.

HERBERT SPENCER: ON THE POOR LAWS

From *Social Statics* (New York, 1896), pp. 146–150, 154–155.

Herbert Spencer (1820–1903) developed a concept of "survival of the fittest" in nature and society a decade before Darwin published his *Origin of Species*. Spencer's ideal society was one that allowed for the elimination of the unfit and the independent success of the individual on his own merits through free competition. Avoiding any interference with the operation of the "law" of natural selection, the State should provide security against foreign aggression, assure domestic tranquillity and enforce contracts. Pure laissez faire, in other words. The enemy for Spencer was Socialism in any form.

Pervading all Nature we may see at work a stern discipline which is a little cruel that it may be very kind. That state of universal warfare maintained throughout the lower creation, to the great perplexity of many worthy people, is at bottom the most merciful provision which the circumstances admit of. It is much better that the ruminant animal, when deprived by age of the vigor which made its existence a pleasure, should be killed by some beast of prey, than that it should linger out a life made painful by infirmities, and eventually die of starvation. By the destruction of all such, not only is existence ended before it becomes burdensome, but room is made for a younger generation capable of the fullest enjoyment; and, moreover, out of the very act of substitution happiness is derived for a tribe of predatory creatures. Note, further, that their carnivorous enemies . . . also weed out the sickly, the malformed, and the least fleet or powerful. . . .

Meanwhile, the well-being of existing humanity and the unfolding of it into this ultimate perfection, are both secured by that same beneficial though severe discipline to which the animate creation at large is subject. It seems hard that an unskillfulness, which with all his efforts he cannot overcome, should entail hunger upon the artisan. It seems hard that a laborer, incapacitated by sickness from competing with his stronger fellows, should have to bear the resulting privations. It seems hard that widows and orphans should be left to struggle for life or death. Nevertheless, when regarded not separately but in connection with the interests of universal humanity, these harsh fatalities are seen to be full of beneficence—the same beneficence which brings to early graves the children of diseased parents, and singles out the intemperate and the debilitated as the victims of an epidemic.

There are many very amiable people who have not the nerve to look this matter fairly in the face. Disabled as they are by their sympathies with present suffering, from duly regarding ultimate consequences, they pursue a course which is injudicious, and in the end even cruel. . . . Similarly, we must call those spurious philanthropists who, to prevent present misery, would entail greater misery on future generations. That rigorous necessity which, when allowed to operate, becomes so sharp a spur to the lazy and so strong a bridle to the random, these paupers' friends would repeal, because of the wailings it here and there produces. Blind to the fact that under the natural order of things society is constantly excreting its unhealthy, imbecile, slow, vacillating, faithless members, these unthinking, though well-meaning, men advocate an interference which not only stops the purifying process, but even increases the vitiation—absolutely encourages the multiplication of the reckless and incompetent by offering them an unfailing provision, and *discourages* the multiplication of the competent and provident by heightening the difficulty of maintaining a family. And thus, in their eagerness to prevent the salutary sufferings that surround us, these sigh-wise and groan-foolish people bequeath to posterity a continually increasing curse. . . .

Should there be any to whom this abstract reasoning is unsatisfactory, a concrete statement of the case will, perhaps, remove their doubts. A poors'-rate [tax] collector takes from the citizen a sum of money equivalent to bread and clothing for one or more paupers. Had not this sum been so taken, it would either have been used to purchase superfluities, which the citizen now does without, or it would have been paid by him into a bank, and lent by the banker to a manufacturer, merchant, or tradesman; that is, it would ultimately have been given in wages either to the producer of the superfluities or to an operative paid out of the banker's loan. But this sum having been carried off as poors'-rate, whoever would have received it as wages must now to that extent go without wages. The food which it represented having been taken to sustain a pauper, the artisan to whom that food would have been given in return for work done, must now to that extent lack food. And thus, as at first said, the transaction is simply a change of the parties by whom the insufficiency of food is felt.

Nay, the case is even worse. Already it has been pointed out that, by suspending the process of adaptation, a poor-law increases the distress to be borne at some future day; and here we shall find that it also increases the distress to be borne now. For be it remembered that of the sum taken in any year to support paupers, a large portion would otherwise have gone to support laborers employed in new productive works—land-drainage, machine-building, &c. An additional stock of commodities would by-and-by have been produced, and the number of those who go short would consequently have been diminished. Thus the astonishment expressed by some that so much misery should exist, notwithstanding the distribution of fifteen millions a year by endowed charities, benevolent societies, and poor-law unions, is quite uncalled for; seeing that the larger the sum gratuitously administered, the more intense will shortly become the suffering. Manifestly, out of a given population, the greater the number living on the bounty of others, the smaller must be the number living by labor; the smaller must be the production of food and other necessaries; and the smaller the production of food and other necessaries, the greater the distress.

DEBATE BETWEEN THOMAS H. HUXLEY AND
BISHOP WILBERFORCE (1860)

From L. Huxley, *Life and Letters of Thomas Henry Huxley* (2 vols., New York, 1900), 1:192ff.

Thomas H. Huxley (1825–1895), a scientist in his own right, became so involved in the defense of Darwin's work that he devoted much of his time to being "Darwin's bulldog," as he called it. The most famous of his debates with the opposition came at a meeting of the British Association for the Advancement of Science in 1860. The champion of the theologians in this case was the very popular and eloquent Bishop Wilberforce of the Anglican Church. Huxley's son Leonard tells the story.

The famous Oxford Meeting of 1860 was of no small importance in Huxley's career. It was not merely that he helped to save a great cause from being stifled under misrepresentation and ridicule—that he helped to extort for it a fair hearing; it was not that he first made himself known in popular estimation as a dangerous adversary in debate—a personal force in the world of science which could not be neglected. From this moment he entered the front fighting line in the most exposed quarter of the field. . . .

[There are] several accounts of the scene: . . . one in the *Life of Darwin* (2:320), another in 1892 *Life* (236ff.), and a third that of *Lyell* (2:335), the slight difference between them representing the difference between individual recollections of eye-witnesses. In addition to these I have been fortunate to secure further reminiscences from several other eye-witnesses. . . .

It was not term-time, nor were the general public admitted; nevertheless the room was crowded to suffocation long before the protagonists appeared on the scene, 700 persons or more managing to find places. The very windows by which the room was lighted down the length of its west side were packed with ladies, whose white handkerchiefs, waving and fluttering in the air at the end of the Bishop's speech, were an unforgettable factor in the acclamation of the crowd. . . .

The clergy, who shouted lustily for the Bishop, were massed in the middle of the room; behind them in the northwest corner a knot of undergraduates . . . who had gathered together beside Professor Brodie, ready to lift their voices, poor minority though they were, for the opposite party. . . .

[There were several speakers on both sides:] Then the Bishop spoke the speech that you know, and the question about his mother being an ape, or his grandmother.

From the scientific point of view, the speech was of small value. It was evident from his mode of handling the subject that he had been "crammed to the throat," and knew nothing at first hand; . . . "he ridiculed Darwin badly and Huxley savagely; but," confesses one of his strongest opponents, "all in such dulcet tones, so persuasive a manner, and in such well turned periods, that I who had been inclined to blame the President for allowing a discussion that could serve no scientific purpose, now forgave him from the bottom of my heart."

The Bishop spoke thus "for full half an hour with inimitable spirit, emptiness, and unfairness." "In a light, scoffing tone, florid and fluent, he assured us there was nothing in the idea of evolution; rock-pigeons were what rock-pigeons had always been. Then, turning to his antagonist with a smiling insolence, he begged to know, Was it through his grandfather or his grandmother that he claimed his descent from a monkey?''

This was the fatal mistake of his speech. Huxley instantly grasped the tactical advantage which the descent to personalities gave him. . . . After Huxley had completed his "forcible and eloquent" answer to the scientific part of the Bishop's argument, [he] proceeded to make his famous retort.

On this (continues the writer in *Macmillan's Magazine*) Mr. Huxley slowly and deliberately arose. A slight, tall figure, stern and pale, very quiet and very grave, he stood before us and spoke those tremendous words—words which no one seems sure of now, nor, I think, could remember just after they were spoken, for their meaning took away our breath, though it left us in no doubt as to what it was. He was not ashamed to have a monkey for his ancestor; but he would be ashamed to be connected with a man who used great gifts to obscure the truth. No one doubted his meaning, and the effect was tremendous. One lady fainted and had to be carried out; I, for one, jumped out of my seat.

The fullest and probably most accurate account of these concluding words is the following, from a letter of the late John Richard Green, then an undergraduate, to his friend, afterwards Professor Boyd Dawkins:

> I asserted—and I repeat—that a man has no reason to be ashamed of having an ape for his grandfather. If there were an ancestor whom I should feel ashamed in recalling it would rather be a man—a man of restless and versatile intellect—who, not content with an equivocal success in his own sphere of activity, plunges into scientific questions with which he has no real acquaintance, only to obscure them by an aimless rhetoric, and distract the attention of his hearers from the real point at issue by eloquent digressions and skilled appeals to religious prejudice.

THOMAS H. HUXLEY: EVOLUTION AND ETHICS
(1893)

The Romanes Lecture (London, 1893).

Huxley was always critical of attempts to base social theories on unfounded assumptions about the "natural" state of man. His acceptance of the Darwinian theory was qualified by doubts of its ability to explain all the facets of human evolution, but he accepted the hypothesis pragmatically on the basis of the availble data. In the following selection Huxley indicates some of his advanced ideas.

As no man fording a swift stream can dip his foot twice into the same water, so no man can, with exactness, affirm of anything in the sensible world that it is. As he utters the words, nay, as he thinks them, the predicate ceases to be applicable; the present has become the past; the "is" should be "was." And the more we learn of the nature of things, the more is it evident that what we call rest is only unperceived activity; that seeming peace is silent but strenuous battle. In every part, at every moment, the state of the cosmos is the expression of a transitory adjustment of contending forces; a scene of strife, in which all the combatants fall in turn. What is true of each part, is true of the whole. Natural knowledge tends more and more to the conclusion that "all the choir of heaven and furniture of the earth" are the transitory forms of parcels of cosmic substance wending along the road of evolution, from nebulous potentiality, through endless growths of sun and planet and satellite; through all varieties of matter; through infinite diversities of life and thought; possibly, through modes of being of which we neither have a conception, nor are competent to form any, back to the indefinable latency from which they arose. Thus the most obvious attribute of the cosmos is its impermanence. It assumes the aspect not so much of a permanent entity as of a changeful process, in which naught endures save the flow of energy and the rational order which pervades it.

We are more than sufficiently familiar with modern pessimism. . . .

We also know modern speculative optimism, with its perfectibility of the species, reign of peace, and lion and lamb transformation scenes; but one does not hear so much of it as one did 40 years ago; indeed, I imagine it is to be met with more commonly at the tables of the healthy and wealthy, than in the congregations of the wise. The majority of us, I apprehend, profess neither pessimism nor optimism. We hold that the world is neither so good, nor so bad, as it conceivably might be: and, as most of us have reason, now and again, to discover that it can be. Those who have failed to experience the joys that make life worth living are, probably, in as small a minority as those who have never known the griefs that rob existence of its savor and turn its richest fruits into mere dust and ashes. . . .

The propounders of what are called the "ethics of evolution," when the "evolution of ethics" would usually better express the object of their speculations, adduce a number of more or less interesting facts and more or less sound arguments, in favor of the origin of the moral sentiments, in the same way as other natural phenomena, by a process of evolution. I have little doubt, for my own part, that they are on the right track; but as the immoral sentiments have no less been evolved, there is, so far, as much natural sanction for the one as for the other. The thief and the murderer follow nature just as much as the philanthropist. Cosmic evolution may teach us how the good and the evil tendencies of man may have come about; but, in itself, it is incompetent to furnish any better reason why what we call good is preferable to what we call evil than we had before. Some day, I doubt not, we shall arrive at an understanding of the evolution of the aesthetic faculty; but all the understanding in the world will neither increase nor diminish the force of the intuition that this is beautiful and that is ugly.

There is another fallacy which appears to me to pervade the so-called "ethics of evolution." It is the notion that because, on the whole, animals and plants have advanced in the perfection of organization by means of the struggle for existence and the consequent "survival of the fittest"; therefore men in society, men as ethical beings, must look to the same process to help them towards perfection. I suspect that this fallacy has arisen out of the unfortunate ambiguity of the phrase "survival of the fittest." "Fittest" has a connotation of "best"; and about "best" there hangs a moral flavor. In cosmic nature, however, what is "fittest" depends on the conditions. Long since, I ventured to point out that if our hemisphere were to cool again, the survival of the fittest might bring about, in the vegetable kingdom, a population of more and more stunted and humbler and humbler organisms, until the "fittest" that survived might be nothing but lichens, diatoms, and such microscopic organisms as those which give red snow its color; while, if it became hotter, the pleasant valleys of the Thames and Isis might be uninhabitable by any animated beings save those that flourish in a tropical jungle. They, as the fittest, the best adapted to the changed conditions, would survive.

Men in society are undoubtedly subject to the cosmic process. As among other animals, multiplication goes on without cessation, and involves severe competition for the means of support. The struggle for existence tends to eliminate those less fitted to adapt themselves to the circumstances of their existence. The strongest, the most self-assertive, tend to tread down the weaker. But the influence of the cosmic processes on the evolution of society is the greater the more rudimentary its civilization. Social progress means a checking of the cosmic process at every step and the substitution for it of another, which may be called the ethical process, the end of which is not the survival of those who may happen to be the fittest, in respect of the whole of the conditions which obtain, but of those who are ethically the best.

As I have already urged, the practice of that which is ethically best—what we call goodness or virtue—involves a course of conduct which, in all respects, is opposed to that which leads to success in the cosmic struggle for existence. In place of ruthless self-assertion it demands self-restraint; in place of thrusting aside, or treading down, all competitors, it requires that the individual shall not merely respect, but shall help his fellows; its influence is directed, not so much to the survival of the fittest, as to the fitting of as many as possible to survive. It repudiates the gladiatorial theory of existence. It demands that each man who enters into the enjoyment of the advantages of a polity shall be mindful of his debt to those who have laboriously constructed it; and shall take heed that no act of his weakens the fabric in which he has been permitted to live. Laws and moral precepts are directed to the end of curbing the cosmic process and reminding the individual of his duty to the community, to the protection and influence of which he owes, if not existence itself, at least the life of something better than a brutal savage.

It is from neglect of these plain considerations that the fanatical individualism of our time attempts to apply the analogy of cosmic nature to society. Once more we have a misapplication of the stoical injunction to follow nature; the duties of the individual to the state are forgotten, and his tendencies to self-assertion are dignified by the name of rights. It is seriously debated whether the members of a community are justified in using their combined strength to constrain one of their number to contribute his share to the maintenance of it; or even to prevent him from doing his best to destroy it. The struggle for existence, which has done such admirable work in cosmic nature, must, it appears, be equally beneficent in the ethical sphere. Yet if that which I have insisted upon is true; if the cosmic process has no sort of relation to moral ends; if the imitation of it by man is inconsistent with the first principles of ethics; what becomes of this surprising theory?

Let us understand, once for all, that the ethical progress of society depends, not on imitating the cosmic process, still less in running away from it, but in combating it. It may seem an audacious proposal thus to pit the microcosm against the macrocosm and to set man to subdue nature to his higher ends, but I venture to think that the great intellectual difference between the ancient times with which we have been occupied and our day, lies in the solid foundation we have acquired for the hope that such an enterprise may meet with a certain measure of success.

Ethical nature may count upon having to reckon with a tenacious and powerful enemy as long as the world lasts. But, on the other hand, I see no limit to the extent to which intelligence and will, guided by sound principles of investigation and organized in common effort, may modify the conditions of existence for a period longer than that now covered by history. And much may be done to change the nature of man himself. The intelligence which has converted the brother of the wolf into the faithful guardian of the flock ought to be able to do something towards curbing the instincts of savagery in civilized men.

KROPOTKIN: MUTUAL AID, A FACTOR OF EVOLUTION (1902)

(London, 1902), pp. 1—3.

The Russian anarchist Prince Peter Kropotkin (1842—1921) offered a startlingly different theory of evolution in his book *Mutual Aid,* from which the following excerpt is taken.

Two aspects of animal life impressed me most during the journeys which I made in my youth in Eastern Siberia and Northern Manchuria. One of them was the extreme severity of the struggle for existence which most species of animals have to carry on against an inclement Nature; the enormous destruction of life which periodically results from natural agencies; and the consequent paucity of life over the vast territory which fell under my observation. And the other was, that even in those few spots where animal life teemed in abundance, I failed to find—although I was eagerly looking for it—that bitter struggle for the means of existence, *among animals belonging to the same species,* which was considered by most Darwinists (though not always by Darwin himself) as the dominant characteristic of struggle for life, and the main factor of evolution.

The terrible snowstorms which sweep over the northern portion of Eurasia in the later part of the winter, and the glazed frost that often follows them; the frosts and the snowstorms which return every year in the second half of May, when the trees are already in full blossom and insect life swarms everywhere; the early frosts and, occasionally, the heavy snowfalls in July and August, which suddenly destroy myriads of insects, as well as the second broods of the birds in the prairies; the torrential rains, due to the monsoons, which fall in more temperate regions in August and September—resulting in inundations on a scale which is only known in America and in Eastern Asia, and swamping, on the plateaus, areas as wide as European States; and finally, the heavy snowfalls, early in October, which eventually render a territory as large as France and Germany, absolutely impracticable for ruminants, and destroy them by the thousands—these were the conditions under which I saw animal life struggling in Northern Asia. They made me realize at an early date the overwhelming importance in Nature of what Darwin described as "the natural checks to over-multiplication," in comparison to the struggle between individuals of the same species for the means of subsistence, which may go on here and there, to some limited extent, but never attains the importance of the former. Paucity of life, under-population—not over-population—being the distinctive feature of that immense part of the globe which we name Northern Asia, I conceived since then serious doubts—which subsequent study has only confirmed—as to the reality of that fearful competition for food and life within each species, which was an article of faith with most Darwinists, and, consequently as to the dominant part which this sort of competition was supposed to play in the evolution of new species.

On the other hand, wherever I saw animal life in abundance, as, for instance, on the lakes where scores of species and millions of individuals came together to rear their progeny; in the colonies of rodents; in the migrations of birds which took place at that time on a truly American scale along the Usuri; and especially in a migration of fallow-deer which I witnessed on the Amur, and during which scores of thousands of these intelligent animals came together from an immense territory, flying before the coming deep snow, in order to cross the Amur where it is narrowest—in all these scenes of animal life which passed before my eyes, I saw Mutual Aid and Mutual Support carried on to an extent which made me suspect in it a feature of the greatest importance for the maintenance of life, the preservation of each species, and its further evolution.

And finally, I saw among the semi-wild cattle and horses in Transbaikalia, among the wild ruminants everywhere, the squirrels, and so on, that when animals have to struggle against scarcity of food, in consequence of one of the above-mentioned causes, the whole of that portion of the species which is affected by the calamity, comes out of the ordeal so much impoverished in vigor and health, that *no progressive evolution of the species can be based upon such periods of keen competition.*

Consequently, when my attention was drawn, later on, to the relations between Darwinism and Sociology, I could agree with none of the works and pamphlets that had been written upon this important subject. They all endeavored to prove that Man, owing to his higher intelligence and knowledge, *may* mitigate the harshness of the struggle for life between men; but they all recognized at the same time that the struggle for the means of existence, of every animal against all its congeners, and of every man against all other men was "a law of Nature." This view, however, I could not accept, because I was persuaded that to admit a pitiless inner war for life within each species, and to see in that war a condition of progress was to admit something which not only had not yet been proved, but also lacked confirmation from direct observation.

On the contrary, a lecture "On the Law of Mutual Aid," which was delivered at a Russian Congress of Naturalists, in January 1880, by the well-known zoologist, Professor Kessler, the then Dean of the St. Petersburg University, struck me as throwing a new light on the whole subject. Kessler's idea was that besides the *law of*

Mutual Struggle there is in Nature *the law of Mutual Aid,* which, for the success of the struggle for life, and especially for the progressive evolution of the species, is far more important than the law of mutual contest. This suggestion—which was, in reality, nothing but a further development of the ideas expressed by Darwin himself in *The Descent of Man*—seemed to me so correct and of so great importance, that since I became acquainted with it (in 1883) I began to collect materials for further developing the idea, which Kessler had only cursorily sketched in his lecture, but had not lived to develop.

NIETZSCHE: THE WILL TO POWER (Notes, 1883–1888)

Der Wille zur Macht, ed. P. Gast, in *Sämtliche Werke,* vol. 9 (Stuttgart, 1964).

Friedrich Nietzsche (d. 1900) was one of the most advanced thinkers of the nineteenth century. At age twenty-four he was appointed to the chair of Classical Philology at the Univerity of Basle. At age forty-four he had become hopelessly insane. In between, he published some of the most thought-provoking works of our time. Proclaiming the freedom of the human spirit, they speak not only to Darwinism but also to psychoanalysis, analytical philosophy, and existentialism. Nietzsche saw the process of evolution as an opportunity for man to take control of his own development—by an act of *will.* Consequently, he was critical of all those nineteenth century tendencies towards "automatic," non-intellectual controls, whether natural or political, over the individual. *The Will to Power* was published posthumously, from Nietzsche's notes.

647. The use of an organ does *not* explain its origin. On the contrary, during most of the time needed to form a particular attribute, it will not help the individual to survive; least of all will it be of any use in his struggle against external circumstances and enemies. . . .

That which promotes the individual's longevity might be unfavorable to his strength or attractiveness; that which preserves him might also limit him and prevent his development. . . . The influence of "environment" is grossly overrated in Darwin: the essential factor in the life process is precisely the tremendous inner power to shape and create forms which utilize and expoit "external circumstances.". . .

684. *The domestication of man:* What definite value can it have? or has domestication in general any definite value?—There are reasons for denying this proposition.

Darwin's school of thought certainly goes to great pains to convince us of the reverse. It would like to show that the effect of domestication is profound and fundamental. . . . Up to now, domestication has produced only superficial results, when it has not produced degeneration. And everything that escapes from the hand and discipline of man returns almost immediately to its original condition. The type remains constant; one cannot "denature nature."

[Biologists] rely on the struggle for existence, the death of the weaker creatures, and the survival of the most robust and gifted; from that they imagine a continuous growth in perfection. We are convinced, on the contrary, that in the struggle for existence chance serves the weak as well as the strong; that cunning often prevails over strength; [and] that *prolificness* in a species is related in an important way to its destruction. . . .

We have so exaggerated the selection of the most beautiful that it far exceeds the drive for beauty in our own race! In fact, the most beautiful creatures often couple with the most debased, and the largest with the smallest. We almost always see males and females take advantage of any chance encounter, showing no taste or selectiveness whatever. . . .

There are no *intermediate forms*. . . . The increasing evolution of creatures is asserted, [but] all evidence for this is lacking. Every type has its *limitations;* beyond these evolution cannot carry it.

My general point of view. First proposition: Man as a species is not progressing. Higher specimens are indeed attained, but they do not survive. The level of the species is not raised.

Second proposition: Man as a species does not represent any sort of progress compared with any other animal. The whole of the animal and vegetable kingdom does not develop from lower to higher, . . . but all simultaneously, haphazardly, confusedly, and at variance. The richest and most complex forms—and the term *higher type* means no more than this—perish more easily; only the lowest succeed in maintaining their apparent indestructibility. The former are seldom attained, and they maintain their superiority only with difficulty; the others are compensated by greater fruitfulness. Also, in the human race, the superior specimens—the happy cases of evolution—are the first to perish amid the fluctuating chances for and against them. They are exposed to every kind of decadence; being extreme, they are already decadent on that account alone. . . . The short duration of beauty, of genius, of the Caesar, is unique; such things are not hereditary. The *type* is inherited [and] there is nothing extreme or particularly "happy" about a type. . . . Not because of Nature's "ill-will," but only because of the concept *superior type.* Any higher type exemplifies an incomparably greater degree of complexity—a greater sum of coordinated elements—but on this account disintegration becomes a thousandfold more threatening. A "genius" is the sublimest machine in existence—hence, the most fragile. . . .

753. I am opposed to Socialism, because it dreams ingenuously of "goodness, truth, beauty, and equal rights" (anarchy pursues the same ideal, but in a more brutal fashion). I am opposed to parliamentary government and the power of the press, because they are means by which the herd become masters.

856. *The will to power.* How those men would have to be constituted who would undertake such a revaluation. Order of rank as the order of power: war and danger are prerequisites for a rank to maintain its existence. The great example: Man in nature—the weakest and shrewdest creature making himself master, putting a yoke on all the less intelligent forces.

859. *Advantage of detachment from one's era.* Detached from the movements of either individualism or collective morality; for even individualism does not recognize the order of rank and would grant one individual the same freedom as another. My concern is not with the degree of freedom which would be granted to one or the other or to all, but with the degree of *power* which one or the other should exercise over his

neighbor or over all; and especially with the question to what extent a sacrifice of freedom, even enslavement, might provide the basis for the emergence of a superior type. In simple terms, *how could one sacrifice the development of mankind* in order to help a higher species than man to come into being?

860. *Concerning rank.* The terrible consequences of "equality"—ultimately, everybody thinks he has a right to every problem. All order of rank has vanished.

898. *The strong of the future.* To what extent necessity, on the one hand, and accident, on the other, have attained to conditions from which a *stronger species* may be reared; this we are now able to understand and consciously *will;* we can now create the conditions under which such an elevation is possible.

Up to now, "education" has always aimed at the needs of society; not the possible needs of the future, but the needs of the existing society. What people wanted were "implements" for this purpose. If the wealth of force were greater, one could imagine a draft being made on them, not to serve the needs of society, but some future need.

Such a task would have to be advanced the more people came to see the extent to which the present form of society was in a stage of transition as—sooner or later—to be no longer able to exist for its own sake alone, but only as an instrument in the hands of a stronger race.

The increased dwarfing of man is precisely the driving force that makes one think of the cultivation of a stronger race—a race with an abundance in those areas where the dwarfed species is weak and gowing weaker: i.e., in will, responsibility, self-reliance, the ability set goals for one's self.

The means would be those taught by history: isolation by means of interests in preservation, which are the opposite of those generally accepted today; exercise in the revaluation of values; distance as pathos; a clear conscience in what is most devalued and prohibited today.

The leveling of the European peoples is the great process which should not be prevented; it should even be accelerated. The need for creating a gulf, a distance, an order of rank, is therefore imperative. . . .

This leveled-down species requires justification as soon as it is attained; its justification is that it exists for the service of a higher and sovereign race which stands upon it and can only be elevated upon its shoulders to the task it is destined to fulfill. Not merely a ruling race whose task would be consummated in ruling alone, but a race with its own vital spheres, with an overflow of energy for beauty, bravery, culture, and manners, even for the most abstract thought; a yea-saying race which would be able to allow itself every great luxury—strong enough to be able to discard the tyranny of virtue's imperatives; rich enough to forgo thrift and pedantry; beyond good and evil; a hothouse for rare and unusual plants.

954. One question keeps coming to mind—a seductive and wicked question, perhaps; let it be whispered to those who have a right to such controversial questions—those strong souls whose self-control is unshaken: Is it not high time, now that the type "herd animal" is evolving more and more in Europe, to set about "breeding" the opposite type consciously and artificially, and to establish its virtues? For the first time, would not the democratic movement itself find its own possible goal, salvation, and justification, if someone appeared who made use of it, so that, besides

its new and sublime development of slavery (for this is what European democracy must finally become), a higher kind of ruling and Caesarian spirits might be produced who would stand upon it . . . and elevate themselves through it? Would this new race climb up to hitherto impossible things, to a broader vision, and to its own earthly tasks?

CHAPTER 25

NINETEENTH-CENTURY NATIONALISM— HUMANE OR INTOLERANT?

If I knew something that would benefit my country but would harm mankind, I would never reveal it, for I am a citizen of humanity first and by necessity, and a citizen of my country second and only by accident.

—*Eighteenth-century philosopher*

Alsace and Lorraine . . . are ours by right of the sword, and we shall dispose of them in virtue of a higher right—the right of the German nation, which will not permit its lost children to remain strangers to the German Reich. We Germans . . . know better than these unfortunates themselves what is good for the people of Alsace. . . . Against their will we shall restore them to their true selves.

—*Heinrich von Treitschke, 1870*

Nationalism has been defined as a state of mind that pervades a large portion of a people but claims to pervade the whole people; it sees the nation-state as the source of all good and all authority; recognizing no power higher than the state, it identifies the collectivity with the Divinity. Thus the spirit of nationalism tends to compete for the loyalty of the citizen against all other affinities, including church and family.

The demand for complete loyalty is a rather recent development. Although nationalism seems to have existed among the ancient Hebrews and the Greek city-states, the modern movement stems largely from the French Revolution. Having overthrown their king and set up a republic, the French revolutionaries thought it only fair and proper to help liberate other European peoples. Napoleon made himself the instrument of this policy, introducing such institutions as civil rights, law codes, and governmental efficiency into the lands he conquered.

But things did not work out as expected. The Spanish, Italians, Germans, and other conquered peoples resisted French benevolent despotism while they set out to discover their own customs, traditions, and identities. National movements of liberation grew up in the subject countries to expel the foreigner, as French armies were defeated all across Europe. But then other oppressors—Austria, Russia, Turkey—came forward to replace the French, and the history of the nineteenth century is a history of national liberation and unification from Greece to Belgium, from Italy to Germany, from Rumania to Serbia and Montenegro. But others remained submerged—the Croatians, Czecks, Poles, Finns, Estonians, Latvians, and Lithuanians in Eastern Europe; and the Irish, Flemish, Basques, and Catalans in the West, for example.

Finally, something larger than these local movements is involved in two competing nationalisms that helped cause both World Wars I and II: Pan-Germanism versus Pan-Slavism. The quotation from Treitschke, above, puts it very bluntly. Those peoples whose language is German or derived from German, including the Scandinavians, Dutch, Flemish, and Swiss, among others, should be forced, if they will not come willingly, into joining the German Empire. And the same goes on the other side for Czechs, Poles, South Slavs, etc., whom Russia claimed as her client peoples.

FICHTE: ADDRESSES TO THE GERMAN NATION (1808)

Reden an die Deutsche Nation (Leipzig, 1824), pp. 152–157, 200–204, 207–208 passim.

After Prussia's defeat at Jena, and the humiliating Treaty of Tilsit (1807), Johann Gottlieb Fichte (d. 1814) began his lectures on German nationalism at the University of Berlin under the very noses of the French occupation forces. His program of regeneration for the "German nation"—which would not even come into existence for another sixty years—was to be based on a new educational system designed to change the character of the German people. "Freedom" was to be the basis of this regeneration, but not the freedom we in the United States and Britain think of. Rather, it was the individual's freedom to identify his will with a personality greater than his own—the personality of the Nation, which Fichte saw as a reflection of God himself.

We have seen how the inhabitants of [France] took up lightly and with great daring . . . the establishment of a perfect state. But they soon abandoned the task [and now] use every means to expunge those deeds from their . . . history. The reason is obvious: the state cannot be built up in accordance with reason by artificial means with whatever materials may be handy; on the contrary, the nation must first be educated up to it.

Only a nation which has first solved the problem of educating perfect men will be able to solve the problem of the perfect state. . . .

True religion in the form of Christianity was the germ of the modern world, whose task it was to make this religion permeate the culture of Antiquity, thereby spiritualizing and sanctifying it. The first step was to rid the religion of the external respect for form and introduce into it the free thinking of Antiquity; foreign countries provided the stimulus for this, but the Germans *did* it. The second step . . . was to discover in ourselves this religion and with it all wisdom; this too was prepared by foreign countries, but completed by the Germans. The next step we have to make . . . is to educate the nation to perfect manhood. . . .

This then is the relationship in which the German nation has stood with regard to the development of the human race in the modern age. . . . In Germany all culture has proceeded from the people. That the Reformation of the Church was first brought before the people and that it succeeded only because it became their affair, we have already seen. But we will show that this single case was not an exception; it has, on the contrary, been the rule.

[In the Middle Ages] there arose cities erected by the people, in which cities every branch of culture sprang into bloom; civic constitutions and organizations developed a high order of excellence; . . . their extensive commerce helped in discovering the world; their [Hanseatic] League was feared by kings; their architectural monuments are still standing. . . . The German burghers were the civilized people, others the barbarians.

The history of Germany, of German strength, German enterprise and inventions, of German monuments and the German spirit—the history of all these during that period is nothing but the history of those cities. . . . Moreover, that period is the only one in German history in which this nation is famous and brilliant. . . . As soon as its blossom is killed by the tyranny and greed of the princes, and as soon as its freedom is trodden under foot, the whole nation gradually sinks lower and lower until we reach the condition we are in at present. But as Germany sinks, so does the rest of Europe, if we consider not the mere appearances but the soul. . . .

The German nation is the only one of the neo-European nations that has shown in practice, by the example of its burgher class for centuries, that it is capable of a republican constitution. . . .

People and Fatherland

People and fatherland, as a support and guarantee of eternity on earth, far transcend the state in the ordinary sense of the word. . . . The aim of the state is positive law, internal peace, and a condition of affairs in which everyone may earn his daily bread and meet the needs of his material existence. . . . But these are only a means to what the love of fatherland really wants, which is that the eternal and divine may blossom in the world and become ever more and more pure, perfect, and excellent. That is why this love of fatherland must itself govern the state and be the supreme, final, and absolute authority. Its first exercise must be to limit the state's choice of means for securing . . . internal peace. . . . A legislation which keeps the higher culture in view will allow to freedom as wide a field as possible, even at the risk of . . . peace and quiet and making the work of governing a little harder and more troublesome. . . .

Then too, love of fatherland must govern the state by holding before it a higher objective than the usual one of maintaining internal peace, property, personal freedom, and well-being for all. For this higher objective alone does the state assemble an armed force. When the question comes of using this force, . . . what spirit is it that in such cases may place itself at the helm [and] make its decisions with sureness and certainty, untroubled by any hesitation? What spirit has an undisputed right to summon everyone, whether he be willing or not, . . . to risk everything including his life? Not the peaceful citizen's love for the constitution, but the devouring flame of higher patriotism. . . .

In this belief our forefathers, . . . the Germans, as the Romans called them, bravely resisted the advancing world-empire of the Romans. . . . Why did the Germans fight for several generations in bloody wars that broke out again and again? . . . A Roman writer [Tacitus] puts these words into the mouth of their leaders: "What was left for them except to maintain their freedom or else to die before they became slaves?" Freedom meant remaining German and continuing to settle their own affairs in accordance with the spirit of their race, continuing their development in the same spirit, and propagating this independence to their posterity, [whereas] all the blessings the Romans offered them meant slavery, because they would have had to become something that was not German, they would have had to become half Roman. They assumed as a matter of course that every man would rather die than become half Roman, and that a true German could only want to live in order to be and remain a German and raise his children as Germans.

MAZZINI: DUTIES TOWARDS YOUR COUNTRY (1858)

From *Pensiero ed Azione,* in *Life and Writings of Joseph Mazzini* (6 vols., London, 1890–1891), 1:226ff.

Giuseppi Mazzini combined the concepts of nationalism and religion. Because Italy had been the battleground for Europe ever since Machiavelli's day, unification and independence were the goals of all Italian patriots. But Mazzini, having lived abroad so many years, championed *all* movements of national liberation. Besides having founded the Young Italy society-in-exile, he helped to organize Young Poland, Young Hungary, and even Young Europe, believing that if every people had its own state peace and harmony would ensue!

Your first duties . . . are towards Humanity. You are *men* before you are either citizens or fathers. If you do not embrace the whole human family in your affection, if you do not bear witness to your belief in the unity of that family—consequent on the Unity of God—and in that fraternity among the peoples which is destined to reduce that unity to action; if, wherever a fellow creature suffers, or the dignity of human nature is violated by falsehood or tyranny—if you are not ready to aid the unhappy and do not feel called upon to fight, if able, for the redemption of the betrayed or oppressed—you violate your law of life, you fail to understand the religion that will be your guide and help in the future. . . .

But, you will say, you cannot attempt united action, since you are all distinct and divided in language, customs, attitudes, and abilities. . . . And [I say,] you will find the means to multiply infinitely your powers and abilities. It was given to you by God when he gave you a country; when . . . he divided Humanity into distinct groups or nuclei over the face of the earth, thus creating the germ of nationalities. Evil governments have mutilated the divine plan, but you can still see it distinctly marked out, at least so far as Europe is concerned, by the great rivers, the mountain ranges, and similar geographical features. . . .

These evil governments did not and do not recognize any country—only their own families or dynasties, an egotism of caste. But the divine plan will inevitably be realized. Natural divisions and the peoples' innate tendencies will take the place of the arbitrary divisions sanctioned by evil governments. The map of Europe will be redrawn. On the ruins of countries owned by kings and privileged classes there will arise Peoples' countries, among which harmony and brotherhood will prevail. . . .

Then will each one of you, fortified by the power and love of many millions, all speaking the same language, endowed with the same will, and educated by the same historical traditions, each of you may then benefit all humanity by your own single effort.

Love your country, O my brothers! Our country is our home, the house that God has given us, with a numerous family in it whom we love and who loves us; a family with whom we more readily sympathize and whom we understand more easily than we do others; and which, from its being geographically centered and homogeneous in its elements, is adapted to a special branch of activity.

Our country is our common workshop, from which the products of our activity are sent forth for the benefit of the whole world; in which the tools and instruments we can most effectively use are collected; and which we may not reject without disobeying the Almighty's plan and diminishing our own strength.

By working for our own country on the right principle, we work for Humanity. Our country is the fulcrum of the lever we have to wield for the common good. If we abandon the fulcrum, we run the risk of making ourselves useless not only to mankind but to our country as well.

Before people can associate with the nations of which humanity is composed, they must have a national existence. There is no true association except among equals. Only through our own country can we have a recognized collective existence.

Humanity is a vast army advancing to the conquest of lands unknown, against enemies both powerful and astute. The peoples are the different corps, the divisions of that army. Each of them has its post assigned to it, and its special operation to execute; and the common victory depends upon the precision with which those distinct operations are carried out. Disturb not the order of battle. . . .

Your country is the sign of the mission God has given you to fulfill towards humanity. . . . The true country is a community of free and equal men, bound together in fraternal accord to work for a common goal. . . .

In the name of the love you bear your country you must peacefully but untiringly combat the existence of privilege and inequality in the land that gave you life.

There is only one legitimate privilege, the privilege of genius when it reveals itself united with virtue. But this is a God-given privilege; in acknowledging it and following its inspiration, you do so freely, after your own reasoning and choice. Every other privilege which requires your submission because of power, inheritance, or other right . . . is a usurpation and a tyranny which you are duty-bound to resist and destroy.

Let your country be your temple, with God at the summit and a people of equals at the base. Accept no other formula, no other moral law, if you would not dishonor both your country and yourselves. Let all other laws be but the gradual regulation of your life by the progressive application of this supreme law. For this purpose, it is necessary that all of you should aid in framing the laws. Laws framed by only a fraction of the citizens can never, in the nature of things, be anything but an expression of the thoughts, hopes, and desires of that fraction. . .

Laws should be the expression of the universal aspiration of the people, promoting the common good. They should be the heartbeat of the Nation, which should, either directly or indirectly, legislate. By yielding up this mission to a few, you substitute the egotism of a class for the Country, which is the union of all classes.

The Country is not simply a piece of territory; it is the Idea to which it gives birth, it is the thought of love, the sense of communion which unites all the sons of that land. So long as one among your brothers has no vote to represent him in the development of the national life, so long as there is one left to vegetate in ignorance where others are educated, so long as a single person able and willing to work languishes in poverty through want of work, you have no Country in the true sense—the Country *of* all, *for* all.

Education, working, and voting are the three pillars of the Nation. Do not rest until you have built them up strongly with your own efforts.

Never deny your sister Nations. Be it yours to evolve the life of your Country in love and strength, free from all servile fears and clawing doubt, maintaining at its base the People; as its guide, the principles of its religious faith, logically and energetically applied; its strength, the united strength of all; its aim, the fulfillment of the mission given to it by God.

So long as you are ready to die for Humanity, the life of your Country will be immortal.

LORD ACTON: ON THE PRINCIPLE OF NATIONALITY (1862)

History of Freedom and Other Essays (London, 1907), pp. 276–298 passim.

The name of Lord Acton (d. 1902) is synonymous with nineteenth-century liberalism. Although he never wrote a book (his lectures and essays were published posthumously), his influence was great. A former Liberal member of Parliament, friend of W.E.

Gladstone, editor of the Catholic monthly *Rambler,* and professor of history at Cambridge University, he planned and organized the original *Cambridge Modern History.* In the following essay he refutes some of the arguments of Mazzini.

. . . Men of speculative or imaginative genius have sought in the contemplation of an ideal society a remedy . . . for evils which they were practically unable to remove. . . . The eighteenth century acquiesced in the oblivion of corporate rights [because] the absolutists cared only for the State, and the liberals only for the individual. . . .

The old despotic policy which made [Poland] its prey had two adversaries—the spirit of English liberty, and the doctrines of [the French] revolution: . . . these two contradicted the theory that nations have no collective rights. At the present day, the theory of nationality is not only the most powerful auxiliary of revolution, but its substance in the movements of the last three years [1859–1862]. This, however, is a recent alliance, unknown to the French Revolution. The modern theory of nationality arose partly as a legitimate consequence [of it], partly as a reaction against it. . . .

Napoleon called a new power into existence by attacking nationality in Russia, by delivering it in Italy, by governing in defiance of it in Germany and Spain. The sovereigns of these countries were deposed or degraded; and a system of administration was introduced which was French in its origin, its spirit, and its instruments. The people resisted the change. The movement against it was popular and spontaneous, because the rulers were absent or helpless; and it was national, because it was directed against foreign institutions. In Tyrol, in Spain, and afterwards in Prussia, the people did not receive the impulse from the government, but undertook of their own accord to cast out the armies and the ideas of revolutionized France. . . .

In 1813, the people rose against their conquerors, in defense of their legitimate rulers. They refused to be governed by usurpers. In the period between 1825 and 1831, they resolved that they would not be misgoverned by strangers. The French administration was often better than that which it displaced, but there were prior claimants for the authority exercised by the French, and at first the national contest was a contest for legitimacy. In the [next] period this element was wanting. No dispossessed princes led the Greeks, the Belgians, or the Poles. The Turks, the Dutch, and the Russians were attacked, not as usurpers, but as oppressors—because they misgoverned, not because they were of a different race. Then began a time when the text simply was, that nations would not be governed by foreigners. Power legitimately obtained and exercised with moderation, was declared invalid. . . . Now nationality became a paramount claim, which was to assert itself alone [and] which . . . was to prevail at the expense of every other cause for which nations make sacrifices. . . . It was appealed to in the name of the most contradictory principles of government, and served all parties in succession, because it was one in which all could unite. Beginning by a protest against the dominion of race over race, its mildest and least developed form, it grew into a condemnation of every State that included different races, and finally became the complete and consistent theory that the State and the nation must be co-extensive.

The outward historical progress of this idea from indefinite aspiration to be the keystone of a political system, may be traced in the life of the man who gave to it the element in which its strength resides—Giuseppe Mazzini. He found Carbonarism impotent against the measures of government, and resolved to give new life to the liberal movement by transferring it to the ground of nationality. Exile is the nursery of nationality, as oppression is the school of liberalism; and Mazzini conceived the idea of Young Italy when he was a refugee at Marseilles. In the same way, the Polish exiles are the champions of every national movement; for to them all political rights are absorbed in the idea of independence, which, however they may differ with each other, is the one aspiration common to them all.

In pursuing the outward and visible growth of the national theory we are prepared for an examination of its political character and value. The absolutism which has created it denies equally the absolute right of national unity which is a product of democracy, and the claim of national liberty which belongs to the theory of freedom. These two views of nationality, corresponding to the French and to the English systems, are connected in name only, and are in reality the opposite extremes of political thought. In one case, nationality is founded on the perpetual supremacy of the collective will, of which the unity of the nation is the necessary condition, to which every other influence must defer, and against which no obligation enjoys authority, and all resistance is tyrannical. The nation is here an ideal unit founded on the race, in defiance of the modifying action of external causes, of tradition, and of existing rights. It overrules the rights and wishes of the inhabitants, absorbing their divergent interests in a fictitious unity; sacrifices their several inclinations and duties to the higher claim of nationality, and crushes all natural rights and all established liberties for the purpose of vindicating itself.

Connected with this theory in nothing except in the common enmity of the absolute state, is the theory which represents nationality as an essential, but not a supreme element in determining the forms of the State. It is distinguished from the other, because it tends to diversity and not to uniformity, to harmony and not to unity; because it aims not at an arbitrary change, but at careful respect for the existing conditions of political life, and because it obeys the laws and results of history, not the aspirations of an ideal future. While the theory of unity makes the nation a source of despotism and revolution, the theory of liberty regards it as the bulwark of self-government, and the foremost limit to the excessive power of the State. . . .

The presence of different nations under the same sovereignty is similar in its effect to the independence of the Church in the State. It provides against the servility which flourishes under the shadow of a single authority, by balancing interests, multiplying associations, and giving to the subject the restraint and support of a combined opinion. . . . Liberty provokes diversity, and diversity preserves liberty by supplying the means of organization. This diversity in the same State is a firm barrier against the intrusion of the government beyond the political sphere which is common to all into the social department which escapes legislation and is ruled by spontaneous laws. . . . That intolerance of social freedom which is natural to absolutism is sure to find a corrective in the national diversities, which no other force could so efficiently provide. The co-existence of several nations under the same State is a test, as well as the best security of its freedom. It is also one of the chief instruments of civilization; and, as such, it is in the natural and providential order, and indicates a state of greater advancement than the national unity which is the ideal of modern liberalism.

If we take the establishment of liberty for the realization of moral duties to be the end of civil society, we must conclude that those states are substantially the most perfect which, like the British and Austrian Empires, include various distinct nationalities without oppressing them. Those in which no mixture of races has occurred are imperfect; and those in which its effects have disappeared are decrepit. A State which is incompetent to satisfy different races condemns itself; a State which labors to neutralize, to absorb, or to expel them, destroys its own vitality; a State which does not include them is destitute of the chief basis of self-government. The theory of nationality, therefore, is a retrograde step in history.

RENAN: WHAT IS A NATION? (1882)

In *Discours et conférences* (Paris, 1887), pp. 277–309 passim.

French philosopher and Orientalist, one of the most broadminded men of his age, Ernest Renan (d. 1892) was as shocked as anybody at the defeat of France in the Franco-Prussian War of 1870. Having been educated for the priesthood, Renan gradually drifted away from the Church but not from religion: two of his greatest works were the six-volume *Origins of Christianity* and the *History of Israel* (3. vols.). His vast knowledge, embracing such German scholars as Hegel, Kant, and Herder, was all the more challenged by the Germany he saw developing after 1870. "What Is a Nation?" is therefore a soul-searching journey for Renan.

I propose to examine with you an idea which may seem simple and clear, but which lends itself to the most dangerous misunderstandings. . . . We today make a serious mistake: we confuse nations with race, attributing to ethnic, or rather, linguistic groups an identity akin to that of actual nations. Let us try to be precise about these difficult questions, where the slightest confusion over word meanings could have the most disastrous consequences. . . .

Since the end of the Roman Empire, or rather since the disintegration of Charlemagne's empire, Western Europe appears to be divided into nations. At certain periods, some of these have sought to achieve hegemony over the others but with no lasting success. That which Charles V, Louis, XIV, or Napoleon I could not achieve probably no one will achieve in the future. The establishment of a new Roman or Carolingian empire has become impossible: the divisions of Europe are too great for any nation to attempt universal domination, which would produce an immediate coalition to return any such nation to its natural limits. . . .

Nations in this sense are something new in history. . . . They are characterized by the fusion of the populations composing them. Nothing similar exists in the Ottoman

Empire, where the Turk, Slav, Greek, Armenian, Arab, Syrian, and Kurd are each as distinct as they were on the day of the conquest. . . . Even by the tenth century all the inhabitants of France were French. After Hugh Capet, any idea of different races in the French population completely disappeared among French writers and poets. The distinction between noble and serf was greatly emphasized, but that distinction was in no way an ethnic distinction. . . .

These great laws of history in Western Europe become clear when we contrast them with events in Eastern Europe. Under the crown of St. Stephen [in Hungary], Magyars and Slavs remain as distinct today as they were 800 years ago. In Bohemia, the Czech and German elements are superimposed like water and oil in a glass. The Turkish policy of separating nationalities according to religion has had the most serious consequences: it has caused the ruin of the Middle East. For, the essential element of a nation is that all of its inhabitants have many things in common but have also forgotten many things. Every French citizen must have forgotten the night of St. Bartholomew and the massacres of the thirteenth century in the South. There are not ten families in France who could prove their Frankish origin. . . .

The nation, according to some theorists, is primarily the work of a dynasty in an ancient conquest that was first accepted and then forgotten by the mass of the people. . . . Does such a law have complete validity? Certainly not. Switzerland and the United States, which absorbed successive additions, have no dynastic basis. . . . It must therefore be admitted that a nation may exist without the dynastic principle, and even that nations formed by dynasties can separate themselves from them without losing their identity. As opposed to dynastic rights, the right of nationality has emerged. On what concrete fact might it be based?

1. Some say it could be based on race. The artificial divisions of the feudal past, created by royal marriages and diplomatic congresses, have lapsed. What remains solid and permanent is the race of the people, which constitutes a legitimate right. According to this theory, the Germans have the right to take back the scattered members of the German family, even if those members do not seek annexation. Thus, one creates a primordial right analogous to the divine right of kings. This is a great fallacy whose dominance would ruin European civilization. . . .

To base one's policy on an ethnographic analysis is to base it on a chimera. The greatest countries—England, France, Italy—are those whose blood is most mixed. Germany is no exception. . . . Race as we historians understand it is something which is formed by history and undone by history. The study of race is of great importance for the study of the history of mankind, but it has no place in politics. . . . Will not the Germans, who have raised so high the banner of ethnography, some day find the Slavs analyzing the names of Saxon and Lusatian villages, seeking the traces of populations long dead, and asking for an accounting of the massacres and mass enslavements to which the Germans . . . subjected their ancestors? It is good for us all to know how to forget.

2. What we have said of race is just as true of language. It may invite us to unite, but does not compel us to do so. . . . Languages are historical formations which tell us very little about the race of those who speak them. In any event, they should not fetter

human freedom when it concerns the fate of the group with whom we wish to unite for life or death. . . .

Let us not abandon the fundamental principle that man is a rational and moral being before he is penned up in this or that language, or before he is a member of this or that race or adheres to this or that culture. Over and above the French, German, or Italian culture, there is a human culture. Look at the great men of the Renaissance. They were neither French, Italian, nor German. By their intimacy with the spirit of antiquity, they had found the secret of the true education of the human mind and devoted themselves to it with all their heart. How well they acted!

3. Neither could religion offer a sufficient foundation for the establishment of a modern nation. . . . One can be French, English, or German by being a Catholic, Protestant, Jew, or agnostic. Religion has become something individual: it concerns the conscience of each person. . . .

4. Community of interests is certainly a strong tie among people. But are interests sufficient to create a nation? I doubt it. The community of interests creates commercial treaties. Nationality is something sentimental as well: it is at once body and soul. A customs union is not a fatherland.

5. Geography, or the so-called natural frontiers, certainly plays a considerable part in the division of nations. . . . But can we say, as some do, that a nation's frontiers are marked on the map and that the nation has the right to decide for itself what it regards as necessary to round out its contours, to reach some mountain or river to which is assigned some hypothetical quality? I know of no doctrine that would be more capriciously disastrous. It could justify any violence. Strategic reasons are evoked. Nothing is absolute, of course, and some concessions have to be made. But concessions should not go too far; otherwise, everybody would demand whatever is strategically convenient, and wars without end would ensue. . . .

A nation is a spirit, . . . a great unity created by a feeling for the sacrifices one has already made and for those one is prepared to make in the future. It implies a past but expresses itself in the present by an obvious fact—the consent of the people and their clearly expressed desire to continue life in common. A nation's existence is . . . a day-to-day plebiscite, just as the individual's existence is a continuous affirmation of life. I am aware that this is less metaphysical than divine right and less barbarous than so-called historical right. . . .

We have eliminated metaphysical and theological abstractions from politics. What is left? Man, his desires, his wants. You may reply that the division and crumbling of nations is the result of a system that leaves those old organisms to the mercy of frequently unenlightened peoples. Clearly, in such matters, no rule should be inflexible, and principles can be applied only in the most general way. . . . Nations are not eternal; they had a beginning, they will have an end. A European confederation will probably supplant them. But not in our century. At present, the existence of nations is good, even necessary. It is a guarantee of liberty, which would be lost in a world with one law and one master.

HYDE: ON THE REVIVAL OF GAELIC (1892)

Douglas Hyde, *Revival of Irish Literature and Other Addresses* (London, 1894), pp. 117–131 passim.

Hoping to sponsor a revival of Gaelic, Douglas Hyde wrote and spoke the language and founded the Gaelic League in 1893. Although he did not succeed in replacing English, his efforts did help to produce Irish nationalism in the twentieth century. Author of such works as a *Literary History of Ireland* and *Love Songs of Connacht,* Hyde was also President of Ireland from 1938 to 1945.

When we speak of "The Necessity for de-Anglicizing the Irish Nation," we mean it not as a protest against imitating what is best in the English people, for that would be absurd, but rather to show the folly of neglecting what is Irish, and hastening to adopt, pell-mell, and indiscriminately, everything that is English, simply because it is English. . . . If we take a bird's-eye view of our island today, and compare it with what it used to be, we must be struck by the extraordinary fact that the nation which was once, as everyone admits, one of the most classically learned and cultivated nations in Europe, is now one of the least so. . . .

I shall endeavor to show that this failure of the Irish people in recent times has been largely brought about by the race diverging during this century from the right path, and ceasing to be Irish without becoming English. I shall attempt to show that with the bulk of the people this change took place quite recently, much more recently than most people imagine, and is, in fact, still going on. I should also like to call attention to the illogical position of men who drop their own language to speak English, of men who translate their euphonious Irish names into English monosyllables, of men who read English books, and know nothing about Gaelic literature, nevertheless protesting as a matter of sentiment that they hate the country which at every hand's turn they rush to imitate.

I wish to show you that in Anglicizing ourselves wholesale we have thrown away with a light heart the best claim we have upon the world's recognition of us as a separate nationality. What did Mazzini say? . . . That we ought to be content as an integral part of the United Kingdom because we have lost the notes of nationality, our language and customs. It has always been very curious to me how Irish sentiment sticks in this halfway house—how it continues apparently to hate the English, and at the same time continues to imitate them; how it continues to clamor for recognition as a distinct nationality and at the same time throws away with both hands what would make it so. . . .

What lies at the back of the sentiments of nationality with which the Irish millions seem so strongly leavened? . . . Of course it is a very composite feeling which prompts them; but I believe that what is largely behind it is the half unconscious feeling that the race which at one time held possession of more than half Europe, which established itself in Greece, and burned infant Rome, is now—almost extirpated and absorbed elsewhere—making its last stand for independence in this island of Ireland; and do what they may the race of today cannot wholly divest itself from the mantle of its own past. Through early Irish literature, for instance, we can best form some conception of what that race really was, which, after overthrowing and trampling on the primitive peoples of half Europe, was itself forced in turn to yield its speech, manners, and independence to the victorious eagles of Rome. We alone of the nations of Western Europe escaped the claws of those birds of prey; we alone developed ourselves naturally upon our own lines outside of and free from all Roman influence; we alone were thus able to produce an early art and literature, *our* antiquities can best throw light upon the pre-Romanized inhabitants of half Europe, and—we are our father's sons. . . .

What the battleaxe of the Dane, the sword of the Norman, the wile of the Saxon were unable to perform, we have accomplished ourselves. We have at last broken the continuity of Irish life, and just at the moment when the Celtic race is presumably about to largely recover possession of its Celtic characteristics, cut off from the past, yet scarcely in touch with the present. It has lost since the beginning of this century almost all that connected it with the era of Cuchullain and of Ossian, that connected it with the christianizers of Europe, that connected it with Brian Boru and the heroes of Clontarf, with the O'Neills and O'Donnells, with Rory O'More, with the Wild Geese, and even to some extent with the men of '98. It has lost all that they had—language, traditions, music, genius, and ideas. Just when we should be starting to build up anew the Irish race and the Gaelic nation—as within our own recollection Greece has been built up anew—we find ourselves despoiled of the bricks of nationality. The old bricks that lasted eighteen hundred years are destroyed; we must now set to, to bake new ones, if we can, on other ground and of other clay. . . . In a word, we must strive to cultivate everything that is most racial, most smacking of the soil, most Gaelic, most Irish, because in spite of the little admixture of Saxon blood in the northeast corner, this island is and will ever remain Celtic at the core.

PAN-GERMANISM VERSUS PAN-SLAVISM

TREITSCHKE: THE IDEA OF THE STATE

From *Politik* (2 Vols., Leipzig, 1897–1898), 1:13, 20, 25, 28–30, 32–35, 37–43 passim.

A disappointed liberal after the revolutions of 1848, Heinrich von Treitschke (d. 1896) became a professor, historian, and member of the Prussian Reichstag. Following the victory over France in 1870, Treitschke became a panegyrist of the House of Hohenzollern. His chauvinism was so extreme that he supported legislation against Poles and Catholics and sanctioned attacks on the Jews. His *History of Germany* (5 vols.) is marked by careful use of sources, good character delineation, and vigorous narrative style.

The state is the people legally united as an independent force. By *people* we mean a number of families living permanently together. . . . [It is] wrong to call the state a necessary evil; rather, it is a sublime necessity. . . . "The state arose to make life possible," [said Aristotle,] "it endured to make life good." . . . Broadly speaking, the evolution of the state is simply the outward form that the inner life of a people takes upon itself, each people attaining to whatever form of government their moral capacity permits. . . .

As Fichte put it so well: "The individual sees in his country the realization of his earthly immortality." This means that the state has a personality in both the legal and the politico-moral sense. Just as the person who is able to exercise his will has a legal personality, so the state has a deliberate will and a juridical personality in the fullest sense. In international treaties, for example, it is the will of the state and not the private wills of the people that manifests itself. . . .

Once we look upon the state as a person, then the multiplicity of states follows. As in the individual, where an ego implies a non-ego, so with states: the state is power precisely in order to assert itself against other, equally independent powers. War and the administration of justice are the principal functions of even the most barbaric states. But those functions are conceivable only when a plurality of states exist side by side. The idea of a single universal empire is therefore odious. . . . Such an empire could never span the whole range of cultures; no one nation could combine all the virtues of aristocracy and democracy. All nations have their limitations, but it is in the very abundance of these limited expressions [of culture] that the genius of humanity is brought out. The rays of the divine light are manifested and refracted by the countless facets of the various nations. Every people has the right to believe that certain attributes of the Divine Reason are developed to the fullest in themselves. The Germans are always in danger of weakening their nationalism by insufficient pride; the average German has very little. . . .

By its nature, history is virile, unsuited to sentimental or feminine characters. Brave people alone have an existence, an evolution, and a future; the weak and cowardly perish, and justly so. The grandeur of history lies in the perpetual conflict of nations. . . . Now, if we reexamine our definition of the state as "the people legally united as an independent force," we find we can rephrase it: The state is the public force for offense and defense. It is power that makes its will prevail, not the people, as Hegel assumed. . . . Submission is the first law of the state: it insists upon obedience; its essence is the accomplishment of its will. . . . A state that cannot carry out its purposes collapses in anarchy. . . . It is not an academy of arts. If a state neglects its strength in order to promote man's idealistic aspirations, it repudiates its own nature and perishes. For the nation this is equivalent to the sin against the Holy Ghost, for it is indeed a mortal error for the state to subordinate itself, for sentiment's sake, to any foreign power, as we Germans have done with England. . . .

This pregnant theory implies, first, a moral supremacy so absolute that the state cannot legitimately tolerate any power above its own, and second, a temporal freedom, with a variety of material resources adequate for its protection. . . . "I recognize no power over me but God and the conqueror's sword," said Gustavus Adolphus. . . . Our ideal is a harmonious community of nations, who make treaties of their own free will and admit restrictions on their sovereignty without abrogating it. The notion of sovereignty must not be rigid but, like all such political concepts, flexible and relative.

In making treaties each state limits its power in certain ways for its own advantage, . . . but every treaty is a voluntary limitation and all international agreements are prefaced with the words *Rebus sic stantibus* ["Things remaining as they are"]. No state can pledge its future to another . . . and each has the right to declare war at its pleasure, thus renouncing its treaties. . . . Each nation should take care to see that its treaties do not outlive their usefulness, lest another power repudiate them by declaring war. . . .

Flexible as the concept of sovereignty may be, there is no self-contradiction in it, only the need to define it adequately. . . . Legally, it is the state's competence to determine its own authority; politically, it means the [ultimate] appeal to arms. . . . A defenseless state may still be called a kingdom, but only out of courtesy; science, whose first principle is accuracy, must boldly affirm that such a country is no longer a state. . . .

Another test of sovereignty is the right of a state to determine the limits of its power. . . . In such matters one must be guided not by historians but by statesmen. When Bismarck once told Kaiser Wilhelm I that the Empire would not go along with a particular action, he replied, "Nonsense! What is the Empire but an extension of Prussia!" . . .

[One more] essential of sovereignty is what Aristotle called *autarkeia*—the quality of being self-sufficient. This means, first, an adequate number of families to assure the continuance of the race, and second, a certain geographical area. . . . Also, the state must have the material resources to defend its theoretical independence by force of arms. . . .

The whole development of European polity tends unmistakably to drive second-rate powers into the background. Up until now Germany has always had too small a share . . . in the partitioning of overseas territories; . . . our existence as a first-rate nation depends on whether we can become a power outside of Europe. If not, we face the appalling prospect of having England and Russia divide up the world between them.

DANILEVSKY: PAN-SLAVISM (1869)

From Nikolai Danilevsky, *Rossiia i Evropa: An Inquiry into the Cultural and Political Relations of the Slav World and the Germano-Roman World* (St. Petersburg, 1869), trans. Robert J. Devlin; pp. 513–514, 523–525, 530–531, 538, 555–556.

The competition between Pan-Slavism and Pan-Germanism dates back to the Middle Ages. Danilevsky (d. 1885), a natural scientist and a sociologist, was a fervent Darwinist and passionate Slavophile, as the following excerpt demonstrates.

In the previous chapter, I . . . [discussed] the hostility of Europe toward Russia and the Slav world— . . . a hostility [that] lies deep in the gulf existing between the Slav world and the Germano-Roman world. . . . I attempted to [supplement] this theoretical approach by indicating the main differences between the Slav and the Germano-Roman cultural-historical types, the fatal predicament to which Westernization or Europeanization has led us, and the extent to which it causes the disease from which Russia's social body suffers—the source of all our social ills. . . . Only historical events can cure this disease and raise the spirit of our society, which now suffers spiritual decay and abasement. However, since the disease has, so far, penetrated only the surface of the social structure, the cure seems both possible and probable. . . .

Such an historical event . . . is seen in the latest phase of the Eastern Question, whose origins are rooted in the course of universal historical development. . . . The importance of the coming struggle leads us to try to understand the objections raised against . . . the full political liberation of all the Slav peoples and the formation of a Pan-Slav union under Russian hegemony. . . .

Religious truth, in the form of eternal Christianity, was discovered and adopted with humility and exaltation by new peoples, who were highly gifted in their spiritual natures. . . . A central tenet of this doctrine was the need to do away with slavery, which, in fact, appeared as a mere transitory phase among the Germano-Roman peoples. They were also richly endowed with political sense and a talent for cultural development—scientific, artistic, and industrial.

But those great gifts were not fated to be fully realized, because the violence of the Latin character, Roman love of power, and Roman state structure . . . distorted Christian truth, and the Church was transformed into the politico-religious despotism of Catholicism. This, combined with feudal despotism, rooted in the violence of German character, and the despotism of scholasticism, rooted in a slavish attitude toward the forms of ancient knowledge, impelled the whole history of Europe toward a severe struggle, which ended in a three-fold anarchy: [First,] a religious anarchy, Protestantism, with the idea of basing religious truth on personal authority. [Second,] a philosophical anarchy, an all-inclusive skeptical materialism, which began to assume the character of a faith and, little by little, replaced religious conviction in men's minds. [Third,] a socio-political anarchy, a contradiction between an ever-growing political democratization and economic feudalism.

Since these anarchies are essentially the forerunners and instruments of decay, they cannot be considered productive investments for the treasury of mankind, and the Germano-Roman cultural-historical type is not an adequate representative of the religious nor of the socio-economic aspect of culture. . . .

From an objective, factual point of view, on the other hand, the Russians and the majority of Slav peoples became the chief preservers, together with the Greeks, of Orthodoxy—the living tradition of religious truth. [They] thus continued the high calling—the destiny—of Israel and Byzantium, to be God's chosen people. . . .

We are entitled to consider the Slavs among the most gifted of the human race in political ability. . . . The Russians do not send out colonists to create new political societies, as did the Greeks in antiquity or the English in modern times. Russia, unlike Rome or England, does not have colonial possessions. The Russian state, since the first days of the Muscovite princes, has been Russia herself gradually, irresistibly spreading on all sides, settling neighboring non-settled territories and assimilating into herself and her national boundaries foreign populations. This basic character of

Russian expansion was misunderstood because of the distortion of the original Russian point of view through Europeanization, the source of every evil in Russia. . . .

Socio-economically, Russia is the only large state which has solid ground under its feet, in which there are no landless masses and in which, consequently, the social edifice does not rest on the misery of the majority of citizens and the insecurity of their situation. [Only in Russia is there] no contradiction between political and economic ideals . . .—a contradiction that threatens [Western] European life. . . . What gives such superiority to the Russian over the European social structure, what gives it an unshakable stability, is peasant land and its common ownership. It is on this health of Russia's socio-economic structure that we base our hopes for the Slav cultural-historical type, which has succeeded for the first time in creating a just and natural system of human activity. This includes man's moral and political relations as well as his mastery over nature as a means of satisfying human needs and wants. . . .

Since the political independence of the race is the necessary foundation of culture, all Slav energies must be directed towards this goal. Independence is necessary for two reasons: without the consciousness of a distinct Slav racial unity, an independent culture is impossible; and without fruitful interaction among the Slav peoples, liberated from foreign powers and from their national divisions, cultural diversity and richness are impossible. A familiar example of the beneficial effects of unity is the interaction between the spiritual developments of Great Russia and the Ukraine.

The importance of political independence is also evident in the cultural sphere: the struggle against the Germano-Roman world . . . will help to eradicate the cancer of an imitative and servile attitude towards the West, which has eaten its way . . . into the Slav body and soul. The moment for this cultural development has now arrived: only with the emancipation of the peasantry could the period of Russian cultural life begin, following the end of her purely state period of life, which was to lead the people from tribal will to civil liberty. First, however, as the sine qua non of success, a great and strong Russia has to face the difficult task of liberating her racial brothers: for this she must steel them and herself in the spirit of independence and Pan-Slav consciousness.

On the basis, therefore, of our analysis of the cultural-historical types and the peculiarities of the Slav world, we may affirm the basic hope that the Slav cultural-historical type will, for the first time in history, achieve a synthesis of all forms of cultural activity, forms which were developed by its predecessors, either in isolation or in incomplete union. We may hope that the Slav type will be the first to [realize] fully all four basic cultural-historical types: . . . the religious, the political, the esthetic-scientific, and the socio-economic.

CHAPTER 26

THE NEW IMPERIALISM, 1880—1914

> The timid man, the lazy man, the man who distrusts his country, the overcivilized man, who has lost the great fighting, masterful virtues, the ignorant man, and the man of dull mind, whose soul is incapable of feeling the mighty lift that thrills "stern men with empires in their brains"—all these, of course, shrink from seeing the nation undertake its new duties; shrink from seeing us build a navy and an army adequate to our needs; shrink from seeing us do our share of the world's work, by bringing order out of chaos in the great, fair tropic islands from which the valor of our soldiers and sailors has driven the Spanish flag.
>
> —*Theodore Roosevelt, On the Philippines, 1899.*

Imperialism, meaning the extension of rule by one people over another, went into a sort of eclipse after the great age of expansionism in the sixteenth and seventeenth centuries. But in the late nineteenth century, due to such factors as industrialism, nationalism, social Darwinism, and new concepts of race and ethnicity, there was a recrudescence of imperialism, which was typified by the United States. After having followed its "Manifest Destiny" from one ocean to the other, over the bodies of many Indian tribes, this country found itself in possession of the Philippine Islands in 1898. As President McKinley put it, they just "dropped into our lap" after the Spanish-American War. Rudyard Kipling, the poet, thought it was a fine chance to bring food, medicine, and education to these "fluttered folk and wild." But the Filipinos, like the Congolese and many other preliterate people, did not want or need anything the white man had to offer. His calico and beads came at too high a price when the native had to look into the barrel of a gun, and when he saw his kinsmen shot down "to encourage the others," as Voltaire once said.

In the following excerpts, Hobson and Lenin discuss some of the possible motives for the new imperialism that helped to produce the First World War. The dates, 1880–1914, are arbitrary, of course. Since the war, some of the principa*ls* have changed, but the princip*les* remain pretty much the same, and so does the great Question: How can the Third World defend itself against East and West alike without adopting their evil ways?

THE PHILIPPINES

PRESIDENT McKINLEY: PHILIPPINE DECISION (1898)

From J.B. Devins, *An Observer in the Philippines* (Boston, 1905), pp. 70–71.

In the following passage, President McKinley explains why he felt the United States should take possession of the Philippines after the defeat of Spain in the Spanish-American War.

. . . I didn't want the Philippines, and when they came to us, as a gift from the gods, I did not know what to do with them. . . . I sought counsel from all sides—Democrats as well as Republicans—but got little help. I thought first we would only take Manila; then Luzon; then other islands, perhaps all. I walked the floor of the White House night after night until midnight; and I am not ashamed to tell you, gentlemen, that I went down on my knees and prayed to Almighty God for light and guidance more than one night.

And one night late it came to me this way—I don't know how it was, but it came: (1) That we could not give them back to Spain—that would be cowardly and dishonorable; (2) that we could not turn them over to France or Germany—that would be bad business and discreditable; (3) that we could not leave them to themselves— they were unfit for self-government—and they would soon have anarchy and misrule over there worse than Spain's was; and (4) that there was nothing left for us to do but to take them all, and to educate the Philipinos, and uplift and civilize and Christianize them, and, by God's grace, do the very best we could by them, as our fellowmen for whom Christ also died. And then I went to bed, and went to sleep, and slept soundly, and the next morning I sent for the chief engineer of the War Department and told him to put the Philippines on the map of the United States, and there they are and there they will stay while I am president!

RUDYARD KIPLING: THE WHITE MAN'S BURDEN (1899)

Poet, novelist, journalist, Rudyard Kipling (1856–1936) was a great popularizer of imperialism. He wrote the following poem to persuade the United States to take the Philippines: two days after it was published, the U.S. Senate voted to take control of the islands.

Take up the White Man's burden—
Send forth the best ye breed—
Go bind your sons to exile
To serve your captives' need;
To wait in heavy harness,
On fluttered folk and wild—
Your new-caught, sullen people,
Half-devil and half-child.

Take up the White Man's burden—
In patience to abide,
To veil the threat of terror
And check the show of pride;
By open speech and simple,
An hundred times made plain
To seek another's profit,
And work another's gain.

Take up the White Man's burden—
The savage wars of peace—
Fill full the mouth of Famine
And bid the sickness cease;
And when your goal is nearest
The end for others sought,
Watch sloth and heathen Folly
Bring all your hopes to nought.

Take up the White Man's burden—
No tawdry rule of kings,
But toil of serf and sweeper—
The tale of common things.
The ports ye shall not enter,
The roads ye shall not tread,
Go make them with your living,
And mark them with your dead.

Take up the White Man's burden—
And reap his old reward:
The blame of those ye better,
The hate of those ye guard—
The cry of hosts ye humor
(Ah, slowly!) toward the light:—
"Why brought he us from bondage,
Our loved Egyptian night?"

Take up the White Man's burden—
Ye dare not stoop to less—
Nor call too loud on Freedom
To cloke your weariness;
By all ye cry or whisper,
By all ye leave or do,
The silent sullen peoples
Shall weigh your Gods and you.

Take up the White Man's burden—
Have done with childish days—
The lightly proffered laurel,
The easy, ungrudged praise.
Comes now, to search your manhood
Through all the thankless years,
Cold, edged with dear-bought wisdom,
The judgment of your peers!

PLATFORM OF THE AMERICAN ANTI-IMPERIALIST LEAGUE
(1899)

The Anti-Imperialist League, *Liberty Tracts*, No. 10 (Chicago, 1900), p. 2.

The following platform was adopted at the Anti-Imperialist Congress in Chicago on October 18, 1899, eight months after the United States had taken over the administration of the Philippines. Composed of various local and regional groups, the League indicates the ambivalence in American society over the government's departure from the traditional anti-colonial position of the founding fathers.

We hold that the policy known as imperialism is hostile to liberty and tends toward militarism, an evil from which it has been our glory to be free. We regret that it has become necessary in the land of Washington and Lincoln to reaffirm that all men, of whatever race or color, are entitled to life, liberty and the pursuit of happiness. We maintain that governments derive their just powers from the consent of the governed. We insist that the subjugation of any people is "criminal aggression" and open disloyalty to the distinctive principles of our government.

We earnestly condemn the policy of the present National Administration in the Philippines. It seeks to extinguish the spirit of 1776 in those islands. We deplore the sacrifice of our soldiers and sailors, whose bravery deserves admiration even in an unjust war. We denounce the slaughter of the Filipinos as a needless horror. We protest against the extension of American sovereignty by Spanish methods.

We demand the immediate cessation of the war against liberty, begun by Spain and continued by us. We urge that Congress be promptly convened to announce to the Filipinos our purpose to concede to them the independence for which they have so long fought and which of right is theirs.

The United States have always protested against the doctrine of international law which permits the subjugation of the weak by the strong. A self-governing state cannot accept sovereignty over an unwilling people. The United States cannot act upon the ancient heresy that might makes right.

Imperialists assume that with the destruction of self-government in the Philippines by American hands, all opposition here will cease. This is a grievous error. Much as we abhor the war of "criminal aggression" in the Philippines, greatly as we regret that the blood of the Filipinos is on American hands, we most deeply resent the betrayal of American institutions at home. The real firing line is not in the suburbs of Manila. The foe is of our own household. The attempt of 1861 was to divide the country. That of 1899 is to destroy its fundamental principles and noblest ideals.

Whether the ruthless slaughter of the Filipinos shall end next month or next year is but an incident in a contest that must go on until the Declaration of Independence and the Constitution of the United States are rescued from the hands of their betrayers. Those who dispute about standards of value while the Republic is undermined will be listened to as little as those who would wrangle about the small economies of the household while the house is on fire. The training of a great people for a century, the aspiration for liberty of a vast immigration are forces that will hurl aside those who in the delirium of conquest seek to destroy the character of our institutions.

We deny that the obligation of all citizens to support their government in times of grave National peril applies to the present situation. If an Administration may with impunity ignore the issues upon which it was chosen, deliberately create a condition of war anywhere on the face of the globe, debauch the civil service for spoils to promote the adventure, organize a truth-suppressing censorship and demand of all citizens a suspension of judgment and their unanimous support while it chooses to continue the fighting, representative government itself is imperiled.

We propose to contribute to the defeat of any person or party that stands for the forcible subjugation of any people. We shall oppose for reelection all who in the White

House or Congress betray American liberty in pursuit of un-American gains. We still hope that both of our great political parties will support and defend the Declaration of Independence in the closing campaign of the century.

We hold, with Abraham Lincoln, that "no man is good enough to govern another man without that man's consent. When the white man governs himself, that is self-government, but when he governs himself and also governs another man, that is more than self-government—that is despotism." "Our reliance is in the love of liberty which God has planted in us. Our defense is in the spirit which prizes liberty as the heritage of all men in all lands. Those who deny freedom to others deserve it not for themselves, and under a just God cannot long retain it."

IMPERIALISM IN THE CONGO: A CASE HISTORY

From E.D. Morel, *King Leopold's Rule in Africa* (London, 1904), pp. 181–186 passim.

The shocking story of King Leopold's exploitation of the African Congo is glimpsed in the following journal by a missionary, A. E. Scrivener, one of the first "outsiders" to penetrate the carefully guarded secrets of Leopold and his company, the International Association of the Congo. This company sold monopolies, beginning in 1882, to private concerns for the exploitation of the region's rubber and other resources, which concerns used a system of forced labor and capital punishment to achieve their ends. It was not until 1908 that international pressure finally forced the Belgian Parliament to stop the worst abuses by annexing the Congo outright.

Everything was on a military basis, but so far as I could see, the one and only reason for it was rubber. It was the theme of everyone's conversation and it was evident that the only way to please one's superiors was to increase the output somehow. I saw a few men come in and the frightened look even now on their faces tells only too eloquently of the awful time they have passed through. As I saw it brought in, each man had a little basket, containing say, four or five pounds of rubber. This was emptied into a larger basket and weighed, and being found sufficient, each man was given a cupful of coarse salt, and to some of the headmen a fathom of calico. . . .

I heard from the white men and some of the soldiers some most gruesome stories. The former white man (I feel ashamed of my color every time I think of him) would stand at the door of the store to receive the rubber from the poor trembling wretches, who after, in some cases, weeks of privation in the forests, had ventured in with what they had been able to collect. A man bringing rather under the proper amount, the white man flies into a rage, and seizing a rifle from one of the guards, shoots him dead on the spot. Very rarely did rubber come in but one or more were shot in that way at the door of the store "to make the survivors bring more next time." Men who had tried to run from the country and had been caught were brought to the station and made to stand one behind the other, and an Albini bullet sent through them. "A pity to waste cartridges on such wretches.'' On ——— removing from the station, his successor almost fainted on attempting to enter the station prison, in which were numbers of poor wretches so reduced by starvation and the awful stench from weeks of accumulation of filth, that they were not able to stand. Some of the stories are unprintable. . . .

Under the present regime a list is kept of all the people. Every town is known and visited at stated intervals. Those stationed near the posts are required to do the various tasks, such as the bringing in of timber and other material. A little payment is made, but that it is in any respect an equivalent it would be absurd to suppose. The people are regarded as the property of the State for any purpose for which they may be needed. That they have any desires of their own, or any plans worth carrying out in connection with their own lives, would create a smile among the officials. It is one continual grind, and the native intercourse between one district and another in the old style is practically non-existent. Only the roads to and from the various posts are kept open, and large tracts of country are abandoned to the wild beasts. The white man himself told me that you could walk on for five days in one direction and not see a single village or a single human being. And this is where formerly there was a big tribe! . . .

From thence on to the Lake we found the road more and more swampy. Leaving Mbongo on Saturday (29th [1903]) we passed through miles of deserted villages, and saw at varying distances many signs of the former inhabitants. . . . Leaving the plain, we . . . followed for three-quarters of an hour the course of a fast-flowing, swollen stream. Then for half an hour through some deserted gardens and amongst the ruins of a number of villages, then a sharp turn to the left through another low-lying bit of grassland. . . .

[At Ngongo, there is an emotional reunion between some surviving relatives of the refugees that Scrivener had picked up along the way and brought with him.]

As one by one the surviving relatives of my men arrived, some affecting scenes were enacted. There was no falling on necks and weeping, but very genuine joy was shown and tears were shed as the losses death had made were told. How they shook hands and snapped their fingers! What expressions of surprise—the wide-opened mouth covered with the open hand to make its evidence of wonder the more apparent. . . .

So far as the State post was concerned, it was in a very dilapidated condition. . . . On three sides of the usual huge quadrangle there were abundant signs of a former population, but we only found three villages—bigger indeed than any we had seen before, but sadly diminished from what had been but recently the condition of the place. . . .

Soon we began talking, and without any encouragement on my part, they began the tales I had become so accustomed to. They were living in peace and quietness when the white man came in from the Lake with all sorts of requests to do this and do that, and they thought it meant slavery. So they attempted to keep the white men out of their country, but without avail. The rifles were too much for them. So they submitted and made up their minds to do the best they could under the altered circumstances. First came the command to build houses for the soldiers and this was done without a murmur. Then they had to feed the soldiers and all the men and women—hangers-on who accompanied them. Then they were told to bring in rubber. This was quite a new thing for them to do. There was rubber in the forest several days away from their home. A small reward was offered, and a rush was made for the rubber; "What strange white men to give us cloth and beads for the sap of a wild vine." They rejoiced in what they thought was their good fortune. But soon the reward was reduced until they were told to bring in the rubber for nothing. To this they tried to demur, but to their great surprise several were shot by the soldiers, and the rest were told, with many curses and blows, to go at once or more would be killed. Terrified, they began to prepare their food for the fortnight's absence from the village, which the collection of the rubber entailed. The soldiers discovered them sitting about. "What, not gone yet!" Bang! bang! bang! And down fell one and another dead in the midst of wives and companions. There is a terrible wail and an attempt made to prepare the dead for burial, but this is not allowed. All must go at once to the forest. And off the poor wretches had to go without even their tinder-boxes to make fires. Many died in the forests from exposure and hunger, and still more from the rifles of the ferocious soldiers in charge of the post. In spite of all their efforts, the amount fell off and more and more were killed. . . .

I was shown round the place, and the sites of former big chiefs' settlements were pointed out. A careful estimate made the population of, say, seven years ago to be 2000 people in and about the post within the radius of, say, a quarter of a mile. All told they would not muster 200 now and there is so much sadness and gloom that they are fast decreasing. . . .

Lying about in the grass within a few yards of the house I was occupying were numbers of human bones, in some cases complete skeletons. I counted 36 skulls and saw many sets of bones from which the skulls were missing. I called one of the men and asked the meaning of it. "When the palaver began," said he, "the soldiers shot so many we grew tired of burying, and very often we were not allowed to bury and so just dragged the bodies out into the grass and left them. There are hundreds all around if you would like to see them." But I had seen more than enough and was sickened by the stories that came from men and women alike of the awful time they had passed through. . . .

In due course we reached Ibali. There was hardly a sound building in the place. . . . Why such dilapidation? The commandant away for a trip likely to extend into three months, the sub-lieutenant away in another direction on a punitive expedition. In other words, station must be neglected and rubber-hunting carried out with all vigor. I stayed here two days and the one thing that impressed itself upon me was the collection of rubber. I saw long files of men come as at Mbongo with their little baskets under their arms, saw them paid their milk-tin-full of salt, and the two yards of calico flung to the head men; saw their trembling timidity, and in fact a great deal more, to prove the state of terrorism that exists and the virtual slavery in which the people are held. . . . So much for the journey to the Lake. It has enlarged my knowledge of the country and also, alas! my knowledge of the awful deeds enacted in the mad haste of men to get rich. So far as I know I am the first white man to go into the *Domaine privé* [private domain] of the King, other than the employees of the State. I expect there will be wrath in some quarters, but that cannot be helped.

CONTEMPORARY CRITIQUES

HOBSON: IMPERIALISM, A STUDY

(New York, 1902), pp. 1–11, 381–383.

J.A. Hobson (1858–1940) was an English economist and journalist. Calling himself "an economic heretic," he criticized classical economics for being too mechanical and for failing to take account of the social and ethical dimensions of Man. In his pioneer study of imperialism, from which the following excerpts are taken, he continued his criticism of capitalism in its attempts to subjugate the less developed areas of the world.

During the nineteenth century the struggle towards nationalism, or establishment of political union on a basis of nationality, has been a dominant factor alike in dynastic movements and as an inner motive in the life of masses of population. That struggle, in external politics, has sometimes taken a disruptive form, as in the case of Greece, Servia, Roumania, and Bulgaria breaking from Ottoman rule, and the detachment of North Italy from her unnatural alliance with the Austrian Empire. In other cases it has been a unifying or a centralizing force, enlarging the area of nationality, as in the case of Italy and the Pan-Slavist movement in Russia. Sometimes nationality has been taken as a basis of federation of states, as in United Germany and North America. . . .

Turning from this territorial and dynastic nationalism to the spirit of racial, linguistic, and economic solidarity which has been the underlying motive, we find a still more remarkable movement. Local particularism on the one hand, vague cosmopolitanism upon the other, yielded to a ferment of nationalist sentiment, manifesting itself among the weaker peoples not merely in a sturdy and heroic resistance against political absorption or territorial nationalism, but in a passionate revival of decaying customs, language, literature, and art; while it bred in more dominant peoples strange ambitions of national "destiny" and an attendant spirit of Chauvinism.

The true nature and limits of nationality have never been better stated than by J. S. Mill:

> A portion of mankind may be said to constitute a nation if they are united among themselves by common sympathies which do not exist between them and others. This feeling of nationality may have been generated by various causes. Sometimes it is the effect of identity of race and descent. Community of language and community of religion greatly contribute to it. Geographical limits are one of the causes. But the strongest of all is identity of political antecedents, the possession of a national history and consequent community of recollections, collective pride and humiliation, pleasure and regret, connected with the same incidents in the past.

It is a debasement of this genuine nationalism, by attempts to overflow its natural banks and absorb the near or distant territory of reluctant and unassimilable peoples, that marks the passage from nationalism to a spurious colonialism on the one hand, Imperialism on the other.

Colonialism, where it consists in the migration of part of a nation to vacant or sparsely peopled foreign lands, the emigrants carrying with them full rights of citizenship in the mother country, or else establishing local self-government in close conformity with her institutions and under her final control, may be considered a genuine expansion of nationality, a territorial enlargement of the stock, language, and institutions of the nation. Few colonies in history have, however, long remained in this condition when they have been remote from the mother country. Either they have severed the connection and set up for themselves as separate nationalities, or they have been kept in complete political bondage so far as all major processes of government are concerned, a condition to which the term *Imperialism* is at least as appropriate as colonialism. The only form of distant colony which can be regarded as a clear expansion of nationalism is the self-governing colony in Australasia and Canada, and even in these cases conditions may generate a separate nationalism based on a strong consolidation of colonial interests and sentiments alien from and conflicting with those of the mother nation. In other "self-governing" colonies, as in Cape Colony and Natal, where the majority of whites are not descended from British settlers, and where the presence of subject or "inferior" races in vastly preponderating numbers, and alien climatic and other natural conditions, mark out a civilization distinct from that of the "mother country," the conflict between the colonial and the imperial ideas has long been present in the forefront of the consciousness of politicians. . . . Our other colonies are plainly representative of the spirit of Imperialism rather than of colonialism. No considerable proportion of the population consists of British settlers living with their families in conformity with the social and political customs and laws of their native land: in most instances they form a small minority wielding political or economic sway over a majority of alien and subject people, themselves under the despotic political control of the Imperial Government or its local nominees. This, the normal condition of a British colony, is well-nigh universal in the colonies of other European countries. The "colonies" which France and Germany establish in Africa and Asia are in no real sense plantations of French and German national life beyond the seas; nowhere, not even in Algeria, do they represent true European civilization; their political and economic structure of society is wholly alien from that of the mother country.

Colonialism, in its best sense, is a natural overflow of nationality; its test is the power of colonists to transplant the civilization they represent to the new natural and social environment in which they find themselves. We must not be misled by names: the "colonial" party in Germany and France is identical in general aim and method with the "imperialist" party in England, and the latter is the truer title. Professor Seeley well marked the nature of Imperialism:

> When a State advances beyond the limits of nationality its power becomes precarious and artificial. This is the condition of most empires, and it is the condition of our own. When a nation extends itself into other territories the chances are that it cannot destroy or completely drive out, even if it succeeds in conquering, them. When this happens it has a great and permanent difficulty to contend with, for the subject or rival nationalities cannot be properly assimilated, and remain as a permanent cause of weakness and danger.

The novelty of the recent Imperialism regarded as a policy consists chiefly in its adoption by several nations. The notion of a number of competing empires is essentially modern. The root idea of empire in the ancient and medieval world was that of a federation of States, under a hegemony, covering in general terms the entire known or recognized world, such as was held by Rome under the so-called *pax Romana*. When Roman citizens, with full civic rights, were found all over the explored world, in Africa and Asia, as well as in Gaul and Britain, Imperialism contained a genuine element of internationalism. With the fall of Rome this conception of a single empire wielding political authority over the civilized world did not disappear. . . . Beneath every cleavage or antagonism, and notwithstanding the severance of many independent kingdoms and provinces, this ideal unity of the empire lived. . . .

This early flower of humane cosmopolitanism was destined to wither before the powerful revival of nationalism. . . . Even in the narrow circles of the cultured classes it easily passed from a noble and passionate ideal to become a vapid sentimentalism, and after the brief flare of 1848 among the continental populace had been extinguished, little remained but a dim smoldering of the embers. . . .

This scramble for Africa and Asia has virtually recast the policy of all European nations, has evoked alliances which cross all natural lines of sympathy and historical association, has driven every continental nation to consume an ever growing share of its material and human resources upon military and naval equipment, has drawn the great new power of the United States from its isolation into full tide of competition; and, by the multitude, the magnitude, and the suddenness of the issues it throws on to the stage of politics, has become a constant agent of menace and of perturbation to the peace and progress of mankind. The new policy has exercised the most notable and formidable influence upon the conscious statecraft of the nations which indulge in it. While producing for popular consumption doctrines of national destiny and imperial missions of civilization, contradictory in their true import, but subsidiary to one another as supports of popular Imperialism, it has evolved a calculating, greedy type of Machiavellianism entitled *Realpolitik* in Germany, where it was made, which has remodelled the whole art of diplomacy and has erected national aggrandisement without pity or scruple as the conscious motive force of foreign policy. Earth hunger and the scramble for markets are responsible for the openly avowed repudiation of treaty obligations which Germany, Russia, and England have not scrupled to defend. The sliding scale of diplomatic language, hinterland, sphere of interest, sphere of influence, paramountcy, suzerainty, protectorate, veiled or open, leading up to acts of forcible seizure or annexation which sometimes continue to be hidden under "Lease," "rectification of frontier," "concession," and the like, is the invention and expression of this cynical spirit of Imperialism. . . .

Analysis of Imperialism, with its natural supports, militarism, oligarchy, bureaucracy, protection, concentration of capital and violent trade fluctuations, has marked it out as the supreme danger of modern national States. The power of the imperialist forces within the nation to use the national resources for their private gain, by operating the instrument of the State, can only be overthrown by the establishment of genuine democracy, the direction of public policy by the people for the people through representatives over whom they exercise a real control. . . .

Imperialism is only beginning to realize its full resources, and to develop into a fine art the management of nations: the broad bestowal of a franchise, wielded by a people whose education has reached the stage of an uncritical ability to read printed matter, favors immensely the designs of keen business politicians, who, by controlling the press, the schools, and where necessary the churches, impose Imperialism upon the masses under the attractive guise of sensational patriotism.

The chief economic source of Imperialism has been found in the inequality of industrial opportunities by which a favored class accumulates superfluous elements of income which, in their search for profitable investments, press ever farther afield: the influence on State policy of these investors and their financial managers secures a national alliance of other vested interests which are threatened by movements of social reform: the adoption of Imperialism thus serves the double purpose of securing private material benefits for favored classes of investors and traders at the public cost, while sustaining the general cause of conservatism by diverting public energy and interest from domestic agitation to external employment.

LENIN: IMPERIALISM, THE HIGHEST STAGE OF CAPITALISM
(1916)

(New York: International Publishers, 1939), pp. 109–111, 123–124, 126–127. Reprinted by permission of International Publishers, Inc.

One year before he took over the leadership of the Russian Revolution in 1917, V.I. Lenin published this scathing attack on imperialism. Calling it the last stage of a dying monopoly capitalism, he found in imperialism all the "inherent contradictions" that his predecessors, Marx and Engels, had found in capitalism, but to an even higher degree.

The enormous dimensions of finance capital concentrated in a few hands and creating an extremely extensive and close network of ties and relationships which subordinate not only the small and medium, but also even the very small capitalists and small masters, on the one hand, and the intense struggle waged against other national state groups of financiers for the division of the world and domination over other countries, on the other hand, cause the wholesale transition of the possessing classes to the side of imperialism. The signs of the times are a "general" enthusiasm regarding its prospects, a passionate defence of imperialism, and every possible embellishment of its real nature. The imperialist ideology also penetrates the working class. There is no Chinese Wall between it and the other classes. The leaders of the so-called "Social-Democratic" Party of Germany are today justly called "social-imperialists," that is, socialists in words and imperialists in deeds; but as early as 1902, Hobson noted the existence of "Fabian imperialists" who belonged to the opportunist Fabian Society in England.

Bourgeois scholars and publicists usually come out in defence of imperialism in a somewhat veiled form, and obscure its complete domination and its profound roots; they strive to concentrate attention on partial and secondary details and do their very best to distract attention from the main issue by means of ridiculous schemes for "reform," such as police supervision of the trusts and banks, etc. Less frequently, cynical and frank imperialists speak out and are bold enough to admit the absurdity of the idea of reforming the fundamental features of imperialism. . . .

The question as to whether it is possible to reform the basis of imperialism, whether to go forward to the accentuation and deepening of the antagonisms which it engenders, or backwards, towards allaying these antagonisms, is a fundamental question in the critique of imperialism. As a consequence of the fact that the political features of imperialism are reaction all along the line, and increased national oppression, resulting from the oppression of the financial oligarchy and the elimination of free competition, a petty-bourgeois-democratic opposition has been rising against imperialism in almost all imperialist countries since the beginning of the twentieth century. . . .

In the United States, the imperialist war waged against Spain in 1898 stirred up the opposition of the "anti-imperialists," the last of the Mohicans of bourgeois democracy. They declared this war to be "criminal"; they denounced the annexation of foreign territories as being a violation of the Constitution, and denounced the "Jingo treachery" by means of which Aguinaldo, leader of the native Filipinos, was deceived (the Americans promised him the independence of his country, but later they landed troops and annexed it). They quoted the words of Lincoln:

> When the white man governs himself, that is self-government, but when he governs himself and also governs another man, that is more than self-government—that is despotism.

But while all this criticism shrank from recognising the indissoluble bond between imperialism and the trusts, and, therefore, between imperialism and the very foundations of capitalism; while it shrank from joining up with the forces engendered by large-scale capitalism and its development—it remained a "pious wish." . . .

We have seen that the economic quintessence of imperialism is monopoly capitalism. This very fact determines its place in history, for monopoly that grew up on the basis of free competition, and precisely out of free competition, is the transition from the capitalist system to a higher social-economic order. We must take special note of the four principal forms of monopoly, or the four principal manifestations of monopoly capitalism, which are characteristic of the epoch under review.

Firstly, monoply arose out of the concentration of production at a very advanced stage of development. This refers to the monopolist capitalist combines, cartels, syndicates, and trusts. We have seen the important part that these play in modern economic life. At the very beginning of the twentieth century, monopolies acquired complete supremacy in the advanced countries. And although the first steps towards the formation of the cartels were first taken by countries enjoying the protection of high tariffs (Germany, America), Great Britain, with her system of free trade, was not far behind in revealing the same basic phenomenon, namely, the birth of monopoly out of the concentration of production.

Secondly, monopolies have accelerated the capture of the most important sources of raw materials, especially for the coal and iron industries, which are the basic and most highly cartelised industries in capitalist society. The monopoly of the most important sources of raw materials has enormously increased the power of big capital, and has sharpened the antagonism between cartelised and non-cartelised industry.

Thirdly, monopoly has sprung from the banks. The banks have developed from modest intermediary enterprises into the monopolists of finance capital. Some three or five of the biggest banks in each of the foremost capitalist countries have achieved the "personal union" of industrial and bank capital, and have concentrated in their hands the disposal of thousands upon thousands of millions which form the greater part of the capital and income of entire countries. A financial oligarchy, which throws a close net of relations of dependence over all the economic and political institutions of contemporary bourgeois society without exception—such is the most striking manifestation of this monopoly.

Fourthly, monopoly has grown out of colonial policy. To the numerous "old" motives of colonial policy, finance capital has added the struggle for the sources of raw materials, for the export of capital, for "spheres of influence," *i.e.,* for spheres of profitable deals, concessions, monopolist profits, and so on; in fine, for economic territory in general. When the colonies of the European powers in Africa, for instance, comprised only one-tenth of that territory (as was the case in 1876), colonial policy was able to develop by methods other than those of monopoly—by the "free grabbing" of territories, so to speak. But when nine-tenths of Africa had been seized (approximately by 1900), when the whole world had been divided up, there was inevitably ushered in a period of colonial monopoly and, consequently, a period of particularly intense struggle for the division and the redivision of the world.

The extent to which monopolist capital has intensified all the contradictions of capitalism is generally known. It is sufficient to mention the high cost of living and the oppression of the cartels. This intensification of contradictions constitutes the most powerful driving force of the transitional period of history, which began from the time of the definite victory of world finance capital.

Monopolies, oligarchy, the striving for domination instead of the striving for liberty, the exploitation of an increasing number of small or weak nations by an extremely small group of the richest or most powerful nations—all these have given birth to those distinctive characteristics of imperialism which compel us to define it as parasitic or decaying capitalism. . . .

The receipt of high monopoly profits by the capitalists in one of the numerous branches of industry, in one of numerous countries, etc., makes it economically possible for them to corrupt certain sections of the working class, and for a time a fairly considerable minority, and win them to the side of the bourgeoisie of a given industry or nation against all the others. The intensification of antagonism between the imperialist nations for the division of the world increases this striving. And so there is created that bond between imperialism and opportunism, which revealed itself first and most clearly in England, owing to the fact that certain features of imperialist development were observable there much earlier than in other countries. . . .

From all that has been said . . . on the economic nature of imperialism, it follows that we must define it as capitalism in transition, or more precisely, as moribund capitalism. It is very instructive in this respect to note that the bourgeois economists, in describing modern capitalism, frequently employ terms like "interlocking," "absence of isolation," etc.; "in conformity with their functions and course of development," banks are "not purely private business enterprises; they are more and more outgrowing the sphere of purely private business regulation." And this very Riesser, who uttered the words just quoted, declares with all seriousness that the "prophecy" of the Marxists concerning "socialisation" has "not come true"!

What then does this word "interlocking" express? It merely expresses the most striking freature of the process going on before our eyes. It shows that the observer counts the separate trees, but cannot see the wood. It slavishly copies the superficial, the fortuitous, the chaotic. It reveals the observer as one who is overwhelmed by the mass of raw material and is utterly incapable of appreciating its meaning and importance. Ownership of shares and relations between owners of private property "interlock in a haphazard way." But the underlying factor of this interlocking, its very base, is the changing social relations of production. When a big enterprise assumes gigantic proportions, and, on the basis of exact computation of mass data, organises according to plan the supply of primary raw materials to the extent of two-thirds, or three-fourths of all that is necessary for tens of millions of people; when the raw materials are transported to the most suitable place of production, sometimes hundreds or thousands of miles away, in a systematic and organised manner; when a single centre directs all the successive stages of work right up to the manufacture of numerous varieties of finished articles, when these products are distributed according to a single plan among tens and hundreds of millions of consumers (as in the case of the distribution of oil in America and Germany by the American "oil trust")—then it becomes evident that we have socialisation of production, and not mere "interlocking"; that private economic relations and private property relations constitute a shell which is no longer suitable for its contents, a shell which must inevitably begin to decay if its destruction be delayed by artificial means; a shell which may continue in a state of decay for a fairly long period (particularly if the cure of the opportunist abscess is protracted), but which will inevitably be removed.

CHAPTER 27

THE EMERGENCE OF FEMINISM, 1848–1900

The very word "woman" (O. Eng. *wifmann*), etymologically meaning a wife, . . . sums up a long history of dependence and subordination, from which the women of today have only gradually emancipated themselves in such parts of the world as come under "Western civilization." Though married life and its duties necessarily form a predominant element in the woman's sphere, they are not necessarily the whole of it; and the "woman's movement" is essentially a struggle for the recognition of equality of opportunity with men, and for equal rights irrespective of sex. . . . The difficulties of obtaining this recognition are obviously due to historical causes combined with the habits and customs which history has produced.—James Williams.

Article "Women," Encyclopedia Britannica, *1911, 28:782.*

This statement from the 1911 *Britannica* indicates the aims and objectives of the feminist movement before World War I. Note that the issues stated here are much broader than voting rights, although the struggle for women's suffrage was being fought out in the streets of London at that very moment. The broader campaign, however, was for equal rights and opportunities all down the line, from employment and economic independence to equality before the law and in the courtroom.

In the selections below, these questions are spelled out in various tracts and manifestoes, beginning with the first Women's Convention at Seneca Falls, New York, in 1848. There Elizabeth Cady Stanton and Lucretia Mott started the modern feminist movement with a stirring Declaration of Independence for Women. In England the great libertarian John Stuart Mill took up the cause, while a short time later Friedrich Engels presented the case for the liberation of women in his *Origin of the Family.*

In Norway, Henrik Ibsen wrote powerful feminist dramas in which the heroines evinced a strong sense of identity and independence, shocking the whole bourgeois establishment—to such an extent that Ibsen found it congenial to spend most of his time in Italy rather than in Norway. Meanwhile, back in America,

Susan B. Anthony was carrying the fight for Women's Suffrage into the camp of the "enemy" by lecturing to men's groups up and down the country, since only men had power to change the laws—which they did finally with the Nineteenth Amendment, ratified in 1920.

A word of caution: Except for the Women's Declaration of Independence, the selections presented here are rather small excerpts from complete essays. We have tried to preserve the original spirit of the writers and to present, in most cases, continuous passages, but some distortion is inevitable and you should consult the full-scale text of any author who piques your curiosity.

THE SENECA FALLS CONVENTION (1848)

From *The History of Woman Suffrage*, ed. E.C. Stanton, *et al.* (6 vols., New York, 1881ff.), 1:70–74.

Although Mary Wollstonecraft had issued the battle cry of the modern feminist movement during the French Revolution (pp. 29–31, above), it was the anti-slavery movement in the 1840s that gave feminism its new militancy, exemplified in the following excerpts from the woman's Declaration of Independence. This document was adopted and publicized by the first Women's Convention, held in Seneca Falls, N.Y., in July 1848.

1. Declaration of Sentiments

When, in the course of human events, it becomes necessary for one portion of the family of man to assume among the people of the earth a position different from that which they have hitherto occupied, but one to which the laws of nature and of nature's God entitle them, a decent respect to the opinions of mankind requires that they should declare the causes that impel them to such a course.

. . . The history of mankind is a history of repeated injuries and usurpations on the part of man toward woman, having in direct object the establishment of an absolute tyranny over her. To prove this, let facts be submitted to a candid world.

He has never permitted her to exercise her inalienable right to the elective franchise.

He has compelled her to submit to laws, in the formation of which she had no voice.

He has withheld from her rights which are given to the most ignorant and degraded men—both natives and foreigners.

Having deprived her of this first right of a citizen, the elective franchise, thereby leaving her without representation in the halls of legislation, he has oppressed her on all sides.

He has made her, if married, in the eyes of the law, civilly dead.

He has taken from her all right in property, even to the wages she earns.

He has made her, morally, an irresponsible being. . . . In the covenant of marriage, she is compelled to promise obedience to her husband, he becoming, to all intents and purposes, her master. . . .

He has monopolized nearly all the profitable employments, and from those she is permitted to follow, she receives but a scanty remuneration. . . .

He allows her in Church as well as State but a subordinate position, claiming Apostolic authority for her exclusion from the ministry. . . .

He has created a false public sentiment by giving to the world a different code of morals for men and women. . . .

He has endeavored, in every way that he could, to destroy her confidence in her own powers, to lessen her self-respect and to make her willing to lead a dependent and abject life. . . .

2. Resolutions

Whereas, The great precept of nature is conceded to be, that "man shall pursue his own true and substantial happiness." Blackstone in his Commentaries remarks, that this law of Nature being coeval with mankind, and dictated by God himself, is of course superior in obligation to any other. . . . No human laws are of any validity if contrary to this; . . . therefore,

Resolved, That all laws which prevent woman from occupying such a station in society as her conscience shall dictate, or which place her in a position inferior to that of man, are contrary to the great precept of nature, and therefore of no force or authority.

Resolved, That woman is man's equal—was intended to be so by the Creator, and the highest good of the race demands that she should be recognized as such. . . .

Resolved, That the same amount of virtue, delicacy, and refinement of behavior that is required of woman in the social state, should also be required of man, and the same transgressions should be visited with equal severity on both man and woman. . . .

Resolved, That the speedy success of our cause depends upon the zealous and untiring efforts of both men and women . . . for the securing to women an equal participation with men in the various trades, professions, and commerce.

Resolved, therefore, That, being invested by the creator with the same capabilities, and the same consciousness of responsibility for their exercise, it is demonstrably the right and duty of woman, equally with man, to promote every righteous cause by every righteous means; and especially in regard to the great subjects of morals and religion, it is self-evidently her right to participate with her brother in teaching them, both in private and in public, by writing and by speaking, . . . in any assemblies proper to be held. . . .

JOHN STUART MILL: THE ENFRANCHISEMENT OF WOMEN (1851)

From *Westminister Review,* July 1851.

John Stuart Mill was an early champion of the cause of Women's Rights, as shown by the following excerpts from his article in the *Westminister Review.* Later, in 1869, he published a classic defense of the cause in his book on *The Subjection of Women.*

There has arisen in the United States, and in the most civilized and enlightened portion of them, an organized agitation on a new question—new, not to thinkers nor to anyone by whom the principles of free and popular government are felt as well as acknowledged, but new, and even unheard of, as a subject for public meetings and practical political action. This question is the enfranchisement of women; their admission, in law and in fact, to equality in all rights, political, civil, and social, with the male citizens of the community.

. . . [This] agitation is not a pleading by male writers and orators *for* women. . . . It is a political movement, practical in its objects, carried on in a form which denotes an intention to persevere. And it is a movement not merely *for* women, but *by* them. . . . On the 23d and 24th of October last, a succession of public meetings was held at Worcester [Mass.] under the name of a "Women's-Rights Convention," of which the president was a woman, and nearly all the chief speakers women; numerously re-enforced, however, by men, among whom were some of the most distinguished leaders in the kindred cause of negro emancipation. . . .

That the promoters of this new agitation take their stand on principles, and do not fear to declare these in their widest extent, . . . will be seen from the resolutions adopted by the Convention, part of which we transcribe:

> *Resolved,* That every human being of full age, and resident for a proper length of time on the soil of the nation, who is required to obey the law, is entitled to a voice in its enactment; that every such person, whose property or labor is taxed for the support of the government, is entitled to a direct share in such government: therefore—
>
> *Resolved,* That women are entitled to the right of suffrage, and to be considered eligible to office; . . . and that every party which claims to represent the humanity, the civilization, and the progress of the age, is bound to inscribe on its banners, "Equality before the Law, without Distinction of Sex or Color.". . .
>
> *Resolved,* That the laws of property, as affecting married persons, demand a thorough revisal, so that all rights be equal between them; that the wife have, during life, an equal control over the property gained by their mutual toil and sacrifices, and be heir to her husband precisely to that extent that he is heir to her, and entitled at her death to dispose by will of the same share of the joint property as he is. . . .

As a question of justice, the case seems to us too clear for dispute. As one of expediency, the more thoroughly it is examined, the stronger it will appear.

That women have as good a claim as men have, in point of personal right, to the suffrage, or to a place in the jury-box, it would be difficult for anyone to deny. It cannot certainly be denied by the United States of America, as a people or as a community. Their democratic institutions rest avowedly on the inherent right of everyone to a voice in the government. . . .

Not only to the democracy of America, the claim of women to civil and political equality makes an irresistible appeal but . . . it is an axiom of English freedom that taxation and representation should be coextensive. Even under the laws which give the wife's property to the husband, there are many unmarried women who pay taxes. It is one of the fundamental doctrines of the British Constitution, that all persons should be tried by their peers; yet women, whenever tried, are tried by male judges and a male jury. To foreigners, the law accords the privilege of claiming that half the jury should be composed of themselves: not so to women. . . . It is an acknowledged dictate of justice to make no degrading distinctions without necessity. In all things, the presumption ought to be on the side of equality. A reason must be given why anything should be permitted to one person, and interdicted to another. But when that which is interdicted includes nearly everything which those to whom it is permitted most prize, and to be deprived of which they feel to be most insulting; when not only political liberty, but personal freedom of action, is the prerogative of a caste; when, even in the exercise of industry, almost all employments which task the higher faculties in an important field, which lead to distinction, riches, or even pecuniary independence, are fenced round as the exclusive domain of the predominant section, scarcely any doors being left open to the dependent class . . .—[it is] a flagrant injustice, . . .

We are firmly convinced that the division of mankind into two castes, one born to rule over the other, is in this case, as in all cases, an unqualified mischief; a source of perversion and demoralization, both to the favored class and to those at whose expense they are favored; producing none of the good which it is the custom to ascribe to it, and forming a bar, almost insuperable while it lasts, to any really vital improvement, either in the character or in the social condition of the human race.

MILL: THE SUBJECTION OF WOMEN (1869)

(2d ed., London, 1869), pp. 1, 49-52, 56-57, 187-188.

The object of this Essay is to explain as clearly as I am able, the grounds of an opinion which I have held from the very earliest period when I had formed any opinions at all on social or political matters, and which, instead of being weakened or modified, has been constantly growing stronger by the progress of reflection and the experience of life: That the principle which regulates the existing social relations between the two sexes—the legal subordination of one sex to the other—is wrong in itself, and now one of the chief hindrances to human improvement; and that it ought to be replaced by a principle of perfect equality, admitting no power or privilege on the one side, nor disability on the other.

.   .   .

The general opinion of men is supposed to be, that the natural vocation of a woman is that of a wife and mother. I say, is supposed to be, because judging from acts—from the whole of the present constitution of society—one might infer that their opinion was the direct contrary. They might be supposed to think that the alleged natural vocation of women was of all things the most repugnant to their nature; insomuch that if they are free to do anything else—if any other means of living, or occupation of their time and faculties, is open, which has any chance of appearing desirable to them—there will not be enough of them who will be willing to accept the condition said to be natural to them. If this is the real opinion of men in general, it would be well that it should be spoken out. I should like to hear somebody openly enunciating the doctrine (it is already implied in much that is written on the subject)—''It is necessary to society that

Mrs. Pankhurst Goes to Jail (1911). One of the leaders in the fight for women's suffrage before World War I, Mrs. Emmeline Pankhurst founded the Women's Social and Political Union in 1903. Her tactic of civil disobedience coupled with her charm and organizational ability eventually won the vote for English women, and in 1928 she was elected to the House of Commons with the support of the Conservatives. (The Granger Collection.)

women should marry and produce children. They will not do so unless they are compelled. Therefore it is necessary to compel them." . . .

It is not a sign of one's thinking the boon one offers very attractive when one allows only Hobson's choice, "that or none." And here, I believe, is the clue to the feelings of those men, who have a real antipathy to the equal freedom of women. I believe they are afraid, not lest women should be unwilling to marry, for I do not think that any one in reality has that apprehension; but lest they should insist that marriage should be on equal conditions; lest all women of spirit and capacity should prefer doing almost anything else, not in their own eyes degrading, rather than marry, when marrying is giving themselves a master, and a master too of all their earthly possessions. . . . But, in that case, all that has been done in the modern world to relax the chain on the minds of women, has been a mistake. They never should have been allowed to receive a literary education. Women who read, much more women who write, are, in the existing constitution of things, a contradiction and a disturbing element; and it was wrong to bring women up with any acquirements but those of an odalisque, or of a domestic servant.

.   .   .

I am far from pretending that wives are in general no better treated than slaves; but no slave is a slave to the same lengths, and in so full a sense of the word, as a wife is. Hardly any slave . . . is a slave at all hours and all minutes; in general he has, like a soldier, his fixed task, and when it is done, or when he is off duty, he disposes, within certain limits, of his own time, and has a family life into which the master rarely intrudes. . . . But it cannot be so with the wife. Above all, a female slave has (in Christian countries) an admitted right, and is considered under a moral obligation, to refuse her master the last familiarity. Not so the wife: however brutal a tyrant she may unfortunately be chained to—though she may know that he hates her, though it may be his daily pleasure to torture her, and though she may feel it impossible not to loathe him—he can claim from her and enforce the lowest degradation of a human being, that of being made the instrument of an animal function contrary to her inclinations.

.   .   .

When we consider the positive evil caused to the disqualified half of the human race by their disqualification—first in the loss of the most inspiriting and elevating kind of personal enjoyment, and next in the weariness, disappointment, and profound dissatisfaction with life, which are so often the substitute for it; one feels that among all the lessons which men require for carrying on the struggle against the inevitable imperfections of their lot on earth, there is no lesson which they more need, than not to add to the evils which nature inflicts, by their jealous and prejudiced restrictions on one another. Their vain fears only substitute other and worse evils for those which they are idly apprehensive of: while every restraint on the freedom of conduct of any of their human fellow creatures . . . dries up *pro tanto* [by so much] the principal fountain of human happiness, and leaves the species less rich, to an inappreciable degree, in all that makes life valuable to the individual human being.

HENRIK IBSEN: A DOLL'S HOUSE (1879)

Trans, W. Archer, 1905, revised.

Henrik Ibsen (d. 1906), one of the greatest playwrights of modern times, was also a feminist, creating such immortal characters as *Hedda Gabler*, Mrs. Alving in *Ghosts*, and Nora Helmer in *A Doll's House*, from which the following scene is taken. Previously Nora has secretly forged a signature to help save the life of her husband, Torvald Helmer. When he later discovers it, although she has repaid the money, he is concerned only about the effect of a "scandal" on his career—and not whether Nora will be sent to jail. Once the danger is past, however, he condescendingly forgives Nora for being such an irresponsible "little chipmunk"; but, by then, she has other ideas.

Nora's Declaration of Independence (Act III)

HELMER. You alarm me, Nora. I don't understand you.

NORA. That's just it, you don't understand me; and I have never understood you—until tonight. No, don't interrupt. Just listen to what I have to say. We must come to a final settlement, Torvald.

HELMER. How do you mean?

NORA. *(Pause.)* Does anything strike you as we sit here?

HELMER. What should strike me?

Anti-Suffragette cartoon, Punch, 1913. After trying in vain to light a fire at home, militant suffragette exclaims: "And to think that only Thursday I burnt two pavilions and a church!" (Punch Publications, Ltd./Art Reference Bureau.)

NORA. We've been married eight years; does it not strike you that this is the first time we two, you and I, man and wife, have talked together seriously?

HELMER. Seriously? What do you mean, *seriously?*

NORA. For eight whole years, and more—ever since the day we first met—we have never exchanged one serious word about serious things. . . .

HELMER. Why, my dearest Nora, what have you to do with serious things?

NORA. There we have it! You have never understood me. I've had great injustice done me, Torvald; first by father, then by you.

HELMER. What! Your father *and* me? We, who have loved you more than all the world?

NORA. *(Shaking her head.)* You have never loved me. You just found it amusing to think you were in love with me.

HELMER. Nora! What a thing to say!

NORA. Yes, it's true, Torvald. When I was living at home with father, he told me his opinions and mine were the same. If I had different opinions, I said nothing about them, because he would not have liked it. He used to call me his doll-child and played with me as I played with my dolls. Then I came to live in your house—

HELMER. What a way to speak of our marriage!

NORA. *(Undisturbed.)* I mean that I passed from father's hands into yours. You arranged everything to your taste and I got the same tastes as you; or pretended to—I don't know which—both, perhaps; sometimes one, sometimes the other. When I look back on it now, I seem to have been living here like a beggar, on hand-outs. I lived by performing tricks for you, Torvald. But that was how you wanted it. You and father have done me a great wrong. It is your fault that my life has come to naught.

HELMER. Why, Nora, how unreasonable and ungrateful! Haven't you been happy here?

NORA. No, never. I thought I was, but I never was.

HELMER. Not—not happy!

NORA. No, only merry. And you have always been so kind to me. But our house has been nothing but a playroom. Here I have been your doll-wife, just as I used to be papa's doll-child. And the children, in turn, have been my dolls. I thought it fun when you played with me, just as the children did when I played with them. That has been our marriage, Torvald.

HELMER. There is some truth in what you say, exaggerated and overblown as it may be. But henceforth it shall be different. Playtime is over; now is the time for education.

NORA. Whose education? Mine, or the children's?

HELMER. Both, my dear Nora.

NORA. Oh, Torvald, you are not the man to teach me to be a fit wife for you.

HELMER. And you can say that?

NORA. And I—how have I prepared myself to educate the children?

HELMER. Nora!

NORA. Did you not say yourself, just now, that you dared not trust them to me?

HELMER. In the excitement of the moment! Why do you dwell on that?

NORA. No—you were perfectly right. That problem is beyond me. There is another to be solved first—I must try to educate myself. You are not the man to help me in that; I must go about it alone. And that is why I am leaving you.

HELMER. *(Jumping up.)* What—do you mean to say—?

NORA. I must stand quite alone if I am ever to know myself and my surroundings; so I cannot stay with you.

HELMER. Nora! Nora!

NORA. I am going at once. I daresay [my friend] Christina will take me in for tonight.

HELMER. You are mad! I shall not allow it! I forbid it!

NORA. It's no use your forbidding me anything now. I shall take with me only what belongs to me; from you I will accept nothing, either now or later.

HELMER. This is madness!

NORA. Tomorrow I shall go home—I mean to what was my home. It will be easier for me to find a job there.

HELMER. Oh, in your blind inexperience—

NORA. I must try to gain experience, Torvald.

HELMER. Forsake your home, your husband, your children! And you don't consider what the world will say.

NORA. I can't pay attention to that. I only know that I must do it.

HELMER. This is monstrous! Can you forsake your holiest duties?

NORA. What do you consider my holiest duties?

HELMER. Need I tell you that? Your duties to your husband and children.

NORA. I have other duties equally sacred.

HELMER. Impossible! What do you mean?

NORA. My duties towards myself.

HELMER. Before all else you are a wife and a mother.

NORA. That I no longer believe. Before all else I believe I am a human being, just as much as you are—or at least that I should try to become one. I know that most people agree with you, Torvald, and that they say so in books. But I can no longer be satisfied with what most people say and what is in books. I must think things out for myself and try to get clear about them.

HELMER. Are you not clear about your place in your own home? Have you not an infallible guide in questions like these? Have you not religion?

NORA. Oh, Torvald, I don't really know what religion is.

HELMER. What do you mean?

NORA. I know nothing but what Pastor Hansen told me when I was confirmed. He explained that religion was this and that. When I get away from all this and stand alone, I will look into that matter too. I will see whether what he taught me is right, or at any rate, whether it is right for me.

HELMER. Oh, this is unheard of! And from so young a woman! But if religion cannot keep you right, let me appeal to your conscience—for I suppose you have some moral feeling? Or, tell me: perhaps you have none?

NORA. Well, Torvald, it's not easy to say. I really don't know—I'm all at sea about these things. I only know that I think quite differently about them. I hear too that the laws are different from what I thought, but I can't believe that they are right. . . .

HELMER. You talk like a child. You don't understand the society in which you live.

NORA. No, I do not. But I shall try to learn. I must make up my mind which is right—society or I.

HELMER. Nora, you are ill; you're feverish. I almost think you are out of your mind.

NORA. I have never felt such clearness and certainty as tonight.

HELMER. You are clear and certain enough to abandon you husband and children?

NORA. Yes, I am.

HELMER. Then there is only one explanation possible.

NORA. What is that?

HELMER. You no longer love me.

NORA. No, I do not.

HELMER. Nora!—How can you say that!

NORA. Oh, I'm so sorry, Torvald, for you have always been so kind to me. But I can't help it. I do not love you any longer.

HELMER. *(Mastering himself with difficulty.)* Are you clear and certain on this point too?

NORA. Yes, quite. That is why I will not stay here any longer.

HELMER. Can you also make clear to me how I have forfeited your love?

NORA. Yes, I can. It was this evening, when . . . I saw that you were not the man I had imagined. . . .

*   *   *   *

HELMER. I would gladly work for you day and night, Nora—bear sorrow and want for your sake. But no man sacrifices his honor, not even for the one he loves.

NORA. Millions of *women* have done so.

HELMER. Oh, you think and talk like a silly child.

NORA. Very likely. But you neither think nor talk like the man I can share my life with. . . . Torvald, I have been living here these eight years with a strange man and borne him three children.—Oh, I can't bear to think of it! I could tear myself to pieces!

HELMER. *(Sadly.)* I see it, I see it; an abyss has opened between us.—But Nora, can it never be bridged?

NORA. As I am now, I am no wife for you.

HELMER. I have the strength to become a different man.

NORA. Perhaps—if your doll is taken away from you.

HELMER. To part—to part from you! No, Nora, no, I can't stand the thought of it.

NORA. *(Going into the room off stage.)* All the more reason for the thing to happen. *(She comes back with outdoor things and a traveling bag.)*

HELMER. Nora, Nora, not now! Wait till tomorrow.

NORA. *(Putting on her coat.)* I can't spend the night in a strange man's house.

HELMER. But can we not live here as brother and sister?

NORA. *(Tying her hat.)* You know very well that wouldn't last. *(Putting on her shawl.)* Goodbye, Torvald. No, I won't go to the children. I know they are in better hands than mine. As I am now, I can be nothing to them.

HELMER. But some time, Nora—some day—?

NORA. How can I tell? I have no idea what will become of me.

HELMER. But you are my wife, now and always!

NORA. Listen, Torvald, when a wife leaves her husband's house, as I am doing, I have heard that in the eyes of the law he is free from all duties towards her. At any rate, I release you from them. You must not feel yourself bound, any more than I shall. There must be perfect freedom on both sides. There, I give you back your ring. Give me mine.

HELMER. That too?

NORA. That too.

HELMER. Here it is.

NORA. Very well. Now it is all over. . . .

FRIEDRICH ENGELS: THE ORIGIN OF THE FAMILY (1884)

Trans. E. Untermann (Chicago, n.d.), pp. 91–93, 96, 98–100, revised.

After Marx died in 1883, Engels put together all the notes and other materials that they had collected on the structure and historical evolution of marriage and the family. Believing that the modern bourgeois family was founded on the "open or concealed slavery of the wife," Engels was convinced that the coming socialist revolution would free all women by absorbing them into "social" production. Then for the first time women would be able to enter marriage as equals, on the basis of love and attraction, instead of for "convenience," or as high-level prostitutes.

Monogamy arose from the concentration of considerable wealth in the hands of a single individual—a man—and from his desire to leave this wealth to his children and to nobody else. This necessitated monogamy on the part of the woman but not on the part of the man, since the woman's monogamy did not interfere at all with the man's open or secret polygamy. However, when the major portion of permanent, inheritable wealth—the means of production—is transformed into social property by the coming revolution, all this anxiety about inheriting and bequeathing will be reduced to a minimum. Then, having arisen from economic causes, will monogamy also disappear when those causes disappear?

One might answer, not without reason, that far from disappearing it will, on the contrary, be fully realized. For with the transformation of the means of production into social property wage-labor will also disappear; so will the proletariat and the necessity for a certain, statistically calculable number of women to surrender themselves for money. Prostitution disappears and monogamy, instead of collapsing, at last becomes a reality—for men as well as for women.

So, in any case the position of men will be greatly altered. But the position of women—*all* women—will also undergo significant change. With the transfer of production into common ownership, the individual family ceases to be the economic unit of society. Private housekeeping is transformed into a social industry. The care and education of children becomes a public affair: society looks after all children alike, whether legitimate or not. This removes the anxiety about the "consequences," which is today the most essential factor—moral as well as economic—that prevents a girl from giving herself completely to the man she loves. Will this not suffice to bring about the gradual growth of unconstrained sexual intercourse and a more tolerant public opinion regarding a virgin's honor or a woman's shame? And finally, have we not seen that in the modern world monogamy and prostitution, while antithetical, are also inseparable—opposite poles of the same state of society? Can prostitution disappear without dragging monogamy with it into the abyss?

Here a new element comes into play, an element which, at the time monogamy was developing, existed at most in germ: individual sex-love.

Before the Middle Ages we cannot speak of individual sex-love. . . . Throughout Antiquity, marriages were arranged by the parents, while the partners quietly accepted their choices. . . . Love relationships in the modern sense occurred in Classical times only outside of official society. . . .

Our sexual love differs essentially from the simple sexual desire—*eros*—of the Ancients. In the first place ours assumes that love is shared by both partners; to this extent the woman is on an equal footing with the man, while in the eros of Antiquity she was often not even consulted. In the second place, our sexual love has an intensity and a duration that makes both partners feel that non-possession or separation are a great calamity. In order to possess one another they risk high stakes, even life itself. . . . And finally, a new moral standard has arisen for judging a sexual relationship: we not only ask, Was it within or outside of marriage? but also, Did it spring from love—reciprocated love? Of course, this new standard fares no better in feudal or bourgeois practice than all the other standards of morality—i.e., it is simply ignored. Neither does it fare any worse, however. . . .

Marriage according to the bourgeois conception was a contract, a legal transaction, and the most important one of all, because it disposed of two human beings, body and soul, for life. . . .

The rising bourgeoisie . . . increasingly recognized freedom of contract in marriage, . . . [which] remained class marriage; but within the class the partners were conceded a certain degree of freedom of choice. On paper, in ethical theory, and in poetic description, nothing was more immutably established than that every marriage is immoral which does not rest on mutual sexual love and perfectly free agreement of husband and wife. In sum, the love marriage was proclaimed as a human right, and indeed not only as . . . one of the rights of man, but also one of the rights of woman. . . .

The ruling class, however, remains dominated by the familiar economic influences, providing instances of freely contracted marriages only in rare cases. . . . Hence, full freedom of marriage can be generally established only with the abolition of capitalist production and property relations, . . . [thereby] removing all the . . . considerations that still exert such a powerful influence on the choice of a marriage partner. Then no other motive will remain except mutual attraction. . . .

What will certainly disappear from monogamy are all the features stamped on it by its origin in property relations: namely, male supremacy and marital indissolubility. The supremacy of the male in marriage is simply the result of his economic supremacy; with the abolition of the latter, the former will disappear too. And the indissolubility of marriage . . . has already been breached at a thousand points. If only those marriages based on love are moral, so only those in which love abides. . . . If affection definitely comes to an end, or is supplanted by a new passionate love, then separation is a blessing for both partners, as well as for society. And people will be spared having to wade through the useless mire of a divorce suit.

What we may now conjecture about the ordering of sexual relations after the impending overthrow of capitalist production is mainly negative, limited for the most part to what will disappear. But what will be new? That will be answered by a new generation—a generation of men who have never known what it is to buy a woman's surrender with money or with any other instrument of social power; a generation of women who have never known what it is to give themselves to a man for any other consideration than true love, or to refuse to give themselves to their lover from the fear of economic consequences. When these people are in the world, they will care little what anybody now thinks they ought to do; they will make heir own practice and form their own opinion about the practice of others. . . .

SUSAN B. ANTHONY: ON WOMEN'S SUFFRAGE

From I. H. Harper, *The Life and Work of Susan B. Anthony* (2 vols., Indianapolis, 1898), 2:997ff.

The following excerpts from a typical speech—usually before men's groups—illustrates the kind of intelligence and resourcefulness that led to the ultimate success of the women's-suffrage movement in the United States. Miss Anthony's motto was: The true republic—men, their rights and nothing more; women, their rights and nothing less.

The Degradation of Disenfranchisement

It is said that women do not need the ballot for their protection because they are supported by men. Statistics show that there are 3,000,000 women in this nation supporting themselves. In the crowded cities of the East they are compelled to work in shops, stores, and factories for the merest pittance. In New York alone there are over 50,000 of these women receiving less than fifty cents a day. Women wage-earners in different occupations have organized themselves into trades unions, from time to time, and made their strikes to get justice at the hands of their employers just as men have done, but I have yet to learn of a successful strike of any body of women. . . .

My friends, the condition of [working] women but represents the utter helplessness of disenfranchisement. The question with you, as men, is not whether you want your wives and daughters to vote, nor . . . whether you yourselves want to vote; but whether you will help to put this power of the ballot into the hands of the 3,000,000 wage-earning women, so that they may be able to compel politicians to legislate in their favor and employers to grant them justice. . . .

It was cruel, under the old regime, to give rich men the right to rule poor men. It was wicked to allow white men absolute power over black men. It is vastly more cruel, more wicked to give all men—rich and poor, white and black, native and foreign, educated and ignorant, virtuous and vicious—this absolute control over women. Men talk of the injustice of monopolies. There never was, there never can be, a monopoly so fraught with injustice, tyranny, and degradation as this monopoly of sex, of all men over all women. Therefore, I not only agree with Abraham Lincoln that, "No man is good enough to govern another man without his consent"; but I say also that no man is good enough to govern a woman without her consent, and further, that all men combined in government are not good enough to govern all women without their consent. There might have been some plausible excuse for the rich governing the poor, the educated governing the ignorant, the Saxon governing the African; but there can be none for making the husband the ruler of the wife, the brother of the sister, the man of the woman, his peer in birth, in education, in social position, in all that stands for the best and highest in humanity. . . .

Men say it is not votes, but the law of supply and demand which regulated wages. The law of gravity is that water shall run downhill, but when men build a dam across the stream, the force of gravity is stopped and the water held back. The law of supply and demand regulates free and enfranchised labor, but disfranchisement stops its operation. What we ask is the removal of the dam, that women, like men, may reap the benefit of the law. Did the law of supply and demand regulate work and wages in the olden days of slavery? This law can no more reach the disenfranchised than it did the enslaved. There is scarcely a place where a woman can earn a single dollar without a man's consent.

There are many women equally well qualified with men for principals and superintendents of schools, and yet, while three-fourths of the teachers are women, nearly all of them are relegated to subordinate positions on half or at most two-thirds the salaries paid to men. The law of supply and demand is ignored, and that of sex alone settles the question. If a business man should advertise for a bookkeeper and ten young men, equally well qualified, should present themselves and, after looking them over, he should say, "To you who have red hair, we will pay full wages, while to you with black hair we will pay half the regular price," that would not be a more flagrant violation of the law of supply and demand than is that now perpetrated upon women because of their sex. . . .

Denied the ballot, the legitimate means with which to exert their influence, and as a rule being lovers of peace, [women] have recourse to prayers and tears, those potent weapons of women and children, and when they fail, must tamely submit to wrong or rise in rebellion against the powers that be. Women's crusades against saloons, brothels and gambling dens, emptying kegs and bottles into the streets, breaking doors and windows and burning houses, all go to prove that disenfranchisement, the denial of lawful means to gain desired ends, may drive even women to violations of law and order. Hence to secure both national and "domestic tranquility," to "establish justice," to carry out the spirit of our Constitution, put into the hands of all women, as you have into those of all men, the ballot, that symbol of perfect equality, that right protective of all other rights.

CHAPTER 28
LENIN AND THE RUSSIAN REVOLUTION

Compiled and Edited by Robert J. Devlin, Ph.D.

Lenin almost missed the revolution! By the time he reached Russia in April 1917, Tsar Nicholas II had been overthrown and a Provisional Government formed which had already called for the election of a constituent assembly—all in the tradition of European liberal revolutions from 1789 to 1848. But Lenin, returning to Russia from his exile in Switzerland, had other ideas on how to run a revolution. His slogans were appealing: "Peace, Land, Bread!" "Worker Control of Production!" "All power to the Soviets!"

In a country burdened with intolerable scarcity, with a disintegrating economy, with a land-hungry peasantry, with a working class that was on the march and a soldiery that was decimated and dispirited, Lenin's slogans struck home. A superb tactician, he waited for the Provisional Government to exhaust its credibility. Unable to successfully prosecute the war or to satisfy the demands of workers, peasants, and soldiers, that government was ripe for a well-timed coup d'état.

If genius is the capacity for taking infinite pains in quest of a remote objective, Lenin had it. Twenty-five years of revolutionary writing and activity had prepared him for his mission. In 1902, in a tract titled *What Is To Be Done?* Lenin had already revised Marx's philosophy to give it the discipline and the strategy needed for a revolutionary movement locked in mortal combat with an authoritarian regime.

Even before he went to Russia, Lenin had decided that the most likely agency to effect a socialist revolution was the popularly elected soviets (councils) of workers' and soldiers' deputies, which had formed in the midst of the February Revolution. With their support and that of the Bolshevik Party, Lenin, together with Leon Trotsky, successfully engineered the seizure of power on the night of October 25.

After February, Bolshevik influence had grown proportionally as the Provisional Government alienated more and more people by its ineffectiveness and procrastination. The problems that would face Russia in wartime had been predicted as early as 1914 by a tsarist bureaucrat, Durnovo. Those same problems brought down the old regime in February 1917 and they would inevitably cut the ground from under the Provisional Government if it too failed to solve them.

Whereas the uprising in February had been unplanned and uncoordinated, the collapse of the Provisional Government was accelerated by Lenin and the Bolshevik Party through the mobilization of popular disaffection. The parties of the Right and Center having been discredited, the Bolsheviks were the only socialist party willing and able to respond forcibly and directly to the forces demanding change.

In the light of history, how will Lenin ultimately be regarded? Great leader or evil genius? Ideologue or opportunist? Marxist or Machiavellian?

THE COMING CRISIS

LENIN: WHAT IS TO BE DONE? (1902)

V.I. Lenin, *Collected Works* (New York: International Publishers, 1929), 4:109–110, 122–123, 198–199, 210ff. Reprinted by permission of International Publishers, Inc.

Son of a provincial tsarist bureaucrat, brother of Alexander Ulianov who was executed for plotting the assassination of the tsar, Lenin threw over a career in law to become a professional revolutionary. He subsequently spent five years in Siberian exile as punishment for his radicalism, where he continued his study of Marx and revolution. But Lenin was not a theorist in the same sense as Marx; he was a strategist, not a grand conceptualizer. In the fifty-five volumes of the latest edition of his collected writings there is but a small fraction that is not of a polemical nature. *What Is To Be Done?*, one of Lenin's most famous works, falls within this category. It is an assault on an opposing faction in the Russian Marxist movement that favored a more open revolutionary party structure that might merge with the Russian labor movement. Although it was written in the heat of a particular controversy at a particular historical juncture, many commentators have come to feel that it represents the heart of "Leninism" and a key to understanding the Russian Revolution. Others argue that Bolshevik policy in 1917 was forged in the midst of the contingencies of the moment. The reader might bear this issue in mind as he peruses these documents.

Without a revolutionary theory there can be no revolutionary movement. . . . The history of all countries shows that the working class, exclusively by its own efforts, is able to develop only trade-union consciousness. . . . The theory of socialism grew out of the philosophical, historical, and economic theories that were elaborated by the educated representatives of the propertied classes, the intellectuals. The founders of modern scientific Socialism, Marx and Engels, themselves belonged to the bourgeois intelligentsia. Similarly in Russia, the theoretical doctrine of Social Democracy arose quite independently of the spontaneous growth of the labor movement; it arose as a natural and inevitable outcome of the development of ideas among the revolutionary socialist intelligentsia. . . .

Subservience to the spontaneity of the labor movement, the belittling of the role of "the conscious element," of the role of Social Democracy, *means, whether one likes it or not, growth of influence of bourgeois ideology among the workers.* . . .

Since there can be no talk of an independent ideology being developed by the masses of the workers in the process of their movement, then *the only choice is:* either bourgeois or socialist ideology. There is no middle course, for humanity has not created a "third" ideology, and, moreover, in a society torn by class antagonism there can never be a non-class or above-class ideology. Hence, to belittle Socialist ideology *in any way,* to *deviate from it in the slightest degree,* means strengthening bourgeois ideology. . . . Therefore our task, the task of Social Democracy, is to *combat spontaneity,* to *divert* the labor movement, with its spontaneous trade-unionist striving, from under the wing of the bourgeoisie and bring it under the wing of revolutionary Social Democracy. . . .

We must have a committee of professional *revolutionaries* . . . irrespective of whether they are students or working men. I assert: 1) That no movement can be durable without a stable organization of leaders to maintain continuity; 2) that the more widely the masses are drawn into the struggle and form the basis of the movement, the more necessary it is to have such an organization and the more stable it must be—otherwise it is much easier for demagogues to sidetrack the more backward sections of the masses; 3) that the organization must consist chiefly of persons engaged in revolution as a profession; 4) that in a country with a despotic government, the more we *restrict* the membership of this organnization to persons who are engaged in revolution as a profession and who have been professionally trained in the art of combating the political police, the more difficult will it be to catch the organization; and 5) the *wider* will be the circle of men and women of the working class or of other classes of society able to join the movement and perform active work in it. . . .

But to concentrate all secret functions in the hands of as small a number of professional revolutionaries as possible does not mean that the latter will "do the thinking for all" and that the crowd will not take an active part in the movement. On the contrary, the crowd will advance from its ranks increasing numbers of professional revolutionaries, for it will know that it is not enough for a few students and working men waging economic war to gather together and form a "committee," but that professional revolutionaries must be trained for years. . . .

It is . . . argued against us that the views on organization here expounded contradict the "principles of democracy." . . . Everyone will probably agree that "broad principles of democracy" presupposes the two following conditions: first, full publicity and second, election to all functions. . . .

Try to picture this in the frame of our autocracy! Is it possible in Russia for all those "who accept the principles of the party program, and render it all the support they can," to control every action of the revolutionary working in secret? Is it possible for all the revolutionaries to elect one of their number to any particular office when, in the interest of the work, he *must conceal his identity* from nine out of ten of these "all"? Ponder a little over the real meaning of the high-sounding phrase . . . and you will realize that "broad democracy" in party organization, amidst the gloom of autocracy and the domination of the gendarmes, is nothing more than a *useless and harmful toy.*

It is a useless toy, because as a matter of fact, no revolutionary organization has ever practiced *broad* democracy, nor could it, however much it desired to do so.

It is a harmful toy, because any attempt to practice the "broad principles of democracy" will simply facilitate the work of the police in making big raids, it will perpetuate the prevailing primitiveness, divert the thoughts of the practical workers from the serious and imperative task of training themselves to become professional revolutionaries to that of drawing up detailed "paper" rules for election systems. Only abroad, where very often people who have no opportunity of doing real live work gather together, can the "game of democracy" be played here and there, especially in small groups.

THE DURNOVO MEMORDANDUM (FEBRUARY 1914)

From *Documents of Russian History, 1914–1917*, ed. F.A. Golder, copyright Appelton-Century-Crofts, Inc. New York, 1927.

In early 1914 Peter N. Durnovo (1844–1915) was concluding a long career as a tsarist functionary, thirty-five years of which were spent in leading posts in the ministries of Justice and Interior. The latter post put him in charge of the tsarist security forces, perhaps the most adept branch of the autocratic regime. Durnovo was a profound conservative, some would say reactionary, but he was a keen observer of Russia's domestic circumstances as well as of Russia's place in the world. The prospect of an outbreak of war in Europe which would see Russian involvement on the side of England and France concerned Durnovo greatly. In his memorandum to Tsar Nicholas II, February 1914, Durnovo outlined his fears for Russia's future. They proved to be prophetic.

The main burden of the war will undoubtedly fall on us, since England is hardly capable of taking a considerable part in a continental war, while France, poor in manpower, will probably adhere to strictly defensive tactics in view of the enormous losses by which war will be attended under present conditions of military technique. The part of a battering-ram, making a breach in the very thick of the German defense, will be ours, with many factors against us to which we shall have to devote great effort and attention. . . . Are we prepared for so stubborn a war as the future war of the European nations will undoubtedly become? This question we must answer, without evasion, in the negative. . . .

For there can be no doubt that the war will necessitate expenditures which are beyond Russia's limited financial means. We shall have to obtain credit from allied and neutral countries, but this will not be granted gratuitously. As to what will happen if the war should end disastrously for us, I do not wish to discuss now. The financial and economic consequences of defeat can be neither calculated nor foreseen, and will undoubtedly spell the total ruin of our entire national economy.

. . . An especially favorable soil for social upheavals is found in Russia, where the masses undoubtedly profess, unconsciously, the principles of socialism. In spite of the spirit of antagonism to the Government in Russian society, as unconscious as the socialism of the broad masses of the people, a political revolution is not possible in Russia and any revolutionary movement must degenerate into a socialist movement. The opponents of the Government have no popular support. The people see no difference between a government official and an intellectual. The Russian masses, whether workmen or peasants, are not looking for political rights, which they neither want nor comprehend.

The peasant dreams of obtaining a gratuitous share of somebody else's land; the workman, of getting hold of the entire capital and profits of the manufacturer. Beyond this, they have no aspirations. If these slogans are scattered far and wide among the populace, and the Government permits agitation along these lines, Russia will be flung into anarchy, such as she suffered in the ever-memorable period of troubles in 1905−6. War with Germany would create exceptionally favorable conditions for such agitation. As already stated, this war is pregnant with enormous difficulties for us and cannot turn out to be a mere triumphal march to Berlin. Both military disasters—partial ones, let us hope—and all kinds of shortcomings in our supply are inevitable. In the excessive nervousness and spirit of opposition of our society, these events will be given an exaggerated importance, and all the blame will be laid on the Government. . . .

In the legislative institutions a bitter campaign against the Government will begin, followed by revolutionary agitations throughout the country, with socialist slogans, capable of arousing and rallying the masses, beginning with the division of the land and succeeded by a division of all valuables and property. The defeated army, having lost its most dependable men, and carried away by the tide of primitive peasant desire for land, will find itself too demoralized to serve as a bulwarrk of law and order. The legislative institutions and the intellectual opposition parties, lacking any real authority in the eyes of the people, will be powerless to stem the popular tide, aroused by themselves, and Russia will be flung into hopeless anarchy, the issue of which cannot be foreseen.

THE PROVISIONAL GOVERNMENT: KERENSKY'S ASSESSMENT

Reprinted from the *Slavonic Review*, London, Vol. 11, No. 31, July 1932 by permission of *The Slavonic and East European Review*.

Alexander Kerensky, head of the Provisional Government from July until October 1917, relates some of the obstacles facing the moderate revolutionaries. The vacuum caused by the collapse of the tsarist regime in February was filled by the "Provisional Executive Committee of the members of the Duma." This so-called *Provisional Government* was to rule Russia until a constituent assembly could be elected for the purpose of drafting a new constitution. With the exception of Kerensky, a Socialist-Revolutionary, the original cabinet was composed entirely of bourgeois members. Kerensky did not become head of the Government until July.

To prevent a civil war was the whole object of the internal policy of the Provisional Government. After the collapse of the monarchy, the Provisional Government, in the midst of war, was obliged to restore, from top to bottom, the administrative apparatus of the state and to fix the foundations of a new state and social order. Two conditions for the attainment of [these] objectives of internal policy prevented the application of a dictatorial or . . . "strong" government. First of all, to form a "strong" dictatorial government . . . it was necessary to have at one's disposal a highly organized and well-functioning administration and police. Such a machinery the Provisional Government did not possess. It had to be created anew under the most difficult circumstances. But until it was established, the government had to replace police compulsion by moral persuasion. . . .

The second condition which determined the internal policy of the Provisional Government was the war. By its very nature the war demanded the closest national unity, which under existing conditions was hard to achieve.

. . . At the front there was a mass of more than ten million soldiers, highly agitated, recognizing only the Left socialist parties as an authority. It was also necessary to maintain the efficiency of thousands of officers whose position was highly precarious. The great majority of these officers recognized the political authority of the bourgeois parties. Of these parties, the Cadets or Constitutional Democrats, led by Professor Miliukov, was the most influential. Up to the fall of the monarchy this party had represented the liberal-radical wing of the bourgeois opposition. However, at the time of the February Revolution, when the old conservative parties disappeared from the scene, the Cadet Party became the chief spokesman of the Right. . . .

The Provisional Government's . . . major purpose was to unite all the creative forces of the country in order (1) to reestablish the functioning of the state apparatus, (2) to create the basis of a new post-revolutionary political and social order, and (3) to continue the defense of the country. The only way of opposing the forces of disruption which were driving the country into chaos and civil war, was to draw into the government the leading representatives of all political parties without exception, whether bourgeois or socialist, which recognized the new order and the supreme authority of the Constituent Assembly. It was clear that the latter had to be summoned, in spite of the war, at the earliest possible date.

It must be said that the collapse of the monarchy came about so unexpectedly for the socialist parties that their leaders did not at once understand their own role in the new political conditions. Suddenly the masses of the people—workers, peasants and soldiers—had obtained an overwhelming power in the life of the state. In the first days of the Revolution it seemed to the leaders of the Left that the deciding role in the administration of the state had already passed into the hands of the Liberals and that the socialist parties, although not part of the government, ought to help the government but only in so far as it did not act against the interests of the working class. This so-called "dualism," the sharing of power between the Soviets and the Government, in the first two months of the February Revolution was partly due to the failure of the socialist parties to appreciate their importance and the part they would have to play in the post-revolutionary period. Conscientiously playing the role of a kind of responsible opposition to the government, the Soviets failed to see that their pressures weakened the broken administrative machinery and the bourgeois classes.

In spite of a generally held opinion, it is precisely the strictly bourgeois original composition of the Provisional Government—in which, out of eleven ministers, I was the only representative of the non-bourgeois democracy—that was the cause of the [great] "weakness of authority" of that government. Moreover—and here again we have a paradox—it was just this cabinet that carried out all the programs of the radical political and social reforms. . . .

As a matter of fact, it was precisely the first "capitalist" cabinet of the Provisional Government which issued a number of decrees on freedom of speech, assembly, inviolability of person; worked out the great agrarian reform (the abolition of non-laboring land tenure and landed property); prepared the law on self-government of county and town councils on the basis of proportional universal suffrage without distinction of sex; introduced workers' control into factories and workshops; gave wide powers to workers' trade unions; introduced the eight-hour working day; laid down the principles of cooperative legislation; formulated the plan for transforming the Empire into a federation of free peoples; drew up the principles of the electoral law for the Constituent Assembly, etc. And all this vast legislative work, which transformed the political and social system of Russia, the Provisional Government carried out without any pressure "from the Soviet democracy." Of its own free will it achieved the social and political ideals of the whole Russian liberation movement, liberal and revolutionary. . . .

ORDER NO. 1 OF THE PETROGRAD SOVIET

From *Documents of Russian History, 1914–1917*, ed. F.A. Golder, copyright Appleton-Century-Crofts, Inc., New York, 1927.

One of the most famous acts associated with the February Revolution, Order No. 1, was issued by the Petrograd Soviet of Workers' and Soldiers' Deputies. Dramatically democratizing the armed forces in recognition of the Petrograd garrison's role in overthrowing the old regime, it enraged the officer corps and other conservative elements. Note the demand for personal dignity in Article 7.

To the garrison of the Petrograd District, to all the military in the guard, army, artillery, and navy, for immediate and strict execution, and to the workers of Petrograd for their information:

The Soviet of Workers' and Soldiers' Deputies has resolved:

1. In all companies, battalions, regiments, parks, batteries, squadrons, in the special services of the various military administrations, and on the vessels of the navy, committees from the elected representatives of the lower ranks of the above-mentioned military units shall be chosen immediately.

2. In all those military units that have not yet chosen their representatives to the Soviet of Workers' Deputies, one representative from each company shall be selected,

to report with written credentials at the building of the State Duma by 10 o'clock on the morning of the second of March.

3. In all its political actions, the military branch is subordinated to the Soviet of Workers' and Soldiers' Deputies and to its own committees.

4. The orders of the Military Commission of the State Duma shall be executed only in such cases as do not conflict with the orders and resolutions of the Soviet of Workers' and Soldiers' Deputies.

5. All kinds of arms, such as rifles, machine guns, armored automobiles, and others, must be kept at the disposal and under the control of the company and battalion committees, and in no case should they be turned over to officers, even at their demand.

6. In the ranks and during their performance of the duties of the service, soldiers must observe the strictest military discipline, but outside the service and the ranks . . . soldiers cannot in any way be deprived of those rights that all citizens enjoy. In particular, standing at attention and compulsory saluting, when not on duty, is abolished.

7. Also, the addressing of the officers with the titles "Your Excellency," "Your Honor," etc. is abolished, and these titles are replaced by . . . "Mister General," "Mister Colonel," etc. Rudeness toward soldiers of any rank, and especially addressing them as "thou" is prohibited, and soldiers are required to bring to the attention of the company committees every infraction of this rule. . . .

The present Order is to be read to all companies, battalions, regiments, ships' crews, batteries, and other combatant and non-combatant commands.

PETROGRAD SOVIET OF WORKERS' AND SOLDIERS' DEPUTIES
March 1, 1917

CAPITAL AND LABOR

Reprinted from *The Russian Provisional Government, 1917: Documents, Volumes II and III,* Selected and edited by Robert Paul Browder and Alexander F. Kerensky, with the permission of the publishers, Stanford University Press. © 1961 by the Board of Trustees of the Leland Stanford Junior University, II, 712.

Marxism posits a central role for the proletariat in a socialist revolution. The following documents illustrate aspects of the class struggle between capital and labor in 1917. First is an agreement reached in early March which established important gains for the Petrograd workers. The succeeding documents, however, show a rising animosity between capital and labor.

An agreement has been reached between the Petrograd Soviet of Workers' and Soldiers' Deputies and the Petrograd Association of Manufacturers on the introduction of an eight-hour working day in factories and mills and on the establishment of factory committees and chambers of conciliation.

I. The eight-hour working day.
1. Pending the promulgation of the law standardizing the working day, the eight-hour working day, . . . applicable to all shifts, is introduced in all factories and mills.
2. On Saturdays the working day is . . . seven hours.
3. The reduction in working hours is to have no effect on workers' wages.
4. Overtime is permitted only with the consent of factory committees.
II. Factory committees.
1. Factory committees, elected from workers of a given enterprise on the basis of universal, equal, etc., suffrage, are to be established in all factories and mills.
2. The functions of these committees are:
a) to represent the workers in a given enterprise in their relations with government or public institutions.
b) to formulate opinions on questions pertaining to the socioeconomic life of workers in a given enterprise.
c) to settle problems arising from interpersonal relations of workers in a given enterprise.
d) to represent workers before the management in matters concerning labor-management relations.
III. Chambers of conciliation.
1. Chambers of conciliation are to be established in all mills and factories for the purpose of settling all misunderstandings arising from labor-management relations.
2. Chambers of conciliation are to consist of an equal number of elected representatives from workers and from management. . . .
3. The electoral procedure for the workers is to be determined by the factory committee. . . .
5. In the eveng that an agreement between workers and employers is not reached, . . . the matter is then to be carried to and settled by the Central Chamber of Conciliation.
6. The Central Chamber of Conciliation is to consist of an equal number of elected representatives from the Soviet of Workers' Deputies . . . and from the Association of Manufacturers.
IV. The removal of foremen and other administrative officials without examining the case in the chamber of conciliation, and their subsequent more violent removal (by physical force) are prohibited.
V. The matter of employees' status must be determined immediately.

[Toward the end of March the Petrograd Association of Manufacturers informed the Provisional Government that the workers' committees were proving successful:]

It should be pointed out with regard to the activities of the factory committees in many plants, that in a number of cases the factory committees have succeeded in introducing some order and discipline into the working masses. In general, it is to be observed that the influence of the committees is greater the more conscious are the workers. Thus, their authority is much greater, for example, in the metalworking plants, and, on the contrary, very low in those industrial concerns where the workers are comparatively less cultured. . . . [From the Central State Archives of the October Revolution, Moscow, 6935/6:77:47.]

[It was not long, however, before the "order and discipline" of the committees was being extended to circumscribe the perquisites of the employers, or even to dominate them. The industrialists' response is illustrated in the following excerpts from a resolution passed at a conference of industrialists held in Petrograd on June 1−2, 1917.]

From A.L. Sidorov *et al.*, eds., *Ekonomicheskoe polozhenie Rossii nakanune Velikoi Oktiabr'skoi sotsialisticheskoi revoliutsii: Dokumenty i materialy* (Moscow, 1957), 1:181−182 (trans. RJD).

1. One of the most important causes of the critical condition of industry at the present time is the growing anarchy in the country. The Provisional Government . . . must employ its full powers for the support of order in the country, the preservation of freedom and the inviolability of person and property, for the defense of the rights of the citizens. . . .

2. Under the existing conditions of the world economy, no other economic system except capitalism is possible for Russia. Thus, any attempt, even partial attempts in individual enterprises, at the implementation of the socialist principle, are fruitless and absolutely harmful. Interference by workers and employees in the administration of the enterprises, and even more, the virtual subordination of the administration of the enterprises to workers and employees, and even outside persons, by means of the establishment of an electoral basis, or of willful removal of members of the administration, the subordination to them of the financial and economic life of the factory by means of the formation of all sorts of control commissions, leads only to anarchy in the enterprises. . . .

4. With regard to the present high level of wages, means to satisfy the demands of the workers can be attained by industry only at the cost of a further increase in prices for goods. This is in conflict with the interests of the state and the population as a whole. . . .

5. The diversion to the front of a significant part of the working element of the country imperatively demands from the remaining population a rise in labor productivity for the satisfaction of the country's need for manufactured goods. Thus, the interests of the state and the population as a whole are contradicted by measures carried out by separate groups [of workers] on their own initiative or under pressure from those who are actually bringing production to a standstill, e.g., the eight-hour working day for workers, six hours for employees, and the case of the change from piece-work wages [to hourly rates]. . . .

[But the workers' movement remained unchecked, and in September the largest organization of industrialists published the following front-page editorial in the first edition of its newspaper.*]

*Izvestiia Vserossiiskogo soiuza obshchestv zavodchikov i fabrikantov, Sept. 14, 1917 (trans. RJD).

The present period in the history of human society assigns to each class a specific historical role, and to struggle for the fulfillment of that role, within the limits good for the whole state, is the duty of every class. . . . The industrialist class throughout the entire world is the class of human progress and culture, the class of technology and science, the class of human genius and organization. The creativity of the industrialist class in all areas of life opens before humanity new horizons for the restructuring of human society. Class struggle is a normal phenomenon of the life of the state, developing and intensifying it, and while it is carried on within the limits of the state, it is undoubtedly an extraordinarily important factor of political life. Russia is no exception.

PEASANTRY IN REVOLT: DISTRICT COMMISSAR'S REPORT (JUNE 14, 1917)

From *Readings in Russian History*, ed. W.B. Walsh (Syracuse University Press, 1963), 3:696f.

Numerous and longstanding grievances of the peasants, some dating back to the terms of serf emancipation in 1861, burst forth in 1917. The first document below reflects the helplessness felt by officials of the Provisional Government in the face of this elemental upsurge. The second document is a commentary from a conservative newspaper published shortly before the October Revolution.

On the 4th of June, at the town of Desna, . . . the Commissar convoked a Peasants' Convention of the Vitebsk Gubernia and of . . . part of the District of Novoalexandrovsk. . . . About 400 representatives, peacefully minded peasants, appeared. Speakers from the extreme left-wing parties (the Socialist Revolutionaries) appeared and excited the whole assembly. [They declared:] "All the land is ours, and you may now take all you need in accordance with the resolutions of the volost committees—fields, forests, meadows, ponds, etc.—and in order to legalize this, so that it will not be considered as a seizure, you have to pay, not to the owners but to the volost committees—the very lowest rent. . . ."

It was suggested that they replace all foresters on privately owned and state owned lands with persons of their own choice. The charge for grinding grain was set at the lowest figure imaginable, and the millers, unwilling to work for such pay, refused to work. In such cases, the volost committees seize the mills. All waters, ponds and rivers are taken over by the volost committees . . . and former tenants are sent away. Private owners are permitted to harvest hay for their own use, but only up to 10 July and on condition that they do it by their own efforts without hired help. So, according to this convention, private owners and their tenants are completely excluded from managing their land, and everything goes over to the hands of the volost or village committees. Persons unqualified for the duties are elected to the volost committees. Those who promise to take all private land from the owners and give it to the peasants are elected. Private owners are entitled only to that which they can cultivate by their own strength. Until this resolution was adopted, I managed, although with great difficulty, to restrain the peasants of the Novoalexandrovsk District from more seizures, illegal grazing, forest cutting, etc. But I am no longer able to do this. When the peasant delegates return from the convention, they recount all the speeches they heard, and they take no notice of my protests, saying that they heard differently at the convention. . . .

The duties of the elected District Commissars are very difficult. When trying to stop seizures, and when remonstrating with the peasants at volost meetings, they cry: "We elected you and if you won't stick with us, we will fire you."

From *Novoe Vremia*, Oct. 3, 1917, in Browder and Kerensky, *Documents*, 2:593–594.

Not a day goes by that news does not appear in the press about the atrocious pogroms which take place in the village. In the spirit of anarchy, the propaganda-inspired masses are not satisfied to seize the lands of the private owners. They also remove the workers from properties, fell forests, and destroy crops.

The nonresistance of the Provisional Government, which limits itself in the struggle with anarchy to mere appeals, which naturally no one takes seriously, has resulted in veritable pogroms by the population in its efforts to seize land. Estates of private owners are destroyed by arson and other ways. Livestock and equipment are seized. Various agricultural enterprises are put out of use completely. The owners and their employees, in so far as they succeed in saving themselves from attacks or actual murder, flee to the cities, leaving their estates to the mercy of fate. The lands remain unsown or are sown in any way hastily, by the usurpers who down in their hearts realize very well their guilt and the insecurity of the seizures. But this is beside the point now.

The formula of Bolshevism, "peace at the front and war in the rear," now assumes a particularly menacing character because any intensification of civil war obviously is immediately reflected in a weakening of our resistance at the front.

We wonder: will our provisional rulers limit themselves now also to appeals to combat the pogroms or will they take other and more vigorous measures?

Reprinted from *The Russian Provisional Government, 1917: Documents, Volumes II and III*, Selected and edited by Robert Paul Browder and Alexander F. Kerensky, with the permission of the publishers, Stanford University Press. © 1961 by the Board of Trustees of the Leland Stanford Junior University.

LENIN'S APRIL THESES (1917)

From *Pravda*, April 7 (20), 1917, in Browder and Kerensky, *Documents*, 3:1205–1207.

The Bolshevik party's initial response to the February Revolution was to join other socialist parties in supporting the Provisional Government. At that time Lenin was living in exile in Switzerland. German socialists prevailed upon the German High Command to allow Lenin to cross Germany in order to reach Russia. The High Command's acquiescence in this plan was not without ulterior motives: They saw the advantage to Germany of giving their enemy an energetic opponent of the "imperialistic war," as

Lenin termed it. And on his arrival in Petrograd he proclaimed the following theses, first to a popular assembly and then to a meeting of Bolshevik faithful, who gave his views a cool reception. The April Theses were also published in *Pravda*, the Bolshevik newspaper.

1. In our attitude toward the war not the slightest concession must be made to "revolutionary defensism," for under the new government of Lvov & Co., owing to the capitalist nature of that government, the war on Russia's part remains a predatory imperialist war. . . .

   In view of the undoubted honesty of the mass of rank and file representatives of revolutionary defensism who accept the war only as a necessity and not as a means of conquest, in view of their being deceived by the bourgeoisie, it is necessary most thoroughly, persistently, and patiently to explain to them their error, to explain the inseparable connection between capital and the imperialist war, to prove that without the overthrow of capital it is *impossible* to conclude the war with a really democratic, non-oppressive peace.

   This view is to be widely propagated among the army units in the field.

2. The peculiarity of the present situation in Russia is that it represents a *transition* from the first stage of the revolution—which, because of the inadequate organization and insufficient class-consciousness of the proletariat, led to the assumption of power by the bourgeoisie—to its second stage which is to place power in the hands of the proletariat and the poorest strata of the peasantry. . . .

3. No support of the Provisional Government; exposure of the utter falsity of all its promises, particularly those relating to the renunciation of annexations. . . .

4. Recognition of the fact that in most of the Soviets of Workers' Deputies our party constitutes a minority, and a small one at that, in the face of the bloc of all the petty-bourgeois opportunist elements, from the People's Socialists, Socialist-Revolutionists, down to the Organization Committees . . . who have yielded to the influence of the bourgeoisie and [who] have been extending this influence to the proletariat as well. . . .

5. Not a parliamentary republic—a return to it from the Soviets of Workers' Deputies would be a step backward—but a republic of Soviets of Workers', Agricultural Laborers', and Peasants' Deputies throughout the land, from top to bottom.

   Abolition of the police, the army, the bureaucracy.*

   All officers to be elected and to be subject to recall at any time, their salaries not to exceed the average of a competent worker. . . .

6. Confiscation of all private lands.

   Nationalization of all lands in the country, and management of such lands by local Soviets of Agricultural Laborers' and Peasants' Deputies. . . .

7. Immediate merger of all banks in the country into one general national bank, over which the Soviet of Workers' Deputies should have control. . . .

---

*Substituting for the standing army the universal arming of the people.

8. Not the "introduction" of Socialism as an immediate task, but the immediate placing of the Soviet of Workers' Deputies in control of social production and distribution of goods.

9. Party tasks:
   A. Immediate calling of a party convention.
   B. Changing the party program, mainly:
      1. Concerning imperialism and the imperialist war.
      2. Concerning our attitude toward the state, and our demand for a "commune state.*
      3. Amending our antiquated minimum program.
   C. Changing the name of the party.†

10. Rebuilding the International.
    Taking the initiative in the creation of a revolutionary International, an International against the social-chauvinists and against the "center."‡

THE JULY DAYS

From P.N. Miliukov, *Political Memoirs, 1905–1917* (Ann Arbor: University of Michigan Press, 1967), p. 470.

The revolutionary upsurge on the part of the workers, peasants, and soldiers, as the year progressed, caused Lenin to admonish his fellow party leaders to get in step: "The country is a thousand times to the left of [the Mensheviks] and a hundred times to the left of [the Bolsheviks]." By early July, stirred up by anarchists and rank-and-file Bolsheviks, the militancy of the soldiers and workers in Petrograd could not be contained. Thousands of armed demonstrators marched on the Taurida Palace, seat of the All-Russian Congress of Soviets, and demanded that the moderate socialist leadership of that body overthrow the Provisional Government and constitute itself a revolutionary government. The following anecdote about the July Days is related by Paul Miliukov, the Constitutional Democratic leader.

. . . Military detachments and crowds of the public streamed day and night during these three days (July 3–5) toward the Taurida Palace where the Soviet was in session, and there they held the Soviet in an uninterrupted state of siege. Instances of the

---

*A state the model for which was given by the Paris Commune.
†Instead of "Social Democracy," whose official leaders throughout the world have betrayed Socialism by going over to the bourgeoisie, . . . we must call ourselves the *Communist Party.*
‡The *center* in international Social Democracy is the tendency vacillating between chauvinists ("defensists") and internationalists.

bloodless struggle flared up, while at times, real chaos threatened. Tsereteli bravely held the line; the sessions continued, delegations were received, proposals were heard and discussed, reports were delivered, decisions were made. At times the crowd demanded that the ministers come outside. They wanted to arrest Tsereteli but could not find him. They caught Chernov on the porch, and a strapping worker shouted out to him in a frenzied voice, shaking his fist in Chernov's face: "Take power, you son of a bitch, when they give it to you." The Kronstadt sailors dragged him into a car as a hostage so that the Soviets would take "all power," and only Trotsky let him go.

DELO NARODA ON THE DEEPENING CRISIS

From *Delo naroda,* September 27 (October 10), 1917, in Browder and Kerensky, *Documents,* 3:1711–1712.

The following article from the Socialist-Revolutionary newspaper *Delo naroda* [Peoples' Affairs] indicates the critical situation facing the population and the Provisional Government after the failure of a right-wing coup led by General Kornilov in late August. The popular mood depicted in the article suggests a mixture of militancy and despair.

Yes, bolshevism is gaining ground in factories and in the Soviets of Workers' Deputies. Bolsheviks are elected to volost committees, to municipal dumas. They and the "left S.R.s" succeed, and sometimes with no special effort, in passing their "left" resolutions: "all power to the Soviets," "peace on all fronts." All this is indisputable. But along with this weariness and apathy of the popular masses is growing, at the same time, another wing—the right, the counterrevolutionary wing—and even pogrom tendencies are ripening. In Moscow, which but recently was regarded as [dominated by the] S.R.s, thanks to the brilliant victory of the S.R.s during the elections to the central municipal duma—in this Moscow, according to recent reports, at the elections to district dumas, the Bolsheviks took first place, the K.D. second, the S.R. third, and the Mensheviks fourth. Moreover, the number of voters dropped 50 percent. The Petrograd Soviet of Workers' Deputies goes over into the hands of the Bolsheviks, and Trotsky is elected president [replacing the Menshevik] Chkheidze. And moreover, of the one thousand members, only 400 participate in the elections. At the Obukhovskii factory where the S.R.s were formerly in complete control, now after the reelection to the Soviet of Workers' Deputies eleven Bolsheviks and two syndicalists are elected, but not one S.R. and not one Menshevik. And moreover, only an insignificant number of workers participate in the elections. Meetings formerly thronged by thousands are now attended only by hundreds. In the villages insignificantly small numbers participate in volost elections—from 3 to 10 percent. . . . The circulation of socialist papers in many places drops; the circulation and influence of the yellow press, on the other hand, increases. Among the popular masses a weariness is observed from conferences, voting, and resolutions. Here and there pogroms flare up. Anarchical speeches begin to sound loudly, such as Bleickhman's recent appeals . . . for assassinations, and settling of accounts with "the whole 'Kornilovshchina,' beginning with Kerensky and Tsereteli. . . ."

With a background of such phenomena, the "country's tendency toward the left" assumes an entirely special character and meaning. We must talk not of the country's leaning toward the left but about the damage to the revolution. Only blind people and fanatics could evaluate these phenomena in any other way. And to all genuine revolutionaries, to whom it should be clear that a revolution can be created only by the will of all the working people, the meaning [to them] of the indicated phenomena is also clear, [with] menacing forebodings for the revolution. If the country's tending toward the left continues, the revolution risks being no better off than at the start. The Bolsheviks and the "left S.R.s" are already proving not to be left enough. They are replaced by the anarchists and syndicalists, on the base of the apathy and inertia of the popular masses.

THE OCTOBER REVOLUTION

MEETING OF THE PETROGRAD SOVIET (OCTOBER 25, 1917)

From *Izvestiia* No. 206, Nov. 7, 1917, in Golder, *Documents*, pp. 616−617.

Leon Trotsky, chairman of the Petrograd Soviet and head of the Soviet's Military Revolutionary Committee (MRC), was the chief public figure in the coup d'état of October 25−26, but the commanding force behind the movement was, of course, Lenin. The following account is from the paper *Izvestiia*, which was not taken over by the Bolsheviks until the next day.

The meeting was opened at 7 P.M. by Trotsky, who said: We learned in the course of the night that the Provisional Government has called for a battalion of picked men from the Tsarskoe Selo, the officers' school from Oranienbaum, and artillery from Pavlovsk. Early in the morning we received information that two [Bolshevik] papers, *Soldat* and *Rabochi Put*, have been closed.

But the MRC was not a passive onlooker, and as a result, all the troops called out by the Government, with the exception of a small group of cadets, have refused to obey orders. In addition, the MRC proposed to the Litovsk regiment that it take upon itself the protection of our newspapers, which was done immediately and the printing presses are working regularly. No attention was paid to the order of the Provisional Government to the cruiser *Aurora* to weigh anchor and leave Petrograd. The cruiser is just where she was yesterday, which is in accordance with the instructions of the MRC. . . .

We were asked if we planned to have an uprising. I replied that the Petrograd Soviet stood for a transfer of power to the hands of the Soviets, and at the present time, today or tomorrow, when the [Second] All-Russian Congress of Soviets opens, this slogan will be put into force. Whether this will lead to an uprising depends not on us but on those who oppose us.

We regard the Provisional Government as nothing more than a pitiful, helpless half-government, which waits the motion of a historical broom to sweep it off, to make room for a real, popular government. The present government has lost everything—support, authority, right, and morale.

But a conflict in the form of an uprising is not in our plan for today or tomorrow, when the All-Russian Congress of Soviets is about to meet. We believe that the Congress will carry through our slogan with considerable force and authority. But if the Government wishes to make use of the hours it still has to live—24, 48, or 72—and comes out against us, then we will counterattack, blow for blow, steel for iron. . . .

From *Documents of Russian History, 1914–1917*, ed. F. A. Golder, copyright Appleton-Century-Crofts, Inc., New York, 1927.

MEETING OF THE PETROGRAD SOVIET (OCTOBER 26, 1917)

From *Izvestiia* No. 207, Nov. 8, 1917, in ibid., pp. 618–619.

The meeting opened at 2:35 P.M. with Trotsky in the chair. He said: In the name of the MRC, I announce that the Provisional Government no longer exists. (Applause.) Some of the Ministers are already under arrest. ("Bravo!") Others soon will be. (Applause.) The revolutionary garrison, under the control of the MRC, has dismissed the Assembly of the Pre-parliament. (Loud applause. "Long live the Military Revolutionary Committee!"). . . . The railway stations, post and telegraph offices, the Petrograd Telegraph Agency, and the State Bank are occupied. . . .

In our midst is Vladimir Ilich Lenin, who, by force of circumstances, was not able to be with us all this time. . . .

Hail the return of Lenin! (Noisy ovation.)

Lenin's Speech

Comrades,

The workers' and peasants' revolution, the need for which the Bolsheviks have emphasized many times, has come to pass.

What is the significance of this revolution? Its significance is that, in the first place, we shall have a soviet government without the participation of any bourgeois of any kind. The oppressed masses will form a government of themselves. The old state machinery will be smashed to bits and in its place will be created a new machinery of government by the soviet organization. From now on, there is a new page in the history

Lenin addressing a meeting in Moscow, May 1920. With a rather high-pitched voiced and not given to histrionics, Lenin's oratorical powers were greatest when addressing smaller groups. The figure in uniform beside the podium is Leon Trotsky. Soviet versions of this picture, however, since the time when Stalin consolidated his power, have all been cropped to eliminate the image of Trotsky, a "nonperson" and "counter-revolutionary." (Culver Pictures.)

of Russia, and the present, third* Russian Revolution will, in its final result, lead to the victory of Socialism.

One of our immediate tasks is to put an end to the war. But in order to end the war, which is closely bound up with the present capitalistic system, it is necessary to overthrow capitalism itself. In doing so we shall have the aid of the world labor movement, which has already begun to develop in Italy, England, and Germany.

An immediate and just offer of peace by us to the international democracy will find everywhere a warm response among the international proletarian masses. In order to secure the confidence of the proletariat, it is necessary to publish at once all the secret treaties.

In the interior of Russia a large part of the peasantry has said: Enough playing with the capitalists; we will go with the workers. So we shall gain the confidence of the peasants by a decree which will wipe out the private property of the landowners. The peasants will see that their only salvation is in union with the workers.

We shall establish the worker's real control over production.

We have now learned how to work together in a friendly way, as evidenced by this revolution. We have the force of mass organization which has conquered over all and which will lead the proletariat to world revolution. We shall now apply ourselves to the building up of a proletarian socialist state in Russia.

Long live the world-wide socialistic revolution!

*Reference to the revolutions of 1905 and February 1917.—Ed.

DISSOLUTION OF THE CONSTITUENT ASSEMBLY
(JANUARY 1918)

From *Izvestiia*, Jan. 20, 1918, in Lenin, *Selected Works*, 2:382−384.

Following the October Revolution, Lenin felt he had to convene the long-promised Constituent Assembly, modeled after the French Constituent Assembly of 1789. It met once on January 18, 1918, after which Lenin dissolved it. He was able to do so because, although the Bolsheviks were a minority in the Assembly, they controlled both the Soviet Executive Committee and the Council of Peoples' Commissars, which had troops available. Exclusive Bolshevik rule, however, did not begin until March 1918 when the Left S-R's, who had been allied with the Bolsheviks, abandoned the coalition over a policy dispute.

At the very beginning of the Russian Revolution the Soviets of Workers', Soldiers', and Peasants' Deputies came to the fore as a mass organization. It brought the toiling and exploited classes together and led them in the fight for full political and economic freedom. During the first period of the revolution the Soviets increased, developed, and grew strong. They learned by experience the futility of compromising with the bourgeoisie, the deception of the bourgeois-democratic parliamentarism, and came to the conclusion that it is not possible to free the downtrodden classes without completely breaking with these forms and compromises. The October Revolution and the taking over of all power by the Soviets constituted such a break.

The Constituent Assembly which was elected on the lists made out before the October Revolution represents the old order, when the compromisers and Cadets were in power. At the time of the voting for the Socialist-Revolutionaries the people were not in a position to decide between the Right Wing—partisans of the bourgeoisie—and the Left Wing, partisans of socialism. This accounts for the fact that the Constituent Assembly, the crown of the bourgeois parliamentary republic, stands in the way of the October Revolution and the Soviet Government. Naturally enough, the October Revolution, which gave power to the Soviets, and through them to the exploited classes, has called forth the opposition of the exploiters. . . .

The laboring classes have learned by experience that the old bourgeois parliament has outlived its usefulness, that it is quite incompatible with the task of establishing socialism, and that the task of overcoming the propertied classes and of laying the basis of a socialistic society cannot be undertaken by a national institution but only by one, such as the Soviet, representing a class. To deny full power to the Soviets . . . in favor of bourgeois parliamentarism or the Constituent Assembly would be a step backward and the death-blow of the October worker-peasant revolution.

The Constituent Assembly which opened on January 18 has . . . a majority of Right Socialist-Revolutionaries, the party of Kerensky, Avksentiev, and Chernov. It is natural that this party should refuse to consider the . . . recommendation of the sovereign organ of the Soviet Government and should refuse to recognize the "Declaration of the Rights of the Toiling and Exploited People," the October Revolution, and the Government of the Soviet. By these very acts the Constituent

Assembly has cut every tie that bound it to the Soviet of the Russian Republic. Under the circumstances the Bolsheviks and Socialist-Revolutionaries of the Left . . . had no choice but to withdraw from the Constituent Assembly.

The majority parties of the Constituent Assembly—the [Right] Socialist-Revolutionaries and Mensheviks—are carrying on an open war against the Soviet, calling . . . for its overthrow, and in this way helping the exploiters in their efforts to block the transfer of the land and the factories to the toilers.

It is clear that this part of the Constituent Assembly can be of help to the bourgeois counterrevolution in its efforts to crush the power of the Soviets. In view of the above, the Central Executive Committee hereby decrees the Constituent Assembly dissolved. . . .

The second sesssion of the Constituent Assembly scheduled for January 19 did not take place. . . .No one except Bolshevik officials was allowed to enter the Taurida Palace. Toward 5 o'clock some of the members came to the palace, . . . but the guard would not let them in.

CHAPTER 29
FASCIST "REVOLUTION" IN ITALY

Young Fascists, on entering the National Fascist Party,
will take the oath before the Political Secretary of the
Fascio di Combattimento, as follows: "In the name of
God and of Italy I swear to carry out without discussion
the orders of the *Duce* and to serve the Cause of the
Fascist Revolution with all my might and if necessary
with my life."
—*Statute of the National Fascist Party, 1932*

The Fascist juggernaut was the invention of Benito Mussolini, who put it together,
by trial and error, from the spare parts of Socialism, Communism, Social
Darwinism, Chauvinism, Elitism, Militarism, Terrorism, Cult of Personality, and
just plain Bluff. The son of a blacksmith, Mussolini (1883–1945) went from editor
of a Socialist newspaper, to propagandist for World War I, to postwar leader of the
Fasci di Combattimento ("combat bands" of terrorists), to member of the Italian
Parliament, to Head of State.

As a member of the Parliament, Mussolini and his thirty-one fellow Fascists
were so successfully obstructionist that they prevented the government from
dealing with its postwar problems. Then in an act of bravado, Mussolini sent his
Fascists in their black shirts to march on Rome, while he himself waited in Milan
to see what would happen. Beyond all expectation, King Victor Emmanuel asked
him to head the government (October 29, 1922). Thus Mussolini won "legally"
what he had been prepared to take by force and terror. Although his party was
only a minority of the Parliament, he soon rectified that situation—not by winning
more seats but by changing the electoral laws.

The following documents illustrate some of the elements in the Fascist
revolution, but since the movement is more one of action than philosophy and
since much of the action is terrorist, you have to interpret the documents carefully
to discover the reality behind the words.

PROGRAM OF THE ITALIAN FASCIST PARTY (AUGUST 1919)

From G.A. Chiurco, *Storia della Rivoluzione Fascista: Anno 1919* (Florence, 1929), 1:240–242).

This program of the Italian Fascist Party in 1919 illustrates the eclectic nature of that weakest of all postwar Italian parties. But as with the later German Nazi Party, it was the quality of its leadership rather than the planks of its program that would pay off.

ITALIANS!
This is the national program of a movement sanely Italian: revolutionary and therefore antidogmatic and antidemagogic; potently innovating because it is beyond prejudicial fixed principles.

We place the enhancement of the values of the revolutionary war above everything and everyone.

Other problems, such as those relating to the bureaucracy, the administrative system, justice, education, the colonies, etc., will be tackled by us once we have created our ruling class.

WE THEREFORE DEMAND:
For the political problem:
a. Universal suffrage with regional . . . proportional representation and woman suffrage and eligibility.

b. The lowering of the minimum age requirement for voters to 18 and for deputies to 25.

c. Abolition of the Senate.

d. The convocation of a national assembly, to meet for three years, whose first task will be the drafting of a Constitution for the State.

e. The establishment of national councils with technical capacities in the fields of labor, industry, transport, social hygiene, communications, etc., to be elected by professional and trade groups and possessing legislative powers as well as the right to elect a general commissary with ministerial powers.

For the social problem:
WE DEMAND
a. The prompt promulgation of a State law establishing an 8-hour legal workday for all workers.

b. A minimum wage law.

c. Worker representatives to participate in the management of industry.

d. Management of public services entrusted to those same proletarian organs (in so far as they may be proven worthy both technically and morally).

e. Prompt and effective settlement of all railway workers' problems as well as those of other transport workers.

f. Modification . . . of disability and old age insurance by lowering the age limit from 65 to 55.

For the military problem:
WE DEMAND
a. Creation of a national militia with short training periods and exclusively for defensive purposes.

b. Nationalization of arms and explosives manufacture.

c. A nationally inspired foreign policy which, by the peaceful competition of civilization, seeks to assert the rights of the Italian nation in the world.

For the financial problem:
WE DEMAND
a. A heavy extraordinary graduated tax on capital to be of such form as to constitute a true PARTIAL EXPROPRIATION of all wealth.

b. Seizure of all possessions of religious associations and the abolition of all episcopal incomes, since these constitute an enormous liability for the Nation and the privilege of a few.

c. The revision of all contracts for war supplies and the seizure of up to 85 percent of war profits.

ITALIANS!
Italian Fascism wishes through its national existence to continue to uphold the rights of the great national spirit which was tempered and hardened by the great test of war; it wishes to keep united—through a form of anti-party and super-party—Italians of all faiths and all productive classes and impel them toward the new and unavoidable battles that must be fought in order to fulfill and enhance the significance of the great revolutionary war. The Fasci di Combattimento want the collective sacrifices of the war to afford Italians that place in international life which the victory has merited them.

For this great work all must enroll in the Fasci di Combattimento.

THE CENTRAL COMMITTEE

MUSSOLINI: CLARIFYING SPEECH OF SEPTEMBER 20, 1922

From *Opera omnia di Benito Mussolini*, ed. E. and D. Susmel (Florence, 1951–1962), 18:411–421 passim.

Before he could hope to take power, Mussolini had to clarify his changing position on such questions as Socialism, democracy, and monarchy, in this prelude to the October 27 March on Rome.

. . . Violence that is lacking in reason must be disavowed. There is, it is true, a form of violence that liberates, but another that fetters. While one kind of violence is moral, certain others are immoral and stupid. It must be adapted to the needs of the time, but not made into a cult. . . . We Fascists must be careful not to spoil our fine victories . . . with acts of . . . gratuitous violence.

. . . You know very well that I do not worship the masses, that new god created by Democracy and Socialism, [which claim that] the masses are right simply because of their numbers. No such thing. On the contrary, . . . the many take the side opposite to what is right. History proves, in fact, that it is always the minorities who produce the great changes in human society. We refuse to worship the masses even when they come endowed with all their sacred callouses on hands and brains. . . . However, we cannot reject them. It was they who came to us. Should we have greeted them with kicks in the shins? . . .

We have had to practice syndicalism and we continue to do so. Some people say: "Your syndicalism will end up indistinguishable from Socialist syndicalism; you will be forced by the logic of events to wage the class struggle." . . . Actually, our syndicalism differs from others' because we categorically deny the right to strike in the public services. We particularly favor class collaboration and are trying, therefore, to imbue our unions with this . . . idea. . . .

Can our political regime be . . . profoundly altered without tampering with the monarchy? . . . I am convinced that the government can be renovated in depth even if the monarchy is left intact. . . . We shall leave [it] alone for another reason: because we believe that a large part of the country would look askance at any transformation of the regime that went as far as that. . . .

I am basically of the opinion that the monarchy has no reason whatever to oppose . . . the Fascist revolution. . . . [But if it did] it would at once become a target. If that happened, we would surely not be able to save it because the issue would be a matter of life and death for us. Whoever sympathizes with us must not hide in the shadows; he should remain in full view. [On the other hand,] we must have the courage to be monarchists. Why [were we formerly] . . . republicans? To some extent because we beheld a king who was not enough of a monarch. The monarchy, in the last analysis, may be said to represent the historical continuity of the nation. That is a very beautiful mission and one of incalculable . . . historical importance.

MUSSOLINI: SPEECH OF JANUARY 3, 1925

From Italy, *Atti del Parlamento Italiano: Camera dei Deputati, Sessione 1924–1925 (XXVII Legislatura), Discussioni,* 3:2028–2032 passim.

After the March on Rome, an outstanding and fearless critic of the Fascist regime was the Socialist Giacomo Matteotti. Then on June 10, 1924, he disappeared, only to be found murdered a short time later in a ditch outside Rome. For the next six months, revulsion against this crime and its Fascist perpetrators fostered the hope that the regime would soon be overthrown. But on January 3, 1925, Mussolini delivered the following speech before the Italian Parliament. The "Aventine secession" refers to those deputies who withdrew from the Parliament to protest Matteotti's murder.

The speech I am about to deliver may not be classifiable as a parliamentary speech in the true sense of the word. Upon its conclusion some of you may find that this speech is connected, if only through the time that has elapsed, with the speech I made in this hall on November 16. Such a speech may not win political applause. Let it be known that I do not seek such applause. I do not wish it; I have already had too much of it. Article 47 of the Constitution states: "The Chamber of Deputies has the right to accuse the Ministers of the King and to have them brought before the High Court of Justice." I ask formally whether anyone in this Chamber or outside this Chamber wants to avail himself of Article 47. . . .

It is I, Gentlemen, who raise this accusation in this hall against myself. It has been said that I have founded a Cheka. Where? When? In what manner? No one can say. In reality there has been a Cheka in Russia which has condemned without trial 150—160,000 persons, according to fairly reliable statistics. The Russian Cheka has perpetrated a systematic terror on all bourgeois classes, . . . a Cheka calling itself *the red sword of the Revolution*. But no Italian Cheka has ever existed. . . .

If I had founded a Cheka, I would have founded it after criteria which I have always used in defending the violence that cannot be expunged from history. I have always said . . . that violence, if it is to be therapeutic, should be surgical, intelligent, and chivalrous. . . .

Now, . . . do you really think that I could give orders on the day after holy Christmas . . . for an act of violence at 10 A.M. on Francesco Crispi Street in Rome, after the most conciliatory speech of my administration?

Surely you remember my June 7 speech. Perhaps you will easily recall that week of burning political passions, . . . such that people began to despair of our being able to establish the necessary bases for that political and civil spirit of compromise that is so essential between opposing factions of the Chamber. . . .

I said to the Opposition: I recognize your ideal right, your contingent right. . . . You can focus your immediate criticism on all the provisions of the Fascist Government.

I remember . . . feeling that in that moment I had spoken profound words of life and laid the basis for that spirit of compromise without which no political assembly is possible. After such a success, how could I . . . after such an overwhelming success, the whole Chamber, including the Opposition, admits, . . . how could I think, unless I was subject to some madness, of committing, let alone a crime, even the mildest, most ridiculous affront against that opponent whom I esteemed because he had a certain bluster, a certain courage, that resembled my own courage and obstinacy in supporting my arguments. . . .

When the life of a citizen is at stake, [the death penalty] must be evoked through a regular, a most regular, process. It was at the end of that month, that has left such an impression on me, that I said: I want the Italian people to have peace, and I tried to normalize political life.

But what has been the response to this principle of mine? First of all, the secession of the Aventine, an unconstitutional and definitely revolutionary secession. Then came a newspaper campaign lasting through June, July, and August, a filthy, contemptible campaign that ridiculed us for three months. The most fantastic, the most frightful, the most macabre lies were spread across all the newspapers. . . .

But, Gentlemen, what butterflies are we chasing? . . . Very well, then. I delcare here before this assembly and before the Italian people that I alone take the political, moral, and historical responsibility for all that has happened. . . . If Fascism means nothing but castor oil and the cudgel and not a superb passion of the best Italian youth, it is my fault! If Fascism is a criminal association, if all acts of violence are the result of a given historical, political, and moral climate, mine is the responsibility for it, because it was I who created this historical, political, and moral climate with a propaganda which lasted from the intervention to this day. . . .

It is clear that the Aventine secession has had profound repercussions throughout the country. Well, then a moment comes when we must say: Enough! When two irreducible elements clash, the solution is force. There has never been another solution in history and never will be.

Now I dare say the problem will be solved. Fascism, as a Government and Party, is at top efficiency. Gentlemen, you have been laboring under an illusion! You thought Fascism was through because I held it down, that the Party was dead because I chastened it and I was cruel enough to say so. But it will not be necessary [to unleash the Fascists] . . . because the Government is strong enough to break the Aventine secession completely and finally.

Italy wants peace, tranquillity, calm in which to work; we will give it to her, by means of love if possible, by force if necessary. Rest assured that within the next 48 hours the entire situation will be clarified. Everyone must realize that what I am planning to do is not one man's whim, it is not a lust for power, it is not ignoble passion, but solely the expression of a boundless and mighty love of Country. [Loud, prolonged, and repeated applause—cries of *Viva Mussolini!*]

SALVEMINI: THE POGROM OF NOVEMBER 1926

From *Fascist Dictatorship in Italy* by Gaetano Salvemini, pp. 147–151, 162. Copyright 1927 by Holt, Rinehart and Winston. Copyright © 1955 by Gaetano Salvemini. Reprinted by permission of Holt, Rinehart and Winston, Publishers.

In addition to teaching at the Universities of Messina, Pisa, and Florence, Professor Salvemini was a noted historian and one-time member of the Italian Parliament, from 1919 to 1921. Arrested as an anti-Fascist in 1925, he went into exile, living most of the time in the United States. He taught at Harvard University from 1930 to 1948 and subsequently became a U.S. citizen. Several of his later books, such as this one, were devoted to the unmasking of Fascist propaganda.

After the attempt on Mussolini's life by a dissident Fascist on October 31, 1926, there occurred throughout Italy a series of attacks on liberals, intellectuals, former statesmen, and other dissidents, as described here by Professor Salvemini.

At Bergamo, the secondary school-teacher Fachery and the lawyer Biolini were flogged. The Fascists looted the house of Count Secco Suardo and of Signor Gavazzeni, ex-Member of Parliament. The first was ferociously beaten and forced to sign a declaration that no violence had been done to him. Signor Gavazzeni was dragged out of his house, beaten and spat at along the streets, and taken outside the city to a place where a gallows had been erected. The Fascists put a noose around his neck, lifted him on a stool and kept him there for some time, as if they were about to hang him. Before letting him go, they beat him nearly to death.

At Como, the Fascists got hold of many of the Opposition and painted their faces in three colors. Amongst the persons who suffered this vile treatment were the proprietor of a clock factory, . . . the proprietor of a cement factory, . . . and Commendatore Rosasco, one of the most important silk weavers of the district. The houses of Signor Noseda, a Member of Parliament, of the lawyer Beltramini Frontini, and the priest Primo Noiana, were sacked. The last named was also severely bludgeoned. The three victims were kept in prison for three days. . . .

At Brescia, the printing establishment of the paper *Il Cittadino di Brescia,* and the headquarters of the Christian-Democratic organization were smashed and burnt: the damages amounted to £18,000. Signor Ducos, Member of Parliament, was flogged.

At Padua, the Fascists sacked the Bishop's Printing Press, the Jewish Synagogue, and the house of the lawyer Toffanin, and occupied the aristocratic Pedrocchi Club, "a den of anti-Fascist slander." . . .

At Treviso, the Fascists destroyed the premises of the chemist Fanoli, the offices of the lawyers Grollo and Visentini, the engineering works of the brothers Ronfini, and the clinic of Dr. Bergamo, Member of Parliament. Before setting fire to this latter building, the Fascists forcibly transferred the 40 patients to the town hospital: three of the sick men died on the way. The brothers Ronfini were dragged through the streets with ropes round their necks, spat upon, and whipped amidst disgusting shouts and insults; outside the city, they were placed beneath a gallows, and for the last time, flogged.

At Venice, the premises and offices of the paper *Il Gazzettino,* and the chambers of the lawyer Cornoldi, the offices of the engineers Samasso, Fano, and Carli, and that of Commendatore Grubisich were wrecked. The sub-editor of the *Gazzettino,* Stringari, Commendatore Grubisich and the workman Mondaini, were flogged till the blood flowed. All the Christian-Democratic clubs of the city, about fifteen in all, save one, were wrecked.

At Trento, the Fascists wrecked the offices of the *Azione Cattolica* (headquarters of the Christian-Democratic organization), the offices and printing press of the paper *Nuovo Trentino,* and the headquarters of the *Sindicato Agrario Industriale,* which is the center of all the Christian-Democratic Cooperatives of the district. The safe of the *Sindicato* was emptied. . . .

At Rome the Fascists wrecked the premises of the newspapers *Mondo, Risorgimento,* and *Voce Repubblicana:* those of the Reformist-Socialist Party, the headquarters of the International Confederation of Transport, the Morara printing premises, and the houses of the journalists Cianci, Giannini, and Mrs. Olga Lerda-Oldberg, of General Bencivenga, Member of Parliament, Signor Sardelli, Member of Parliament, Signor Ferrari, ex-Grand Master of the Freemasons. . . .

At Naples, the Fascists sacked the houses of the following: Senator Benedetto Croce, ex-Minister, the world-famous philosopher; the Members of Parliament

Rodinò, ex-Minister, Labriola, ex-Minister, Presutti, a professor of the University, Bracco, the well-known dramatist, Lucci, Janfolla, Sandulli; of the journalists Scaglione, Marvasi, Scarfoglio; and of the citizens Bordiga, Colozza, Pistolesi. Colozza was seriously wounded. Labriola's library, rich in works on economics, and that of Bracco, one of the finest theatrical collections in Italy, were both entirely ruined. . . .

When it is said that there is no disorder in Italy under the Fascist Government, the statement is a half truth which is worse than the blackest lie. Today there are no longer disorders of the kind provoked by the "Bolshevists" in 1919 and 1920. There is no longer the disorder of the civil war of 1921 and 1922. But there are disorders of a new kind: beatings, woundings, killings, perpetrated by the members of the Party in power on their opponents.

THE FASCIST LABOR CHARTER (1927)

From Benito Mussolini, *The Corporate State* (Florence, 1936), pp. 65ff.

Early on, the Corporate State was heralded as one of the great innovations of Fascism. In 1927 the Labor Charter was promulgated by the Grand Council of Fascism, setting forth the principles that were to be a solution to the evils of capitalism, the class struggle, and the Communist dictatorship of the proletariat. In 1934 another law, the Law of Corporations, was issued to flesh out the principles of the Labor Charter. But as with Mussolini's article on the "doctrine of Fascism," so with the theory of the Corporate State: one has to look for the facts behind the theory.

The Corporate State and Its Organization

1. The Italian Nation is an organism having ends, a life, and means superior in power and duration to the single individuals or groups of individuals composing it. It is a moral, political, and economic unit which finds its integral realization in the Fascist State.

2. Work in all its forms—intellectual, technical, and manual—both organizing and executive, is a social duty. On this score and only on this score is it protected by the State.

From the national standpoint the mass of production represents a single unit; it has a single object, namely, the well-being of individuals and the development of national power.

3. There is complete freedom of professional or syndical organization. But only unions that are legally recognized and subject to State control have the right of legal representation of the whole category of employers and workers for which they are constituted; they have the right to protect their interests in their relations with the State or with professional associations; they stipulate collective labor contracts binding on all those belonging to the category; they levy their dues and exercise with regard to them functions of public interest that devolve upon them.

4. Solidarity between the various factors of production is concretely expressed by the Collective Labor Contract, which conciliates the opposing interests of employers and workers, subordinating them to the higher interests of production.

5. The Labor Court is the organ by means of which the State intervenes in order to settle labor controversies, whether arising from the observance of contracts or other existing rules or from the formulation of new labor conditions.

6. Legally recognized professional associations ensure legal equality between employers and workers, control the discipline of production and labor, and promote the improvement of both.

Corporations constitute the unitary organization of all the forces of production and integrally represent their interests.

In view of this integral representation, since the interests of production are the interests of the nation, the corporations are recognized by law as State organs.

As representing the unitary interests of production, corporations may enforce binding regulations for the discipline of labor relations as well as for the coordination of production, whenever they are empowered to do so by the affiliated associations.

7. The Corporate State considers that private enterprise in the sphere of production is the most effective and useful instrument in the interest of the nation.

In view of the fact that private organization of production is of national concern, the organizer of the enterprise is responsible to the State for the direction given to production. Collaboration between the forces of production gives rise to reciprocal rights and duties. The worker, whether technician, employee, or laborer, is an active collaborator in the economic enterprise, the direction of which rests with the employer who is responsible for it.

8. Professional associations of employers are needed to promote by all means the increase and improvement of production and to reduce costs. Organs representing those who exercise a liberal profession or art, and associations of civil servants should promote the interests of art, science, and letters with a view to improving production and achieving the moral aims of the syndical system.

9. State intervention in economic production arises when private initiative is lacking or insufficient, or when the political interests of the State are involved. Such intervention may be in the form of control, assistance, or direct management.

10. Judicial action cannot be invoked in collective labor controversies unless the corporative organ has first attempted conciliation.

In the case of individual controversies concerning the interpretation and enforcement of collective labor contracts, professional associations may use their good offices to attempt conciliation. . . .

Collective Labor Contracts

11. Collective labor contracts are stipulated between first-grade associations under the direction and control of the central organizations, but the option of substitution is allowed the higher-grade associations in cases specified in the law and statutes.

All collective labor contracts shall, under penalty of nullification, contain precise rules on such matters as disciplinary relations, probationary period, terms of remuneration, and hours of work. . . .

Employment Bureaus

23. Labor employment bureaus are established on a mutual basis, subject to the control of the corporative organs. Employers are required to engage workers through these bureaus, freedom of choice being allowed them among those figuring on lists of the bureau, with precedence for those who are members of the Fascist Party and Fascist Syndicates, according to their seniority of enrollment. . . .

Welfare, Education, and Instruction

26. Welfare measures are a further expression of the principle of collaboration and the employer and worker should both bear a proportional share of the cost. The State, through the corporative organs and professional associations, shall see to the coordination and unity, as far as possible, of the systems and institutes for welfare.

CHURCH-STATE ACCORDS (FEBRUARY 11, 1929)

From *Documents on International Affairs: 1929*, ed. J.W. Wheeler-Bennett (London, 1930), pp. 216–241 passim.

One of Mussolini's lasting achievements was the rapprochement between the Holy See and the Italian State. Ever since the unification of Italy in 1870, the papacy had refused to recognize the Kingdom of Italy under the House of Savoy. Now both Pope Pius XI and Mussolini saw advantages to be gained from a settlement of their differences; they were ready, therefore, to make compromises. Preliminary question: Which side made most of them?

1. Conciliation Treaty

In the name of the Most Holy Trinity.

Whereas the Holy See and Italy have recognized the desirability of eliminating every reason for dissension between them and arriving at a final settlement of their reciprocal relations which shall be consistent with justice and with the dignity of both High Contracting Parties, and which by permanently assuring to the Holy See a position *de facto* and *de jure* which shall guarantee absolute independence for the fulfillment of its exalted mission in the world, permits the Holy See to consider as finally and irrevocably settled the Roman Question which arose in 1870 by the annexation of Rome to the Kingdom of Italy, under the Dynasty of the House of Savoy;

And whereas it was obligatory, for the purpose of assuring the absolute and visible independence of the Holy See, likewise to guarantee its indisputable sovereignty in international matters, it has been found necessary to create under special conditions the Vatican City, recognizing the full ownership, exclusive and absolute dominion and sovereign jurisdiction of the Holy See over that City;

His Holiness the Supreme Pontiff Pius XI and His Majesty Victor [Emmanuel] III, King of Italy, have agreed to conclude a treaty. . . .

Art. 1. Italy recognizes and reaffirms the principle established in the first Article of the Italian Constitution dated March 4, 1848, according to which the Catholic Aspotolic Roman religion is the only State religion. . . .

Art. 3. Italy recognizes the full ownership, exclusive dominion, and sovereign authority and jurisdiction of the Holy See over the Vatican as at present constituted, together with all its appurtenances and endowments, thus creating the Vatican City. . . .

Art. 8. Considering the person of the Supreme Pontiff to be sacred and inviolable, Italy declares any attempt against His person or any incitement to commit such attempt to be punishable by the same penalties as all similar attempts . . . against the person of the King.

All offenses or public insults committed within Italian territory against the person of the Supreme Pontiff, whether by means of speeches, acts, or writings, shall be punished in the same manner as offenses and insults against the person of the King.

Art. 26. The Holy See considers that the agreements signed today offer an adequate guarantee for assuring to it, together with the requisite liberty and independence, the pastoral administration of the Roman Diocese and of the Catholic Church throughout Italy and the entire world, and it declares the Roman Question to be definitely and irrevocably settled and therefore eliminated, and recognizes the Kingdom of Italy under the Dynasty of the House of Savoy, with Rome as the capital of the Italian State. . . .

2. The Financial Convention

Whereas the Holy See and Italy, following upon the stipulations of the Treaty by means of which the Roman Question has been finally settled, consider it to be requisite and necessary that their financial relations be regulated by a separate Convention which shall, however, form an integral part of such Treaty:

And whereas the Supreme Pontiff—considering from a lofty point of view the great prejudice suffered by the Apostolic See by reason of the loss of the Patrimony of St. Peter, represented by the former Papal States and the property belonging to ecclesiastical bodies, and, on the other hand, the ever-increasing demands made upon the Church, even in the City of Rome alone; and moreover considering the financial position of the State and the economic conditions of the Italian people (especially after the War)—has seen fit to limit the request for indemnity to what is strictly necessary, by asking for . . . much less than what the State should have paid to the Holy See: . . .

And whereas the Italian State . . . considers compliance with the request for payment of such sum to be its bounden duty:

The High Contracting Parties . . . have agreed as follows:

Art. 1. Italy agrees to pay the Holy See . . . the sum of 750,000,000 Italian lire, and at the same time to deliver to the Holy See . . . a sum in Italian 5-percent Consolidated Bearer Bonds equivalent to the value of 1,000,000,000 Italian lire.

Art. 2. The Holy See agrees to the above conditions in final settlement of its financial relations with Italy from the events of 1870. . . .

3. The Concordat

In the name of the Most Holy Trinity.

Whereas, from the very beginning of the negotiations between the Holy See and Italy for settlement of the Roman Question, the Holy See itself suggested that the Treaty relating to this question be accompanied, as its necessary complement, by a Concordat intended to settle the conditions governing religion and the Church in Italy; . . .

His Holiness Pius XI, the Supreme Pontiff, and His Majesty Victor [Emmanuel] III, King of Italy, have agreed to enter into a Concordat. . . .

Art. 24. Royal or State nomination in the appointment to benefices throughout Italy . . . [is hereby] abolished . . .

Art. 29. The laws of the Italian State concerning ecclesiastical matters shall be revised . . . and brought into harmony with the principles which inspired the Treaty concluded with the Holy See and the present Concordat. . . .

b) The legal status of those religious asssociations . . . which are approved by the Holy See, whose headquarters is in Italy, and who are legally represented there by persons of Italian nationality or domiciled in Italy [is hereby] recognized . . .

d) All religious Foundations, of whatever kind, shall be sanctioned, provided they serve the people's religious needs. . . .

Art. 30. The administration and management of property belonging to any ecclesiastical institution or religious association shall be carried out under the supervision and control of the proper Church authorities, without any intervention on the part of the Italian Government. . . .

Art. 34. Desirous of restoring to the institution of marriage, which is the basis of the family, that dignity which is in keeping with the Catholic traditions of the Italian people, the Italian State recognizes the sacrament of marriage as legal for civil purposes when administered according to Canon Law. . . .

Art. 36. The teaching of Christian doctrine, in the form admitted by Catholic tradition, is considered by Italy to be the basis and apex of public education. For this reason Italy agrees that religious education, which is now given in the public elementary schools, be in the future extended to and developed in secondary schools according to a programme to be agreed upon between the Holy See and the State. Such instruction shall be imparted by teachers and professors who are priests or members of religious orders . . . and by lay teachers . . . [certified] by the Ordinary of the Diocese. . . .

Art. 37. In order to make possible the religious instruction and assistance of youths entrusted to their care, the heads of Government associations for physical training and for instruction preceding military training . . . shall arrange their timetables in such way as not to prevent the carrying out of their religious duties. . . .

Art. 43. The Italian State recognizes the organizations connected with the *Azione Cattolica Italiana* [Catholic Action] in so far as they shall—as provided by the Holy See—carry out their activities outside any political party, and under the immediate direction of the Church hierarchy, for the diffusion and practice of Catholic principles. . . .

Art. 45. In so far as they shall not be in accord with the provisions of the present Concordat, . . . the Governmental laws, regulations, ordinances, and decrees now in force shall be abrogated upon the coming into force of the present Concordat. . . .

THE DOCTRINE OF FASCISM (1932)

"La dottrina del Fascismo," *Enciclopedia italiana* (Milan, 1932), 14:847ff.

Although Mussolini had originally boasted that Fascism was a movement without any theoretical trappings, once in power he apparently felt the need for some sort of doctrine. With the help of the philosopher Giovanni Gentile, the Duce produced the following rationale for his movement. The lofty tone of the rhetoric, however, contrasts with the silencing of all opposition in Italy by beatings, exile, imprisonment, and other forms of "persuasion."

Like all sound political conceptions, Fascism is both action and thought; action in which a doctrine is immanent, and a doctrine arising out of a given set of historical forces in which it remains embedded and on which it works from within. Hence its form is correlated to contingencies of time and space, but it also has a content of thought which makes it an expression of truth in the higher region of the history of thought. It is not possible to exert a spiritual influence in the world as a human will dominating others unless one has a conception of both the transient and the particular reality within which one must act, and of the permanent and universal reality in which the former has its being and its life. To know men one must know man, and to know man one must be familiar with reality and its laws. There is no concept of the State which is not fundamentally a concept of life: philosophy or intuition, a system of ideas which develops logically or is concentrated in a vision or a faith, but which is always, in potential at least, an organic conception of the world.

Thus many of the practical manifestations of Fascism—such as party organization, system of education, discipline—can be understood only when seen in the light of its general attitude toward life, a spiritualized attitude. The world seen through Fascism is not the superficial, material world, in which man is an individual separated from all others, standing by himself, governed by a natural law that drives him instinctively toward selfish and momentary pleasures; Fascism sees not only the individual but the nation and the country, individuals and generations bound together by a moral law, with common traditions and a mission which, suppressing the instinct for a life enclosed within a brief round of pleasure, creates a higher life founded on duty and free from the limitations of time and space, in which the individual, by self-sacrifice, by self-denial, by death itself, can achieve that completely spiritual existence wherein lies his value as a man.

It is therefore a spiritualized conception arising from the general reaction of the present against the flabby materialistic positivism of the nineteenth century. Anti-positivistic, but positive; neither sceptical nor agnostic; neither pessimistic nor passively optimistic as are, in general, the doctrines (all negative) that place the center of life outside man, who with his free will can and must create his own world.

Fascism wants man to be active, putting all his energies into action; it wants him to be manfully aware of the difficulties that exist and to be ready to face them. It conceives of life as a struggle, in which it behooves man to win for himself a really worthy place, first of all by equipping himself (physically, morally, and intellectually) to become the instrument for winning it. As for the individual so for the nation and for mankind. Hence the high value of culture in all its forms (artistic, religious, scientific) and the enormous importance of education. Hence also the essential value of work, by which man conquers nature and creates the human world (economic, political, ethical, intellectual).

This positive conception of life is obviously an ethical one. It pervades the whole field of reality as well as the human activities which control it. No action is exempt from moral judgment; no activity can be separated from the value which a moral purpose confers on everything. Therefore life as perceived by the Fascist is serious, austere, and religious; the whole of life is poised in a world sustained by moral forces and subject to spiritual values. The Fascist disdains the "life of comfort."

The Fascist conception of life is a religious one in which man is seen in his immanent relationship with a higher law and with an objective will transcending the individual and raising him to conscious membership in a spiritual society. Whoever sees in the Fascist regime nothing but mere opportunism has not understood that Fascism is not only a system of government but also and above all a system of thought.

Fascism is also a historical conception; man is man only by virtue of the spiritual process to which he contributes as a member of the family, the social group, the nation, and history, to which all nations make their contribution. From this comes the great value of tradition, in records, language, customs, and rules of social life. Outside history man is nothing. Fascism is therefore opposed to all Jacobin utopias and innovations. It does not believe that "Happiness" is possible on earth as conceived by the economic literature of the eighteenth century and it therefore rejects the teleological notion that at some future time mankind will achieve a final solution of all its difficulties.

Such a notion runs counter to experience, which teaches that life is in continual flux and evolution. In politics Fascism aims at realism; in practice it hopes to solve those problems that arise spontaneously from historical conditions and which of themselves find or suggest their own solutions. Only by entering into reality and mastering the forces at work within it can one act on man and on nature.

Anti-individualistic, the Fascist conception of life favors the State; it accepts the individual only in so far as his interests coincide with those of the State, which is the conscience and universal will of man in his historical existence. It is opposed to classical Liberalism, which arose as a reaction to absolutism and which ended its historical function when the State became the conscience and will of the people. Liberalism denied the State in the name of the individual; Fascism reasserts the rights of the State as expressing the real essence of the individual. And if liberty is to be the attribute of real men and not the abstract puppets envisaged by individualistic Liberalism, then Fascism stands for liberty, and for the only liberty worth having, the liberty of the State. The Fascist conception of the State is all-embracing; outside it no human or spiritual values can exist. In this sense Fascism is totalitarian and the Fascist State—synthesis and unity of all values—interprets, develops, and energizes the whole life of a people.

No individuals or groups (political parties, associations, unions, social classes) outside the State. Fascism is therefore opposed to Socialism, which sees in history nothing but the class struggle and ignores the amalgamation of classes into one economic and moral reality in the State. Fascism is likewise opposed to trade-unionism as a class weapon. But Fascism recognizes the real needs that gave rise to Socialism and trade-unionism and wishes to bring them under the control of the State and give them a purpose in the corporative system in which divergent interests are reconciled within the unity of the State.

Individuals form classes according to their interests; they form trade unions according to their economic activities; but above all they form the State, which is more than mere numbers, more than the sum total of individuals forming the majority of the nation. Fascism is therefore opposed to Democracy, which equates a nation with the majority, lowering it to the level of the largest number. But Fascism is the purest form of democracy if the nation is conceived, as it should be, qualitatively and not quantitively, as an idea, the most powerful because the most moral, the most coherent, the most true, expressing itself in the nation as the conscience and will of the few, even of the One, which idea tends to become the conscience and will of the mass or the whole group ethically molded by natural and historical forces into a nation, advancing as a single conscience and a single will along the same line of development and spiritual formation. Not a race or a geographic region, but a people historically perpetuating itself, a multitude unified by a single idea, which is the will to life and to power, conscious of self and personality.

In so far as it is embodied in a State, this higher personality becomes the nation. It is not the nation that generates the State, as the old naturalistic concept had it during the formation of state theories in the nineteenth century. Rather the nation is formed by the State, which gives will and effective life to a people made aware of their moral unity.

The right to national independence derives not from any literary or idealistic form of self-consciousness, still less from a more or less passive and unconscious acceptance of a *de facto* situation, but from an active, self-conscious political will expressing itself in action and ready to demonstrate its rights, that is to say, from a State already coming into being. The State, indeed, is the universal ethical will, the creator of right.

The nation as the State is a living, ethical entity only in so far as it develops. Inactivity is death. Therefore the State is not only the Authority which governs and gives legal forms and spirituality to individual wills, but it is also a Power that makes its will felt and respected beyond its own frontiers, thus demonstrating its universality in all the decisions necessary to its development. This implies organization and expansion, in potential at least. Thus it can be likened to the human will, which sees no limits to its development and realizes itself by proving its limitlessness.

The Fascist State, as a higher and more powerful form of personality, is a force, but a spiritual force, which assumes all the forms of the moral and spiritual life of man. Its functions cannot be limited to those of order and peace keeping as Liberalism assumed. The State is no mere mechanical device for defining the spheres in which individuals may properly exercise their supposed rights. The Fascist State is the form, the inner standard, and the discipline of the whole person; it permeates the will no less than the intellect. It stands for a principle which becomes the central motive of man as a member of civilized society, piercing into the heart of the man of action as well as of the thinker, of the artist as well as of the scientist; it is the soul of the soul.

Fascism, in short, is not only the law-giver and founder of institutions, but an educator and promoter of spiritual life. It aims at refashioning not only the forms but the content of life: man, his character, and his faith. To this end it requires discipline and authority, entering into man's soul and ruling with undisputed sway. Therefore it has chosen as its emblem the Lictor's rods, the symbol of unity, strength, and justice.

STATUTE OF THE NATIONAL FASCIST PARTY (1932)

From Mussolini, *Fascism: Doctrine and Institutions* (Rome, 1935), pp. 198−217 passim.

The following statute was adopted on November 12, 1932, regularizing some of the techniques and procedures that facilitated the Italian dictatorship.

Art. 1. The National Fascist Party is a civil militia, under the orders of Il Duce, in the service of the Fascist State.

Art. 2. The National Fascist Party is composed of *Fasci di Combattimento,* which are grouped in each province into a Federation. . . .

No Fasci di Combattimento may be formed or dissolved without the authorization of the Secretary of the National Fascist Party.

In every provincial capital a University Fascist Group shall be established.

To each Fasci di Combattimento shall be attached a [Youths'] *Fascio Giovanile di Combattimento* and a women's Fascio, which shall in turn establish a girls' group of Fascists.

To the Federation of Fasci di Combattimento shall be joined the provincial association of Schools, of Public Employment, of Railways, of Posts and Telegraphs, of Employees in State Industrial Concerns, and the Section of District Doctors belonging to the Association of Public Employment.

Art. 3. The Black Shirt is the Fascist uniform and must be worn only on prescribed occasions. . . .

Art. 14. The Fascist Levy takes place on April 21, Labor Day. The Fascist Levy consists in the promotion of *Balilla* to the ranks of the *Avanguardisti,* and of the Avanguardisti to the ranks of the Young Fascists, and of the latter to the National Fascist Party and the Fascist Militia. . . .

Young Fascists, on entering the National Fascist Party, will take the oath before the Political Secretary of the Fascio di Combattimento, as follows:

> In the name of God and of Italy I swear to carry out without discussion the orders of Il Duce and to serve the Cause of the Fascist Revolution with all my might and if necessary with my life. . . .

Art. 20. Any Fascist who is expelled from the National Fascist Party shall be outlawed from public life.

CHAPTER 30
GERMANY FROM WEIMAR TO HITLER

> We proceed . . . from the very correct principle that the
> size of the lie always involves a certain element of
> credibility. . . . In view of the primitive simplicity of the
> [people's] mind, it is more readily captivated by a big lie
> than by a small one.
>
> —*Adolf Hitler,* Mein Kampf.

The Second German Reich lasted only half a century when it was defeated by the Allied Powers and by the German revolutionaries. The Armistice of 1918 marked the collapse of the German Army, while the Leftist revolution drove the Kaiser into exile and established a democratic republic at Weimar.

Unfortunately for the new government, it was forced to ratify the harsh terms of the Versailles Treaty, accept the burden of reparations payments, and sign the war-guilt clause acknowledging Germany's sole blame for the start of World War I. Added to these handicaps was the fact that Germany had had no experience with democracy and that a catastrophic inflation wiped out the savings of the middle classes in 1923. It is a wonder then that Weimar was able not only to survive but to be well on the way to solving its political and economic problems by 1929 when the worldwide depression hit Germany and produced an ideal environment for a demagogue—an orator who capitalizes on discontent, promising immediate solution to all social problems and frequently, as in the case of Hitler, appealing to such base instincts as race prejudice and class antagonisms. He was also able to capitalize on the "war guilt" clause of the Versailles Treaty and the extremely high reparations payments demanded by the Allies.

The following documents illustrate several aspects of the "German problem." Two literary works—Fallada's *Little Man, What Now?* and Lilo Linke's autobiography—show something of the frustrations facing young people in the Weimar Republic. Then we follow Hitler's rise from charter member of a small workers' party to head of the state, where he put into practice many of the diabolical schemes proposed in his earlier *Mein Kampf.*

Finally, we have to face the reality of the extermination camps, where not only Jews but other members of Hitler's proclaimed "inferior species"—Poles, Slavs, French, as well as dissident Germans—were tortured and killed. Was there a political purpose to the death camps? Hannah Arendt, a leading political philosopher of our time, thinks there was.

THE WEIMAR REPUBLIC

FALLADA: LITTLE MAN, WHAT NOW? (1932)

From *Little Man, What Now?* by Hans Fallada trans. Eric Sutton, copyright © 1933, 1961 by Simon and Schuster, Inc. Reprinted by permission of SIMON & SCHUSTER, a Division of Gulf & Western Corporation, pp. 16–19, 367–370.

Rudolf Ditzen (pseud. Hans Fallada) was one of many distinguished intellectuals who came to maturity in Weimar Germany. His novel *Little Man, What Now?* won him almost instant international acclaim. In it he captures the stress and heartbreak of those years that helped prepare the way for Nazism. In the first of the following selections, Johannes Pinneberg, a white-collar worker, meets the family of his fiancée Emma ("Bunny") Mörschel—a family that is not only blue-collar but socialist as well.

At the kitchen table sat a tall man in gray trousers, gray waistcoat, and white flannelette shirt, without coat or collar: slippers on his feet. A lined yellow face, with little sharp eyes behind a pair of pince-nez, a gray moustache, and an almost white beard.

As Pinneberg and Emma came in, he let the *Volkstimme* [socialist paper] drop.

"So you're the boy that wants to marry my daughter? Glad to hear it, sit down. You must take time to think it over, though."

Bunny had put on an apron and was helping her mother. Frau Mörschel said angrily: "I wonder where that young rascal's got to. Supper will be spoilt."

"Overtime," said Herr Mörschel laconically; and winking at Pinneberg, he added: "I suppose you work overtime sometimes, don't you?"

"Yes," said Pinneberg; "fairly often."

"But without pay—?"

"Unfortunately, yes. The boss says . . ."

Herr Mörschel went right on: "That's why I'd rather have a working man for my daughter. When my boy works overtime he gets paid for it."

"Herr Kleinholz says . . ." began Pinneberg afresh.

"What the bosses say, young man," observed Herr Mörschel, "we've known a long time. It doesn't interest us. What does interest us is what they do. Any wage agreement in your job?"

"I believe so."

"Belief belongs to religion. The worker has nothing to do with religion. There's sure to be an agreement; and you'll find it provides that overtime must be paid. Why should I have a son-in-law that doesn't get paid for overtime?"

Herr Mörschel, after planting this poser, leaned back complacently. Pinneberg shrugged his shoulders.

"Because you clerks are not organized," Herr Mörschel explained kindly. "Because you don't stick together and back each other other up. So they treat you as they like."

"But I am organized," objected Pinneberg. "I belong to a Trades Union."

"Emma! Mother! Our young man belongs to a Trades Union! Who would have thought it? Well!" The tall Mörschel cocked his head and observed his future son-in-law with half-closed eyes. "What's your Union called, my boy? Out with it."

"The German Employees' Union," said Pinneberg, more warmly.

Mörschel was so overcome that his tall form was quite convulsed. "The G.E.U.! Mother, Emma, hold me tight. And the lad calls that a Trades Union. The bosses kind of like it, don't they? God bless my soul, children, what a joke!"

"Look here," said Pinneberg, now furious. "You're quite wrong. We're not financed by the employers. We pay our contributions ourselves."

"Yes, and I can guess what your officers do with them. Well, Emma, you've found a grand lad, I must say."

Pinneberg looked appealingly at Emma, but she did not catch his eye.

"People like you, so I've heard," went on Mörschel, "think you're a cut above us working men."

"No."

"Yes. And why? Because you're paid by the month instead of the week. Because you work overtime without pay. Because you don't mind being paid under scale. Because you never go out on strike. Because you're always scabs."

"It's not just a question of money," said Pinneberg. "We think differently from most working men, our needs are different."

"Think different!" said Mörschel. "Think different! You think just like any proletarian."

"I believe not," said Pinneberg. "I, for instance . . ."

"You, for instance," said Mörschel, fixing him with an evil leer. "You, for instance, have had an advance, eh?"

"Advance?"

"Yes. An advance on Emma. Not very nice behavior. Very proletarian habit, too."

"I . . ." began Pinneberg; he grew very red, and longed to pull the place about their ears.

Frau Mörschel said sharply: "No more from you, father. That's all over. Keep your nose out of it."

.   .   .   .   .   .

[Two years later, in the depth of the Depression, Pinneberg is out of work and nearly destitute. He is in downtown Berlin to pick up his unemployment relief and buy some food for the baby.]

Pinneberg walked on and on, until he reached the Friedrichstrasse, but anger and fury were becoming rather stale. Such had been his fate, he could rage against it if he liked, but to what purpose?

In former days Pinneberg had often walked down the Friedrichstrasse, it was an old haunt of his and he noticed how many more girls there were. For some time now, of course, they had not all been regulars, there had been much unfair competition in late years; even eighteen months ago he had heard in the shop that many wives of men out of work had gone on the street to earn a few marks.

It was true—indeed it was obvious; many of them were so utterly without attraction or prospects of success, or, if they had any looks, greed, and greed for money, was written on their faces.

Pinneberg thought of Bunny and the boy. "We aren't so bad off," Bunny would often say. She was certainly right.

There still seemed a certain amount of excitement among the police, all the patrols were doubled, and every minute or two he passed a pair of officers parading the pavement. Pinneberg had nothing against the police, they had to exist, of course, especially the traffic police; but he could not help feeling that they looked irritatingly well-fed and clothed, and behaved, too, in rather a provocative way. They walked among the public like teachers among school-children during the play interval:— Behave properly, or—!

Well, let them be.

For the fourth time Pinneberg was pacing that section of the Friedrichstrasse that lies between the Leipziger and the Linden. He could not go home, he simply revolted at the thought. When he got home, everything was again at a dead end, life flickered into a dim and hopeless distance. But here something still might happen. It was true the girls did not look at him; a man with so threadbare a coat, such dirty trousers and without a collar did not exist for the girls on the Friedrichstrasse. If he wanted anything of that kind, he had better go along to Schlesischer; there they did not mind appearances so long as the man could pay. But did he want a girl?

Perhaps he did, he was not sure, he thought no more of the matter. He just wanted to tell some human being what his life had once been, the smart suits he had had, and talk about—

He had entirely forgotten the boy's butter and bananas, it was now nine o'clock and all the shops would be shut! Pinneberg was furious with himself, and even more sorry than angry; he could not go home emptyhanded, what would Bunny think of him? Perhaps he could get something at the side-door of a shop. There was a great grocer's shop, radiantly illuminated. Pinneberg flattened his nose against the window. Perhaps there was still someone about. He must get that butter and bananas!

A voice behind him said in a low tone: "Move on please!"

Pinneberg started—he was really quite frightened. A policeman stood beside him. Was the man speaking to him?

"Move on there, do you hear?" said the policeman, loudly now.

There were other people standing at the shop-window, well-dressed people, but to them the policeman had undoubtedly not addressed himself. He meant Pinneberg.

"What? But why—? Can't I—?"

He stammered; he simply did not understand.

"Are you going?" asked the policeman. "Or shall I—?"

The loop of his rubber club was slipped round his wrist, and he raised the weapon slightly.

Everyone stared at Pinneberg. Some passers-by had stopped, a little crowd began to collect. The people looked on expectantly, they took no sides in the matter; on the previous day shop-windows had been broken on the Friedrich and the Leipziger.

The policeman had dark eyebrows, bright resolute eyes, a straight nose, red cheeks, and an energetic moustache.

"Well?" said the policeman calmly.

Pinneberg tried to speak; Pinneberg looked at the policeman; his lips quivered, and he looked at the bystanders. A little group was standing round the window, well-dressed people, respectable people, people who earned money.

But in the mirror of the window still stood a lone figure, a pale phantom, collarless, clad in a shabby ulster and tar-smeared trousers.

Suddenly Pinneberg understood everything; in the presence of the policeman, these respectable persons, this gleaming window, he understood that he was outside it all, that he no longer belonged here and that he was rightly chased away; he had slipped into the abyss, and was engulfed. Order and cleanliness; they were of the past. So too were work and safe subsistence. And past too were progress and hope. Poverty was not merely misery, poverty was an offence, poverty was evil, poverty meant that a man was suspect.

"Do you want one on the bean?" asked the policeman.

Pinneberg obeyed; he was aware of nothing but a longing to hurry to the Friedrichstrasse station and catch his train and get back to Bunny.

Pinneberg was conscious of a blow on his shoulder, not a heavy blow, but just enough to land him in the gutter.

"Beat it!" said the policeman. "And be quick about it!"

Pinneberg went; he shuffled along in the gutter close to the curb and thought of a great many things, of fires and bombs and street shooting and how Bunny and the baby were done for: it was all over . . . but really his mind was vacant.

LILO LINKE: RESTLESS DAYS, A GERMAN GIRL'S AUTOBIOGRAPHY (1935)

From *Restless Days: A German Girl's Autobiography* by Lilo Linke. Copyright 1935 by Alfred A. Knopf, Inc, and renewed 1963 by Lilo Linke. Reprinted by permission of Alfred A. Knopf, Inc., pp. 385–390.

Lilo Linke (b. 1906) was active in the Young Democratic League in Germany before Hitler came to power. In her autobiography she describes the complex situation that existed as a result of the Depression, the Versailles Treaty, and the fragmentation of political parties.

After a few months' work in the office of the financial paper, I was promoted to the post of the editor's private secretary. Again, a new field of experience opened up to me, more intricate and confusing than even that of politics. . . . Dr. Berger, my chief, was in every regard an outstanding personality. Important for me was that he was generous enough to become my teacher instead of being annoyed at my lack of knowledge, and that he possessed the genial ability to explain a complicated process in its essential outline so that I could understand what I was writing down for him.

I began my studies at a most exciting time, but not in the least a pleasant time. Financial and economic difficulties drove at a maddening pace towards the final crisis and dominated fatefully the whole life of Germany. It was no consolation that other countries suffered from the same plague, although not to the same extent.

The outstanding events of [1929] were the creation and signing of the Young Plan in Paris, which definitely fixed the number and magnitude of Germany's annual payments to its former enemies. For thirty-seven years we were bound to pay an increasing amount, millions and millions and millions, and for twenty-two further years we had to contribute to the repayment of the debt which the Allies owed to the U.S.A. The Young Conference was followed by the first Hague Conference, held to discuss and solve the political side of the problem.

The Republican parties were prepared to sign the treaty, not because they felt any enthusiasm for it, but because it brought comparatively low payments for the next ten years, the premature evacuation of the occupied German territory, the cessation of certain control-institutions imposed on Germany, and similar immediate advantages. Ten years was a long time, and we all still hoped that by then an agreement could be reached for a reconstruction of Europe on a basis of friendship and equality by which the Treaty of Versailles would be torn to shreds. Reason would win, it only needed time.

Week after week our paper tried to explain this attitude, but the Right was not inclined to listen. For the first time Hugenberg, the leader of the German Nationals, joined forces with Hitler, who was becoming daily more powerful. Both lifted their arms to heaven, imploring God to take notice of this ruthless desire of the Allies to confirm the wicked spirit of Versailles by enslaving two further generations. Never, never should this happen. Germany should rise as one man and stamp the treaty underfoot, and all those German statesmen who had signed it or ever negotiated another one should be considered traitors and sentenced to penal servitude.

In the midst of this agitation Stresemann died.* On the 3rd of October, early in the morning, the telephone rang in the office; I lifted the receiver and, surprised, I heard Ernst's voice. I was only rarely in touch with him. He asked for Dr. Berger, who was not there yet, and then he said:

"Tell him that Stresemann is dead—we have just received the news. He died about six hours ago—unconscious; a stroke had paralysed his right side. Yesterday he had taken part in a conference of his parliamentary party. Good-bye, my dear. I hope you are well."

"Thank you, Ernst. Good-bye."

For a while I sat motionless. This was terrible. With Stresemann more than our Foreign Minister had died. As Hindenburg had become the symbol for the Right, so Stresemann had become for us the embodiment of an ideal—the ideal of international understanding and cooperation. The Left had [a scarcity] of great men. Our leaders had

---

*Gustav Stresemann: Foreign minister of the Weimar Republic from 1923 until his death in 1929.—Ed.

been killed or had died, they were too worn-out by the ceaseless struggle or were too old to master the situation any longer. A Social Democratic lawyer was reported to have expressed what many of us felt:

"There is nothing but offal on the Left."

Stresemann, only slowly becoming a Republican and always remaining a liberal, had been eagerly accepted by us for his foreign policy, which we held to be the only possible one. He, whom we once thought the least inspiring of all statesmen, had a thousand times during the six years of his leadership strengthened our belief in the League of Nations as the instrument of our aims. He was one of the few respected and known outside their own parties—a rare occurrence because of the high walls which secluded one political group from the others and because of the intensity with which each led its separate life.

No sooner had Dr. Berger written his obituary article than he had to leave for Mannheim, where the Democratic Party was holding its national conference. Here he delivered a great speech—which I knew by heart because I had typed it so carefully—on a democratic social and economic program. Passionately he repudiated the idea of class-war, confessed his belief in the necessity of private property as the basis of all individual freedom, and declared that democracy could not stand mass distress, but that it also possessed the means of abolishing it. . . .

The conference rose enthusiastically to its feet and cheered him for minutes on end. Here was at last a man who had the courage not only to defend, but to glorify their own belief, which was daily more violently attacked from all sides and only timidly spoken of by its own disciples. To their immense disappointment two representatives of the Young Democratic League rose a short while after and asserted that the capitalist system had failed—the young generation was deserting the flag.

It was no good to go on assuming that a common basis for all the different groups and classes in Germany could be found. The break between them became daily wider and more irreparable. The Plebiscite of the Right "against the Young Plan and war-guilt lie" proved just as unsuccessful as those arranged in former years by the Left, but the poison of the defamatory agitation remained in the body of the community, and we watched its effects with anxiety.

In my own family the political antagonism was growing past endurance. In October Fritz had finished his apprenticeship in an old-established export house, at the precise moment when the firm went bankrupt—a minor incident compared with such events as the breakdown of the Frankfurt General Insurance Company and the Civil Servant's Bank or the enforced reorganization and amalgamation of the Deutsche Bank and the Disconto-Gesellschaft, which all happened in the course of the year and dangerously damaged the whole economic life of Germany. Yet for my brother the bankruptcy of his firm overshadowed all the other happenings, since it meant that he lost his job. His three years' training was in vain—there was not a single export firm which was not forced to dismiss as many of its employees as possible.

Coming home from the office, I found him brooding in a corner with the expression of a beaten dog. He felt humiliated by the fact that I, a girl, was working and earning money whilst he was idle and without a pfennig in his pockets, reduced to the state of a proletarian. I tried to console him:

"Don't worry, you will find another job. And besides, it isn't in the least your fault. Nobody can blame you. Millions suffer the same."

He looked at me with wild hatred:

"Yes, that's just it—millions! If it isn't my fault, whose fault is it? I tell you—your friends, the French, the English, the Americans, and all those damnable nations who inflict on us one dishonorable penalty after the other—they are to blame for all this. Before the war the whole world bought German goods. My firm exported to Africa, to the German colonies. Hundreds of thousands we turned over every year. But they have robbed us of our colonies, of all our former markets. They have stolen the coal-mines in the Saar and in Upper Silesia, they squeeze millions of marks out of our bleeding country. We'll never rise again unless we free ourselves by another war."

"Don't be foolish, Fritz. Things are bad in the whole world."

"I don't care about the world. I care only about Germany, which you and your pacifists have delivered into the hands of our enemies. I despise you, you are not worthy to call yourself a German."

"Call me what you like, it's all the same to me, but don't be ridiculous, my dear boy."

"I'll show you how ridiculous I am!"

He moved towards me threateningly. There was a mad fanaticism in his eyes:

"Force—only by force can we save ourselves."

"It looks as if you are prepared to draw your sword even against me."

"I'll stop your laughing!"

But before he could hit me, I had run out of the room. I had no desire to roll about on the floor with him. Often such scenes involved not only the two of us, but my parents, aunts, and cousins as well, who all formed a united front against me. It was impossible to argue, because none of them was approachable by reason. We no longer spoke the same language. . . .

PROGRAM OF THE GERMAN WORKERS' PARTY (1920)

From *National Socialism*, ed. R.E. Murphy, U.S. Department of State, 1943, pp. 222—225.

Hitler joined the German Workers' Party just after the war, in 1919. Six months later the party issued its twenty-five point program and shortly thereafter changed its name to the National Socialist German Workers' Party (NSDAP). Hitler, with his great oratorical ability, easily captured its leadership.

1. We demand the union of all Germans to form a Greater Germany on the basis of the right of national self-determination.

2. We demand equality of rights for the German people in its dealings with other nations and the abolition of the Peace Treaties of Versailles and Saint-Germain.

3. We demand land and territory for the nourishment of our people and the settlement of our surplus population.

4. Only members of the nation may be citizens of the State and only those of German blood, whatever their creed, may be members of the nation. No Jew, therefore, may be a member of the nation.

5. Those who are not citizens of the State may live in Germany only as guests, subject to the laws for aliens.

7. We demand that the State make its first priority the industry and livelihood of the citizens of the State. If it is not possible to feed the entire population, foreign nationals should be excluded from the Reich.

11. We demand . . . the abolition of all income not earned by work.

16. We demand the creation and maintenance of a healthy middle class.

23. . . . It must be forbidden to publish newspapers that are not conducive to the national welfare. We demand legal prosecution of all tendencies in art and literature that are likely to disintegrate our national life, and the suppression of institutions which militate against the above standards.

24. We demand liberty for all religious denominations in the State so long as they are not a danger to, and do not militate against, the moral feelings of the German race.

The party stands for positive Christianity, but does not bind itself . . . to any particular confession. It combats the Jewish-materialist spirit. . . .

25. That all of the foregoing may be realized, we demand the creation of a strong central power of the State [and] the unquestioned authority of the politically centralized Parliament over the entire Reich and its organizations. . . .

ADOLF HITLER

MEIN KAMPF

(Munich: F. Eher, 1932), pp. 197–203, 311–314.

After the failure of the Beer-hall Putsch in 1923, Adolf Hitler was sentenced to five years in jail. He served only nine months before his release, but during that time he dictated the first volume of "My Battle" to one of his disciples. The book soon became the bible of National Socialism, and after Hitler came to power in 1933 copies of it were presented to all newlyweds.

On Propaganda

The function of propaganda is not the scientific education of the individual; it is imparting to the people certain facts, procedures, and necessities, whose importance can be brought home to the masses only by this means. The art of propaganda consists in doing this so skillfully that a general conviction is created of the reality of a fact, the necessity of a procedure, the correctness of the necessity, etc. . . .

All propaganda must be made to appeal to the masses, and its intellectual level should therefore be in accordance with the most limited intelligence of those being addressed. Thus, the greater the mass it is intended to reach, the lower its purely intellectual level. . . .

The more unassuming its intellectual quality, and the more emotional its appeal to the masses, the more successful it will be. This, and not the approval of a few longheads or young aesthetes, is the best test of a propaganda campaign. . . . The art of propaganda consists in awakening the imagination of the masses and in finding the psychologically correct way to win their attention and even their hearts. . . .

[Since] the receptive capacity of the masses is very limited, their understanding meager, and their forgetfulness enormous, . . . all effective propaganda must stick to a few essential points, driven home by slogans, until even the last person understands what is meant by a particular term. . . .

The function of propaganda is not . . . to weigh and pass judgment on conflicting rights, giving each side its due, but exclusively to emphasize the single right which we are asserting. Its task is not to make an objective study of the truth and, in so far as it favors the other side, present it to the masses in all honesty; its task is to present only that aspect of the truth that favors our side.

The broad masses of a nation are not made up of diplomats or professors of public law, nor even of persons capable of making a reasoned judgment, but only of grown-up children constantly wavering between one idea and another. If our propaganda even once accords the glimmer of truth to the other side, a basis for doubt is laid concerning our own cause. The masses cannot distinguish where the error of the other side ends and our own begins. In such a case they become hesitant and suspicious, especially if the enemy does not make the same mistake but heaps all the blame on his adversary. Isn't it then clear that the people end up believing the enemy's propaganda, which was more unified and consistent, rather than our own? And that, of course, in a people such as the Germans that suffers from a mania for objectivity! . . .

The great majority of a nation is . . . ruled by sentiment and emotion rather than by sober reasoning. Its sentiment, however, is not complicated but simple and consistent. Devoid of multiple shadings, it has only negative and positive notions: love and hate, right and wrong, truth and falsehood; never half this or half that. . . .

No matter how brilliant the technique, however, it will not succeed unless one fundamental principle is kept constantly in mind: Propaganda must be confined to a few points, which are repeated over and over. Here, as so often happens in this world, persistence is the first and most essential requirement for success. . . .

The function of propaganda is not to provide an interesting diversion for blasé young gentlemen, but to win over the masses, whose slowness of understanding needs a certain amount of time to absorb information; only constant repetition thousands of times over will succeed in imprinting an idea on the memory of the crowd. Any change that is made in the message must emphasize the same conclusion. A slogan must, of course, be presented from different angles, but in the end the same unchanging formula has got to be reasserted. Only in this way can propaganda be consistent and forceful in its effect.

Nation and Race

Even the most superficial observation shows that Nature's limited form of propagation is a fundamental, almost rigid law of all her many expressions of the vital urge. Each animal mates only with a member of its own species: titmouse mates only with titmouse, finch with finch, stork with stork, fieldmouse with fieldmouse, dormouse with dormouse, wolf with she-wolf etc.

Only extreme circumstances can change this, *e.g.,* primarily captivity or some other cause that prevents mating within the same species. But Nature detests such intercourse with all her might, her most obvious protest being the fact that the hybrid is sterile or the fertility of later offspring is limited. In most cases she takes away the power of resistance to disease or enemy attack.

This is only natural, since any crossing of two beings that are not at exactly the same level produces an intermediate form between the level of the two parents, which means that the offspring will probably be superior to the biologically lower parent but not as high as the higher parent. Consequently, it will eventually succumb in any struggle against the higher species. Such mating is contrary to the will of Nature to favor the selective improvement of life in general. . . .

This urge for racial purity, universally valid in the world of Nature, results not only in the sharp outward distinction of the various races, but also in the uniform characteristics within each species: the fox remains a fox, the goose a goose, the tiger a tiger, etc. The only differences that can exist within the species are variations in strength, intelligence, dexterity, endurance, etc., among individual specimens. But you will never find a fox showing good-will toward geese nor a cat being friendly toward mice. . . .

If Nature does not desire the mating of weaker with stronger individuals, even less does she desire that a superior race should mingle their blood with that of an inferior race, since in such a case all her work through hundreds of thousands of years to establish a higher stage of being could be ruined.

History provides innumerable proofs of this. It shows with frightful clarity that every mingling of Aryan blood with that of inferior peoples resulted in the downfall of the cultured people. In North America, for example, whose population is largely Teutonic and who mated little with the lower colored peoples, we find a different kind of humanity and culture from those of central and South America, where the predominantly Latin immigrants often mated with the aborigines on a large scale. Here we have a clear and distinct example of the effect of racial mixture. But in North America the Teutonic inhabitant, who has kept his race pure, rose to be master of the continent, and will remain so as long as he does not fall victim to the defilement of the blood.

The results of miscegenation, therefore, are always the following:

(a) Lowering the level of the superior race;

(b) Physical and mental degeneration, leading to a slow but sure decline in health and vitality.

To bring about such a development, then, is nothing less than to sin against the will of the eternal Creator. . . .

HITLER'S SPEECHES

From *The Speeches of Adolf Hitler, 1922–39*. ed. Norman H. Baynes, Volume I; by Oxford University Press under the auspices of the Royal Institute of International Affairs, London, 1942. Reprinted by permission.

Kultur

Simultaneously with this political purification of our public life, the Government of the Reich will undertake a thorough moral purging of the body corporate of the nation. The entire educational system, the theatre, the cinema, literature, the press, and [radio]— all these will be used as means to this end and valued accordingly. They must all serve for the maintenance of the eternal values present in the essential character of our people. Art will always remain the expression and the reflection of the longings and the realities of an era. The neutral international attitude of aloofness is rapidly disappearing. Heroism is coming forward passionately and will in future shape and lead political destiny. It is the task of art to be the expression of this determining spirit of the age. Blood and race will once more become the source of artistic intuition.—Speech in the Reichstag, March 23, 1933. [Source: *Dokumente der deutschen Politik* (1935), 1:28–29.]

The Press

The press should draw from the past the lesson of the necessity for cooperation in training the people's judgment in accordance with the principles of those eternally valid laws which govern life. The press must itself never fall into the error of wishing to judge an historic achievement on the basis of the confusing succession of single happenings: it must take the greatness of the task which is set us by our time as the basis from which it judges the single happenings, the single phenomena of our day. Only so will it avoid the damage to its own prestige which will result if . . . its judgment of these events . . . is proved to be false.—Address to representatives of the foreign press, April 6, 1933. (Source: *Dokumente*, 1:254-225.)

Women

. . . Providence has entrusted to woman the cares of that world which is peculiarly her own, and only on the basis of this smaller world can the man's world be formed and built up. . . . Every child that a woman brings into the world is a battle, a battle waged for the existence of her people. Man and woman must therefore mutually value the respect each other when they see that each performs the task which Nature and Providence have ordained. It is not true, as Jewish intellectuals assert, that respect depends upon the overlapping of the spheres of activity of the sexes: this respect demands that neither sex should try to do that which belongs to the other's sphere. . . .

We National Socialists have for many years protested against bringing woman into political life; that life in our eyes was unworthy of her. . . . The program of our National Socialist Women's Movement has in truth but one single point, and that point is the Child—that tiny creature which must be born and should grow strong, for in the child alone the whole life-struggle gains its meaning. . . .—Address to women at the Nuremberg Parteitag, September 8, 1934. (Source: *Frankfurter Zeitung*, 9/9/34.)

The Anti-Jewish Laws

[On September 15, 1935, anti-Jewish laws were passed at a special session of the Reichstag. Hitler's justification for the introduction of these laws was relatively brief. He referred to the insult to the German flag in the United States and to the agitation in favor of a boycott of German goods; then he continued:]

This international unrest in the world would unfortunately seem to have given rise to the view amongst the Jews within Germany that the time has come openly to oppose Jewish interests to those of the German nation. . . . The only way [open] to deal with the problem is [through] legislative action. The German Government is . . . controlled in this by the thought that through a single secular solution it may be possible still to [establish] a ground on which the German people may find a tolerable relation towards the Jewish people. Should this hope not be fulfilled and [should] the Jewish agitation both within Germany and in the international sphere . . . continue, then the position must be examined afresh.

[Hitler then proposed that the three "Nuremberg laws" be adopted. First was the Law on the Flags of the Reich; second, the Law respecting Reich Citizenship; and third, the Law for the Protection of German Blood and German Honor.]

The first two laws repay the debt of gratitude to the Movement under whose symbol Germany has recovered her freedom, since it implements the program of the National Socialist Party in an important point. The second is an attempt to regulate by law a problem which, should this attempt fail, must then be handed over by law to the National Socialist Party for a final solution.—Address to the Reichstag in Nuremberg, September 15, 1935. (Source: *Völkischer Beobachter*, 9/16/35.)

IDEOLOGY AND TERROR

NAZI MEDICAL EXPERIMENTS

From Nuremberg Document #3249-PS: Testimony of Dr. Franz Blaha, a Czechoslovakian prisoner.

The open secret of the Nazi concentration camps was finally documented when the Allied armies entered the camps and when the War Crimes Trials at Nuremberg disclosed the medical experiments and the mass murders.

From the middle of 1941 to the end of 1942, some 500 operations were performed on healthy prisoners [at Dachau]. These were for the instruction of SS medical students

Landsberg Concentration Camp. After the German defeat in World War II, an American Army colonel tries to convince a group of German civilians that they bear some responsibility for the horrors of the concentration camps. *(Wide World Photos.)*

and doctors and included operations on the stomach, gall bladder, and throat. They were performed by students and doctors with only two years training, although they were very dangerous and difficult. . . . Many prisoners died on the operating table and many others from later complications. I performed the autopsies. . . . Doctors supervising the operations were Lang, Muermelstadt, Wolter, Ramsauer, and Kahr. . . .

During my time at Dachau I was familiar with many kinds of experiments carried on there. The victims never volunteered but were forced to submit to these operations. Dr. Klaus Schilling conducted malaria experiments on about 1200 people between 1941 and 1945. Himmler personally ordered him to conduct these experiments. The victims were either bitten by mosquitoes or given injections of malaria sporozoites; treatments included quinine, pyrifer, neosalvarsam, antipyrin, pyramidon, and a drug called 2516 Behring. I performed autopsies on those who died from these experiments. About 30–40 died from the malaria itself, and 300–400 from later diseases that were fatal because of the physical condition resulting from the malaria attack. There were also deaths from overdoses of neosalvarsan and pyramidon. . . .

In 1942 and 1943 experiments were conducted by Dr. Sigmund Rascher to determine the effects of changes in air pressure. As many as 25 persons at a time were put into a specially constructed van where pressure could be increased or decreased at will, in order to see the effects of high altitude and rapid descent by parachute. . . . Most of the victims in these experiments died from internal hemorrhaging of the lungs or brain. Survivors coughed blood when taken out of the van. It was my job to remove the bodies as soon as they were dead and send the internal organs to Munich for study. About 400–500 prisoners were experimented on. . . .

Dr. Rascher also conducted cold-water experiments to find ways of reviving airmen who fell in the ocean. The subject was placed in ice water and kept there until unconscious. Blood was taken from his neck and tested with each degree change in his body temperature. . . . The lowest body temperature obtained was 19° C., but most of the men died at 25° or 26°. When they were removed from the water, attempts were made to revive them by artificial sunlight, hot water, electrotherapy, or animal warmth. For the latter, prostitutes were used, the body of the unconscious man being placed between two of the women. Himmler was present at one such experiment. . . . About 300 prisoners were used. The majority died. Of those who survived, many became mentally deranged. . . .

Liver-puncture experiments were performed on healthy people and on others who had diseases of the stomach and gall bladder. A needle was jabbed into the person's liver and a small piece extracted. No anaesthetic was used. The experiment was very painful and often had serious results when the stomach or a large blood vessel was punctured. Many persons died of these tests, involving Polish, Russian, Czech and German prisoners. . . .

It was a common practice to remove the skin from dead prisoners, which I was ordered to do on many occasions. Drs. Rascher and Wolter in particular asked for the skin from backs and chests. It was chemically treated, placed in the sun to dry, and then cut into various sizes for use as saddles, riding breeches, gloves, slippers, and ladies' handbags. Tattooed skin was especially valued by SS men. Russians, Poles, and other inmates were used in this way, but it was forbidden to cut the skin of a German prisoner. . . . Sometimes we did not have enough bodies with good skin and Rascher would say, "All right, you will get the bodies." The next day we would receive 20 or 30 bodies of young people, [who] had been shot in the neck or struck on the head so the skin would not be injured. . . .

MASS MURDER OF JEWS

From Nuremberg Document #3868-PS: Testimony of Rudolf Hoess.

I have been continually associated with the administration of concentration camps since 1934, serving at Dachau until 1938 and at Sachsenhausen from 1938 to 1940, when I was appointed Commandant of Auschwitz. I commanded Auschwitz until 1 December 1943, and estimate that at least 2,500,000 victims were executed and exterminated there by gassing and burning; at least another half-million succumbed to starvation and disease, making a total of about 3,000,000. This figure represents about 70–80 percent of all persons sent to Auschwitz as prisoners, the remainder having been selected and used for slave labor in the concentration-camp industries; included among the executed and burned were about 20,000 Russian prisoners. . . . The rest of the victims included about 100,000 German Jews and a large number of citizens, mostly Jewish, from Holland, France, Belgium, Poland, Hungary, Czechoslovakia, Greece, and other countries. . . .

The "final solution" of the Jewish question meant the complete extermination of all the Jews in Europe. I was ordered to establish extermination facilities at Auschwitz in June 1941. . . . I visited Treblinka to see how they carried out their exterminations. The camp commander told me that he had liquidated 80,000 in half a year. He was chiefly concerned with liquidating all the Jews from the Warsaw Ghetto. He used monoxide gas, but I did not think his methods were very efficient. So when I set up the extermination building at Auschwitz, I used Cyklon B, . . . a crystallized prussic acid . . . dropped into the death chamber through a small opening. It took from 3 to 15 minutes to kill the people, . . . depending on weather conditions. We knew the people were dead when their screaming stopped. . . .

Another improvement . . . was that we built our gas chambers to accommodate 2000 people at a time, whereas the Treblinka chambers accommodated only 200. . . . We selected our victims as follows: two doctors examined the incoming prisoners. As they were marched past one of the doctors, he would make spot decisions: those fit for work were sent into the camp; the others went immediately to the extermination plants. Children of tender years were invariably exterminated, since they were unfit for work because of their youth.

Still another improvement . . . was that, while the victims at Treblinka almost always knew they were to be exterminated, we sought to fool them into thinking they were going to a delousing process. Of course, they frequently realized our real intentions, and we sometimes had riots and difficulties from that. Women would often hide their children under their clothes, but of course when we found them we sent the children in to be exterminated. We were required to carry out these exterminations secretly, but . . . the stench from the continuous burning of bodies permeated the entire area and everybody in the surrounding communities knew that the exterminations were going on at Auschwitz.

ARENDT: IDEOLOGY AND TERROR

From *The Origins of Totalitarianism* by Hannah Arendt, copyright © 1951, 1958, 1966 by Hannah Arendt; renewed 1979 by Mary McCarthy West. Reprinted by permission of Harcourt Brace Jovanovich, Inc. and George Allen & Unwin, Ltd., pp. 442–45, 466–468

One of the leading political analysts of our time, Hannah Arendt (d. 1975) succeeded not only in relating the Nazi and Soviet treatment of minorities to the illiberal trends of the nineteenth century, but also in showing why it is difficult for the average person to believe the horrors of the concentration camps. The totalitarian state succeeded in doing what was previously thought impossible, in going beyond the murder of the individual to the obliteration of a person's very existence—while he or she is still alive!

. . .The murderer who kills a man—a man who has to die anyway—still moves within the realm of life and death familiar to us; both have indeed a necessary connection on which the dialectic is founded, even if it is not always conscious of it. The murderer leaves a corpse behind and does not pretend that his victim has never existed; if he wipes out any traces, they are those of his own identity, and not the

Buchenwald. (Wide World Photos.)

memory and grief of the persons who loved his victim; he destroys a life, but he does not destroy the fact of existence itself.

The Nazis, with the precision peculiar to them, used to register their operations in the concentration camps under the heading "under cover of the night." . . . The radicalism of measures to treat people as if they had never existed and to make them disappear in the literal sense of the word is frequently not apparent at first glance, because both the German and the Russian system are not uniform but consist of a series of categories in which people are treated very differently. In the case of Germany, these different categories used to exist in the same camp, but without coming into contact with each other: frequently, the isolation between the categories was even stricter than the isolation from the outside world. Thus, out of racial considerations, Scandinavian nationals during the war were quite differently treated by the Germans than the members of other peoples, although the former were outspoken enemies of the Nazis. The latter in turn were divided into those whose "extermination" was immediately on the agenda, as in the case of the Jews, or could be expected in the predictable future, as in the case of the Poles, Russians and Ukranians, and into those who were not yet covered by instructions about such an over-all "final solution," as in the case of the French and Belgians. In Russia, on the other hand, we must distinguish three more or less independent systems. First, there are the authentic forced-labor groups that live in relative freedom and are sentenced for limited periods. Secondly, there are concentration camps in which the human material is ruthlessly exploited and the mortality rate is extremely high, but which are essentially organized for labor purposes. And, thirdly, there are the annihilation camps in which the inmates are systematically wiped out through starvation and neglect. . . .

There are no parallels to the life in the concentration camps. Its horror can never be fully embraced by the imagination for the very reason that it stands outside of life and death. It can never be fully reported for the very reason that the survivor returns to the world of the living, which makes it impossible for him to believe fully in his own past experiences. It is as though he had a story to tell of another planet, for the status of the inmates in the world of the living, where nobody is supposed to know if they are alive or dead, is such that it is as though they had never been born. Therefore all parallels create confusion and distract attention from what is essential. Forced labor in prisons and penal colonies, banishment, slavery, all seem for a moment to offer helpful comparisons, but on closer examination lead nowhere.

Forced labor as a punishment is limited as to time and intensity. The convict retains his rights over his body; he is not absolutely tortured and he is not absolutely dominated. Banishment banishes only from one part of the world to another part of the world, also inhabited by human beings; it does not exclude from the human world altogether. Throughout history slavery has been an institution within a social order; slaves were not, like concentration-camp inmates, withdrawn from the sight and hence the protection of their fellow-men; as instruments of labor they had a definite price and as property a definite value. The concentration-camp inmate has no price, because he can always be replaced; nobody knows to whom he belongs, because he is never seen. From the point of view of normal society he is absolutely superfluous, although in times of labor shortage, as in Russia and in Germany during the war, he is used for work. . . .

Concentration camps can very aptly be divided into three types corresponding to three basic Western conceptions of life after death: Hades, Purgatory, and Hell. To Hades correspond those relatively mild forms, once popular even in non-totalitarian countries, for getting undesirable elements of all sorts—refugees, stateless persons, the asocial and the unemployed—out of the way; as DP camps, which are nothing other than camps for persons who have become superfluous and bothersome, they have survived the war. Purgatory is represented by the Soviet Union's labor camps, where neglect is combined with chaotic forced labor. Hell in the most literal sense was embodied by those types of camp perfected by the Nazis, in which the whole life was thoroughly and systematically organized with a view to the greatest possible torment.

All three types have one thing in common: the human masses sealed off in them are treated as if they no longer existed, as if what happened to them were no longer of any interest to anybody, as if they were already dead and some evil spirit gone mad were amusing himself by stopping them for a while between life and death before admitting them to eternal peace. . . .

If the propaganda of truth fails to convince the average person because it is too monstrous, it is positively dangerous to those who know from their own imaginings what they themselves are capable of doing and who are therefore perfectly willing to believe in the reality of what they have seen. Suddenly it becomes evident that things which for thousands of years the human imagination had banished to a realm beyond human competence can be manufactured right here on earth, that Hell and Purgatory, and even a shadow of their perpetual duration, can be established by the most modern methods of destruction and therapy. To these people (and they are more numerous in any large city than we like to admit) the totalitarian hell proves only that the power of man is greater than they ever dared to think, and that man can realize hellish fantasies without making the sky fall or the earth open. . . .

The first essential step on the road to total domination is to kill the juridical person in man. This was done, on the other hand, by putting certain categories of people outside the protection of the law and forcing at the same time, through the instrument of denationalization, the nontotalitarian world into recognition of lawlessness; it was done, on the other, by placing the concentration camp outside the normal penal system, and by selecting its inmates outside the normal judicial procedure in which a definite crime entails a predictable penalty. Thus criminals, who for other reasons are an essential element in concentration-camp society, are ordinarily sent to a camp only on completion of their prison sentence. Under all circumstances totalitarian domination sees to it that the categories gathered in the camp—Jews, carriers of diseases, representatives of dying classes—have already lost their capacity for both normal or criminal action. Propagandistically this means that the "protective custody" is handled as a "preventive police measure," that is, a measure that deprives people of the ability to act. Deviations from this rule in Russia must be attributed to the catastrophic shortage of prisons and to a desire, so far unrealized, to transform the whole penal system into a system of concentration camps.

The inclusion of criminals is necessary in order to make plausible the propagandistic claim of the movement that the institution exists for asocial elements. Criminals do not properly belong in the concentration camps, if only because it is harder to kill the juridical person in a man who is guilty of some crime than in a totally innocent person. If they constitute a permanent category among the inmates, it is a concession of the totalitarian state to the prejudices of society, which can in this way most readily be accustomed to the existence of the camps. In order, on the other hand, to keep the camp system itself intact, it is essential as long as there is a penal system in the country that criminals should be sent to the camps only on completion of their sentence, that is when they are actually entitled to their freedom. Under no circumstances must the concentration camp become a calculable punishment for definite offenses.

The amalgamation of criminals with all other categories has moreover the advantage of making it shockingly evident to all other arrivals that they have landed on the lowest level of society. It soon turns out, to be sure, that they have every reason to envy the lowest thief and murderer; but meanwhile the lowest level is a good beginning. Moreover it is an effective means of camouflage: this happens only to criminals and nothing worse is happening than what deservedly happens to criminals.

The criminals everywhere constitute the aristocracy of the camps. . . . What places the criminals in the leadership is not so much the affinity between the supervisory personnel and criminal elements . . . as the fact that only criminals have been sent to the camp in connection with some definite activity. They at least know why they are in a concentration camp and therefore have kept a remnant of their juridical person. . . .

To the amalgam of politicals and criminals with which concentration camps in Russia and Germany started out, was added at an early date a third element which was soon to constitute the majority of all concentration-camp inmates. This largest group has consisted ever since of people who had done nothing whatsoever that, either in their own consciousnesss or the consciousness of their tormentors, had any rational connection with their arrest. In Germany, after 1938, this element was represented by masses of Jews, in Russia by any groups which, for any reason having nothing to do with their actions, had incurred the disfavor of the authorities. These groups, innocent in every sense, are the most suitable for thorough experimentation in disfranchisement and destruction of the juridical person, and therefore they are both qualitatively and quantitatively the most essential category of the camp population. This principle was most fully realized in the gas chambers which, if only because of their enormous capacity, could not be intended for individual cases but only for people in general. In this connection, the following dialogue sums up the situation of the individual: "For what purpose, may I ask, do the gas chambers exist?"—"For what purpose were you born?" It is this third group of the totally innocent who in every case fare the worst in the camps. Criminals and politicals are assimilated to this category; thus deprived of the protective distinction that comes of their having done something, they are utterly exposed to the arbitrary. The ultimate goal, partly achieved in the Soviet Union and clearly indicated in the last phase of Nazi terror, is to have the whole camp population composed of this category of innocent people. . . .

While the classification of inmates by categories is only a tactical, organizational measure, the arbitrary selection of victims indicates the essential principle of the institution. If the concentration camps had been dependent on the existence of political adversaries, they would scarcely have survived the first years of the totalitarian regimes. One only has to take a look at the number of inmates at Buchenwald in the years after 1936 in order to understand how absolutely necessary the element of the innocent was for the continued existence of the camps. "The camps would have died out if in making its arrests the Gestapo had considered only the principle of opposition," and toward the end of 1937 Buchenwald, with less than 1,000 inmates, was close to dying out until the November pogroms brought more than 20,000 new arrivals. In Germany, this element of the innocent was furnished in vast numbers by the Jews since 1938; in Russia, it consisted of random groups of the population which for some reason entirely unconnected with their actions had fallen into disgrace. But if in Germany the really totalitarian type of concentration camp with its enormous majority of completely "innocent" inmates was not established until 1938, in Russia it goes back to the early thirties, since up to 1930 the majority of the concentration-camp population still consisted of criminals, counterrevolutionaries and "politicals" (meaning, in this case, members of deviationist factions). Since then there have been so many innocent people in the camps that is is difficult to classify them—persons who had some sort of contact with a foreign country, Russians of Polish origin (particularly in the years 1936 to 1938), peasants whose villages for some economic reason were liquidated, deported nationalities, demobilized soldiers of the Red Army who happened to belong to regiments that stayed too long abroad as occupation forces or had become prisoners of war in Germany, etc. But the existence of political opposition is for a concentration-camp system only a pretext, and the purpose of the system is not achieved even when under the most monstrous terror, the population becomes more or less voluntarily co-ordinated, *i.e.*, relinquishes its political rights. The aim of an arbitrary system is to destroy the civil rights of the whole population, who ultimately become just as outlawed in their own country as the stateless and homeless. The destruction of a man's rights, the killing of the juridical person in him, is a prerequisite for dominating him entirely. And this applies not only to special categories such as criminals, political opponents, Jews, homosexuals, on whom the early experiments were made, but to every inhabitant of a totalitarian state. Free consent is as much an obstacle to total domination as free opposition. The arbitrary arrest which chooses among innocent people destroys the validity of free consent, just as torture—as distinguished from death—destroys the possibility of opposition. . . .

Total terror, the essence of totalitarian government, exists neither for nor against men. It is supposed to provide the forces of nature or history with an incomparable instrument to accelerate their movement. This movement, proceeding according to its own law, cannot in the long run be hindered; eventually its force will always prove more powerful than the most powerful forces engendered by the actions and the will of men. But it can be slowed down and is slowed down almost inevitably by the freedom of man, which even totalitarian rulers cannot deny, for this freedom . . . is identical with the fact that men are being born and that therefore each of them *is* a new beginning, begins, in a sense, the world anew. From the totalitarian point of view, the fact that men are born and die can only be regarded as an annoying interference with higher forces. Terror, therefore, as the obedient servant of natural or historical movement has to eliminate from the process not only freedom in any specific sense, but the very source of freedom which is given with the fact of the birth of man and resides in his capacity to make a new beginning. In the iron band of terror, which destroys the plurality of men and makes out of many the One who unfailingly will act as though he himself were part of the course of history or nature, a device has been found not only to liberate the historical and natural forces, but to accelerate them to a speed they never would reach if left to themselves. Practically speaking, this means that terror executes on the spot the death sentences which Nature is supposed to have pronounced on races or individuals who are "unfit to live," or History on "dying classes," without waiting for the slower and less efficient processes of nature or history themselves. . . .

The inhabitants of a totalitarian country are thrown into and caught in the process of nature or history for the sake of accelerating its movement; as such, they can only be executioners or victims of its inherent law. The process may decide that those who today dominate races and individuals . . . are tomorrow those who must be sacrificed. What totalitarian rule needs to guide the behavior of its subjects is a preparation for each of them equally well for the role of executionor [or] victim. This two-sided preparation, the substitute for a principle of action, is the ideology.

CHAPTER 31
WAR IN OUR TIME

Truman used the atomic bomb to end a war that seemed
to him limitless in its horrors. And then, for a few
minutes or hours in August 1945, the people of
Hiroshima endured a war that actually was limitless in
its horrors. . . . A new kind of war was born at
Hiroshima, and what we were given was a first glimpse
of its deadliness. . . . After Hiroshima, the first task of
political leaders everywhere was to prevent its recurrence.

—M. Walzer, Just and Unjust Wars (1977)

For obvious reasons, war has become a preoccupation of twentieth-century
politics. In the first reading that follows, the United States Strategic Bombing
Survey presents a factual report of the damage done by the atomic bombs that
were dropped on Hiroshima and Nagasaki. The loss of life that resulted from those
two relatively small nuclear devices exceeded 100,000 people, and the physical
destruction of the two cities was almost total, their recovery slow and painful,
although today they are entirely rebuilt and very modern indeed.

Following these case studies of the effects of nuclear war are excerpts from two
modern analyses of the problem of war itself: Professor Geoffrey Blainey of the
University of Melbourne considers the close relationship that seems to exist
between war and peace; and Professor John G. Stoessinger, formerly acting
director of the Political Affairs Division at the United Nations, explores some of
the underlying reasons why nations go to war.

Two questions: Is war inevitable? And if so, can its most serious effects be
controlled?

THE ATOMIC BOMBING OF HIROSHIMA AND NAGASAKI

From "The Effects of Atomic Bombs on Health and Medical Services in Hiroshima and Nagasaki," in *The
United States Strategic Bombing Survey* (Washington, D.C., 1948).

Despite its objective tone, the following report of the bombing of the two Japanese cities
in August 1945 manages to convey much of the drama, suffering, and confusion that
remained with the survivors both immediately and long after the event. It is little wonder

Hiroshima Before and After. 1. Before: The Industrial Promotion Hall. (Courtesy of the Hiroshima Peace Cultural Foundation.) *2. After:* The same building completely gutted. In the foreground are the remains of the Sei Hospital; sign on the post (lower right) informs passers-by that the writer still lives. (Photo by Shigeo Hayashi from Hiroshima and Nagasaki: The Physical, Medical and Social Effects of the Atomic Bombings by the Committee for the Compilation of Materials on Damage Caused by the Atomic Bombs in Hiroshima and Nagasaki. © 1981 by Hiroshima City and Nagasaki City. By permission of Basic Books, Inc., Publishers, New York.

that the Japanese are among the most antiwar people in the world today. Although it is argued that the bombings were justified in terms of the lives saved on both sides by comparison with the hundreds of thousands of casualties that would have resulted from an invasion of Japan, it must be recognized that many people consider the United States to have been guilty of genocide in Hiroshima and Nagasaki.

Status of Medical Care Prior to Bombing

Generally speaking, the Japanese are not accustomed to good medical care as one uses the term in the light of practice in the Western world. . . . Though the number of physicians per unit of population compares favorably with that in the United States, the average physician is poorly trained and the character of medicine which he practices is far below Western standards. . . .

The average Japanese hospital is a small private hospital which consists of 10 to 50 beds. Actually, the term "beds" is used loosely in this respect since few of them have Western-style beds. The rooms in such hospitals are very much like rooms in Japanese homes with tatami floors and beds made by spreading bedding upon the floor. It is thus impossible to give an accurate bed capacity, this figure actually representing the number that can be crowded into the available space. On the other hand, the larger city institutions and university hospitals are usually well equipped, of modern construction, and use Western beds throughout. Despite this fact, there are in every city large numbers of these small Japanese-style hospitals. Too, a large percentage of the population never go to hospitals, but they are born, have their illnesses and babies, and die in their own homes. Most of the births in Japan are attended by midwives. Hiroshima and Nagasaki did not differ from the usual medium-sized Japanese city. Hiroshima had two Army hospitals and an Army-Navy relief hospital in addition to the civilian institutions. The Red Cross Hospital and the Communications Hospital were modern structures and were the better institutions of the city. In addition there were many small Japanese hospitals scattered over the city. In the spring of 1945 a medical college was started in Hiroshima and the first class had matriculated. Though no school building was available they were being taught in one of the local hospitals at the time of the bombing. The supply of doctors and nurses seemed up to Japanese standards and it was thought that the city was well provided with medical care.

The situation in Nagasaki differed from Hiroshima in that it possessed one of the finest medical centers in Japan. The University Hospital was the pride of the city and was reputed to be second to none in Japan except the Imperial University Hospital in Tokyo. It was a large modern unit consisting of many buildings and contained about 500 beds. This number represented more than three-quarters of the hospital facilities in the city. The Medical College was located near the hospital and had a large staff of well-trained teachers. There were in addition a tuberculosis sanatorium and many small private and industrial hospitals. Here too, the number of physicians and nurses seemed to be adequate in comparison to other Japanese cities.

Since most of the other large cities of Japan had been subjected to demolition and incendiary raids during late 1944 and 1945 it was natural for Nagasaki and Hiroshima to expect similar treatment. Hiroshima contained no large war industries and had been bombed on one previous occasion only. At that time a single B-29 had dropped several demolition bombs on a suburban district, but there was little damage done. Nagasaki had experienced demolition bombing on several occasions but these raids were directed at key industrial plants. On 1 August 1945, 6 bombs were dropped on the University Hospital hitting the operating room and laboratories and resulting in the death of 3 students and 30–40 other casualties. Many patients were then evacuated as an air-raid precaution. . . . Officials proceeded with the creation of large firebreaks. This work was started in March 1945 and continued until the time of the atomic bombing. Thousands of homes were thus destroyed and their occupants were required to leave the city. It was estimated by the Prefectural Health Officer that 150,000 people were evacuated from Hiroshima from March to August 1945, of whom probably 10,000 had returned. Similar preparations were being carried out in Nagasaki but they appear to have been on a somewhat smaller scale.

The Atomic Bombing

It was upon the previously described conditions that the atomic bombs were dropped on Hiroshima on 6 August and on Nagasaki three days later. In order to appreciate the conditions at the time of the blast and immediately thereafter it will be well to reconstruct the scene in Hiroshima as best it can be determined from talking with survivors.

The morning of 6 August 1945 began bright and clear. At about 0700 there was an air-raid alarm and a few planes appeared over the city. Many people within the city went to prepared air-raid shelters, but since alarms were heard almost every day the general population did not seem to have been greatly concerned. About 0800 an all-clear was sounded after the planes had disappeared. At this hour of the morning many people were preparing breakfast. This fact is probably important since there were fires in charcoal braziers in many of the homes at this time. Some of the laboring class were at work but most of the downtown business people had not gone to work. Consequently, a large percentage of the population was in their homes and relatively few were in the more strongly constructed business buildings.

After the all-clear sounded persons began emerging from air-raid shelters and within the next few minutes the city began to resume its usual mode of life for that time of day. It is related by some survivors that they had watched planes fly over the city. At about 0815 there was a blinding flash. Some described it as brighter than the sun, others likened it to a magnesium flash. Following the flash there was a blast of heat and wind. The large majority of people within 3,000 feet of ground zero were killed immediately. Within a radius of about 7,000 feet almost every Japanese house collapsed. Beyond this range and up to 15,000−20,000 feet many of them collapsed and others received serious structural damage. Persons in the open were burned on exposed surfaces, and within 3,000−5,000 feet many were burned to death while others received severe burns through their clothes. In many instances clothing burst into spontaneous flame and had to be beaten out. Thousands of people were pinned beneath collapsed buildings or injured by flying debris. Flying glass particularly produced many non-lethal injuries. . . .

Shortly after the blast, fires began to spring up over the city. Those who were able made a mass exodus from the city into the outlying hills. There was no organized activity. The people appeared stunned by the catastrophe and rushed about as jungle animals suddenly released from a cage. Some few apparently attempted to help others from the wreckage, particularly members of their family or friends. Others assisted those who were unable to walk alone. However, many of the injured were left trapped beneath collapsed buildings as people fled by them in the streets. Pandemonium reigned as the uninjured and slightly injured fled the city in fearful panic. Teams which had been previously organized to render first aid failed to form and function. Those closer to ground zero were largely demobilized due to injuries and death. However, there were physically intact teams on the outskirts of the city which did not function. Panic drove these people from the city just as it did the injured who could walk or be helped along. Much of the city's fire-fighting equipment was damaged beyond use so that soon the conflagrations were beyond control.

In Nagasaki a similar but slightly less catastrophic picture occurred. The blast was not centered over the main business section of the city but was up the valley about 2 miles. There were large industrial plants, hospitals, the medical school and partially built-up residential areas near the ground zero. The terrain in this area was uneven with large hills which shielded certain areas. Due to the shielding factor and the distance of the explosion from the center of the city, Nagasaki was less completely destroyed than Hiroshima and the panic was apparently less.

The Fate of Medical Facilities

The fate of the hospitals in Hiroshima is particularly interesting in the light of this chaos and destruction. Many of the smaller hospitals and clinics were located in the center of the city and were of typical Japanese construction. For instance, the Shima Surgical Hospital was only 100 feet from ground zero. It was partly brick but largely wooden construction. The blast blew it flat and it is believed that all of the occupants were killed immediately. The remains of the building burned, and the spot is now [1948] a mass of flattened rubble. The Tada Hospital was partly reinforced concrete and partly wooden construction. Located at 2,600 feet from ground zero it was completely demolished, and the only remnants were the concrete foundation and the gutted and broken concrete portions of the building. The exact fate of its occupants could not be definitely determined but it is believed that they were all killed by the blast and succeeding fire. Another building of medical nature which was located near the center of the blast was the Japan Red Cross Office Building. It was only 740 feet from ground zero and was almost completely demolished. The windows, window casements, and doors were blown out and even the concrete structure was broken by the downward thrust of the blast. The building was then gutted by fire and all occupants perished. The Hiroshima Army Hospitals No. 1 and No. 2 were located within 1,500−2,000 feet of ground zero. It is reported that 80 percent of the personnel and all of the patients (500 in No. 1 and 650 in No. 2) were killed. The ultimate fate of the surviving 20 percent of the personnel is not known, but on the basis of other experiences at this distance, it is probable that a large percentage of them died of injuries or radiation effects. The hospital buildings collapsed and burned. The Red Cross Hospital, which was the city's largest and best hospital, was located 4,860 feet from ground zero. The basic structure of the building, which is reinforced concrete, remained virtually intact. However, window casements were blown out or twisted and torn on the side near the blast and the interior was seriously damaged by falling plaster, broken partitions, and falling ceilings. There were 90 percent casualties of the occupants of this building and the damage was so great that the hospital ceased operations for several weeks after the bombing. It did, however, serve as a first-aid station and out-patient clinic in the interim. Practically all the instruments and supplies in this hospital were completely destroyed or damaged beyond repair. The Hiroshima Communications Hospital was located at a similar distance from the ground zero, 4,900 feet. It, too, was of reinforced concrete construction. Though the concrete framework of the building remained intact, it suffered even more severe damage than the Red Cross Hospital. . . .

Thus it may be said of Hiroshima that essentially all of the civilian hospitals and 2 large Army hospitals were located within 5,000 feet of ground zero and were functionally completely destroyed. Those within 3,000 feet were totally destroyed and the mortality rate of the occupants was practically 100 percent. Two large hospitals of reinforced concrete construction were located 4,860 and 4,900 feet from ground zero. The basic structure remained erect but there was such severe interior damage that neither was able to continue operation as a hospital. The casualty rate in these 2 hospitals was approximately 90 percent. . . .

The destruction of hospitals in Nagasaki was even more outstanding than that in

Hiroshima. Since the Nagasaki University Hospital contained over three-quarters of the hospital beds in the city, it represented the bulk of the city's hospital facilities. The center of the hospital grounds was only 2,400 feet from ground zero and from a functional standpoint the hospital was completely obliterated. Most of the buildings were of reinforced-concrete construction but a great deal of wood was used in interior construction and fittings. The basic structure of all these buildings remained essentially intact but there was severe damage otherwise. The blast effects were very severe and almost every building was gutted by fire. . . .

In summary, it may be said of the hospital facilities in Nagasaki that over 80 percent of the hospital beds and the Medical College were located within 3,000 feet of ground zero and were completely destroyed. . . . The mortality of occupants of this group of buildings was about 75−80 percent.

Restoration of Hospitals after Bombing

An amazing feature of the atomic bombings to one going into the area later was the poor recuperative powers of the population towards the restoration of all types of facilities. Though this was probably less so in the medical field than in others, it was still alarmingly apparent. The panic of people immediately after the bombing was so great that Hiroshima was literally deserted. It was apparently less true of Nagasaki and this was probably due to the fact that the city was less completely destroyed, but the same apathy was there. The colossal effects of the bombs and the surrender following shortly thereafter seemed to have completely stunned the people. The effects of the typhoons of September and early October may have contributed to this psychological reaction.

Since the most outstanding feature of the atomic bombs was the high rate of human casualties, it was natural that this was the greatest problem in the areas following the bombing. But even in this regard the progress was astoundingly slow and haphazard. Other evidences of restoration were almost completely absent. For instance, at the time the Medical Division visited Hiroshima, 3 months after the bombing, the first street car was beginning operation, people wandered aimlessly about the ruins, and only a few shacks had been built as evidence of reoccupation of the city. No system for collection of night soil or garbage had been instituted. Leaking water pipes were seen all over the city with no evidence of any attention. It was reported that following the bombing several days were required for disposal of the dead and they were simply piled into heaps . . . without [any] attempts at identification or enumeration. Street cars were burned as a method of cremating the bodies within. All in all, there appeared to be no organization and no initiative.

The care of the wounded immediately after the bombing was essentially nil in Hiroshima. Beyond the sphere of family ties there seemed to be little concern for their fellow man. It is true that essentially all of the medical supplies were destroyed by the bombing and that there were no hospitals and little with which to work. For the first 3 days there was no organized medical care. At the end of this time the Prefectural Health Department was successful in getting a portion of the surviving physicians together and to begin ministering to the wounded who remained in the city. Up until this time all nursing and medical care had been on an individual basis. The more seriously injured were placed in the few remaining public buildings on the outskirts of the city. Many of them had died but many seriously burned cases remained. Small stacks of medical supplies which had been stored in caves outside the city were brought out but were soon exhausted. With all medical supplies gone and practically none being brought in, the treatment of the injured seems to have consisted largely of offering a place of refuge. There is no doubt that many died who might have been saved by modern competent medical care. As time elapsed, many of the small hospitals and clinics were able to reopen and offer some help. Japanese medical authorities and other scientists visited the city in order to appraise the nature and extent of the damage, but they did not contribute materially to the care of the sick and injured. Finally, medical teams consisting of medical students and physicians were sent into the area from the larger cities such as Tokyo, Osaka, and Kyoto. They assisted materially in administering medical care but were handicapped by the overwhelming size of the task and the lack of supplies. The Red Cross Hospital was cleared of wreckage and finally reopened without any repair of the building. In many respects it was fortunate that such a large proportion of the injured fled to nearby towns and villages. Except for Kure, which had been largely destroyed by incendiary bombing, the facilities in these areas were relatively intact.

Most of the fatalities due to flash burns and secondary injuries occurred within a few days after the bombing. The peak of deaths due to radiation effects was not reached until late August or early September. Very few cases suffering from radiation died after 1 October and deaths due to other causes had practically ceased by this time. Thus, during October the essential medical care was directed almost exclusively toward burn cases, most of which were flash burns. A large number were still in hospitals but the vast majority of these patients could be treated as out-patients. By 1 November adequate hospital space was available, but it was still of emergency nature and medical supplies were inadequate. Many of the burns remained unhealed. Inadequate medical care, poor nutrition, and secondary infection were important factors in this delayed healing.

The effects of the atomic bombing of Nagasaki were very similar to those in Hiroshima. Even though it followed the bombing of Hiroshima by 3 days, wartime secrecy, general confusion and the short lapse of time did not allow the population of Nagasaki any particular advantage from the previous experience. The psychological reaction of the people was essentially the same and the chaos in the city seems to have been almost as great. A very important difference between the two cities was that Nagasaki was not so completely destroyed. Further, the bomb blast was centered over a more industrial area and the character of the buildings resulted in less extensive fires. But, from the medical standpoint, the bombing was particularly catastrophic because the bulk of the city's hospital facilities were located within a radius of 3,000 feet of the center of the explosion. The destruction of the University Hospital and the Medical College was so great that the buildings left standing could not be reoccupied even for emergency medical care. Other hospitals and clinics, including the Tuberculosis Sanatorium, had burned to a heap of ashes. The only remaining facilities were small, private clinics and hospitals and many of them were seriously damaged. Essentially no organized medical care was carried out for several days after the bombing. The

Shinkosen Hospital was established in an old school building for the care of bomb victims, but it was woefully inadequate. At one time it harbored over 500 victims. Fortunately, there was a large medical depot at Omura, 20 miles away. Such large stocks of supplies were on hand here that Nagasaki did not suffer in this respect as did Hiroshima. Another school building was converted into an infectious disease hospital.

At the time the Allied Military Government entered Nagasaki, about 1 October [1945], the population was found to be apathetic and profoundly lethargic. Even at this time the collection of garbage and night soil had not been reestablished, restoration of other public facilities was lacking, and the hospital facilities were inadequate. . . .

When Nagasaki was visited . . . about three months after the bombing, conditions were still very primitive. A visit to the Infectious Disease Hospital revealed that the school building in which it was located had been seriously damaged by bombing and no repairs had been made. The roof was partially destroyed, there were no window-panes, and the building was filthy. All the patients, both male and female, were in adjacent beds in the same ward. Members of their families were present and were going in and out at will. The hospital had a capacity of 35 beds and contained 21 patients: 18 cases of dysentery and 3 cases of typhoid fever, at the time of the visit. There were no isolation precautions in practice. The only medicine and supplies were those furnished by the Military Government. Because of these conditions the Military Government had taken over a Japanese Army Hospital of 103 beds and 12 bassinets and was converting it for use as a Japanese civilian hospital. . . . The Omura General Hospital . . . was in excellent condition and was being used for the care of atomic bomb victims. Thus . . . by 1 November some semblance of medical care and sanitary procedures had been reestablished in Nagasaki, but the facilities were still inadequate. The entire program had to be directed and forced by the Americans though they did not enter the area until nearly 2 months after the bombing.

GEOFFREY BLAINEY: THE CAUSES OF WAR

Reprinted with permission of Macmillan Publishing Co., Inc. and Macmillan London from *The Causes of War* by Geoffrey Blainey. © Geoffrey Blainey, 1973, pp. 245–249.

Geoffrey Blainey is professor of economic history in the University of Melbourne. After having studied the history of all wars fought since 1700, Blainey seeks to answer such questions as: What makes wars long or short? What makes for the persistence of feud-wars between two nations? What factors produce "world" wars, as distinct from two-nation wars? And what do the stages in the outbreak of peace reveal about stages in the outbreak of war? Following are his conclusions.

1. There can be no war unless at least two nations prefer war to peace.

2. Just as peace comes only through the agreement of the fighting nations, so war comes only through the agreement of nations which had previously been at peace.

3. The idea that one nation can be mainly blamed for causing a war is as erroneous

Picasso, Guernica, 1937. *Inspired by the terror bombing of a Northern Spanish town by German planes in the Civil War of 1936 – 1939, this painting seems to capture the horror of modern war better than any other. It did not, of course, prevent the calculated bombing of defenseless civilians in later wars—all the Conventries, Dresdens, and Hiroshimas of World War II and the ongoing genocide in Southeast Asia. (Museo del Prado.)*

as the idea that one nation can be mainly praised for causing the end of a war. Most current explanations of war, however, rest on these errors.

4. If it is true that the breakdown of diplomacy leads to war, it is also true that the breakdown of war leads to diplomacy.

5. While the breakdown of diplomacy reflects the belief of each nation that it will gain more by fighting than by negotiating, the breakdown of war reflects the belief of each nation that it will gain more by negotiating than by fighting.

6. Neutrality, like war and peace, depends on agreement. Sweden and Switzerland, for instance, have remained neutral for more than a century and a half not only because they chose neutrality but because warring nations permitted them to remain neutral.

7. War and peace are more than opposites. They have so much in common that neither can be understood without the other.

A Framework of Causes

8. War and peace appear to share the same framework of causes. The same set of factors should appear in explanations of the

    outbreak of war;
    widening of war by the entry of new nations;
    outbreak of peace;
    surmounting crises during a period of peace; and,
    of course, the ending of peace.

9. When leaders of rival nations have to decide whether to begin, continue or end a war, they are, consciously or unconsciously, asking variations of the same question: they are assessing their ability or inability to impose their will on the rival nation.

10. In deciding for war or peace national leaders appear to be strongly influenced by at least seven factors:

i. military strength and the ability to apply that strength efficiently in the likely theatre of war;

ii. predictions of how outside nations will behave if war should occur;

iii. perceptions of whether there is internal unity or discord in their land and in the land of the enemy;

iv. knowledge or forgetfulness of the realities and sufferings of war;

v. nationalism and ideology;

vi. the state of the economy and also its ability to sustain the kind of war envisaged;

vii. the personality and experience of those who share in the decision.

11. Wars usually begin when two nations disagree on their relative strength, and wars usually cease when the fighting nations agree on their relative strength. Agreement or disagreement emerges from the shuffling of the same set of factors. Thus each factor is capable of promoting war or peace.

12. A change in one factor—the defection of an ally or the eruption of strife in the land of the enemy—may dramatically alter a nation's assessment of its bargaining position. In the short term that factor could wield an influence which seems irrationally large.

13. When nations prepare to fight one another, they have contradictory expectations of the likely duration and outcome of the war. When those predictions, however, cease to be contradictory, the war is almost certain to end.

14. Any factor which increases the likelihood that nations will agree on their relative power is a potential cause of peace. One powerful cause of peace is a decisive war, for war provides the most widely accepted measure of power.

15. Even a decisive war cannot have permanent influence, for victory is invariably a wasting asset.

16. A formula for measuring international power is essential: ironically the most useful formula is warfare. Until the function of warfare is appreciated, the search for a more humane and more efficient way of measuring power is likely to be haphazard.

Varieties of War

17. To precede war with a formal "declaration of war" is usually regarded as normal behavior, but the evidence since 1700 suggests that it was abnormal. The Japanese surprise attack on Pearl Harbor in 1941 belonged to a strong international tradition.

18. Wars confined to two nations were fought usually on the geographical fringes rather than near the core of world power.

19. A general war or a world war began usually as a war between two nations and then became a series of wars which were interlocked and were fought simultaneously. An explanation of a general or many-sided war would therefore be structurally similar to the explanation of several two-sided wars.

20. A civil war was most likely to develop into an international war when one side in the civil war had ideological, racial or other links with an outside nation.

21. A general war was usually, by the standards of the age, a long war. Even in the era of nuclear weapons a general war—if it occurs—will probably be a long war.

22. It is doubtful whether any war since 1700 was begun with the belief, by *both* sides, that it would be a long war.

23. The idea that great advances in the technology of warfare inevitably led to shorter wars was held by many generations but falsified by many wars.

Flaws in Current Theories of War and Peace

24. Most of the popular theories of war—and the explanations by many historians of individual wars—blame capitalists, dictators, monarchs or other individuals or pressure groups. These theories, however, explain rivalry and tension rather than war: rivalry and tension between two countries can exist for generations without producing war.

25. Governments' aims and ambitions are vital in explaining each war, but to emphasize ambitions and to ignore the *means* of implementing ambitions is to ignore the main question which has to be explained. For the outbreak of war and the outbreak of peace are essentially decisions to implement aims by new *means*. To attempt to explain war is to attempt to explain why forceful *means* were selected.

26. The evidence of past wars does not support the respectable theory that an uneven "balance" of power tends to promote war. If the theory is turned upside down, however, it has some validity.

27. The evidence of past wars does not support the scapegoat theory and its assumption that rulers facing internal troubles often started a foreign war in the hope that a victory would promote peace at home.

28. The evidence of past wars does not support the "one pair of hands" theory of war: the belief that a nation busily making money will have no spare energy or time for the making of war.

29. The idea that the human race has an innate love of fighting cannot be carried far as an explanation of war. On the statistical evidence of the last three or thirteen centuries it could be argued with no less validity that man has an innate love of peace. Since war and peace mark fluctuations in the relations between nations, they are most likely to be explained by factors which themselves fluctuate than by factors which are "innate."

30. War-weariness in a nation often promotes peace and war-fever promotes war, but there have been notable instances where war-weariness promoted war.

31. The Manchester theory argues that increasing contact between nations—through common languages, foreign travel and the exchange of commodities and ideas—dispels prejudice and strongly promotes peace. The evidence for this theory, however, is not convincing.

32. No wars are unintended or "accidental." What is often unintended is the length and bloodiness of the war. Defeat too is unintended.

33. Changes in society, technology and warfare in the last three centuries spurred some observers to suggest that international relations were thereby so revolutionized

that past experience was largely irrelevant. There is much evidence, however, to suggest that there is considerable continuity between the era of cavalry and the era of intercontinental missiles.

JOHN G. STOESSINGER: WHY NATIONS GO TO WAR

From *Why Nations Go To War*, 2nd Edition, by John G. Stoessinger.©1978 by St. Martin's Press and reprinted by permission of the publisher, pp. 221–233 passim.

On the eve of World War II, John G. Stoessinger fled from Nazi-occupied Austria to Czechoslovakia. Three years later he fled again via Siberia to China, where he lived for seven years. In 1947 he came to the United States, received his Ph.D. degree from Harvard in 1954, and taught at Harvard, M.I.T., Columbia, and Princeton. From 1967 to 1974 Dr. Stoessinger served as acting director of the Political Affairs Division at the United Nations. He is now professor of political science at the City University of New York. Among his numerous publications are: *Nations in Darkness: China, Russia, America;* and *Henry Kissinger: The Anguish of Power.*

"If you look too deeply into the abyss," said Nietzsche, "the abyss will look into you." The face of war in our time is so awesome and so terrible that the first temptation is to recoil and turn away. Who of us has not despaired and concluded that the entire spectacle of war was a manifestation of organized insanity? Who of us has not had moments in which he has been tempted to dismiss the efforts of those working for peace as futile Sisyphean labor? Medusa-like, the face of war, with its relentless horror, threatens to destroy anyone who looks at it for long.

Yet we must find the courage to confront the abyss. I deeply believe that war is a sickness, though it may be mankind's "sickness unto death." No murderous epidemic has ever been conquered without exposure, pain, and danger, or by ignoring the bacilli. But in the end, man's faculty of reason and his courage have prevailed and even the plague was overcome. The Black Death that ravaged our planet centuries ago today is but distant memory.

I know that the analogy between sickness and war is open to attack. It has been fashionable to assert that war is not an illness but, like aggression, an ineradicable part of human nature. I challenge this assumption. While aggression may be inherent in us all, war is learned behavior and, as such, can be unlearned and, ultimately, selected out entirely. There have been other habits of mankind that seemed impossible to shed. In the Ice Age, when people lived in caves, incest was perfectly acceptable. No one except mother and sister was around. Today, incest is virtually gone. Cannibalism provides an even more dramatic case. Thousands of years ago, human beings ate each other and drank each other's blood. That too was part of "human nature." Even a brief century ago, millions of Americans believed that God had ordained white people to be free and black people to be slaves. Why else would He have created them in different colors? Yet, slavery, once a part of "human nature," was abolished because human beings showed a capacity for growth. The growth came slowly, after immense suffering, but it *did* come. "Human nature" had been changed. Like slavery and cannibalism, war too can be eliminated from mankind's arsenal of horrors.

It seems, however, that men abandon their bad habits only when catastrophe is close at hand. The intellect alone is not enough. Men must be shaken, almost shattered, before changing. A grave illness must pass its crisis before it is known whether the patient will live or die. Most appropriately, the ancient Chinese had two characters for crisis: one connoting danger and the other, opportunity. The danger of extinction is upon us, but so is the opportunity for a better life for all men on this planet.

We must therefore make an effort to look Medusa in the face and to diagnose the sickness. Diagnosis is no cure, of course, but it is the first and the most necessary step. I shall attempt this diagnosis by suggesting certain common themes. . . . I hesitate to state these . . . as definitive conclusions and prefer instead to set them forth in the hope that they might engage the reader in a dialogue. If he is challenged and pursues my quest to greater depth, I shall have been well served.

The first general theme that compels attention is that no nation that began a major war in this century emerged a winner. Austria-Hungary and Germany, which precipitated World War I, went down to ignominious defeat; Hitler's Germany was crushed into unconditional surrender; the North Korean attack was thwarted by collective action and ended in a draw; although the Vietnam war ended in a Communist victory, it would be far too simple to blame the Communists exclusively for its beginning; the Arabs who invaded the new Jewish state in 1948 lost territory to the Israelis in four successive wars; and Pakistan, which wished to punish India through preemptive war, found itself dismembered in the process. In all cases, those who began a war came out a cropper. The nature or the ideology of the government that started a war seems to have made little, if any, difference. Defeat came to aggressors whether they were capitalists or Communists, white or non-white, Western or non-Western, rich or poor. . . .

In the atomic age, war between nuclear powers is suicidal; wars between small countries with big friends are likely to be inconclusive and interminable; hence, decisive war in our time has become the privilege of the impotent. . . . No nuclear power can tell another: "Do as I say or I shall kill you," but is reduced to saying: "Do as I say or I shall kill us both," which is an entirely different matter. Thus, when everybody is somebody, nobody is anybody. But it is not only nuclear countries that cannot win wars against each other. A small country with a good tie to a big ally also can no longer be defeated. The wars in Korea, Vietnam, and the Middle East all illustrate this point. . . . The paradox of war in the atomic age may be summarized as follows: the power of big states vis-à-vis each other has been reduced if not altogether cancelled out, while the power of small and friendless states vis-à-vis each other has been proportionately enhanced.

In our time, unless the vanquished is destroyed completely, a victor's peace is seldom lasting. Those peace settlements that are negotiated as a basis of equality are much more permanent and durable. In 1918, Germany was defeated but not crushed. Versailles became the crucible for Hitler's Germany, which was then brought down only through unconditional surrender. The Korean settlement was negotiated between undefeated equals. Both sides were unhappy, but neither side was so unhappy that it wished to overturn the settlement and initiate yet another war. An uneasy armistice or truce was gradually recognized as a possible basis for a peace settlement. The relative insecurity of each side thus became the guarantor of the relative security of both. Israel learned this lesson in October 1973. The victor's peace of 1967 had left the Arabs in a state of such frustration that they were compelled to try their hand once more at war. With their dignity restored in 1973, they found it psychologically possible to meet with Israelis in a face-to-face diplomatic encounter for the first time in a quarter of a century.

Turning to the problem of the outbreak of war, . . . case studies indicate the crucial importance of the personalities of leaders. . . . The outbreak of World War I illustrates this point quite clearly. Conventional wisdom has blamed the alliance system for the spread of the war. Specifically, the argument runs, Kaiser Wilhelm's alliance with Austria dragged Germany into the war against the Allied Powers. This analysis, however, totally ignores the role of the Kaiser's personality during the gathering crisis. Supposing Wilhelm had had the fortitude to continue his role as mediator and to restrain Austria instead of engaging in paranoid delusions and accusing England of conspiring against Germany? The disaster might have been averted and then the conventional wisdom would have praised the alliance system for saving the peace instead of blaming it for causing the war. In truth, the emotional balance or lack of balance of the German Kaiser turned out to be absolutely crucial. Similarly, the relentless mediocrity of the leading personalities on all sides no doubt contributed to the disaster. Looking at the outbreak of World War II, there is no doubt that the victor's peace of Versailles and the galloping inflation of the 1920s brought about the rise of Nazi Germany. But once again, it was the personality of Hitler that was decisive. A more rational leader would have consolidated his gains and certainly would not have attacked the Soviet Union. And if Russia had to be attacked, then a rational man would have made contingency plans to meet the Russian winter instead of counting blindly on an early victory. In the Korean War, the *hubris* of General MacArthur probably prolonged the conflict by two years, and in Vietnam, the fragile egos of at least two American presidents who could not face the facts first escalated the war quite disproportionately and then postponed its ending quite unreasonably. In the Middle East, the volatile personality of Gamal Abdel Nasser was primarily responsible for the closing of the Gulf of Aqaba which precipitated the Six-Day War of 1967. . . .

The case material reveals that perhaps the most important single precipitating factor in the outbreak of war is misperception. Such distortion may manifest itself in four different ways: in a leader's image of himself; a leader's view of his adversary's character; a leader's view of his adversary's intentions toward himself; and finally, a leader's view of his adversary's capabilities and power. Each of these is of such importance that it merits separate and careful treatment.

There is a remarkable consistency in the self-images of most national leaders on the brink of war. Each confidently expects victory after a brief and triumphant campaign. Doubt about the outcome is the voice of the enemy and therefore incomprehensible. This recurring atmosphere of optimism is not to be dismissed lightly by the historian as an ironic example of human folly. It assumes a powerful emotional momentum of its own and thus itself becomes one of the causes of war. Anything that fuels such optimism about a quick and decisive victory makes war more likely and anything that dampens it becomes a cause of peace.

This common belief in a short, decisive war is usually the overflow from a reservoir of self-delusions held by the leadership about both itself and the nation. The Kaiser's appearance in shining armor in August 1914 and his promise to the German nation that its sons would be back home "before the leaves had fallen from the trees," was matched by similar scenes of overconfidence and military splendor in Austria, Russia, and in the other nations on the brink of war. Hitler's confidence in an early German victory in Russia was so unshakable that no winter uniforms were issued to the soldiers and no preparations whatsoever made for the onset of the Russian winter. In November 1914, when the mud of autumn turned to ice and snow, the cold became the German soldier's bitterest enemy. . . . When North Korea invaded South Korea, her leadership expected victory within two months. . . . In Pakistan, Yahya Khan hoped to teach Indira Gandhi a lesson modelled on the Six-Day War in Israel. And in Vietnam, every American escalation in the air or on the ground was an expression of the hope that a few more bombs, a few more troops, would bring decisive victory. . . .

Distorted views of the adversary's character also help to precipitate a conflict. As the pressure mounted in July 1914, the German Kaiser explosively admitted that he "hated the Slavs, even though one should not hate anyone." This hatred no doubt influenced his decision to end his role as mediator and to prepare for war. Similarly, his naive trust in the honesty of the Austrian leaders prompted him to extend to them the blank-check guarantee that dragged him into war. In reality, the Austrians were more deceitful than he thought and the Russians more honest. Worst of all, the British leadership which worked so desperately to avert a general war was seen by Wilhelm as the center of a monstrous plot to encircle and destroy the German nation. Hitler, too, had no conception of what Russia was really like. He knew nothing of the history and depth of the Russian land and believed that it was populated by subhuman barbarians who could be crushed with one decisive stroke and then be made to serve as slaves for German supermen. This relentless hatred and contempt for Russia became a crucial factor in Hitler's ill-fated assault of 1941. Perhaps the most important for the American military intervention in Vietnam was the misperception of the American leadership about the nature of Communism in Asia. President Lyndon Johnson committed more than half a million combat troops to an Asian land war because he believed that Communism was still a monolithic octopus with North Vietnam its tentacle. He did this more than a decade after the death of Stalin, at a time when Communism had splintered into numerous ideological and political fragments. His total ignorance of Asia in general and of Vietnam in particular made him perceive the Vietnam war in terms of purely Western categories: a colossal shoot-out between the forces of Communism and those of anti-Communism. The fact that Ho Chi Minh saw the Americans as the successors of French imperialism whom he was determined to drive out was completely lost upon the President. Virtue, righteousness, and justice were fully on his side, he thought. America, the child of light, had to defeat the child of darkness in a twentieth-century crusade. . . .

If a leader on the brink of war believes that his adversary will attack him, the chances of war are fairly high. If both leaders share this perception about each other's intent, war becomes a virtual certainty. The mechanism of the self-fulfilling prophecy is then set in motion. If leaders attribute evil designs to their adversaries, and if they nurture these beliefs for long enough, they will eventually be proven right. The mobilization measures that preceded the outbreak of World War I were essentially defensive measures triggered by the fear of the other side's intent. The Russian czar mobilized because he feared an Austrian attack; the German Kaiser mobilized because he feared the Russian "steamroller." The nightmare of each then became a terrible reality. Stalin was so imprisoned by the Marxist dogma that capitalists would always lie that he disbelieved Churchill's truthful warnings about Hitler's murderous intent to which he was so blind that Russia almost lost the war. Eisenhower and Dulles were so convinced that the Chinese would move against the French in Indochina in the way they had against MacArthur's UN forces, that they committed the first American military advisers to Vietnam. The Chinese never intervened but the Americans had begun their march along the road to self-entrapment in the Vietnam quagmire. . . .

A leader's misperception of his adversary's power is perhaps the quintessential cause of war. It is vital to remember, however, that it is not the actual distribution of power that precipitates a war; it is the way in which a leader thinks that power is distributed. A war will start when nations disagree over their perceived strength. The war itself then becomes a dispute over measurement. Reality is gradually restored as war itself cures war. And the war will end when the fighting nations perceive each other's strength more realistically.

Germany and Austria-Hungary in 1914 had nothing but contempt for Russia's power. This disrespect was to cost them dearly. Hitler repeated this mistake a generation later and his perception led straight to his destruction. One of the clearest examples of another misperception of this kind took place in the Korean War. MacArthur, during his advance through North Korea toward the Chinese border, stubbornly believed that the Chinese Communists did not have the capability to intervene. When the Chinese did cross the Yalu River into North Korea, MacArthur clung to the belief that he was facing 40,000 men while in truth the figure was closer to 200,000. And when the Chinese forces temporarily withdrew to assess their impact on MacArthur's army, the American general assumed that the Chinese were badly in need of rest after their encounter with superior Western military might. And when the Chinese attacked again and drove MacArthur all the way back to South Korea, the leader of the UN forces perceived this action as a "piece of treachery worse even than Pearl Harbor." The most amazing aspect of this story is that the real facts were quite available to MacArthur from his own intelligence sources, if only the general had cared to look at them. But he knew better and thus prolonged the war by two more years. Only at war's end did the Americans gain respect for China's power and take care not to provoke her again beyond the point of no return. Yet in the Vietnam war, the American leadership committed precisely the same error vis-à-vis North Vietnam. Five successive presidents believed that Ho Chi Minh would collapse if only a little more military pressure would be brought to bear on him either from the air or on the ground. The North Vietnamese leader proved them all to be mistaken and only when America admitted that North Vietnam could not be beaten, did the war come to an end. In both Korea and Vietnam the price of reality came high indeed. As these wars resolved less and less, they tended to cost more and more in blood and treasure. The number of dead on all sides bore mute testimony to the fact that America had to fight two of the most terrible and divisive wars in her entire history before she gained respect for the realities of power on the other side. . . .

Thus, on the eve of each war, at least one nation misperceives another's power. In that sense, the beginning of each war is a misperception or an accident. The war itself then slowly, and in agony, teaches man about reality. And peace is made when reality has won. The outbreak of war and the coming of peace are separated by a road that leads from misperception to reality. The most tragic aspect of this truth is that war has continued to remain the best teacher of reality and thus has been the most effective cure for war.

CHAPTER 32

SCIENCE AND PHILOSOPHY IN A "HERACLITEAN" AGE

Ours is, with a vengeance, a "Heraclitean" period, in which forms and fixity have all but disappeared. We live in a kaleidoscopic world . . . in which forms cannot be smashed because they hardly exist.

—Bruce Mazlish, "Our 'Heraclitean' Period"

Given Einstein's concept of relativity and space-time, Max Planck's quantum theory, and Werner Heisenberg's indeterminacy principle, modern science, like modern art, seems indeed to have entered a period "without forms or fixity."

In the first excerpt that follows, Sigmund Freud, himself an iconoclast of high order, questions whether man's basic unhappiness may not be a function of his civilization. The higher homo sapiens climbs the ladder of "progress" the further he gets from his basic animal nature and the more he must combat his primitive instincts—which, ironically, have helped him to "rise" up to now.

In the second excerpt, Gary Zukav, a popularizer of science—would that there were more like him!—explains the difference between quantum mechanics based on the microcosm of subatomic particles, and the physics of Sir Isaac Newton based on the everyday world.

Then, a biologist, Dr. Lewis Thomas, finds that ignorance is a major contributor of science today. As we discover how little we know about our world, we are driven into a kind of scientific work-ethic in order to learn more. However, it is becoming clear that some things may be unknowable, such as how a beetle thinks, or *if* it does. But speculation, hypothesis-formation and -testing are all in the grand manner of the post-Galilean scientific tradition.

One might define that tradition by saying that science is a method of *systematized* discovery: systematized, because it has a rational approach to the problems it chooses to define and study; because it uses observation, experiment, and record-keeping to test its hypotheses; and because it holds (or should hold) all conclusions as tentative pending further research and discovery. Then just when you might be thinking, after all that, that the conclusions of scientists would have to coincide, how thrilling to discover that these rational researchers disagree all along the line—almost as much as theologians disagreed in the sixteenth century! I say *thrilling* because it all fits nicely with our concept of a democracy in which people may disagree violently but still seem able to get the work done.

In the last article below, Professor Mazlish explains how and why ours is a Heraclitean age, in which almost all forms were smashed, even before World War I, by some of the men we have already mentioned: Einstein, Planck, and Freud, among others. Finally, as a cultural historian, Mazlish applies his theory to other fields, including modern art, with some surprising results.

FREUD: EROS VERSUS THE DEATH WISH

From Sigmund Freud, *Das Unbehagen in der Kultur* (Vienna, 1930), pp. 23−25, 80−85, 97−98.

To exaggerate the impact of Sigmund Freud (d. 1939) on twentieth-century psychology would be difficult indeed. He has made it impossible for any thinking person to ignore the irrational and the subconscious, either in the individual or in the collectivity, and we have him to thank for such useful concepts as the id, the ego, the superego, and the libido. The following excerpt is from one of his later works, which explores the relationship between unhappiness and culture.

What does man's behavior show to be the purpose and intention of his life? What does he ask of life and what does he want to get from it? The answer is scarcely in doubt: People seek happiness: they want to be happy and they want to stay happy. This striving has both a positive and a negative aspect. On the one hand, man seeks to avoid pain and displeasure, and on the other hand, he endeavors to experience the greatest amount of pleasure. In the narrower sense the word, *happiness* refers only to the latter. Given this duality in his aims, man's activity develops in two directions, depending on which of the two aims he seeks—either principally or exclusively—to achieve.

So we see that what determines the purpose of life is simply the pleasure principle. This principle dominates man's mental processes from the very beginning. There is no doubt as to its purposiveness, although its plan of action runs counter to the whole universe, the macrocosm as well as the microcosm. There is no possibility of its being realized, since all the laws of the universe are opposed to it. One is tempted to say that the intention of making people "happy" was not included in the scheme of Creation. What we call happiness in the strictest sense comes from the rather sudden gratification of needs that have been largely dammed up. In the nature of things, this is possible only once in a while. If a situation desired by the pleasure principle is prolonged, it produces a feeling of only mild contentment. We are so constituted that we gain intense pleasure only from a contrast, and very little satisfaction from a fixed state of things. Our chances of happiness, therefore, are already limited by our constitution. Unhappiness is much more readily experienced. We are threatened with pain and suffering from three sources: from our own body, which is doomed to deterioration and cannot even do without pain and fear as warning signals; from the outside world, which often attacks us with powerful, merciless, and destructive might; and finally, from our relations with our fellow humans. The suffering from this source is perhaps the most painful of all. We tend to see it as a sort of gratuitous excess, although it can be no less inevitable than the suffering from other sources. . . .

The element of truth in all this, which people are prone to disavow, is that man is not a gentle creature who wants to be loved and will, at most, defend himself when attacked. On the contrary, he is a creature whose instinctual endowments include a powerful measure of aggression. Consequently, his neighbor is for him not only a potential helper or sex object, but also someone on whom he is tempted to satisfy his aggressiveness, one whose capacity to work without pay he will exploit, and whom he will use sexually without his consent; cause him pain, torture him, or kill him. *Homo homini lupus* [man is a wolf toward other men]. Who, given all his experience of life and history, would dare dispute this proposition? As a rule, this cruel aggressiveness awaits some provocation or aligns itself with some other purpose whose goal might also have been reached by milder means. Under favorable circumstances and without the mental counterforces which ordinarily inhibit it, it may also manifest itself spontaneously, revealing man as a savage beast with no regard for his fellows. Anyone who calls to mind the atrocities committed by the Huns during their racial migrations, or by the people called Mongols under Genghis Khan and Tamerlane, or by the pious Crusaders at the capture of Jerusalem, or even, indeed, the horrors of World War [I]—anyone who recalls these things will have to acknowledge the truth of this point of view.

The existence of this aggression tendency, which we can see in ourselves, and assume, correctly, to exist in others, is the factor that impedes our relations with our neighbors and costs civilization so dear. As a result of this mutual hostility among men, civilized society is continually threatened with disintegration. The advantage of work in common is insufficient to hold it together; instinctive passions are stronger than rational interests. Civilization has to apply its greatest effort to limit man's aggressive instincts and check their manifestations by psychological-reaction concepts: hence, the development of methods to move people toward the identifications and aim-inhibiting relationships of love; hence, the restrictions on sex life; hence also, the ideal commandment to love one's neighbor as oneself—a commandment that is fully justified by the fact that nothing else runs so exactly contrary to man's original nature. In spite of everything, these efforts of civilization have not achieved very much up to now. Society tries to prevent the crudest excesses of violence by taking upon itself the right to use violence against criminals, but the law cannot reach the more cunning and refined manifestations of human agressiveness. There comes a time when each of us has to abandon as illusory the expectations which we placed upon our fellow creatures when we were young—a time when we discovered how much trouble and pain had been added to our life by their ill-will. Nevertheless, it would be unfair to blame civilization for trying to eliminate strife and competition from human activity. Those things are undoubtedly necessary, but opposition is not always enmity; it is merely made an *occasion* for enmity if abused.

The Communists think they have found the way of deliverance from evil. Man, they claim, is wholly good and well-disposed toward his neighbor, but the institution of private property has corrupted him. The private ownership of wealth gave him power and with it the temptation to mistreat his neighbor; while the man who is denied possession is bound to rebel hostilely against his oppressor. Once private property is abolished, all wealth held in common, and everyone allowed to share in its enjoyment, then ill-will and hostility are supposed to disappear from society. Since everybody's needs would be satisfied, no one would have any reason to regard anyone else as his enemy, and all would willingly do whatever work was necessary.

Now, I am not concerned with any economic criticism of the communist system; I cannot investigate whether the abolition of private property is either expedient or advantageous. What I can see, however, is that the psychological premises on which the system is based are untenable and illusory. Abolishing private property does deprive the aggressive urge of one of its instruments—a strong one, certainly, but by no means the strongest. However, the differences in power and influence that are misused by aggressiveness have not been changed nor has its nature. Aggressiveness was not born of property. It reigned almost absolutely in primitive times, when property was very scarce, and it shows up in the nursery almost before property has lost its primal, anal form; it is the basis of every relation of affection and love among people, with the possible exception of the mother's relation to her male child. If personal rights to material wealth are abolished, there still remain the prerogatives of sexual relationships, which are bound to be a source of the greatest jealousy and most violent hostility among men who are in other respects equal. If we removed this factor too by allowing complete sexual freedom, thereby abolishing the family—the germ-cell of society—it is hard to see what new paths civilization might take. But one thing is predictable: that the perdurable feature of human nature [aggressiveness] would go with civilization wherever it went. . . .

I hold the position, therefore, that the inclination to aggression is an original, self-acting, instinctual disposition in man and . . . that it constitutes the greatest impediment to civilization. At one point in the course of this inquiry I was led to the idea that civilization was a special process which mankind undergoes, and I am still intrigued by that idea. I would now add that civilization is a process in the service of Eros, whose purpose is to combine individual human beings, and after that families, then races, peoples, and nations, into one great unity: Mankind. Why this has to happen I do not know, but the work of Eros is precisely that. These collections of men are to be bound libidinally to one another; neither necessity alone nor the advantages of work in common will hold them together. But man's aggressive instinct, the hostility of each against all and all against each, opposes this aim of civilization. The aggressive instinct is the derivative and chief representative of the death instinct, which we have found alongside Eros and which shares world domination with it.

Now I think the meaning of civilization is no longer obscure. It is the struggle between Eros and Death, between the life instinct and the instinct of destruction, as it works itself out in the human species. This struggle is what all life essentially consists in, and the evolution of civilization may be simply described, therefore, as the struggle for life of the species Man.

GARY ZUKAV: EINSTEIN DOESN'T LIKE IT (QUANTUM MECHANICS)

From pp. 52−54 "Einstein Doesn't Like It" in *The Dancing Wu Li Masters* by Gary Zukov. Copyright © 1979 by Gary Zukov. By permission of William Morrow & Company.

Although Einstein made major contributions to its development, he did not like quantum mechanics. Maybe you won't either, but in the excerpt below Gary Zukav explains the difference between the old physics of Sir Isaac Newton and the newer quantum theory. Quantum theory does not replace Newtonian physics, it includes it and goes beyond it to deal with the realities inside the atom, where the old physics does not apply.

. . . Imagine an object moving through space. It has both a position and a momentum which we can measure. This is an example of the old (Newtonian) physics. (Momentum is a combination of how big an object is, how fast it is going, and the direction that it is moving.) Since we can determine both the position and the momentum of the object at a particular time, it is not a very difficult affair to calculate where it will be at some point in the future. If we see an airplane flying north at two hundred miles per hour, we know that in one hour it will be two hundred miles farther north if it does not change its course or speed.

The mind-expanding discovery of quantum mechanics is that Newtonian physics does not apply to subatomic phenomena. In the subatomic realm, we cannot know both the position *and* the momentum of a particle with absolute precision. We can know both, approximately, but the more we know about one, the less we know about the other. We can know either of them precisely, but in that case, we can know nothing about the other. This is Werner Heisenberg's uncertainty principle. As incredible as it seems, it has been verified repeatedly by experiment.

Of course, if we picture a moving particle, it is very difficult to imagine not being able to measure both its position and momentum. Not to be able to do so defies our "common sense." This is not the only quantum mechanical phenomenon which contradicts common sense. Commonsense contradictions, in fact, are at the heart of the new physics. They tell us again and again that the world may not be what we think it is. It may be much, much more.

Since we cannot determine both the position and momentum of subatomic particles, we cannot predict much about them. Accordingly, quantum mechanics does not and cannot predict specific events. It does, however, predict *probabilities*. Probabilities are the odds that something is going to happen, or that it is not going to happen. Quantum theory can predict the probability of a microscopic event with the same precision that Newtonian physics can predict the actual occurrence of a macroscopic event.

Newtonian physics says, "If such and such is the case now, then such and such is going to happen next." Quantum mechanics says, "If such and such is the case now, then the *probability* that such and such is going to happen next is . . . (whatever it is calculated to be)." We never can know with certainty what will happen to the particle that we are "observing." All that we can know for sure are the probabilities for it to behave in certain ways. This is the most that we can know because the two data which must be included in a Newtonian calculation, position and momentum, cannot both be known with precision. *We must choose,* by the selection of our experiment, which one we want to measure most accurately.

The lesson of Newtonian physics is that the universe is governed by laws that are susceptible to rational understanding. By applying those laws we extend our knowledge of, and therefore our influence over, our environment. Newton was a religious person. He saw his laws as manifestations of God's perfection. Nonetheless, Newton's laws served man's cause well. They enhanced his dignity and vindicated his importance in the universe. Following the Middle Ages, the new field of science ("Natural Philosophy") came like a fresh breeze to revitalize the spirit. It is ironic that, in the end, Natural philosophy reduced the status of men to that of helpless cogs in a machine whose functioning had been preordained from the day of its creation.

Contrary to Newtonian physics, quantum mechanics tells us that our knowledge of what governs events on the subatomic level is not nearly what we assumed it would be. It tells us that we cannot predict subatomic phenomena with any certainty. We can only predict their probabilities.

Philosophically, however, the implications of quantum mechanics are psychedelic. Not only do we influence our reality, but, in some degree, we actually *create* it. Because it is the nature of things that we can know either the momentum of a particle or its position, but not both, *we must choose* which of these two properties we want to determine. Metaphysically, this is very close to saying that we *create* certain properties because we choose to measure those properties. Said another way, it is possible that we create something that has position, for example, like a particle, because we are intent on determining position and it is impossible to determine position without having some *thing* occupying the position that we want to determine.

Quantum physicists ponder questions like, "Did a particle with momentum exist before we conducted an experiment to measure its momentum?"; "Did a particle with position exist before we conducted an experiment to measure its position?"; and "Did any particles exist at all before we thought about them and measured them?" *"Did we create the particles that we are experimenting with?"* Incredible as it sounds, this is a possibility that many physicists recognize.

John Wheeler, a well-known physicist at Princeton, wrote:

> May the universe in some strange sense be "brought into being" by the participation of those who participate? . . . The vital act is the act of participation. "Participator" is the incontrovertible new concept given by quantum mechanics. It strikes down the term "observer" of classical theory, the man who stands safely behind the thick glass wall and watches what goes on without taking part. It can't be done, quantum mechanics says.*

*J.A. Wheeler, K.S. Thorne, and C. Misner, *Gravitation* (San Francisco, 1973), p. 1273.

The languages of eastern mystics and western physicists are becoming very similar. Newtonian physics and quantum mechanics are partners in a double irony. Newtonian physics is based upon the idea of laws which govern phenomena and the power inherent in understanding them, but it leads to impotence in the face of a Great Machine which is the universe. Quantum mechanics is based upon the idea of minimal knowledge of future phenomena (we are limited to knowing probabilities) but it leads to the possibility that our reality is what we choose to make it.

LEWIS THOMAS: DEBATING THE UNKNOWABLE

From "Debating the Unknowable" by Lewis Thomas in *The Atlantic Monthly*, July 1981, pp. 49–51. Reprinted by permission of Harold Ober Associates Incorporated. Copyright © 1981 by The Atlantic Monthly.

Dr. Lewis Thomas, a biologist, is chancellor of the Memorial Sloan-Kettering Cancer Center. This article is based on a lecture in the 1981 Colloquium on Common Learning held by the Carnegie Foundation for the Advancement of Teaching.

The greatest of all the accomplishments of twentieth-century science has been the discovery of human ignorance. We live, as never before, in puzzlement about nature, the universe, and ourselves most of all. It is a new experience for the species. A century ago, after the turbulence caused by Darwin and Wallace had subsided and the central idea of natural selection had been grasped and accepted, we thought we knew everything essential about evolution. In the eighteenth century there were no huge puzzles; human reason was all you needed in order to figure out the universe. And for most of the earlier centuries, the Church provided both the questions and the answers, neatly packaged. Now, for the first time in human history, we are catching glimpses of our incomprehension. We can still make up stories to explain the world, as we always have, but now the stories have to be confirmed and reconfirmed by experiment. This is the scientific method, and once started on this line we cannot turn back. We are obliged to grow up in skepticism, requiring proofs for every assertion about nature, and there is no way out except to move ahead and plug away, hoping for comprehension in the future but living in a condition of intellectual instability for the long time.

It is the admission of ignorance that leads to progress, not so much because the solving of a particular puzzle leads directly to a new piece of understanding but because the puzzle—if it interests enough scientists—leads to *work*. There is a similar phenomenon in entomology known as stigmergy, a term invented by Grassé, which means to "to incite to work." When three or four termites are collected together in a chamber they wander about aimlessly, but when more termites are added, they begin to build. It is the presence of other termites, in sufficient numbers at close quarters, that produces the work: they pick up each other's fecal pellets and stack them in neat columns, and when the columns are precisely the right height, the termites reach across and turn the perfect arches that form the foundation of the termitarium. No single termite knows how to do any of this, but as soon as there are enough termites gathered together they become flawless architects, sensing their distances from each other although blind, building an immensely complicated structure with its own air-conditioning and humidity control. They work their lives away in this ecosystem built by themselves. The nearest thing to a termitarium that I can think of in human behavior is the making of language, which we do by keeping *at* each other all our lives, generation after generation, changing the structure by some sort of instinct.

Very little is understood about this kind of collective behavior. It is out of fashion these days to talk of "superorganisms," but there simply aren't enough reductionist details in hand to explain away the phenomenon of termites and other social insects: some very good guesses can be made about their chemical signaling systems, but the plain fact that they exhibit something like a collective intelligence is a mystery, or anyway an unsolved problem, that might contain important implications for social life in general. This mystery is the best introduction I can think of to biological science in college. It should be taught for its strangeness, and for the ambiguity of its meaning. It should be taught to premedical students, who need lessons early in their careers about the uncertainties in science.

College students, and for that matter high school students, should be exposed very early, perhaps at the outset, to the big arguments currently going on among scientists. Big arguments stimulate their interest, and with luck engage their absorbed attention. Few things in life are as engrossing as a good fight between highly trained and skilled adversaries. But the young students are told very little about the major disagreements of the day; they may be taught something about the arguments between Darwinians and their opponents a century ago, but they do not realize that similar disputes about other matters, many of them touching profound issues for our understanding of nature, are still going on and, indeed, are an essential feature of the scientific process. There is, I fear, a reluctance on the part of science teachers to talk about such things, based on the belief that before students can appreciate what the arguments are about they must learn and master the "fundamentals." I would be willing to see some experiments along this line, and I have in mind several examples of contemporary doctrinal dispute in which the drift of the argument can be readily perceived without deep or elaborate knowledge of the subject.

There is, for one, the problem of animal awareness. One school of ethologists devoted to the study of animal behavior has it that human beings are unique in the possession of consciousness, differing from all other creatures in being able to think things over, capitalize on past experience, and hazard informed guesses at the future. Other, "lower," animals (with possible exceptions made for chimpanzees, whales, and dolphins) cannot do such things with their minds; they live from moment to moment with brains that are programmed to respond, automatically or by conditioning, to contingencies in the environment. Behavioral psychologists believe that this automatic or conditioned response accounts for human mental activity as well, although they dislike that word "mental." On the other side are some ethologists who seem to be more generous-minded, who see no compelling reasons to doubt that animals in general are quite capable of real thinking and do quite a lot of it—thinking that isn't as dense as human thinking, that is sparser because of the lack of language and the resultant lack of metaphors to help the thought along, but thinking nonetheless.

The point about the argument is not that one side or the other is in possession of a more powerful array of convincing facts; quite the opposite. There are not enough facts to sustain a genuine debate of any length; the question of animal awareness is an unsettled one. In the circumstance, I put forward the following notion about a small beetle, the mimosa girdler, which undertakes three pieces of linked, sequential behavior: finding a mimosa tree and climbing up the trunk and out to the end of a branch; cutting a longitudinal slit and laying within it five or six eggs; and crawling back on the limb and girdling it neatly down into the cambium. The third step is an eight-to-ten-hour task of hard labor, from which the beetle gains no food for itself—only the certainty that the branch will promptly die and fall to the ground in the next brisk wind, thus enabling the larvae to hatch and grow in an abundance of dead wood. I propose, in total confidence that even though I am probably wrong nobody today can prove that I am wrong, that the beetle is not doing these three things out of blind instinct, like a little machine, but is thinking its way along, just as we would think. The difference is that we possess enormous brains, crowded all the time with an infinite number of long thoughts, while the beetle's brain is only a few strings of neurons connected in a modest network, capable therefore of only three *tiny* thoughts, coming into consciousness one after the other: find the right tree; get up there and lay eggs in a slit; back up and spend the day killing the branch so the eggs can hatch. End of message. I would not go so far as to anthropomorphize the mimosa tree, for I really do not believe plants have minds, but something has to be said about the tree's role in this arrangement as a beneficiary: mimosas grow for twenty-five to thirty years and then die, unless they are vigorously pruned annually, in which case they can live to be a hundred. The beetle is a piece of good luck for the tree, but nothing more: one example of pure chance working at its best in nature—what you might even wish to call good nature.

This brings me to the second example of unsettlement in biology, currently being rather delicately discussed but not yet argued over, for there is still only one orthodoxy and almost no opposition, yet. This is the matter of chance itself, and the role played by blind chance in the arrangement of living things on the planet. It is, in the orthodox view, pure luck that evolution brought us to our present condition, and things might just as well have turned out any number of other, different ways, and might go in any unpredictable way for the future. There is, of course, nothing chancy about natural selection itself: it is an accepted fact that selection will always favor the advantaged individuals whose genes succeed best in propagating themselves within a changing environment. But the creatures acted upon by natural selection are themselves there as the result of chance: mutations (probably of much more importance during the long period of exclusively microbial life starting nearly 4 billion years ago and continuing until about one billion years ago); the endless sorting and re-sorting of genes within chromosomes during replication; perhaps recombination of genes across species lines at one time or another; and almost certainly the carrying of genes by viruses from one creature to another.

The argument comes when one contemplates the whole biosphere, the conjoined life of the earth. How could it have turned out to possess such stability and coherence, resembling as it does a sort of enormous developing embryo, with nothing but chance events to determine its emergence? Lovelock and Margulis, facing this problem, have proposed the Gaia Hypothesis, which is, in brief, that the earth is itself a form of life, "a complex entity involving the Earth's biosphere, atmosphere, oceans and soil; the totality constituting a feedbuck or cybernetic system which seeks an optimal physical and chemical environment for life on this planet." Lovelock postulates, in addition, that "the physical and chemical condition of the surface of the Earth, of the atmosphere, and of the oceans has been and is actively made fit and comfortable by the presence of life itself."

This notion is beginning to stir up a few signs of storm, and if it catches on, as I think it will, we will soon find the biological community split into fuming factions, one side saying that the envolved biosphere displays evidences of design and purpose, the other decrying such heresy. I believe that students should learn as much as they can about the argument. In an essay in *Coevolution* (Spring 1981), W. F. Doolittle has recently attacked the Gaia Hypothesis, asking, among other things, ". . . how does Gaia know if she is too cold or too hot, and how does she instruct the biosphere to behave accordingly?" This is not a deadly criticism in a world where we do not actually understand, in anything like real detail, how even Dr. Doolittle manages the stability and control of his own internal environment, including his body temperature. One thing is certain: none of us can instruct our body's systems to make the needed corrections beyond a very limited number of rather trivial tricks made possible through biofeedback techniques. If something goes wrong with my liver or my kidneys, I have no advice to offer out of my cortex. I rely on the system to fix itself, which it usually does with no help from me beyond crossing my fingers.

Another current battle involving the unknown is between sociobiologists and antisociobiologists, and it is a marvel for students to behold. To observe, in open-mouthed astonishment, one group of highly intelligent, beautifully trained, knowledgeable, and imaginative scientists maintaining that all behavior, animal and human, is governed exclusively by genes, and another group of equally talented scientists asserting that all behavior is set and determined by the environment or by culture, is an educational experience that no college student should be allowed to miss. The essential lesson to be learned has nothing to do with the relative validity of the facts underlying the argument. It is the argument itself that is the education: we do not yet know enough to settle such questions.

BRUCE MAZLISH: OUR "HERACLITEAN" PERIOD

From "Our Heraclitean Period" by Bruce Mazlish in the *The Nation*, April 22, 1961, pp. 336–38. Copyright 1961 *Nation* magazine, The Nation Associates, Inc. Reprinted by permission.

In the following article, Professor Mazlish analyzes our present situation and suggests what we may have to do before we can go into the new age that is "struggling to be born." An intellectual historian, Mazlish moves freely through the fields of science, art,

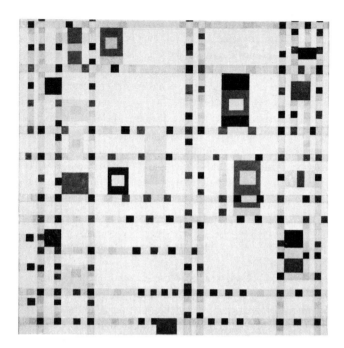

Mondrian, Broadway Boogie Woogie. Abstract painters are often fascinated by the related qualities of music. Mondrian's form-smashing differs from that of Picasso, Duchamp, Léger, and others, by his creation of rigid geometric designs unlike anything found in life. (Mondrian, Piet. Broadway Boogie Woogie, 1942–1943. Oil on canvas. 50×50". Collection, the Museum of Modern Art, New York. Given anonymously.)

music, literature, and history—a rare feat. He brings the cultural developments of the last century and a half into focus, and raises some provocative issues that you will probably have to deal with at some time in your life.

There is a temptation, in a time of atom-smashing (and the consequent shattering of cities like Hiroshima and Nagasaki), to conclude that ours is a time of form-smashing as well. We may be led, by easy analogy, to think of our society as being swept by an almost unprecedented unsettling: a destruction of forms, a sweep of iconoclasm. Against this view, however, I propose a contrary—or different—picture: that ours is, with a vengeance, a "Heraclitean" period, in which forms and fixity have all but disappeared. We live in a kaleidoscopic world (as we shall see, modern, abstract art reflects this fact) in which forms cannot be smashed because they hardly exist.

Such, I suggest, is our present situation. How have we arrived at it? I think the answer is to be sought in an examination of the true iconoclasts who have preceded us. For form-smashing in the Western world did occur; and it occurred, not in our time, but largely before World War I, in the period stretching from about 1830 on. We can trace the lineaments of this movement in a number of fields: the moral (involving the "human sciences"), the scientific and the artistic. Naturally, we can only touch here on the highlights, and even that with acknowledged temerity.

One of the most "shattering" declarations of this earlier iconoclasm can be found in Bernard Shaw's *Man and Superman* (1901–1903). Tanner is shocking his poor Ann. "I am ten times more destructive now that I was then," he explains to her. "The moral passion has taken my destructiveness in hand and directed it to moral ends. I have become a reformer, and like all reformers, an iconoclast. I no longer break cucumber frames and burn gorse bushes: I shatter creeds and demolish idols." To Ann's bored comment that "Destruction can only destroy," Tanner retorts: "Yes. That is why it is so useful. Construction cumbers the ground with institutions made by busybodies. Destruction clears it and gives us breathing space and liberty." As we see here, the line between iconoclasm and vandalism—destruction for its own sake—is thin; Tanner knows that he must destroy, but he does not know what he wishes to construct in the cleared space.

Shaw, of course, is a fairly late comer to the excavation site of nineteenth-century faiths and ideals. Before him, to take some random but key examples, there was Karl Marx, who knew precisely what shape he wished to emerge at the end of the bourgeois form of culture; Friedrich Nietzsche, with his "transvaluation of all values"; Charles

Duchamp, Nude Descending a Staircase, 1913. When Teddy Roosevelt saw this work in the 1913 Armory Exhibit, he left in a huff, exclaiming to reporters, "Not only was there no nude, there wasn't even a stair-case!" (Philadelphia Museum of Art: The Louise and Walter Arensberg Collection.)

Darwin, who broke the image of man as a being separate from the rest of the animals; and, contemporary with Shaw, Sigmund Freud, who destroyed, among other things, the dichotomy between civilized, rational man, and primitive, passional man. The iconoclasm of these men, and others like them, produced the "Heraclitean" aspect of our present time in what I have loosely called the moral field.

For our purposes, two aspects of Marx's work need to be singled out: his theory of ideology and his theory of dialectical materialism. The first suggested that our ideas are merely reflections or psychic projections—not independent, eternal truths—of our material conditions or production. And the second—the theory of dialectical materialism—implied that these material conditions are always changing. The initial effect of the two theories was to tear aside the veil of illusion put up by the bourgeoisie, and to show that its law, morality and religion were so many prejudices: the result, therefore, was a repudiation of existing values. The more long-range effect was to destroy "absolutes" and "fixities" of any kind (and this in spite of Marx's attempt to establish a Communist absolute in place of what he had destroyed), and to leave only a world of shifting appearances.

Nietzsche completed the "transvaluation of all values." He showed that there is no one truth of morality, but merely a number of perspectives, of which none can claim to be absolute. As he remarks in *Beyond Good and Evil* (1886), every philosophy or world-view is merely the confession of its originator. But Nietzsche does not leave the matter there; he seeks the springs in our soul which give rise to our particular confession. To obtain this information he invites us to plunge into our own depths, in search of a new awareness of self, a new self-consciousness: it is a novel form of philosophic skin-diving, for which we must nerve ourselves. The result is his discovery that altruism may be a deception, that intention may be only an outward sign or symbol: in short, that "Everything deep loves masks."

From Nietzsche's "transvaluation" emerges a new view of truth and a new perspective on the self. Our personalities are no longer fixed, for behind them lurks only the seething cauldron of a formless "will to power." And this interpretation accords—how this would delight Nietzsche's philologist's heart!—with the very origin of the word "personality," from the Latin "persona," meaning a mask, the mask used in a play. The self which is left to us after Nietzsche is no longer an essence but a series of masks which we assume. (From this point on, the line to existentialism, where "existence precedes essence," is clear.)

It is difficult to say how much of Nietzsche's work was influenced by Darwin, but both men were occupied with the notion of existence as a struggle. Out of Darwin's "natural history" of struggle came a major revision of man's image of himself as a unique, fixed figure in the universe. The first step in this direction had been taken by Galileo, who "naturalized" man by demonstrating that the planet he inhabits is similar to the heavenly bodies. The next step was prepared by Linnaeus, in 1755, when he revised his classificatory scheme to include *homo sapiens:* henceforth, man was no longer a being totally different in kind from the other animals, midway between them and the angels, but only a natural being further up the classificatory scale. Linnaeus's scheme, however, was static; into this *rigor mortis* Darwin breathed life. The result: by showing man as descended from other animals (the *Descent of Man*, 1871, concluding what the *Origin of Species*, 1859, had begun) he succeeded in eliminating the second discontinuity—to use the nice phrase of Jerome Bruner—that between man and the animal world.

The success of Darwin's work had numerous and powerful effects. One was to substitute, in the period following, the predominance of biological for physical science, and thus to substitute images of life processes for those relating to mechanical systems. Another, and the greater, effect was to introduce the idea of evolution, of constant and unremitting change, as the dominant mode of viewing the world. The result was that, throughout that world, all things, man included, had now to be conceived of as being in a perpetual state of variation.

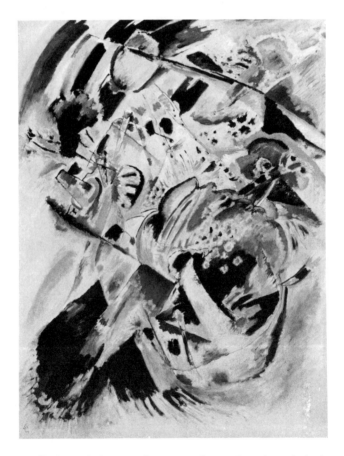

Kandinsky, Painting Number 199 (Winter). Even the painting's title has now become abstract. But does a painting—any more than a piece of music—really need a title? Of course, every painting should be viewed originally in its true colors before one looks at a reproduction. (The Solomon R. Guggenheim Museum.)

Darwin had removed one discontinuity; it was reserved for Sigmund Freud to remove another. He eliminated the distance between the primitive and the civilized man, between the child and the adult, a between the pervert and the normal person. By treating man as a natural object, amenable to the same objective, disinterested approach as previously used by man on the non-human materials of nature, Freud, like Darwin, helped "naturalize " man. In short, he put man on a sliding scale.

Freud, along with Marx, Nietzsche, Darwin, and many others whom we have not even touched upon, have left us—modern man—in a world characterized by an acceptance of the notion of change and by an awareness of the shifting nature of reality: physical, social and personal. Not only have our previously fixed ideas and values been transvalued; they have been shattered in an Alcibiadean fury of iconoclasm. All the masks on the gods have been torn off.

It is my contention, then, that the real form-smashing in Western civilization occurred before World War I, and that it took its dominant tone from thinkers in the human or moral sciences (and I place Darwin in this group). Color and strength were given to this development by work in art, music, and literature, and in the natural sciences. Though I am emphasizing the primary place of iconoclasm in the human sciences, attention must also be given to the highlights from these other fields, and the thesis as to iconoclasm as a pre-World War I phenomenon tested by their evidence.

In general, we tend to forget how dated and no longer à la mode modern art is. In reality, however, almost all the important work, leading from the Impressionists to, say, the movement of cubism, futurism, and abstractionism, and to the innovating work of the early Picasso and of men like Braque, Léger, Gris, Klee and Kandinsky, was accomplished before the actual holocaust of the First World War. The landscape of art which we inhabit today differs little, though it is better explored, from that of 1914. It is a landscape from which all existing forms have been swept away, so that it might be ready for some new construction yet to be decided on. The closest equivalent to Tanner in modern art could well be Piet Mondrian, with his clear, more or less empty, canvases.

So, too, in music, Wagner strained against the limits of tonality in the nineteenth century, and set the stage for its breaking in the twentieth. Arnold Schönberg's *Pierrot Lunaire,* with its weird wandering and haunting sense of homelessness—because there is no key—shattered the world of music in 1912. A year later, Stravinsky's *Rites of Spring,* with its jarring turn to "primitivism" and its exciting use of dissonance and bi-tonality, added its energy to the overthrow of the old forms.

By World War I, James Joyce was already wading in the stream of consciousness: a literary method abandoning conventional, logical, "fixed" associations among words in order to arrive at a new, variable "logic" of emotional association. He rebelled against accepted values, as well as against literary forms. Thus, in *Portrait of the Artist as a Young Man* (1916), he announced: "I will not serve that in which I no longer believe, whether it call itself my home, my fatherland, or my church."

So, too, Ezra Pound and others had set the stage for T. S. Eliot's *The Wasteland* (not itself published till 1922) which, both by form and content, pointed up the empty, desolate and lonely landscape inhabited by modern man. Thus, Eliot's method in the poem is to transcend ordinary space and time in favor of a felt order of space and time—we jump back and forth from Elizabethan to modern times, from the north to the south of Europe—and to use words for their evocative effects. There is little effort at normal, public, "fixed" communication. And this coincides with Eliot's view as to the breakdown of our shared civilization. Our culture, Eliot is saying, is merely "A heap of broken images"; our heritage meaningless, "withered stumps of time told upon the wall." It is Tanner's world of "shattered creeds and demolished idols" par excellence.

What of the world of natural science? Once again, we tend to forget how early non-Euclidean geometry first made its appearance. It was around the 1830s that three great and original minds—Gauss, Lobachevski and Bolyai—began to question the self-evident nature of Euclid's parallel axiom. True, as C.P. Snow has so well expressed it, "the discovery was hung up for thirty years—by Gauss's timidity, Bolyai's lack of professional power, the miserable behavior of Lobachevski's colleagues." But it finally broke through with Riemann's dissertation "On the Hypotheses Underlying Geometry" (1854, but not published till 1868), where the talk is of hypotheses, not axioms, and of hypothetical truths, dependent upon the validity of certain assumptions, rather than of categorical and self-evident propositions. In place of one absolute, fixed geometry, there were several, all equally tenable. No wonder Bolyai exclaimed: "I have created a new and wonderful world!"

He had also destroyed. With his co-workers in mathematics, he had begun the undermining of the notion that nature and her laws are fixed, self-evident entities. Einstein's work in relativity (the initial effort dating from 1905) extended the non-Euclidean shaking to the ideas of absolute space and time, and did for physics what had been done in the new geometry. Only Heisenberg's work, on the indeterminacy principle, falls after World War I, in 1927. By that time, however, the destruction was complete: the simple, visual picture of both the atom and the universe had been completely shattered. The old form had gone, and in its place stood a mathematical equation in, as Heisenberg put it, "an abstract space of many dimensions."

Here we must stop. I have outrun my knowledge—and perhaps yours—of modern science. I have taken, with great boldness and elan, various examples from the human sciences, art, music and literature to illustrate my thesis, some might say to fit it. In spite, however, of any arbitrariness that might be involved, I think the first part of my general thesis will stand: an unprecedented burst of iconoclasm has swept the Western world, not in our time, but in the period roughly stretching from 1830 to 1914. The result, at least for those at the frontier of thought (and overlooking the present "conservative" attempt to return to the past), has been a widespread "denial of faiths, abandonment of traditions, and repudiation of values."

All of this has come about in the name of iconoclasm: an iconoclasm which destroyed in order to prepare the ground for new idols and ideals. What, however, has been the result of that iconoclasm? Have the new forms arisen?

Here I come to the second part of my thesis: ours is a "Heraclitean" period, in which we do not smash forms—because we no longer believe in forms at all. In this post-iconoclastic era, there are no absolutes, whether of morals and values or of space and time; nor are there "fixed" views, whether of the self or of society. In place of dogmas, we have ideologies; in place of faiths, we have psychic projections. Instead of man's occupying a unique, clearly defined and unchanging place in the world, he is, as a species, continuous with the animal world and, as a "civilized" being close to the child and the primitive (an image confirmed in our time, for example, by the art of Klee and Picasso). Modern man is a little like the player in Gilbert and Sullivan, engaged in a game, "On a cloth untrue, with a twisted cue, and elliptical billiard balls."

All is perspective and process. In such a world, there are no statues to deface. As one of my friends has remarked: "Who today is smashing religion? You couldn't find a single atheist in public life, or an acknowledged immoralist (I hasten to add that I use the term in its pre-beatnik sense; that pale protest merely illustrates my point from the other side) in artistic life." His lament is like Villon's, "Where are the iconoclasts of yesteryear"; and just as forlorn.

In a sense, then, ours is a unique period. Previous eras have been unsettled, subject to rapid change and iconoclastic (even in the literal sense). But always, when x-idol was attacked, it was attacked in the name of an alternative, y-idol, or at least in the hope of an alternative. Today, there is no y. There is only process. Our motto might be: "Change for change's sake," for no new forms—no fixities—seem to emerge from the change. It is not by accident, then, that our dominant philosophies are pragmatism or existentialism (or logical analysis, which seeks to do away entirely with the metaphysical idols) and our scientific ethos one of operationalism or instrumentalism.

It is exactly this state of affairs, however, which is our challenge. Do we accept the existing situation (and there is much to be said for this)? Are we comfortable with it? Or do we seek to go back to old, conventional forms? Or to create new forms? Are there any such looming on the horizon?

Hitherto, to use Matthew Arnold's phrases, we have been

Wandering between two worlds, one dead,
The other powerless to be born.

I have tried to suggest why our world is "dead," in the sense that it is living largely in terms of the landscape bequeathed to us by the iconoclasm of the period which ended . . . half a century ago. What will the new world look like? We shall only know after we recognize our situation as a "Heraclitean" one and, from this awareness, seek to discover our "true" bearings.

CHAPTER 33
OF GOD AND MAN

Moved by love, God is eternally resolved to reveal
himself. But as love is the motive so love must also be
the end; for it would be a contradiction for God to have
a motive and an end which did not correspond. His love
is a love for the learner, and his aim is to win him.

—*Søren Kierkegaard*

When Napoleon asked one of his advisers why there seemed to be no evidence of
God in his thinking, the adviser replied, "Sire, I have no need of that hypothesis."
The prevailing "hypotheses" of the nineteenth century were rationalism,
positivism, and scientism.

In the twentieth century our faith in those optimistic devices has been
challenged by the reality of two World Wars, the rise of totalitarianism, and the
instant incineration of cities by atomic weapons. As a result, more and more
serious thinkers are devoting themselves to questions of God and the nature of
existence. Many if not most of these thinkers are religious philosophers rather than
theologians.

For various reasons, Russians have been in the forefront of these speculations;
so it is appropriate that the first selection below is from one of the best-known
Russian novelists. In one segment of his *Brothers Karamazov,* Dostoevsky
imagines what might have happened if Jesus has returned to earth during the
heyday of the Spanish Inquisition, when the Church was burning heretics as an
"act of the faith" (auto-da-fé).

The second selection, from a leading exponent of the Social Gospel, argues that
the church should lead the fight against the evils caused by man's inhumanity to
man, especially the evils of modern industrial society. This movement, also
known as "Christian Socialism," was espoused by such nineteenth-century greats
as Robert Southey, Samuel Taylor Coleridge, and Thomas Carlyle.

Next, C.E.M. Joad, the late English critic and philosopher, explains why he
changed from a rationalist to a Christian as a result of the prevalence of evil in the
world, especially the evil of Hitler. Finally, the most original of all twentieth-
century philosophies, existentialism, is explained by three of its leading expo-
nents: Jean-Paul Sartre, an atheist; Martin Buber, a Jew who was strongly
influenced by the Christian Søren Kierkegaard; and Paul Tillich, a German
Protestant theologian who fled Hitler's Germany and came to the United States in
1933. As its name suggests, existentialism is concerned with the questions: What

does it mean to exist? Does existence precede essence? Does man, alone among living things, have the responsibility to define himself? And, in so doing, to define his morality, his values, and his purpose in life? Is man's freedom the source of his forlornness?

DOSTOEVSKY: THE GRAND INQUISITOR

Feodor Dostoevsky, *Notes from Underground & The Grand Inquisitor*, trans. R.E. Matlaw, 1960. Reprinted by permission of the publisher, E.P. Dutton, New York. Pp. 122–130.

Feodor Dostoevsky (d. 1881) included this story in his novel *The Brothers Karamazov*. But "The Grand Inquisitor" became so popular that it was published separately as a novella in its own right. During the Spanish Inquisition of the sixteenth century, the story goes, the people had prayed so hard for Christ's coming that He actually appears at a child's funeral and raises her from the dead:

. . . At that moment the cardinal himself, the Grand Inquisitor, passes by the cathedral. He is an old man, almost ninety, tall and erect, with a withered face and sunken eyes from which a light like a fiery spark gleams. Oh, he is not in his gorgeous

El Greco, The Grand Inquisitor, Don Fernando Nino de Guevara. Thanks to Dostoevsky, we are transported back to the Renaissance and the Counterreformation in Spain. El Greco's portrait shows a man of restless and penetrating mind, quite capable of the convoluted thinking imagined by Dostoevsky. (Metropolitan Museum of Art, Bequest of Mrs. H.O. Havemeyer, 1929. The H.O. Havemeyer Collection.)

cardinal's robes, that he had flaunted before the people the day before when he was burning the enemies of the Roman Church—no, at the moment he was only wearing his old, coarse monk's cassock. At a distance behind him come his sombre assistants and slaves and the "holy guard." He stops at the sight of the crowd and watches it from a distance. He had seen everything; he had seen them set the coffin down at His feet, seen the girl rise up. His face darkens. He knits his thick gray brows and his eyes gleam with a sinister fire. He holds out his finger and bids the guards take Him. And such is his power, so completely are the people cowed into submission and trembling obedience to him, that the crowd immediately makes way for the guards, and in the midst of the tomblike silence that has suddenly fallen they lay hands on Him and lead Him away. The crowd instantly as one man bows down to the earth before the old inquisitor. He blesses the people in silence and passes on. The guards lead their prisoner to the close, gloomy vaulted dungeon in the ancient palace of the Holy Inquisition and shut Him in it. The day passes and is followed by the dark, burning "breathless" night of Seville. The air is "fragrant with laurel and lemon." In the pitch darkness the iron door of the dungeon is suddenly opened and the Grand Inquisitor himself slowly comes in with a light in his hand. He is alone; the door is closed at once behind him. He stands in the doorway and for a long time, a minute or two, gazes into His face. At last he goes up slowly, sets the light on the table and speaks.

"Is it You? You?" but receiving no answer, he adds at once, "Don't answer, be silent. Indeed, what can You say? I know too well what You would say. And You have no right to add anything to what You had said of old. Why, then, have You come to hinder us? For You have come to hinder us, and You know that. But do You know what will happen tomorrow? I do not know who You are and I don't care to know whether it is You or only a semblance of Him, but tomorrow I will condemn You and burn You at the stake as the worst of heretics. And the very people who today kissed Your feet, tomorrow at the faintest sign from me will rush to heap up the embers of Your fire. Do You know that? Yes, maybe You know it," he added with earnest reflection, never for a moment taking his eyes off the prisoner. . . .

The old man has told Him He hasn't the right to add anything to what He has said of old. One may say it is the most fundamental feature of Roman Catholicism, . . . "All has been given by You to the Pope," they say, "and all, therefore, is still in the Pope's hands, and there is no need for You to come now at all. You must not meddle, for the time at least. . . . Have You the right to reveal to us one of the mysteries of the world from which You have come? . . . No, You have not; that You may not add to what has been said of old, and may not take from men the freedom You exalted when You were on earth. Whatever You reveal anew will encroach on men's freedom of faith; for it will be manifest as a miracle, and the freedom of their faith was dearer to You than anything in those days fifteen hundred years ago. Did You not often say then, 'I will make you free?' But now You have seen these 'free' men," the old man adds suddenly, with a pensive smile. "Yes, we've paid dearly for it," he goes on, looking sternly at Him, "but at last we have completed that work in Your name. For fifteen centuries we have been wrestling with Your freedom, but now it is ended and over for good. Do You not believe that it's over for good? You look at me meekly and do not even deign to be angry with me. But let me tell You now, today, people are more persuaded than ever that they are completely free, yet they have brought their freedom to us and laid it humbly at our feet. But that has been our doing. Was this what You did? Was this Your freedom?''

. . . "Only now" (he is speaking of the Inquisition of course) "for the first time it has become possible to think of the happiness of men. Man was created a rebel; and how can rebels be happy? You were warned,'' he says to Him. ''You had no lack of admonitions and warnings, but You did not listen to those warnings; You rejected the only way by which men might be made happy, but fortunately, when You departed, You handed the work on to us. You affirmed by Your word, You gave us the right to bind and to unbind, and now, of course, You cannot even think of taking that right away from us. Why, then, do You come to hinder us?

''The wise and dread spirit, the spirit of self-destruction and non-existence,'' the old man goes on, ''the great spirit talked with You in the wilderness, and we are told in the books that he 'tempted' You. Is that not so? And could anything truer be said than what he revealed to You in three questions and what You rejected, and what in the books is called 'the temptations'? And yet if there has ever been on earth a real stupendous miracle, it took place on that day, on the day of the three temptations. The statement of those three questions was itself the miracle. If it were possible to imagine simply for the sake of argument that those three questions of the dread spirit had perished utterly from the books, and that we had to restore them and to invent and formulate them anew, to restore them to the books, and to do so had gathered together all the wise men of the earth—rulers, chief priests, learned men, philosophers, poets—and set them the task to invent, to formulate three questions, such as would not only fit the occasion, but express in three words, in a mere three human phrases, the whole future history of the world and of humanity—do You believe that all the wisdom of the earth united together could have invented anything in depth and force equal to the three questions which were actually put to You then by the wise and mighty spirit in the wilderness? From those questions alone, from the miracle of their statement, we can see that we are not dealing with the fleeting human intelligence, but with the absolute and eternal. For in those three questions the whole subsequent history of mankind is, as it were, brought together into one whole and foretold, and in them are united all the unsolved historical contradictions of human nature throughout the world. At the time it could not have been so clear since the future was unknown; but now that fifteen hundred years have passed, we see that everything in those three questions was so justly divined and foretold, and has been so truly fulfilled, that nothing can be added to them or taken from them.

''Judge Yourself who was right—You or he who questioned You then? Remember the first question: its meaning, in other words, was this: 'You would go into the world, and are going with empty hands, with some promise of freedom which men in their simplicity and their natural unruliness cannot even understand, which they fear and dread—since nothing has ever been more insupportable for a man and a human society than freedom. Do You see these stones in this parched and barren wilderness? Turn them into bread, and mankind will run after You like a flock, grateful and obedient, though for ever trembling, lest You withdraw your hand and deny them Your bread.' But You would not deprive man of freedom and rejected the offer, thinking, what is that freedom worth, if obedience is bought with bread? You replied that man lives not by bread alone. But do You know that for the sake of that earthly bread the spirit of the earth will rise up against You and fight with You and overcome You, and all will follow him, crying, 'Who can compare with this beast? He has given us fire from heaven!' Do You know that centuries will pass, and humanity will proclaim through the mouth of their wisdom and science that there is no crime, and therefore no sin, there is only hunger? 'Feed men, and then demand virtue from them!' That's what they'll write on the banner, which they will raise against You, and with which they will destroy Your temple. Where Your temple stood a new building will rise; the terrible tower of Babel will be built again, and though, like the one of old it will not be finished, yet You might have prevented that new tower and have cut short the sufferings of men for a thousand years; for they will come back to us after a thousand years of agony with their tower. They will seek us again, hidden underground in the catacombs, for we shall again be persecuted and tortured. They will find us and cry to us, 'Feed us, for those who have promised us fire from heaven haven't given it!' And then we shall finish building their tower, for he finishes the building who feeds them. And we alone shall feed them in Your name, and declare falsely that it is in Your name. Oh, never, never can they feed themselves without us! No science will give them bread so long as they remain free. In the end they will lay their freedom at our feet, and say to us, 'Make us your slaves, but feed us.' They will understand themselves, at last, that freedom and bread enough for all are inconceivable together, for they will never, never be able to share among themselves. They will be convinced, too, that they can never be free, for they are weak, sinful, worthless, and rebellious. You promised them the bread of heaven, but, I repeat again, can it compare with earthly bread in the eyes of the weak, ever sinful and ignoble race of man? And if for the sake of the bread of Heaven thousands and tens of thousands shall follow You, what is to become of the millions and tens of thousands of millions of creatures who will not have the strength to forgo the earthly bread for the sake of the heavenly? Or do You care only for the tens of thousands of the great and strong dear to You while the millions, numerous as the sands of the sea, who are weak but love You, must exist only for the sake of the great and strong? No, for the weak are dear to us too. They are sinful and rebellious, but in the end they too will become obedient. They will marvel at us and look upon us as gods, because we are ready to endure the freedom which they have found so dreadful and to rule over them—so awful will it seem to them to be free. But we will tell them that we are Your servants and rule them in Your name. We will deceive them again, for we will not let You come to us again. That deception will be our suffering, for we will be forced to lie. That is the significance of the first question in the wilderness, and that is what You rejected for the sake of the freedom which You exalted above everything. Yet that question contains the great secret of this world. Had You chosen "bread," You would have satisfied the universal and everlasting craving of human beings and of the individual to find someone to worship. So long as man remains free he strives for nothing so incessantly and so painfully as to find as quickly as possible someone to worship. But man seeks to worship what is established beyond dispute, so indisputably that all men would agree at once to worship it. For these pitiful creatures are concerned not only to find what one or the other can worship, but to find something that all would believe in and worship; what is essential is that all may be *together* in it. This craving for *community* of worship is the chief misery of every man individually and of all humanity from the beginning of time. For the sake of common worship they've slain each other with the sword. They have set up gods and challenged one another, "Put away your gods and come worship ours, or we will kill you and your gods!' And so it will be to end of the world, even when gods disappear from the earth; they will fall down before idols just the same. You knew, You could not but have known that fundamental secret of human nature, but You rejected the one infallible banner which was offered You, to make all men bow down to You alone—the banner of earthly bread; and You rejected it for the sake of freedom and the bread of Heaven. Behold what else You did. And all again in the name of freedom! I tell You that man is tormented by no greater anxiety than to find someone to whom he can hand over quickly that gift of freedom with which the unhappy creature is born. But only he who can appease their conscience can take over their freedom. In bread there was offered to You an indisputable banner; give bread, and man will worship You, for nothing is more indisputable than bread. But if someone else gains possession of his conscience—oh! then he will cast away Your bread and follow after him who has ensnared his conscience. In that You were right. For the secret of man's being is not only to live but to have something to live for. Without a firm conception of the object of life, man would not consent to go on living, and would rather destroy himself than remain on earth, though he had bread in abundance. That is true. But what happened? Instead of taking men's freedom from them, You make it greater than ever! Did You forget that man prefers peace, and even death, to freedom of choice in the knowledge of good and evil? Nothing is more seductive for man than his freedom of conscience, but at the same time nothing is a greater torture. And yet, instead of providing a firm foundation for setting the conscience of man at rest forever, You chose all that is exceptional, vague, and enigmatic; You chose what is utterly beyond the strength of men, acting as though You did not love them at all—You who came to give Your life for them! Instead of taking possession of men's freedom, You increased it, and burdened the spiritual kingdom of mankind forever with its sufferings. You wanted man's free love. You wanted him to follow You freely, enticed and captured by You. In place of the rigid ancient law, man was hereafter to decide for himself with free heart what is good and what is evil, having only Your image before him as his guide. But did You not think he would at last dispute and reject even Your image and Your truth, if he were oppressed with the fearful burden of free choice? They will cry aloud at last that the truth is not in You, for they could not have been left in greater confusion and suffering than You have caused, laying upon them so many cares and unanswerable problems.

    "So that You Yourself laid the foundation for the destruction of Your kingdom, and no one is more to blame for it. Yet what was offered You? There are three powers, and only three powers that can conquer and capture the conscience of these impotent rebels forever, for their own happiness—those forces are miracles, mystery and authority. You rejected all three. . . ."

RAUSCHENBUSCH: CHRISTIANITY AND THE SOCIAL CRISIS

(New York, 1907), pp. xi–xii, 2–3, 10–11, 41, 54, 57–58, 85–86, 91–92, 285–286.

At the beginning of the twentieth century, Walter Rauschenbusch, a professor in the Rochester Theological Seminary, Rochester, New York, formulated some of the basic problems of our age. Then he asked the churches professing to follow the teachings of Christ what they proposed to do about them. We are still waiting for the answer, but no one has put the question more poignantly or more forcefully. The contemporaneity of Dr. Rauschenbusch's work is evident from the following excerpts from one of his best-known books, *Christianity and the Social Crisis.*

Introduction

Western civilization is passing through a social revolution unparalleled in history for scope and power. Its coming was inevitable. The religious, political, and intellectual revolutions of the past five centuries, which together created the modern world, necessarily had to culminate in an economic and social revolution such as is now upon us.

By universal consent, this social crisis is the overshadowing problem of our generation. The industrial and commerical life of the advanced nations are in the throes of it. In politics all issues and methods are undergoing upheaval and realignment as the social movement advances. In the world of thought all the young and serious minds are absorbed in the solution of the social problems. Even literature and art point like compass needles to this magnetic pole of all our thought.

The social revolution has been slow in reaching our country. We have been exempt, not because we had solved the problems, but because we had not yet confronted them. We have now arrived, and all the characteristic conditions of American life will henceforth combine to make the social struggle here more intense than anywhere else. The vastness and the free sweep of our concentrated wealth on the one side, the independence, intelligence, moral vigor, and political power of the common people on the other side, promise a long-drawn grapple of contesting forces which may well make the heart of every American patriot sink within him.

It is realized by friend and foe that religion can play, and must play, a momentous part in this irrepressible conflict.

The Church, the organized expression of the religious life of the past, is one of the most potent institutions and forces in Western civilization. Its favor and moral influence are wooed by all parties. It cannot help throwing its immense weight on one side or the other. If it tries not to act, it thereby acts; and in any case its choice will be decisive for its own future.

Apart from the organized Church, the religious spirit is a factor of incalculable power in the making of history. In the idealistic spirits that lead and in the masses that follow, the religious spirit always intensifies thought, enlarges hope, unfetters daring, evokes the willingness to sacrifice, and gives coherence in the fight. Under the warm breath of religious faith, all social institutions become plastic. The religious spirit removes mountains and tramples on impossibilities. Unless the economic and intellectual forces are strongly reinforced by religious enthusiasm, the whole social movement may prove abortive, and the New Era may die before it comes to birth.

It follows that the relation between Christianity and the social crisis is one of the most pressing questions for all intelligent men who realize the power of religion, and most of all for the religious leaders of the people who give direction to the forces of religion. . . .

The Historical Roots of Christianity: The Hebrew Prophets

The life and thought of the Old Testament prophets are more to us than classical illustrations and sidelights. They are an integral part of the thought life of Christianity. From the beginning the Christian Church appropriated the Bible of Israel as its own book and thereby made the history of Israel part of the history of Christendom. That history lives in the heart of the Christian nations with a very real spiritual force. The average American knows more about David than about King Arthur, and more about the exodus from Egypt than about the emigration of the Puritans. Throughout the Christian centuries the historical material embodied in the Old Testament has been regarded as not merely instructive, but as authoritative. The social ideas drawn from it have been powerful factors in all attempts of Christianity to influence social and political life. In so far as men have attempted to use the Old Testament as a code of model laws and institutions and have applied these to modern conditions, regardless of the historical connections, these attempts have left a trail of blunder and disaster. In so far as they have caught the spirit that burned in the hearts of the prophets and breathed in gentle humanity through the Mosaic Law, the influence of the Old Testament has been one of the great permanent forces making for democracy and social justice. However our views of the Bible may change, every religious man will continue to recognize that to the elect minds of the Jewish people God gave so vivid a consciousness of the divine will that, in its main tendencies, at least, their life and thought carry a permanent authority for all who wish to know the higher right of God. Their writings are like channel buoys anchored by God, and we shall do well to heed them now that the roar of an angry surf is in our ears. . . .

Our modern religious horizon and our conception of the character of a religious leader are so different [from theirs] that it is not easy to understand men who saw the province of religion chiefly in the broad reaches of civic affairs and international relations. Our philosophical and economic individualism has affected our religious thought so deeply that we hardly comprehend the prophetic views of an organic national life and of national sin and salvation. We usually conceive of the community as a loose sandheap of individuals and this difference in the fundamental point of view distorts the utterances of the prophets as soon as we handle them. For instance, one of the most beautiful revival texts is the invitation: "Though your sins be as scarlet, they shall be as white as snow; though they be red like crimson, they shall be as wool." The words are part of the first chapter of Isaiah, [who] throughout the chapter deals with the national condition of the Kingdom of Judah and its capital. He describes its devastation; he ridicules the attempts to appease the national God by redoubled sacrifices; he urges instead the abolition of social oppression and injustice as the only way of regaining God's favor for the nation. If they would vindicate the cause of the helpless and oppressed, then he would freely pardon; then their scarlet and crimson guilt would be washed away. The familiar text is followed by the very material promise of economic prosperity, and the threat of continued war: "If ye be willing and obedient, ye shall eat the good of the land; but if ye refuse and rebel, ye shall be devoured with the sword." . . . He offered a new start to his nation on condition that it righted social wrongs. We offer free pardon to individuals and rarely mention social wrongs.

. . . The prophets demanded right moral conduct as the sole test and fruit of religion, and that the morality which they had in mind was not the private morality of detached pious souls but the social morality of the nation. This they preached, and they backed their preaching by active participation in public action and discussion. . . .

Their religious concern was not restricted to private religion and morality, but dealt pre-eminently with the social and political life of their nation. Would they limit its range today?

. . . Their sympathy was wholly and passionately with the poor and oppressed. If they lived today, would they place the chief blame for poverty on the poor and give their admiration to the strong? . . .

The Social Aims of Jesus

The historical background which we have just sketched must ever be kept in mind in understanding the life and purpose of Jesus. He was not merely an initiator, but a consummator. . . . He took the situation and material furnished to him by the past and molded that into a fuller approximation to the divine conception within him. He embodied the prophetic stream of faith and hope. He linked his work to that of John the Baptist as the one contemporary fact to which he felt most inward affinity. . . .

He would have nothing to do with bloodshed and violence. When the crowds that were on their way to the Passover gathered around him in the solitude on the Eastern shore of the lake and wanted to make him king and march on the capital, he eluded them by sending his inflammable disciples away in the boat, and himself going up among the rocks to pray till the darkness dispersed the crowd. [Matt. 14:22−23]. Alliance with the Messianic force-revolution was one of the temptations which he confronted at the outset and repudiated [Matt. 4:8−10]; he would not set up God's Kingdom by using the devil's means of hatred and blood. With the glorious idealism of faith and love Jesus threw away the sword and advanced on the entrenchments of wrong with hand outstretched and heart exposed. . . .

There was a revolutionary consciousness in Jesus; not, of course, in the common use of the word "revolutionary," which connects it with violence and bloodshed. But Jesus knew that he had come to kindle a fire on earth. Much as he loved peace, he knew that the actual result of his work would be not peace but the sword. His mother in her song had recognized in her own experience the settled custom of God to "put down the proud and exalt them of low degree,'' to "fill the hungry with good things and to send the rich empty away'' [Luke 1:52−53]. . . . The son of Mary expected a great reversal of values. The first would be last and the last would be first [Mark 10:31]. He saw that what was exalted among man was an abomination before God [Luke 16:15], and therefore these exalted things had no glamour for his eye. This revolutionary note runs even through the Beatitudes where we should least expect it. The point of them is that henceforth those were to be blessed whom the world had not blessed, for the Kingdom of God would reverse their relative standing. Now the poor and the hungry and sad were to be satisfied and comforted; the meek who had been shouldered aside by the ruthless would get their chance to inherit the earth, and conflict and persecution would be inevitable in the process [Matt. 5:1−12].

We are apt to forget that his attack on the religious leaders and authorities of his day was of revolutionary boldness and thoroughness. He called the ecclesiastical leaders hypocrites, blind leaders who fumbled in their casuistry, and everywhere missed the decisive facts in teaching right and wrong. Their piety was no piety; their law was inadequate; they harmed the men whom they wanted to convert [Matt. 23]. Even the publicans and harlots had a truer piety than theirs [Matt. 21:23−32]. If we remember that religion was still the foundation of the Jewish state, and that the religious authorities were the pillars of existing society, much as in medieval Catholic Europe, we shall realize how revolutionary were his invectives. . . .

Jesus was not a mere social reformer. Religion was the heart of his life, and all that he said on social relations was said from the religious point of view. He has been called the first socialist. He was more; he was the first real man, the inaugurator of a new humanity. But as such he bore within him the germs of a new social and political order. He was too great to be the Saviour of a fractional part of human life. His redemption extends to all human needs and powers and relations. Theologians have felt no hesitation in founding a system of speculative thought on the teachings of Jesus, and yet Jesus was never an inhabitant of the realm of speculative thought. He has been made the founder and organizer of a great ecclesiastical machine, which derives authority for its offices and institutions from him, and yet "hardly any problem of exegesis is more difficult than to discover in the gospels an administrative or organizing or ecclesiastical Christ." There is at least as much justification in invoking his name today as the champion of a great movement for a more righteous social life. He was neither a theologian nor an ecclesiastic, nor a socialist. But if we were forced to classify him either with the great theologians who elaborated the fine distinctions of scholasticism; or with the mighty popes and princes of the Church who built up their power in his name; or with the men who are giving their heart and life to the propaganda of a new social system—where should we place him?

The Present Crisis

. . . Will some [Edward] Gibbon of Mongol race sit by the shore of the Pacific in A.D. 3000 and write on the "Decline and Fall of the Christian Empire"? If so, he will probably describe the nineteenth and twentieth centuries as the golden age when outwardly life flourished as never before, but when that decay which resulted in the gradual collapse of the twenty-first and twenty-second centuries was already far advanced. Or will the twentieth century mark for the future historian the real adolescence of humanity, the great emancipation from barbarism and from the paralysis of injustice and the beginning of a progress in the intellectual, social, and moral life of mankind to which all past history has no parallel?

C.E.M. JOAD: GOD AND EVIL

C .E. M. Joad, *God and Evil;* by Harper & Row Publishers, 1943, and by Curtis Brown, Ltd., London. Pp. 9−15, 17−20, 103−104.

Professor Joad (1891−1953) was a renowned rationalist and head of the philosophy department in Birbeck College, University of London, when, as he explains, he became a convert to religion, much to the surprise of his contemporaries.

As a young man at Oxford, I participated, as was natural to my age and generation, in prolonged and frequent discussions of religion which, finding me a Christian, left me as they did many of my generation, an agnostic, an agnostic who entertained a deep-seated suspicion of all dogmatic creeds and, since after all I knew most about it and was in the full-tide of reaction against it,—a particular suspicion of the dogmatic doctrines of Christianity as preached by the Church of England.

As an agnostic, I felt convinced of two things: first, in regard to the matters which fall within the sphere of religion, that we did not and probably could not know the truth; secondly, in regard to the so-called religious truths that I had been taught, as, for example, that God created the world as stated in Genesis at a certain point in time, and at another point in time sent His Son into it to redeem mankind, that it was improbable that they were true and certain that they could not be *known* to be true. In the confidence of this conviction I proceeded, to all intents and purposes, to turn my back upon the whole subject. As a teacher of philosophy, I naturally had occasion to concern myself with topics which bordered upon the sphere of theology, but my treatment of such matters was purely conventional and my discourses conformed, I am afraid, to that rather pessimistic definition of a lecture as the transferring of a certain amount of miscellaneous information from the notebook of the lecturer to the notebooks of the students without passing through the minds of either.

In course of time I came to be known as a rationalist, and in this capacity was frequently in demand for lectures and articles which adopted an attitude hostile to revealed religion in general, and to the Christian Church in particular. . . .

Meanwhile, science, philosophy, [economics,] and, as time went on, increasingly politics, absorbed my attention. It was only after the coming of the Nazis that my mind began again to turn in the direction of religion. As the years passed and the situation worsened, articles on religious topics over my name began to appear, paragraphs on religion crept into books devoted ostensibly to other matters, religious references and illustrations embellished discussions of economics, politics, and the future of society, until on the outbreak of war the subject leapt straight into the forefront of my consciousness where it has remained ever since.

I have ventured upon this brief sketch of a spiritual Odyssey because I take it to be not untypical. From conversations and discussions, especially with students, I surmise that the revival of interest in religion is widespread; that the subject has leaped into the forefront of their consciousness too. This topical relevance of religion derives from two sources.

1. The Relation between Politics and Religion

. . . [The] connection between politics and religion subsists at all times, but in quiet times of peace it usually remains implicit. The peculiar circumstances of the last twenty-five years have, however, combined to thrust it into the foreground of men's consciousness. . . . Political doctrines such as Fascism and Communism assumed for the twentieth century the status which religious doctrines possessed in the nineteenth; they are not, that is to say, doctrines in regard to means to an agreed end, but doctrines in regard to ends about which there is no agreement. It is from this source that the intolerance which the protagonists of the different contemporary ideologies feel for one another derives. . . .

The young men of the late twenties and thirties, wanting desperately to believe, have found no suitable object upon which to focus their faith. . . . [Consequently,] they have sought, in political and social creeds, substitute channels through which the springs of idealist aspiration and emotional veneration might find an outlet. . . .

2. The Obtrusiveness of Evil

The other source of the specifically topical interest in religion is to be found in the obtrusiveness of evil. It may perhaps be plausibly argued that there is no more evil abroad in Western civilization than there was at the end of the last century, but it cannot be denied that what there is of it is more obtrusive. I am not referring to evils arising from the relation between the sexes upon which the Church has laid such exclusive stress. . . . I mean the evils of cruelty, savagery, oppression, violence, egotism, aggrandisement, and lust for power. So pervasive and insistent have these evils become that it is at times difficult to avoid concluding that the Devil has been given a longer rope than usual for the tempting and corrupting of men. In so far as evil becomes more obtrusive, it becomes correspondingly more difficult to explain it away by the various methods which have been fashionable during the last twenty years.

There was, for example, the explanation of evil in terms of economic inequality and injustice. Socialist writers had taught my generation that bad conditions were the cause of human wretchedness; of human wretchedness and also of human wickedness. Poverty, Shaw was insisting with unmatched force and incomparable eloquence, was the supreme sin; supreme if only because it was the source of all the others. . . .

And the moral? That evil is due to bad social conditions. Now you can reform bad social conditions by Act of Parliament, substituting comfort, cleanliness, security, and financial competence for discomfort, dirt, insecurity, and want. Therefore, presumably, you can make men virtuous, or at any rate as nearly virtuous as makes no matter, by Act of Parliament.

There was a later explanation of evil in terms of early psychological maltreatment and consequent psychological maladjustment. . . . Evil, then, according to this view, was the result not of bad social, but of bad psychological conditions; not so much of an imperfect society, as of an imperfect family, an ill-directed nursery, and a wrongly run school. Reform society, said the Socialist, and evil will disappear. Reform the school and the family, the psychoanalysts added, and society will reform itself and, once again, evil will disappear.

Common to both these views was the assumption that evil consisted in the lack of something whose presence would be good. Thus fear and envy are evils because they indicate a lack of psychological adjustment; poverty, because it indicates a lack of material goods. . . .

The answer to these questions is, it would seem, all too obvious. Evil is not *merely* a by-product of unfavorable circumstances; it is too widespread and too deep-seated to admit of any such explanation; so widespread, so deep-seated that one can only conclude that what the religions have always taught us is true, and that evil is endemic in the heart of man.

I am claiming no credit for this conclusion. On the contrary it is ground for humiliation to have come to it so late. There has always been evil in the world, and it is only poverty of imagination which refuses to accept its significance until it struts prominent and repulsive upon the stage of one's times. . . .

The simple truth is that one cannot help oneself. To be confronted with a universe which contains evil as an ultimate and ineradicable fact, to know that there is no defense against it save in the strength or rather in the weakness of one's own character, no hope of overcoming it save through the efficacy of one's own unaided efforts—*this* I find to be a position almost intolerably distressing. For one cannot help but know that one's character is not strong enough, one's efforts not efficacious; at least, that they are not, if unaided. For our burden in the world, as it has become, is indeed greater than we can bear, if we have nothing more secure to rely on than the integrity of our own puny reasons and the wavering uncertainty of our own ethical judgments. It follows that either one must supinely acquiesce in the evil one cannot resolve, or else. . . . There are two alternatives.

The first, since the world is evil, is to escape from it and to find, first in withdrawal, and, as an ultimate hope, in Nirvana, the true way of life. The second is to face evil and to seek to overcome it, even to take it up and absorb it into one's own life, transcending it and enlarging one's own personality with what one has transcended. The first is the way of the East, the second of Christianity. My temperament and disposition incline me to the second, but the second I know to be impossible unless I am assisted from without. By the grace of God, we are assured, such assistance may be obtained and evil may be overcome; otherwise, there is no resource and no resistance.

EXISTENTIALISM

JEAN-PAUL SARTRE: EXISTENTIALISM

From Jean-Paul Sartre, *Existentialism,* trans. Bernard Frechtman, Philosophical Library, Inc., 1947, pp. 15−21, 27−28, 43−44, 58, passim. Reprinted by permission.

One of the leading figures of postwar-II existentialism, Jean-Paul Sartre (d. 1980), was strongly influenced by the German philosopher Martin Heidegger. Both saw man as a lonely and forlorn figure who bears the heavy burden of responsibility for his own life and value system. The works of Sartre—*Being and Nothingness, The Devil and the Good Lord,* and plays such as The *Flies* and *No Exit*—continue to be popular both in France and abroad. Sartre shared a close friendship with Simone de Beauvoir (see her autobiographical essays and diaries) and they contributed greatly to each other's work. In the following excerpts, Sartre distinguishes between theistic and atheistic existentialism and explains his own version.

Actually, [existentialism] is the least scandalous, the most austere of doctrines. It is intended strictly for specialists and philosophers. Yet it can be defined easily. What complicates matters is that there are two kinds of existentialist; first, those who are Christian, among whom I would include Jaspers and Gabriel Marcel, both Catholic; and on the other hand the atheistic existentialists, among whom I class Heidegger, and then the French existentialists and myself. What they have in common is that they think that existence precedes essence, or, if you prefer, that subjectivity must be the starting point.

Just what does that mean? Let us consider some object that is manufactured, for example, a book or a paper-cutter: here is an object which has been made by an artisan whose inspiration came from a concept. He referred to the concept of what a paper-cutter is and likewise to a known method of production, which is part of the concept, something which is, by and large, a routine. Thus, the paper-cutter is at once an object produced in a certain way and, on the other hand, one having a specific use; and one can not postulate a man who produces a paper-cutter but does not know what it is used for. Therefore, let us say that, for the paper-cutter, essence—that is, the ensemble of both the production routines and the properties which enable it to be both produced and defined—precedes existence. Thus, the presence of the paper-cutter or book in front of me is determined. Therefore, we have here a technical view of the world whereby it can be said that production precedes existence.

When we conceive God as the Creator, He is generally thought of as a superior sort of artisan. Whatever doctrine we may be considering, whether one like that of Descartes or that of Leibnitz, we always grant that *will* more or less follows understanding or, at the very least, accompanies it, and that when God creates He knows exactly what He is creating. Thus, the concept of man in the mind of God is comparable to the concept of paper-cutter in the mind of the manufacturer, and, following certain techniques and a conception, God produces man, just as the artisan, following a definition and a technique, makes a paper-cutter. Thus, the individual man is the realisation of a certain concept in the divine intelligence. . . .

Atheistic existentialism, which I represent, is more coherent. It states that if God does not exist, there is at least one being in whom existence precedes essence, a being who exists before he can be defined by any concept, and that this being is man, or, as Heidegger says, human reality. What is meant here by saying that existence precedes essence? It means that, first of all, man exists, turns up, appears on the scene, and, only afterwards, defines himself. If man, as the existentialist conceives him, is indefinable, it is because at first he is nothing. Only afterward will he be something, and he himself will have made what he will be. Thus, there is no human nature, since there is no God to conceive it. Not only is man what he conceives himself to be, but he is also only what he wills himself to be after this thrust toward existence.

Man is nothing else but what he makes of himself. Such is the first principle of existentialism. It is also what is called subjectivity. . . . But what do we mean by this, if not that man has a greater dignity than a stone or table? For we mean that man first exists, that is, that man first of all is the being who hurls himself toward a future and who is conscious of imagining himself as being in the future. Man is at the start a plan which is aware of itself, rather than a patch of moss, a piece of garbage, or a cauliflower; nothing exists prior to this plan; there is nothing in heaven; man will be what he will have planned to be. Not what he will want to be. Because by the word ''will'' we generally mean a conscious decision, which is subsequent to what we have already made of ourselves. I may want to belong to a political party, write a book, get married; but all that is only a manifestation of an earlier, more spontaneous choice that is called ''will.'' But if existence really does precede essence, man is responsible for what he is. Thus, existentialism's first move is to make every man aware of what he is and to make the full responsibility of his existence rest on him. And when we say that a man is responsible for himself, we do not only mean that he is responsible for his own individuality, but that he is responsible for all men. . . .

If, on the other hand, existence precedes essence, and if we grant that we exist and fashion our image at one and the same time, the image is valid for everybody and for our whole age. Thus, our responsibility is much greater than we might have supposed, because it involves all mankind. If I am a workingman and choose to join a Christian trade-union rather than be a communist, and if by being a member I want to show that the best thing for man is resignation, that the kingdom of man is not of this world, I am not only involving my own case—I want to be resigned for everyone. As a result, my action has involved all humanity. To take a more individual matter, if I want to marry, to have children; even if this marriage depends solely on my own circumstances or passion or wish, I am involving all humanity in monogamy and not merely myself. Therefore, I am responsible for myself and for everyone else. I am creating a certain image of man of my own choosing. In choosing myself, I choose man. . . .

Dostoievsky said, ''If God didn't exist, everything would be possible.'' That is the very starting point of existentialism. Indeed, everything is permissible if God does not exist, and as a result man is forlorn, because neither within him nor without does he find anything to cling to. He can't start making excuses for himself.

If existence really does precede essence, there is no explaining things away by reference to a fixed and given human nature. In other words, there is no determinism, man is free, man is freedom. On the other hand, if God does not exist, we find no values or commands to turn to which legitimize our conduct. So, in the bright realm of values, we have no excuse behind us, nor justification before us. We are alone, with no excuses.

That is the idea I shall try to convey when I say that man is condemned to be free. Condemned, because he did not create himself, yet, in other respects is free; because, once thrown into the world, he is responsible for everything he does. The existentialist does not believe in the power of passion. He will never agree that a sweeping passion is a ravaging torrent which fatally leads a man to certain acts and is therefore an excuse. He thinks that man is responsible for his passion.

The existentialist does not think that man is going to help himself by finding in the world some omen by which to orient himself. Because he thinks that man will interpret the omen to suit himself. Therefore, he thinks that man, with no support and no aid, is condemned every moment to invent man. . . .

There can be no other truth to take off from than this: *I think; therefore, I exist.* There we have the absolute truth of consciousness becoming aware of itself. Every theory which takes man out of the moment in which he becomes aware of himself is, at its very beginning, a theory which confounds truth, for outside the Cartesian *cogito,* all views are only probable, and a doctrine of probability which is not bound to a truth dissolves into thin air. In order to describe the probable, you must have a firm hold on the true. Therefore, before there can be any truth whatsoever, there must be an absolute truth; and this one is simple and easily arrived at; it's on everyone's doorstep; it's a matter of grasping it directly.

Secondly, this theory is the only one which gives man dignity, the only one which does not reduce him to an object. The effect of all materialism is to treat all men, including the one philosophizing, as objects, that is, as an ensemble of determined reactions in no way distinguished from the ensemble of qualities and phenomena which constitute a table or a chair or a stone. We definitely wish to establish the human realm as an ensemble of values distinct from the material realm. . . .

Moreover, to say that we invent values means nothing else but this: life has no meaning *a priori.* Before you come alive, life is nothing; it's up to you to give it a meaning, and value is nothing else but the meaning that you choose. In that way, you see, there is a possibility of creating a human community.

MARTIN BUBER: BETWEEN MAN AND MAN (1929)

Reprinted with permission of Macmillan Publishing Co., Inc., and Routledge & Kegan Paul Ltd. from *Between Man and Man.* Copyright © 1965 by Macmillan Publishing Co., Inc. Pp. 13–14.

"When Dag Hammarskjöld's plane crashed in Northern Rhodesia, the Secretary General of the United Nations had with him the manuscript of a translation that he was making of Martin Buber's classic work *I and Thou.* It is because of this book and the philosophy of dialogue that it presents that Dag Hammarskjöld repeatedly nominated Martin Buber for a Nobel Prize in literature. *I and Thou* is recognized today as among the handful of writings that the twentieth century will bequeath to the centuries to come, but for many readers this compact and poetic little book needs an introduction to be properly understood and . . . appreciated. More than any other work of Buber's, *Between Man and Man* provides this introduction. . . ." So writes Maurice Friedman, a leading Buber scholar.

Martin Buber (d. 1965) was born in Vienna and educated at German universities. He taught philosophy in Germany until Hitler came to power; then, in 1938, he became professor of philosophy at the University of Jerusalem. After his retirement in 1951 he continued writing his special brand of existentialism., combining especially the philosophy of the Hasidim with the Christian philosophy of Søren Kierkegaard.

A Conversion

In my early years the "religious" was for me the exception. There were hours that were taken out of the course of things. From somewhere or other the firm crust of everyday was pierced. Then the reliable permanence of appearances broke down; the attack which took place burst its laws asunder. "Religious experience" was the experience of an otherness which did not fit into the context of life. It could begin with something customary, with the consideration of some familiar object, but which then became unexpectedly mysterious and uncanny, finally lighting a way into the lightning-pierced darkness of the mystery itself. But also, without any intermediate stage, time could be torn apart—first the firm world's structure, then the still firmer self-assurance flew apart and you were delivered to fulness. The "religious" lifted you out. Over there now lay the accustomed existence with its affairs, but here illumination and ecstacy and rapture held, without time or sequence. Thus your own being encompassed a life here and a life beyond, and there was no bond but the actual moment of the transition.

The illegitimacy of such a division of the temporal life, which is streaming to death and eternity and which only in fulfilling its temporality can be fulfilled in face of these, was brought home to me by an everyday event, an event of judgment, judging with that sentence from closed lips and an unmoved glance such as the ongoing course of things loves to pronounce.

What happened was no more than that one forenoon, after a morning of "religious" enthusiasm, I had a visit from an unknown young man, without being there in spirit. I certainly did not fail to let the meeting be friendly, I did not treat him any more remissly than all his contemporaries who were in the habit of seeking me out about this time of day as an oracle that is ready to listen to reason. I conversed attentively and openly with him—only I omitted to guess certain questions which he did not put. Later, not long after, I learned from one of his friends—he himself was no longer alive—the essential content of these questions; I learned that he had come not casually, but borne by destiny, not for a chat but for a decision. He had come to me in this hour. What do we expect when we are in despair and yet go to a man? Surely a presence by means of which we are told that nevertheless there is meaning.

Since then I have given up the "religious" which is nothing but the exception, extraction, exaltation, ecstacy; or it has given me up. I possess nothing but the everyday out of which I am never taken. The mystery is no longer disclosed, it has escaped or it has made its dwelling here where everything happens as it happens. I know no fulness but each mortal hour's fulness of claim and responsibility. Though far from being equal to it, yet I know that in the claim I am claimed and may respond in responsibility, and know who speaks and demands a response.

I do not know much more. If that is religion then it is just everything, simply all that is lived in its possibility of dialogue. Here is space also for religion's highest forms. As when you pray you do not thereby remove yourself from this life of ours but in your praying refer your thought to it, even though it may be in order to yield it; so too in the unprecedented and surprising, when you are called upon from above, required, chosen, empowered, sent, you with this your mortal bit of life are referred to, this moment is not extracted from it, it rests on what has been and beckons to the remainder which has still to be lived, you are not swallowed up in a fulness without obligation, you are willed for the life of communion.

MARTIN BUBER: I AND THOU (1923)

From Martin Buber, *I and Thou*, First Part. Translated by Walter Kaufman. Copyright © 1970 by Charles Scribner's Sons and Walter Kaufman. Reprinted with the permission of Charles Scribner's Sons and T. and T. Clark. Pp. 54–57.

The world is twofold for man in accordance with his twofold attitude.

The attitude of man is twofold in accordance with the two basic words he can speak.

The basic words are not single words but word pairs.

One basic word is the word pair I-You.

The other basic word is the word pair I-It; but this basic word is not changed when He or She takes the place of It.

Thus the I of man is also twofold.

For the I of the basic word I-You is different from that in the basic word I-It.

*

Basic words do not state something that might exist outside them; by being spoken they establish a mode of existence.

Basic words are spoken with one's being.

When one says You, the I of the word pair I-You is said, too.

When one says It, the I of the word pair I-It is said, too.

The basic word I-You can only be spoken with one's whole being.

The basic word I-It can never be spoken with one's whole being.

*

There is no I as such but only the I of the basic word I-You and the I of the basic word I-It.

When a man says I, he means one or the other. The I he means is present when he says I. And when he says You or It, the I of one or the other basic word is also present.

Being I and saying I are the same. Saying I and saying one of the two basic words are the same.

Whoever speaks one of the basic words enters into the word and stands in it.

*

The life of a human being does not exist merely in the sphere of goal-directed verbs. It does not consist merely of activities that have something for their object.

I perceive something. I feel something. I imagine something. I want something. I sense something. I think something. The life of a human being does not consist merely of all this and its like.

All this and its like is the basis of the realm of It.

But the realm of You has another basis.

*

Whoever says You does not have something for his object. For wherever there is something there is also another something; every It borders on other Its; It is only by virtue of bordering on others. But where You is said there is no something. You has no borders.

Whoever says You does not have something; he has nothing. But he stands in relation.

*

We are told that man experiences his world. What does this mean?

Man goes over the surfaces of things and experiences them. He brings back from them some knowledge of their condition—an experience. He experiences what there is to things.

But it is not experiences alone that bring the world to man.

For what they bring to him is only a world that consists of It and It and It, of He and He and She and She and It.

I experience something. . . .

*

Those who experience do not participate in the world. For the experience is "in them" and not between them and the world.

The world does not participate in experience. It allows itself to be experienced, but it is not concerned, for it contributes nothing, and nothing happens to it.

*

The world as experience belongs to the basic word I-It.

The basic word I-You establishes the world of relation.

*

Three are the spheres in which the world of relation arises.

The first: life with nature. Here the relation vibrates in the dark and remains below language. The creatures stir across from us, but they are unable to come to us, and the You we say to them sticks to the threshold of language.

The second: life with men. Here the relation is manifest and enters language. We can give and receive the You.

The third: life with spiritual beings. Here the relation is wrapped in a cloud but reveals itself, it lacks but creates language. We hear no You and yet feel addressed; we answer—creating, thinking, acting: with our being we speak the basic word, unable to say You with our mouth.

But how can we incorporate into the world of the basic word what lies outside language?

In every sphere, through everything that becomes present to us, we gaze toward the train of the eternal You; in each we perceive a breath of it; in every You we address the eternal You, in every sphere according to its manner.

PAUL TILLICH: BEING AND LOVE

In *Moral Principles of Action*, ed. Ruth Nanda Anshen (New York: Harper, 1952), pp. 661ff.

A leading existential theologian and religious philosopher, Paul Tillich (d. 1965) was born and educated in Germany, where he taught theology at the universities of Berlin, Marburg, Dresden, and Leipzig. When Hitler came to power in 1933, Tillich was dismissed as professor of philosophy at the University of Frankfurt. Reinhold Niebuhr then invited him and his family to come to New York, where he joined the faculty of the Union Theological Seminary. In 1954 he became University Professor at Harvard, continuing his provocative lecturing and teaching, the source of his "greatest anxiety and greatest happiness," as he put it.

Ontology is the rational explanation of the structure of Being itself. Philosophy always was and always will be in the first place ontology, whether the philosophers admit it or not. . . . Even a skeptical epistemology such as present-day logical positivism is based on a hidden interpretation of the structure of Being itself.

Ontology deals with the structure of Being itself, not with the nature of a special being or a special realm of beings. Ontology asks the question: What does it mean that something *is* and is not *not?* The ontological question presupposes the attitude of a man who has experienced the tremendous shock of the possibility that there is nothing, or—more practically speaking—who has looked into the threatening abyss of nothingness. Such a man is called a philosopher.

If we speak of the ontology of Love, we indicate that Love belongs to the structure of Being itself, that every special being with its special nature participates in the nature of Love since it participates in Being itself. The participation of a being in the nature of Love can happen even as the negation of love, as indifference, or as hate.

The thesis that Love is in the nature of Being itself must be tested by its adequacy to interpret life in all its aspects. Especially, it must be able to give a uniting ground to the different forms of what is called love. It must be shown that without the ontological approach the other approaches remain without a foundation.

Every ontology is fragmentary because of the finiteness of the human mind. So the ontology of Love cannot reach the form of a closed system. Hegel distorted his ontology of Love . . . when he transformed [it] into a closed system. It became a loveless mechanism—which has hidden some of his significant insights into the ontology of Love.

Theology as far as it uses the *logos** is philosophical. Consequently it includes an ontology, an interpretation of Being itself. This is expressed in the basic statement of every doctrine of God, that God is Being-Itself. God is not *a* being, not even the highest one. The atheistic protest against such an assertion is justified and must be a permanent tool of theological thought. God as *a* being is below Being itself; He has something above Himself, He is an idol. The fight against this idol is the theological truth of atheism.

**Logos:* in philosophy, the rational principle in the universe; in theology, the Word of God. In Christianity, the Word is Jesus (John 1:1-14).—Ed.

BIBLIOGRAPHY OF SOURCES
(by chapters)

Chapter 16. THE ENLIGHTENMENT.
Voltaire, *Letters Concerning the English Nation* (London, 1733).
————. *Dictionnaire philosophique* (Paris, 1764).
————. *Candide, ou optimisme* (Paris, 1759).
Montesquieu, *The Spirit of Laws*, trans. T. Nugent (London, 1878).
Rousseau, *Emile*, in *Oeuvres complètes* (38 vols., Paris, 1788–1793), vol. 10.
Adam Smith, *The Wealth of Nations* (London, 1776).

Chapter 17. THE FRENCH REVOLUTION, 1787–1799.
Jean Egret, *La Pré-Révolution française, 1787–1788* (Paris, 1962), trans. W. Camp (Chicago, 1978).
Cahier of Grievances of the Third Estate of Carcassonne, in *Archives parlementaires* (Paris, 1879 et seq.), 2:532ff.
Sieyès, Abbé, *Qu'est-ce que le Tiers Etat?* (Paris, 1888).
Declaration of the Rights of Man and the Citizen, trans. Thomas Paine, *The Rights of Man* (London, 1792), 1:49–50.
Lafayette, *Mémoires, correspondances et manuscrits* (6 vols., Paris, 1837).
Civil Constitution of the Clergy, in *Archives parlementaires*, 21:80–81.
Manifesto of the Duke of Brunswick, in ibid. 16:378.
Jacobin Circular, in *The Constitutions and Other Select Documents Illustrative of the History of France, 1789–1901*, ed. F.M. Anderson (Minneapolis, 1904), pp. 127–128.
Decree of 15 December 1792, in *Le Moniteur Universel* (Paris, 1858), 14:755.
La levée en masse, 23 août 1793, in *Archives parlementaires*, 72:674–675.
"What is a Sans-culotte?" Archives Nationales F^7 4775^{48}.
Maximilien Robespierre, *Oeuvres*, ed. M. Bouloiseau (10 vols., Paris, 1967).
Law of 22 Prairal, in Anderson, ed., *Constitutions of France*, pp. 154–156.
Gracchus Babeuf, *Conspiration pour l'Egalité, dite de Babeuf*, ed. P. Buonarroti (Brussels, 1828).
Edmund Burke, *Reflections on the Revolution in France* (London, 1790).
Mary Wollstonecraft, *A Vindication of the Rights of Woman* (Paris, 1792).

Chapter 18. NAPOLEON.
Napoleon, *Mémoires pour servir à l'histoire de France* (8 vols., Paris, 1823–1825).
Correspondance de Napoléon I (32 vols., Paris 1858–1869).
Lettres inédites de Napoléon Ier, ed. L. Lecestre (2 vols., Paris, 1897).
"Napoleonic Catechism," in *Grand dictionnaire universel du XIXe siècle*, 3:567.
Staël, Madame de, *Oeuvres complètes* (Paris, 1820–21).

Louis de Bourienne, *Memoirs of Napoleon Bonaparte* (Paris, 1829), trans. R. Phipps (4 vols., New York, 1895).
Rémusat, Comtesse de, *Mémoires* (Paris, 1802–1808), trans. C. Hoey and J. Lillie (New York, 1880).
Chaptal de Chanteloup, Jean Comte de, *Mes souvenirs sur Napoléon,* ed. A. Chaptal (Paris, 1893).

Chapter 19. ROMANTICISM, REACTION, AND RECONSTRUCTION.

Rousseau, *Confessions,* livre premier (Paris, 1880).
Goethe, *Dichtung und Wahrheit,* trans. J. Oxenford (London, 1848).
Heine, H., *Die romantische Schule,* trans. S. Fleischmann (New York, 1882).
Blake, William, "Mock on, Mock on, Voltaire, Rousseau."
Wordsworth, William, "The Tables Turned."
Coleridge, Samuel Taylor, "Kubla Khan."
The Holy Alliance, in Robinson and Beard, *Readings in Modern European History,* 1:384.
Metternich, *Memoirs of Prince Metternich* (New York, 1880–1889).
The Carlsbad Decrees, in Meyer, *Corpus juris confoederationis Germanicae,* 2:138ff.
Musset, Alfred de, *La confession d'un enfant du siècle* (Paris, 1887).

Chapter 20. THE INDUSTRIALIZATION OF SOCIETY.

Toynbee, Arnold, *Lectures on the Industrial Revolution of the 18th Century in England* (London, 1884).
Young, Arthur, *The Farmer's Tour through the East of England* (London, 1771).
Great Britain, Board of Agriculture, *General Report of the Agricultural State, and Political Circumstances, of Scotland,* 1814.
————. *Observation on the Results of the Population Act, 41 Geo. III, 9* (London, 1802).
Baines, E., *History of Cotton Manufacture in Great Britain* (London, 1835).
Great Britain, Factory Act of 1802, in *Statutes at Large,* 43:632f.
————. *Parliamentary Papers,* 1831–1832, Vol. 15, "Sadler's Commission Report," and 1842, Vol. 16, "Ashley Mines Commission Report."
Ure, Andrew, *Philosophy of Manufactures* (1835).
Hansard, *Parliamentary Debates,* 3d Ser. 19:912, "Mr. Cobett's Discovery," July 18, 1833.
Great Britain, *Statutes of the United Kingdom,* 73;985f.:3–4, William IV. ca. 103, The English Factory Act of 1833.

Chapter 21. LAISSEZ FAIRE.

Bentham, Jeremy, *A Manual of Political Economy,* in *Works* (11 vols., Edinburgh, 1843).
Malthus, Thomas R., *An Essay on the Principle of Population as It Affects the Future Improvement of Society* (London, 1798).
Ricardo, David, *Principles of Political Economy and Taxation,* ed. E. Gonner (London, 1891).
Carlyle, Thomas, *Past and Present* (3d ed., New York, 1895).
Smiles, Samuel, *Self-Help* (Boston, 1860).

Chapter 22. POLITICAL LIBERALISM AND ITS ENEMIES.

Hansard, *Parliamentary Debates,* 3d Ser. 2:1061f., Lord Russell Introduces the First Reform Bill, March 1, 1831.

The People's Charter (London, 1832).

Jenkins, Evan, *Chartism Unmasked* (London, 1840).

Mill, John Stuart, *Considerations on Representative Government* (London, 1861).

———. *On Liberty* (London, 1859; Boston, 1864).

Tocqueville, Alexis de, *De la démocratie en Amérique* (2 vols., Paris, 1835–1840).

Louis Napoleon, "Proclamation to the People," 1851, in Anderson, *Constitutions and other Documents* (Minneapolis, 1904), p. 539f.

Bismarck, Otto von, *Reflections and Reminiscences,* trans. A. Butler (2 vols., London, 1898).

Great Britain, *Public General Statutes,* Reform Act of 1867, 2:1082f: 30–31 Victoria, c. 102.

Chapter 23. SOCIALISM IN THE NINETEENTH CENTURY.

Owen, Robert, *Life of Robert Owen, Written by Himself* (London, 1858).

Blanc, Louis, *Histoire de dix ans* (5 vols., Paris, 1841–1844).

Marx and Engels, *The Manifesto of the Communist Party* (London, 1888).

Fabian Society, *The Basis of the Fabian Society* (London, 1886).

Bernstein, Eduard, *Die Voraussetzungen des Sozialismus und die Aufgaben des Sozialdemokratie* (Stuttgart, 1899, 1921).

Kropotkin, Peter, *Anarchism, Its Philosophy and Ideal* (London, 1897).

Leo XIII, *De Rerum novarum,* in the *American Catholic Review,* July 1891.

Chapter 24. DARWINISM.

Darwin, Charles, *On the Origin of Species* (London, 1859).

———. *The Descent of Man* (London, 1871).

Spencer, Herbert, *Social Statics* (New York, 1896).

Huxley, Leonard, *Life and Letters of Thomas Henry Huxley* (2 vols., New York, 1900).

Huxley, Thomas Henry, *Evolution and Ethics* (London, 1893).

Kropotkin, Peter, *Mutual Aid, a Factor of Evolution* (London, 1902).

Nietzsche, Friedrich, *Der Wille zur Macht,* ed. P. Gast in *Sämtliche* Werke, Vol. 9 (Stuttgart, 1964).

Chapter 25. NINETEENTH CENTURY NATIONALISM.

Fichte, Johann, *Reden an die Deutsche Nation* (Leipzig, 1824).

Mazzini, Giuseppi, *Pensiero ed Azione,* in *Life and Writings of Joseph Mazzini* (6 vols., London, 1890–1891).

Lord Acton, *History of Freedom and Other Essays* (London, 1907).

Renan, Ernest, *Discours et conférences* (Paris, 1887).

Hyde, Douglas, *Revival of Irish Literature and Other Addresses* (London, 1894).

Treitschke, Heinrich, *Politik: Vorlesungen gehalten an der Universität zu Berlin,* ed. M. Cornicelius (2 vols., Leipzig, 1897–1898).

Danilevsky, Nikolai, *Rossiia i Evropa: An Inquiry into the Cultural and Political Relations of the Slav World and the Germano-Roman World (St. Petersburg, 1869).*

Chapter 26. THE NEW IMPERIALISM.

Devins, J.B., *An Observer in the Philippines* (Boston, 1905).

Kipling, Rudyard, "The White Man's Burden."

Anti-Imperialist League, *Liberty Tracts,* No. 10 (Chicago, 1900).
Morel, E.D., *King Leopold's Rule in Africa* (London, 1904).
Hobson, J.A., *Imperialism, A Study* (New York, 1902).
Lenin, V.I., *Imperialism, the Highest Stage of Capitalism* (New York: International Publishers, 1939).

Chapter 27. THE EMERGENCE OF FEMINISM.
The History of Woman Suffrage, ed. E.C. Stanton et al. (6 vols., New York, 1881–1922).
Mill, J.S., "The Enfranchisement of Women," in *Westminster Review,* July, 1851.
———. *The Subjection of Women* (2d ed., London, 1869).
Ibsen, Henrik, *A Doll's House,* trans. W. Archer (London, 1905).
Engels, Friedrich, *The Origin of the Family,* trans. E. Untermann (Chicago, n.d.).
Harper, I.H., *The Life and Work of Susan B. Anthony* (2 vols., Indianapolis, 1898).

Chapter 28. LENIN AND THE RUSSIAN REVOLUTION.
Lenin, V.I., *Collected Works* (New York: International Publishers, 1929).
———. *Selected Works* (Moscow: Foreign Language Publishing House, 1950–1952).
Golder, F.A., ed., *Documents of Russian History, 1914–1917* (New York: Century, 1927).
Von Mohrenschildt, D., ed., *The Russian Revolution of 1917: Contemporary Accounts* (Oxford University Press, 1971).
Walsh, W.B., ed., *Readings in Russian History* (3 vols., Syracuse University Press, 1963).
Browder, R.P. and Kerensky, A.F., eds. *The Russian Provisional Government, 1917: Documents* (3 vols., Stanford University Press, 1961).
Kerensky, A.F., "The Policy of the Provisional Government of 1917," in *The Slavonic and East European Review,* Vol. 11 (1932), pp. 1–19.
Miliukov, P.N., *Political Memoirs, 1905–1917* (Ann Arbor: University of Michigan Press, 1967).
Sidorov, A.L. et al., eds., *Ekonomicheskoe polozhenie Rosii nakanune Velikoi Oktiabr'skoi sotsialisticheskoi revoliutsii: Dokumenty i materialy* (3 vols., Moscow, 1957).
Izvestiia Vserossiiskogo soiuza obshchestv zavodchikov i fabrikantov, September 14, 1917.

Chapter 29. FASCIST "REVOLUTION" IN ITALY.
Mussolini, Benito, *The Corporate State* (Florence, 1936).
———. *Fascism: Doctrine and Institutions* (Rome, 1935).
———. *Opera omnia,* ed. E. and D. Susmel (Florence, 1951–1962).
———. "La dottrina del Fascismo," in *Enciclopedia italiana* (1932).
Italy, *Atti del Parlamento Italiano: Camera dei Deputati, Sessione 1924–25 (28 Legislatura): Discussioni* (Rome, 1926).
Documents on International Affairs, 1929, ed. J.W. Wheeler-Bennett (London, 1930).
Salvemini, Gaetano, *The Fascist Dictatorship in Italy* (New York, 1927).

Chapter 30. GERMANY FROM WEIMAR TO HITLER.
U.S. Department of State, *National Socialism,* ed. R.E. Murphy (Washington, D.C., 1943).
Fallada, Hans, *Little Man, What Now?* (New York, 1933).
Linke, Lilo, *Restless Days, A German Girl's Autobiography* (New York, 1935).

Hitler, Adolf, *Mein Kampf* (Munich, F. Eher, 1932).
———. *Speeches*, ed. N.H. Baynes (2 vols., Oxford, 1942).
U.S. Department of State, *Nuremberg Documents* #3249-PS and #3868-PS.
Arendt, Hannah, *The Origins of Totalitarianism* (2d ed., New York, 1958).

Chapter 31. WAR IN OUR TIME.
"The Effects of Atomic Bombs on Health and Medical Services in Hiroshima and Nagasaki," in *The United States Strategic Bombing Survey* (Washington, D.C., 1948).
Blainey, Geoffrey, *The Causes of War* (New York, 1973).
Stoessinger, John G., *Why Nations Go to War* (2d ed., New York, 1978).

Chapter 32. SCIENCE AND PHILOSOPHY IN A "HERACLITEAN" AGE.
Freud, Sigmund, *Das Unbehagen in der Kultur* (Vienna, 1930).
Zukav, Gary, *The Dancing Wu Li Masters: An Overview of the New Physics* (New York, 1979).
Thomas, Lewis, "Debating the Unknowable: When the Scientific Method Won't Work," in *The Atlantic Monthly*, July 1981.
Mazlish, Bruce, "Our 'Heraclitean' Period," in *The Nation*, Vol. 192 (New York, April 22, 1961).

Chapter 33. OF GOD AND MAN.
Dostoevsky, Feodor, *Notes from Underground and the Grand Inquisitor*, trans. R.E. Matlaw (New York, 1960).
Rauschenbusch, Walter, *Christianity and the Social Crisis* (New York, 1907).
Joad, C.E.M., *God and Evil* (New York, 1943).
Sartre, Jean-Paul, *Existentialism*, trans. Bernard Frechtman (New York, 1947).
Buber, Martin, *Between Man and Man*, trans. R.G. Smith (New York, 1965).
———. *I and Thou*, trans. W. Kaufman (New York, 1970).
Tillich, Paul, "Being and Love," in Ruth Nanda Anshen, *Moral Principles of Action* (New York, 1952).